The History of the Western Highlands and Isles of Scotland

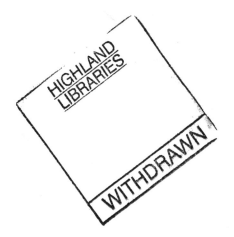

The History of the Western Highlands and Isles of Scotland

Donald Gregory

Introduction to this edition
by *Martin MacGregor*

JOHN DONALD

This edition first published in Great Britain in 2008 by
John Donald, an imprint of Birlinn Ltd

West Newington House
10 Newington Road
Edinburgh
EH9 1QS

www.birlinn.co.uk

ISBN 10: 1 904607 57 8

ISBN 13: 978 1 904607 57 1

Introduction to this edition © Martin MacGregor 2008

This main text of this book is a facsimile of the 1881 edition of

The History of the Western Highlands and Isles of Scotland
Donald Gregory
published by
Hamilton, Adams and Co., London
and
Thomas D. Morison, Glasgow

The right of Martin MacGregor to be identified as the author
of the introduction to this edition has been asserted by him in accordance
with the Copyright, Designs and Patents Act, 1988

British Library Cataloguing-in-Publication Data
A catalogue record for this book is available on request
from the British Library

Printed and bound in Britain by Cpod, Trowbridge

Introduction

Martin MacGregor
Department of Scottish History,
University of Glasgow

DONALD GREGORY was a scion of the astonishing Gregory dynasty which lit up the intellectual firmament of Scotland from the seventeenth to the nineteenth centuries with its achievements in medicine, mathematics, science, philosophy and language. His father, James, in Robert Burns's estimation the last of the Scottish Latinists, removed the dynasty from Aberdeen to Edinburgh, where he held chairs in medicine, became first physician to the king, and engaged in an energetic and at times disputatious public life. History does not seem to feature seriously on the family radar before Donald. Two possible stimuli for his choice of vocation are a belief, reflected in his earliest researches and publications, in an ultimate MacGregor ancestry for his lineage; and the influence of his mother, Isabella MacLeod, whose father was sheriff of Ross-shire, and who seems to have played a significant role in the education of her eleven children. Donald, born in 1803 along with a twin brother, William, died tragically young in 1836, but had already seen five of his siblings predecease him. His death, on 21 October, must have been unexpected, for the preface to *The History of the Western Highlands and Isles of Scotland, from A.D. 1493 to A.D. 1625, with a brief introductory sketch, from A.D. 80 to A.D. 1493*, is dated April 1836, and in it he looks to the future. 'It was my intention to have added a dissertation on the manners, customs and laws of the Highlanders, in which I had made considerable progress. Lack of space, however, has forced me to postpone, but by no means to abandon my design.'

Published more or less simultaneously was *The Highlanders of Scotland, their origin, history and antiquities: with a sketch of their manners and customs, and an account of the clans into which they were divided*, by William Forbes Skene (1809–92). The two men were the moving spirits behind the Iona Club, established in 1833 'to investigate and illustrate the History, Antiquities and early Literature of the Highlands of Scotland'; 'to supply an hiatus in the Historical Literature of Scotland which had long been observed and regretted', and to take steps 'towards substituting an authentic history of this interesting portion of Scotland, and of the literature, manners, and character of its inhabitants, for the fables and errors which have so long prevailed on these subjects'. Amplification of the second of these assertions came at the club's third meeting in 1834, when an honorary diploma was conferred upon Patrick Fraser Tytler, 'the author of a History of Scotland, now in progress, being the first work of the kind in which the History of the Highlands has been assigned a place, at all commensurate with the importance of the subject'.

The Iona Club's research agenda was nothing if not ambitious. Through the publication, in instalments, of *Collectanea*, the club aimed 'to bring together, in one work, all the documents illustrative of Highland history'. These would be complemented by *Transactions*, 'devoted to brief dissertations and illustrative observations, arising out of the documents printed in the *Collectanea*; to extracts from, and remarks upon, various family histories, and similar works of *secondary* authority, but still containing many curious facts connected with the Highlands; and to short statements of the public business of the Club'. From the outset the club had a Gaelic committee but, in 1835, a committee was established specifically 'to report on the propriety of publishing, *an edition of the select works of the best Gaelic Bards, with illustrative notes,* under the auspices of the Club'. All this enterprise did not outlive Donald Gregory. An Extraordinary General Meeting held on 17 November 1836 recorded:

> that the Club regard, with feelings of the deepest sorrow and regret, the loss they have sustained by the lamented death of their Secretary, Donald Gregory, Esq. to whose talents and unwearied exertions on their behalf they owe so much, and whose loss will long be felt by them, as well as by all who were on habits of friendship with him, or take an interest in the history and antiquities of their native country . . .

The Iona Club only ever met once again, on 15 December 1838, when it was agreed to cease operations because of lack of funds. Included in a recapitulation of its achievements was 'the preservation of the valuable and extensive collection of documents made by the late Mr Donald Gregory'.

The 1830s marked the birth of modern scholarship on the history of the Scottish Highlands, and Skene and Gregory – trained for the bar, joint-secretaries to the Society of Antiquaries of Scotland, and with maternal Highland connections – were its founding fathers. To them we might subjoin James Browne, whose *History of the Highlands and of the Highland Clans* appeared in four volumes between 1835 and 1838. Browne aimed to provide a 'comprehensive digest' of Highland history rather than fresh research, but explicitly aligned himself with the rationalism of Gregory and Skene, even if he rejected Skene's line that the Highlanders were the direct descendants of the 'northern Picts'.

Of what had Highland history consisted before 1836? During the seventeenth century, the 'classical tradition' of Gaelic history and genealogy, as practised in Scotland by professional learned lineages such as the MacMhuirichs, on behalf of the major territorial clans which patronised them, gave way before a genre of family or 'genealogical histories' which remained active up to the mid-nineteenth century. These histories were highly partisan accounts of the specific kindred to whom the author belonged or was affiliated, written in manuscript and nearly always in English, and drawing on a wide array of sources including oral tradition. In turn these metamorphosed into a 'clan history' genre which comes on stream in numbers in the late nineteenth century, although the earliest specimen may be 'A Seneachie', *An Historical and Genealogical Account of the Clan MacLean* (1838). We can distinguish the clan histories from the earlier genealogical histories, partly because they are published works rather than manuscripts, and partly because their contents do not represent one 'pure' genealogical history, but amalgams of several such accounts, along with other material, such as fresh injections of oral tradition or documentary evidence. We might describe them as 'phase two' genealogical histories. Another genre which may have come to the fore in the post-Ossianic era, although its roots doubtless take us back at least as far as the late seventeenth century and figures such as Robert Kirk, Martin Martin and Edward Lhwyd, was Highland ethnology. Notable examples in Gregory's lifetime were David Stewart of Garth's *Sketches of the character, manners and present state of the Highlanders of Scotland* (1821), and James Logan's *The Scottish Gael: or, Celtic manners, as preserved among the Highlanders* (1831).

Skene's *Highlanders of Scotland* clearly paid homage of a sort to this genre, as would Gregory's proposed 'dissertation on manners', had he lived to complete it. The earliest reviewers of his *History* felt that the 'dissertation on manners' would probably have been a bigger hit with the reading public than a work which they saw as somewhat dry, localised and limited, even if likely to prove of substantial benefit to future historians. It was a verdict which Gregory had anticipated in his preface, and from which he would not have dissented:

The necessity for minute research implied in a work like the present, has a tendency to prevent the author from drawing those general conclusions which are so desirable in all historical works, and which may occur more readily to those who peruse the result of his labours without any previous knowledge of the subject. This defect seems to be almost inseparable from the pursuits of the antiquary, who, in fact, generally acts as a pioneer to the historian. I shall be satisfied, therefore, if this work prove of service to a future writer on the History of the Highlands, and assist him in forming those general views which give to history its chief value.

Nearly two hundred years on, Gregory's *History* remains the best available narrative account of its chosen time and place. Explaining why involves more than the obvious cynical response that very few have cared enough to follow the trail he blazed. In settling on his subject, Gregory demonstrated a strategic vision far removed from the myopia of the antiquarian: the same vision that characterised the Iona Club's mission to ground Highland historiography upon secure foundations. He comprehended the history of the west Highlands in three great phases. The first was the Kingdom or Lordship of the Isles, dominated initially by the Scandinavians, and latterly, in the fourteenth and fifteenth centuries, by the Clan Donald. The third was the era of military support for endangered Stewart monarchy, through the Civil Wars of the seventeenth century, to Jacobitism. Both, in Gregory's estimation, had received adequate attention from historians, although he devotes a fifth of his book to a corrective overview of the first phase. The second phase, from 1493 and the forfeiture of the MacDonald Lordship, to 1625 and the death of James VI, Gregory regarded as a 'perfect blank', which was all the more reprehensible for being in inverse proportion to the plenitude of the sources. The key theme was the series of attempts to restore MacDonald hegemony in the west, which ended in failure with the death of the last serious claimant, Dòmhnall Dubh, in 1545; and the struggle to fill the vacuum. The main contenders were the crown, the Campbell earls of Argyll, the Gordon earls of Huntly and the MacKenzies of Kintail, and the main casualties were the MacLeods of Lewis and the MacDonalds of Islay – Clan Donald South – both of which were dismembered in the early seventeenth century.

Gregory set about filling the gap through a six-year research programme, launched by public announcement, and drawing upon a largely metropolitan web of archivists, antiquarians and professional Gaels, as well as the contemporary west Highland landed elite. He accessed the public records in London and Dublin as well as Edinburgh. To the modern Scottish historian, accustomed to the ready availability in printed editions of key governmental records such as the *Acts of the Lords of Council*, the *Accounts of the Lord High Treasurer*, and the *Register of the Privy Council*, it is humbling to read Gregory's numerous footnotes to the original manuscript volumes; or to note his extensive use of Highland material in the Denmylne MSS, housed in the then Advocates' Library, nearly a century before its publication in the Scottish History Society's *Highland Papers* series. Many landowners gave him access to their private papers, while his network brought into his personal possession nuggets like the confessions of those implicated in the assassination of Sir John Campbell of Cawdor in February 1592, accounts which contribute hugely to what is undoubtedly one of the high points of his *History*. But Gregory did not stop with the formal documentary record. He was equally assiduous in his pursuit of 'the traditions of the country', garnered both from a rich harvest of the 'genealogical histories' and from information gathered orally via his professional Gaelic contacts or through regular fieldwork in the west Highlands. Gregory was as convinced of tradition's genuine historical potential as he was alert to its propensity for error and exaggeration.

The resultant melding of sources has a distinctly modern, indeed postmodern, flavour. In terms of Highland historiography it is redolent of the approach of later twentieth-century pioneers like William Matheson and Eric Cregeen. But this is only because, after Gregory's time, and perhaps in part as a consequence of the institutionalising within universities from the late nineteenth century onwards of a split between Scottish historical and Celtic studies, tradition became a devalued historical currency. Approaching Gregory in terms of his own antecedents, we can see that he grows naturally and logically out of the genealogical histories, which also combined documentary record and tradition. Where Gregory leaves them and their successors, the clan histories, far behind is, firstly, in the scale, ambition and professionalism of his research programme, and his more systematic and critical attitude to the sources; and secondly, in his writing a general history which, although still clan-orientated – at three points Gregory halts his narrative to give surveys of the fortunes of all the major western clans – nevertheless broke decisively with the partisan 'one kindred' paradigm. The results are seen at their groundbreaking best in set-pieces such as the account of the battle of Kinloch-lochy or Blàr nan Lèine in 1544; the death of Sir John Campbell of Cawdor, which Gregory first demonstrated to be part of the same nationwide conspiracy that also resulted in the death of the 'bonny earl of Moray'; and 'the Great Rebellion of the Clan Donald of Isla', in 1614–15.

It would be alarming indeed if the modern historian could not point to shortcomings in a work first published in 1836. Of the significant sources unavailable to Gregory, we might highlight the riches of the Vatican archives, and proper editions of the Irish annals. His use of the genealogical histories is at points over-credulous, as in the dates he takes from 'MacMhuirich' – the *Red Book of Clanranald* – for the deaths of two early-sixteenth-century Clanranald chiefs; or, more seriously, in his tendency to present as gospel what these texts say about succession to the chiefship of clans. Gregory makes a robust case for his decision to focus solely upon the west, although this may depend less upon the cohesion bestowed upon the region by its geography or history, and more upon the influence of Skene's thesis that there was a racial distinction between the 'Dalriadic' Highlanders of Argyll and the aboriginal 'Pictish' Highlanders of the eastern and northern mainland. In his preface Gregory says:

> the history of the eastern highlanders cannot properly be blended with that of the western highlanders; and if introduced into the same work, would only serve to distract the attention of the reader . . . the measures employed at first for their coercion, and afterwards for their advancement in civilisation, came naturally to be separate from those directed to the subjugation (if I may use the phrase) and improvement of the Eastern tribes.

This thesis still awaits proper scrutiny. Indeed a pernicious consequence of the quality of his *History*, for which Gregory cannot be held responsible, is that the history of the late medieval west Highlands and Islands has come to stand proxy for the whole. It is striking, however, how often his narrative returns to the strategic importance of the Great Glen and the fortresses and power centres along it; and to Lochaber as a crucible where east met west, as the dominance of the MacDonald Lords gave way to the competing jurisdictions of Argyll and Huntly, and their dependent kindreds. The forfeiture of 1493 and its immediate repercussions cry out for a broader Highland perspective, as does the reign of James VI where, for instance, the major pan-Highland acts of parliament of 1587 and 1594 barely register with Gregory.

The charge of lack of context can be applied equally to Gregory's presentation of west Highland history as something

separate from that of the nation as a whole, which sits somewhat paradoxically with his criticism of Scottish historians
for ignoring the region in their own accounts. The history
of the Reformation, we are told, 'is to be traced almost exclusively in the history of the Lowlands; at least, the history of
the Highlands and Islands presents little that is interesting
on this subject'. We gain no real sense from Gregory of the
wider fiscal issues which profoundly shaped the Highland
policies of James IV and James VI. Gregory describes the
ancestors of his eastern Highlanders as 'secured from any
sweeping change, by the rugged nature of the country they
inhabited', and it seems clear from comments elsewhere that
he believed the same to hold true for the late-medieval west.

It follows naturally that Gregory believed in west Highland
history as a slow and erratic voyage from rudeness to civilisation, and that the means by which redemption was to be
delivered to these 'wild and remote districts', and the 'wild
tribes' inhabiting them, could only be from without, in the
form of Stewart monarchy and feudal law. The turbulent
epoch inaugurated by the forfeiture of 1493 furnished him
with no lack of data to paint a portrait of an anarchic society.
Gregory attributes the outcomes of the battles of Flodden
and Glenlivet (1594) to Highland indiscipline, and refers elsewhere to 'the usual system of indiscriminate plunder which
characterised a Highland inroad'. Yet the construction of his
narrative artificially enhances the mayhem. He notes periods
of tranquillity – 1506–13, 1520–27, 1532–39 – purely in the passing,
before moving on to the real business of the next eruption. It
is here that we miss the counterpoise which his 'dissertation
on manners' might have brought. We gain little sense of how
society functioned; of whether it was changing, or capable of
change; of how the MacDonald Lordship endured so long, and
took so long to die. Instead we are left with 'ancient and
inveterate custom', and its polar opposite, feudalism. Whereas
modern scholarship increasingly emphasises a relationship

between late-medieval Scots law and Gaelic custom and practice which was fluid, complementary and capable of compromise, Gregory says that the succession of a MacLeod heiress in the mid-sixteenth century, 'though quite intelligible on the principles of feudal law, was totally opposed to the Celtic customs that prevailed, to a great extent, throughout the Highlands and Islands'. By 1613, he notes 'the greater progress made by the feudal system in the Highlands and Islands than in Ireland'.

Gregory's *History* is structured around the reigns of the Stewarts from James IV to James VI, with five of the nine chapters devoted to the reign of the latter. This is true to his belief that effective Stewart monarchy was the best guarantor of progress in the west, especially when exercised *in propria persona*. It was through 'free personal intercourse between himself and these warlike chiefs' that James V 'soon acquired as much influence in the Isles as had been enjoyed by his gallant and chivalrous sire'. The three long royal minorities of the sixteenth century had the corresponding effect of 'retarding the civilisation of the Highlands and Islands'. Gregory passes positive verdicts on most of the Stewarts, but his faith in the munificent and unbounded blessings of royal government nosedives initially with James VI, who is found distinctly lacking in 'the higher motives which have made some monarchs the benefactors of mankind'. James is rebuked for repeatedly aborting projected royal expeditions to the west between 1596 and 1607 due to his 'natural timidity'; for an over-reliance on lieutenants as royal surrogates; and for making crude and precipitate policy decisions to fulfil his 'golden visions' of the west as a rainbow's end which could save him from his largely self-induced 'pecuniary embarrassments'. After a decade of such blundering, it comes as a shock to reach December 1608 and James's instructions to the Commissioners for the Isles, and to read that these were 'productive of so much benefit, that from this time we may trace the gradual and permanent improvement of the Isles and adjacent Highlands'. The stage is set for Gregory's remarkable and highly tendentious presentation of the Statutes of Iona of 1609 as the fulcrum on which his whole history turns, the sole origin 'of that overflowing loyalty to the house of Stewart for which the Highlanders have been so highly lauded':

> There is no room to doubt that the chiefs who followed Montrose in the great civil war were actuated by a very different spirit from their fathers; and it is well worthy of notice that this difference was produced in the course of a single generation, by the operation of measures which first began to take effect after the year 1609.

Subtlety is not the hallmark of the palette employed by Gregory to explain human behaviour and motivation. There is more than a touch of Victorian melodrama about a cast of characters which includes 'bold and chivalrous' kings, 'numerous and warlike' clans, 'wily chiefs' and 'crafty barons'. Again we feel the lack of depth which the 'dissertation on manners' might have brought. Key and complex figures like Lachlan Mòr MacLean of Duart and Sir Seumas (James) MacDonald remain firmly one-dimensional. The former is 'early familiarised with scenes of blood and rapine', and has an 'innate disposition to violence'. Sir Seumas, a true tragic hero in the Dòmhnall Dubh mould, who spent much of his life striving in vain to reach a negotiated settlement with a government indisposed to listen, is poorly represented by reference to 'the natural violence of his temper', although Gregory does note later that his letters 'are not those of a barbarian, such as his indictment describes him; but, on the contrary, indicated a mind well cultivated for the period'. In the case of two earlier leading MacDonalds, Aonghas Òg and Dòmhnall Gallda, Gregory can find no better explanation for their conduct than insanity. Far more penetrating and interesting is his ambivalent portrayal of the Campbells. They are 'ancient and distinguished', certainly, and clearly seen as civilising agents, yet highly problematic in the scale of the power they accrue; an outcome neither anticipated nor desired by James IV, emphatically reversed by James V, but restored with interest come the reign of James VI, when Gregory lays at their door responsibility for the instabilities which afflicted the South Isles between 1600 and 1615.

We return finally to the indisputable fact that, for all the cracks in the edifice wrought by the passage of time, Donald Gregory's *History* still stands. It has deserved to do so because it lets the evidence speak. Its author cared less for the sound of his own voice than for that of the sources, gathered and assembled by immense effort and 'minute research'. It is a privilege to pay homage to a true historian who did not consider himself worthy of the name. His first and only book is both a fitting memorial, and a monument to what we have lost.

FURTHER READING

Acts of the Lords of the Isles, 1336–1493, eds. J and RW Munro (Scottish History Society: Edinburgh 1986)

Bannerman, JWM, 'The Lordship of the Isles', in *Scottish Society in the Fifteenth Century*, ed. JM Brown (London 1977), 209–40

Boardman, S, *The Campbells 1250–1513* (Edinburgh 2006)

Cathcart, A, *Kinship and Clientage: Highland Clanship 1451–1609* (Leiden 2006)

Collectanea de Rebus Albanicis (Iona Club: Edinburgh 1839 or 1847)

Gregory, D, *Inquiry into the Early History of the Clan Gregor, with a View to Ascertain the Causes which led to their Proscription in 1603* (Edinburgh 1831)

Gregory, D, 'A Short Obituary relating to the Highlands', *Archaeologia Scotica* 3 (1831), 317–28

Gregory, D, *Historical Notices of the Clan Gregor, from Authentic Sources, Part 1* (Edinburgh 1831). This comprehended both papers just cited. For more on Gregory's role in the compilation of 'The Chartulary of the Clan Gregor', see the references to him in the first volume of AGM MacGregor, *History of the Clan Gregor* (Edinburgh 1898)

MacGregor, M, 'The Genealogical Histories of Gaelic Scotland', in *The Spoken Word: Oral Culture in the British Isles, 1500–1850*, eds. A Fox and D Woolf (Manchester 2002), 196–239

MacGregor, M, 'The Statutes of Iona: Text and Context', *Innes Review* 57 (2006), 111–81

Oxford Dictionary of National Biography, eds. HGC Matthew and B Harrison (Oxford 2004), vol. 23 (articles on Donald Gregory and others of his family)

Sellar, WDH, 'Marriage, Divorce and Concubinage in Gaelic Scotland', *Transactions of the Gaelic Society of Inverness* 51 (1978–80), 464–93

Sellar, WDH, 'Celtic Law and Scots Law: Survival and Integration', *Scottish Studies* 29, 1–27

Steer, KA and Bannerman, JWM, *Late Medieval Monumental Sculpture in the West Highlands* (Edinburgh 1977)

HISTORY

OF THE

WESTERN HIGHLANDS AND ISLES

OF

SCOTLAND.

The History

OF THE

Western Highlands

AND

Isles of Scotland,

From A.D. 1493 to A.D. 1625,

WITH A

Brief Introductory Sketch,

From A.D. 80 to A.D. 1493.

BY

Donald Gregory,

Joint Secretary to the Society of Antiquaries of Scotland; Secretary to the Iona Club;
Honorary Member of the Ossianic Society of Glasgow;
Honorary Member of the Society of Antiquaries, Newcastle-on-Tyne;
and Member of the Royal Society of Antiquaries of the
North at Copenhagen.

SECOND EDITION.

TO

THE RIGHT HONOURABLE GODFREY WILLIAM

LORD MACDONALD,

A BARONET OF NOVA SCOTIA:

OTHERWISE STYLED,

nuill na'n Eilean,

OR

MacDonald of the Isles:

HEIR-MALE OF JOHN, LAST LORD OF THE ISLES;

THIS WORK,

CONTAINING MANY PARTICULARS OF THE HISTORY OF HIS LORDSHIP'S
ILLUSTRIOUS ANCESTORS, THE LORDS OF THE ISLES,

IS, WITH PERMISSION,

DEDICATED BY

HIS LORDSHIP'S MOST OBEDIENT SERVANT,

THE AUTHOR.

TABLE OF CONTENTS.

INTRODUCTION.

A. D. 80-1493.

CHAPTER I.

A.D. 1493–1513.

CHAPTER II.

A.D. 1513-1542.

CHAPTER III.

A.D. 1542-1560.

CHAPTER IV.

A.D. 1561-1585.

CHAPTER V.

A.D. 1585-1595.

The feud between the Macdonalds and Macleans again
    breaks out, ... 230

CHAPTER VI.

A.D. 1595-1603.

CHAPTER VII.

A.D. 1603-1610.

CHAPTER VIII.

A.D. 1610–1615.

3

CHAPTER IX.

A.D. 1615-1625.

the Isles and a great part of the adjacent coast, during
the fourteenth and fifteenth centuries, under the sway
of one powerful family, while the eastern clans had no
similar community of interest, and owned no similar
controlling power:—these were the chief causes of the
distinction which, in later times, was found to exist
between the Western and Eastern Highlanders. The
history of the latter cannot properly be blended with that
of the former; and, if introduced into the same work,
would only serve to distract the attention of the reader.
A perusal of the following pages will show that, during
a great portion of the period I have endeavoured to
illustrate, the Western Clans had a common object which
frequently united them in hostility to the government.
In this way, the measures employed at first for their
coercion, and afterwards for their advancement in civilisation, came naturally to be separate from those directed
to the subjugation (if I may use the phrase) and improvement of the Eastern tribes. In the public records
of Scotland, with scarcely an exception, the distinction
I have pointed out is acknowledged either directly or
indirectly. So much for the reasons which induced me
to select, for the subject of the present work, the history
of the West Highlands and Isles.

Having chosen this subject, I very soon perceived
that the history of this portion of the Scottish Highlands might advantageously be divided into three portions. The first portion might embrace its early history,
and the rise and fall of the great Lordship of the Isles;

PREFACE TO FIRST EDITION.

It may naturally be asked by those who read only the title-page of the present work, why it should have been limited to the history of a portion merely of what are commonly called the Highlands of Scotland, as well as to a particular period of that history. I shall endeavour to explain in a few words the reasons which have induced me thus to limit my subject.

Various causes contributed, in former times, to divide the Scottish Highlands into two sections, between which there existed a well-defined line of demarcation. The West Highlands and Isles formed one of these sections: the Central Highlands, and all those districts in which the waters flowed to the East, formed the other. The great mountain-ridge, called, of old, *Drumalban*, from which the waters flowed to either coast of Scotland, was the least of these causes of distinction. The numerical superiority of the *Dalriads* on the west, and of the *Picts* on the east side of Drumalban, and the frequent wars between these nations; the conquest, and occupation for nearly four hundred years, of the Hebrides, by the warlike Scandinavians; and, lastly, the union of

the Isles and a great part of the adjacent coast, during
the fourteenth and fifteenth centuries, under the sway
of one powerful family, while the eastern clans had no
similar community of interest, and owned no similar
controlling power:—these were the chief causes of the
distinction which, in later times, was found to exist
between the Western and Eastern Highlanders. The
history of the latter cannot properly be blended with that
of the former; and, if introduced into the same work,
would only serve to distract the attention of the reader.
A perusal of the following pages will show that, during
a great portion of the period I have endeavoured to
illustrate, the Western Clans had a common object which
frequently united them in hostility to the government.
In this way, the measures employed at first for their
coercion, and afterwards for their advancement in civilisation, came naturally to be separate from those directed
to the subjugation (if I may use the phrase) and improvement of the Eastern tribes. In the public records
of Scotland, with scarcely an exception, the distinction
I have pointed out is acknowledged either directly or
indirectly. So much for the reasons which induced me
to select, for the subject of the present work, the history
of the West Highlands and Isles.

Having chosen this subject, I very soon perceived
that the history of this portion of the Scottish Highlands might advantageously be divided into three portions. The first portion might embrace its early history,
and the rise and fall of the great Lordship of the Isles;

the second might trace the immediate effects of the forfeiture of that Lordship, and bring the history down to the time when, by the exertions of James VI., the Western Highlanders, from being frequently in rebellion against the royal authority, had begun to be distinguished for their loyalty; and the third might record their exertions in support of the house of Stewart, increasing in energy in proportion as the hopes of that unfortunate family became more desperate.

The great power and resources of the old Kings of the Isles, and of the more modern Lords of the Isles, have forced the history of the first of the periods above mentioned on the attention of many of our historians. Moreover, the national records, hitherto discovered, referring to this period, are comparatively scanty, and offer few materials for adding to what has already been written on this branch of the subject. Again, the numerous historical works which have appeared on the great civil war, and on all the later struggles of the house of Stewart, have made us tolerably familiar with the conduct and relative position of the leading Highland clans during the third period.

These considerations alone would have influenced me in choosing for my subject the history of the second period—that, namely, from A.D. 1493 to A.D. 1625, which was as nearly as possible a perfect blank; but when I discovered that our national records and other sources of authentic information were full of interesting and important matter bearing upon this portion of the

history of the West Highlands and Isles, I no longer
hesitated.

It is now six years since, desirous of procuring information from every quarter, I announced to the public
the task I had imposed upon myself, and stated the
leading objects of the present work. I am bound to
acknowledge that I have received, in consequence, from
many private sources, information which, but for that
announcement, I never might have heard of, and of which
it will be perceived that I have made considerable use.

To the late Right Honourable Lord Macdonald; to
the late Sir John Campbell of Ardnamurchan, Bart.;
to the late Sir William Macleod Bannatyne, and the late
John Norman Macleod of Macleod; to the Right Honourable Lord Macdonald; Sir John Campbell of Ardnamurchan, Bart.; Sir Donald Campbell of Dunstaffnage,
Bart.; Murdoch Maclaine of Lochbuy, Esq.; Hugh
Maclean of Coll, Esq.; Alexander Maclean of Ardgour, Esq.; Captain Macdougall of Macdougall, R.N.;
Dugald Campbell of Craignish, Esq.; Major Campbell
of Melfort; Alexander Campbell of Ardchattan, Esq.;
Lieut.-Colonel Macniel of Barra; Captain Stewart,
Ardshiel; and John Stewart of Fasnacloich, Esq.; I
am indebted for being permitted to examine their
ancient family papers, from which I have derived much
curious information.

Cosmo Innes, Esq., gave me access to the valuable
charter chest of Kilravock, from an inspection of which
I added greatly to the information I had previously col-

lected. Captain Alexander Macneill, younger, of Colonsay, allowed me to peruse some of the ancient charters and papers of the Gigha family, which have lately come into his possession.

The late Sir William Macleod Bannatyne; Sir George S. Mackenzie of Coul, Bart.; Colonel Sir Evan J. M. Macgregor of Macgregor, Bart.; George Macpherson Grant, Esq., of Ballindalloch and Invereshie; John Gregorson of Ardtornish, Esq.; Colin Campbell, Esq., Jura; Lauchlan Mackinnon of Letterfearn, Esq.; the Rev. Dr. Norman Macleod, Glasgow; the Rev. Angus Maclaine, Ardnamurchan; the Rev. Alexander Mackenzie Downie; Charles Cameron, Esq., barrister-at-law; Lieut.-Colonel Cameron, Clunes; Captain Donald Cameron, Stone; Colin Macrae, Esq., Nairn Grove; John Macdonnel, Esq., Keppoch; Angus Macdonnell, Esq., Inch; Donald Macrae, Esq., Auchtertyre, Kintaill; Dr. Mackinnon, Kyle, Sky; Dr. Maclean, Isle of Rum; Dr. Maceachern, Arasaig; Mr. Lauchlan Maclean, Glasgow; and Mr. Hugh Macdonald, Dervaig, Mull—have assisted me either by submitting to my inspection copies of various family histories, which have been of much service, by pointing out various useful sources of information, or by communicating authentic traditions; and I have everywhere found a disposition to forward as much as possible the inquiries in which I have been engaged.

The use I have made of the public records will readily be perceived; and, in this department, my researches have been facilitated by the kindness of the learned

Deputy Clerk Register, Mr. Thomas Thomson, and of
Mr. Alexander Macdonald, who have pointed out to me
many curious original documents.

To the Curators of the Advocates' Library, I, in
common with many others engaged in historical pursuits, feel much indebted for the ready access afforded
to the valuable MS. collections of the Faculty of Advocates.

Frequent communications with my friends, Mr. Alexander Sinclair, Mr. Cosmo Innes, and Mr. William F.
Skene, have assisted me to clear up several points
hitherto doubtful; and Mr. Robert Pitcairn, editor of that
curious work, the Criminal Trials, has enabled me to
add considerably to my collections. I am likewise
under great obligations to Mr. David Laing, the active
secretary of the Bannatyne Club.

I did not neglect to examine the Scottish MSS. in
the British Museum, in which I received much assistance from Mr. Joseph Stevenson. Mr. Tytler communicated to me some valuable documents (since published) connected with the history of the Isles, from the
State Paper Office, London. Lastly, such information
as I required from the Irish records and historical MSS.
was communicated to me most readily by Mr. John
D'Alton, barrister-at-law, Dublin, from his own valuable
historical and genealogical collections.

In order the better to arrange the information thus
collected, and to make myself acquainted with such
traditions as were not alluded to in the family histories,

or, if alluded to, were without dates or otherwise defective, I made frequent visits to the West Highlands and
Isles; and succeeded in satisfying myself on many
doubtful points. In these journeys I conversed with
every individual supposed to be well informed that I had
the good fortune to meet; and the information thus
gained proved of essential service afterwards, when I
came to prepare the following pages for press.

Such have been the sources of my information. Of
the use I have made of it, it does not become me to
speak; but I may at least say, that I have striven to be
impartial. The necessity for minute research implied
in a work like the present, has a tendency to prevent
the author from drawing those general conclusions
which are so desirable in all historical works, and which
may occur more readily to those who peruse the result
of his labours without any previous knowledge of the
subject. This defect seems to be almost inseparable
from the pursuits of the antiquary, who, in fact, generally acts as a pioneer to the historian. I shall be satisfied, therefore, if this work prove of service to a future
writer on the History of the Highlands, and assist him
in forming those general views which give to history
its chief value.

It was my intention to have added a dissertation on
the manners, customs, and laws of the Highlanders, in
which I had made considerable progress. Want of
space, however, has forced me to postpone, but by no
means to abandon my design. When I resume it, I

hope to be able to bring forward from my collections, which are increasing every day, many new illustrations of these subjects.

The Introduction of the present Work embraces what I have called the first historical period of the West Highlands and Isles. Such an Introduction seemed indispensable; and, while it is necessarily brief, I have taken the opportunity of correcting some of the more glaring errors of former writers.

EDINBURGH, 10 AINSLIE PLACE,
April, 1836.

INTRODUCTION.

THE object of the present work is to trace the history of the territories once owned by the great Lords of the Isles, from the time of the downfall of that princely race, in the reign of James IV. of Scotland, until the accession of Charles I. to the throne of Great Britain. But, for the better understanding of the subject, it appears absolutely necessary to give a brief sketch, *first*, of the early history of these territories; and, *secondly*, of the rise, progress, and fall of the. potent family of the Isles.

To enter into any speculation regarding the early inhabitants of the country, would, in a work of this nature, be superfluous, and inconsistent with the necessary brevity of an Introduction. The facts bearing on the subject are, unfortunately, few in number. From the Roman authors, who afford the earliest accurate information regarding the tribes of North Britain, it appears A. D. 80-300. that, during the two centuries after the invasion of Agricola, A.D. 80, Scotland was inhabited by two nations only—the *Caledonii*, and the *Mæatae*. Of these, the Caledonii alone inhabited the Highlands; and, indeed, all modern Scotland north of the Friths of Forth and Clyde. After the third century, the names of Caledonii and Mæatae disappear, and we

4

find the Romans terming their northern opponents *Picti* and *Attacotti.* Historians seem now to have agreed that the Picts were, in fact, the Caledonians under a new name; that they were a Celtic race; and that, until the sixth century, they continued to be the sole nation north of the Friths—being divided into two great branches—the *Dicaledones* inhabiting the more mountainous and more rugged districts north and west of the Grampian range, and the *Vecturiones* inhabiting the more level districts between the Grampians and the German Ocean. Thus the former corresponded to the Highlanders of the present day, whilst the latter possessed the Lowlands, from the plains of Moray on the north to Fife and Strathearn on the south. In the

A. D. 503.
beginning of the sixth century, a new people was added to the inhabitants of Scotland, north of Forth and Clyde—for, at that period, the Irish *Scots*, frequently called the *Dalriads*, effected a settlement in the western districts of the Highlands. At this time, the country south of the Friths was occupied by the Strathclyde Britons; but the subsequent conquest of Northumberland and the Lothians, by the Angles, before the close of the sixth century, added that nation to the inhabitants of the south of Scotland. During the sixth, seventh, and eighth centuries, the history of Scotland presents nothing but a succession of conflicts between these four nations, which produced but little permanent change in their relative situations. In the

A. D. 843.
ninth century, however, a revolution took place, the nature of which it is almost impossible to determine, from the unfortunate silence of all the older authorities, whilst the fables of the later historians are quite unworthy of credit. But it is certain,

that the result of this revolution was the nominal union of most of the tribes under KENNETH MACALPIN, a King of the Scottish or Dalriadic race, and the consequent spread of the name of Scotland over the whole country. However this important event might affect the population of the rich and fertile Lowlands, it seems perfectly clear, that the Dicaledones, or Picts, who formed the bulk of the Highland population in these early times, were secured from any sweeping change, by the rugged nature of the country they inhabited. In these Dicaledones, therefore, we see the ancestors of the great mass of the modern Highlanders, excepting those of Argyleshire; among whom, in all probability, the Dalriadic blood predominated. The name of *Albanich*, which, as far back as we can trace, is the proper appellation of the Scottish Highlanders, seems to prove their descent from that tribe which gave to Britain its earliest name of *Albion*, and which may, therefore, be considered as the first tribe that set foot in this island.

The earliest inhabitants of the Western Isles or Ebudes (corruptly Hebrides), were probably a portion of the Albanich, Caledonians, or Picts. In some of the southern islands, particularly Isla, this race must have been displaced or overrun by the Dalriads on their first settlement; so that, at the date of the Scottish Conquest, the Isles, like the adjacent mainland, were divided between the Picts and Scots. The change produced in the original population of the Western Isles, by the influx of the Scots—a cognate Celtic race—was, however, trifling, compared with that which followed the first settlements of the Scandinavians in the Isles, towards the end of the ninth century.

From the chronicles both of England and Ireland, it appears that these northern pirates commenced their ravages in the British Isles a hundred years before this time, and many of them were thus well acquainted with the Western Isles prior to their effecting a permanent settlement in them. An important revolution in Norway led to this settlement. About the year 880, the celebrated Harald Harfager established himself as the first King of all Norway, after bringing into subjection a number of the petty kings of that country. Many of the most violent of Harald's opponents sought to escape his vengeance, by leaving their native land, and establishing themselves in the Scottish Isles, from the numerous harbours of which they afterwards issued in piratical fashion, to infest the coasts of Norway. King Harald was not of a nature to allow such insults to pass unpunished. He pursued the pirates to their insular fastnesses, and not only subdued them, but added the Isles to the crown of Norway. In the following year, the *Vikingr* of the Isles revolted and renewed their piratical expeditions; but were speedily reduced to obedience by Ketil, a Norwegian of rank, despatched by Harald to the Isles for that purpose. Ketil, however, having ingratiated himself with the principal Islanders, soon declared himself King of the Isles, independent of Norway, and held this rank for the rest of his life. According to the Norse Sagas, all the race of Ketil were either dead, or had left the Isles, about the year 900; and, for nearly forty years after this date, the history of the Isles is very obscure.

Aulaf MacSitric, son of the Danish King of Northumberland, and called by the historians, "*Rex pluri-*

A. D. 880.

A. D. 888.

A. D. 890.

A. D. 938.

marum insularum," fought at the great battle of Brunanburg; and, on his death, he seems to have been succeeded by Maccus MacArailt Mac-Sitric, probably his nephew, who was contemporary with, and is said to have been brought under subjection by Edgar, the greatest of the Anglo-Saxon Kings. Gofra MacArailt, King of the Isles, died, according to the

A. D. 990.

Irish annalists, in 989; and, in the following year, the Hebrides were conquered by Sigurd, the second of that name, Earl of Orkney, who placed as his deputy, or Jarl, over them, an individual named Gilli. Sigurd seems to have lost his Hebridean conquests after a time, as we read of a Ragnal MacGofra, King of the

A. D. 1004.

Isles, who died A.D. 1004. On his death, however, Sigurd had resumed possession of the Isles, which he held at the time of the celebrated

A. D. 1014.
A. D. 1034.

battle of Clunatarf, in Ireland, in which he was killed. Twenty years later, the Hebrides were conquered by Earl Thorfin, the son of Sigurd, from which we may infer that, in the interval, they had been independent. Thorfin possessed the Isles

A. D. 1064.

till his death, after which they seem to have formed part of the dominions of Diarmed MacMaelnambo, a potent Irish prince, who died A.D. 1072.

The next King of the Isles that we can trace, is God-red, the son of Sitric (supposed to have been one of the Irish Ostmen), who reigned in the Isle of Man. To him succeeded his son, Fingal, who, after a desperate struggle, was dispossessed of his kingdom by

Cir. A. D. 1077.

another Godred, the son of Harald the Black. This Godred, surnamed *Crovan*, or the White Handed, is the undoubted ancestor of that dynasty of Kings of Man and the Isles which terminated by the death of Magnus, the son of Olave, A.D. 1265. Godred Crovan was first known as a leader of the Norwegians under Harald *Hardrada*, King of Norway, at the battle of Stainford Bridge,

A. D. 1066. where the latter was defeated and slain by Harald, King of England. Escaping from England, Godred seems to have fled to the Isles, where he gradually formed a party strong enough to enable him to expel Fingal from the Isle of Man. But his conquests were not confined to the Isles; he likewise subjugated Dublin (which had for nearly two centuries been the seat of a principality, formed by the Scandinavian Vikingr) and a great part of Leinster. He was, besides, very successful in war against the Scots, whose King, at this time, was Malcolm III., commonly called Malcolm Canmor. For a length of time the claims of Norway to the dominion of the Isles had been neglected; but they were now revived, and triumphantly re-established by King Magnus Barefoot, who, at the head of an imposing force, subjugated

A. D. 1093. the Isles, and, expelling Godred Crovan, placed on the throne his own son, Sigurd. Godred died two years afterwards, in the island of Isla, leaving three sons, Lagman, Harald, and Olave. On

A. D. 1103. the death of Magnus Barefoot, who fell in an expedition against Ulster, Sigurd, becoming King of Norway, returned to his native dominions, when the Islanders, apparently with Sigurd's consent, took for their King, Lagman, the eldest son of Godred Crovan. This Prince, after a reign of seven years, the most important event of which was an unsuccessful rebellion against him by his brother Harald, abdicated.

his throne, and, assuming the cross, went on a pil-
grimage to Jerusalem, where he died. On this, the
nobility of the Isles applied to Murchard O'Brien,
King of Ireland, to send them a Prince of his own blood
to act as Regent during the minority of Olave, the
surviving son of Godred Crovan. In compliance with
this request, the Irish King sent to the Isles a certain
A. D. IIII.   Donald MacTade, who ruled for two years,
but made himself so obnoxious by his tyr-
anny and oppression, that the insular chiefs rose against
A. D. III3.   him with one accord, and forced him to fly
to Ireland, whence he never returned. Olave,
son of Godred Crovan, soon afterwards ascended the
throne, which he filled for forty years. His reign was
peaceful; but he conducted himself so as to preserve
his kingdom from aggression. This Olave is, by the
Norse writers, surnamed *Bitling* or *Klining*, from his
diminutive stature; whilst, in the Highland traditions,
he is called *Olave the Red*. He was the father of
Godred the Black, who succeeded him; and one of
his daughters, *Ragnhildis*, was married to *Somerled*,
Prince or Lord of Argyle, from which marriage sprung
the dynasty so well known in Scottish history as the
Lords of the Isles.

From whatever race, whether Pictish or Scottish, the
inhabitants of the Isles in the reign of Kenneth
MacAlpin were derived, it is clear that the settlements
and wars of the Scandinavians in the Hebrides, from
the time of Harald Harfager to that of Olave the Red,
a period of upwards of two centuries, must have produced
a very considerable change in the population. As in all
cases of conquest, this change must have been most
perceptible in the higher ranks, owing to the natural

tendency of invaders to secure their new possessions,
where practicable, by matrimonial alliances with the
natives. That, in the Hebrides, a mixture of the
Celtic and Scandinavian blood was thus effected at an
early period, seems highly probable, and by no means
inconsistent with the ultimate prevalence of the Celtic
language in the mixed race, as all history sufficiently
demonstrates. These remarks regarding the population
of the Isles, apply equally to that of the adjacent mainland districts, which, being so accessible by numerous
arms of the sea, could hardly be expected to preserve
the blood of their inhabitants unmixed. The extent to
which this mixture was carried is a more difficult question, and one which must be left, in a great measure, to
conjecture; but, on the whole, the Celtic race appears
to have predominated. It is of more importance to
know which of the Scandinavian tribes it was that
infused the greatest portion of northern blood into the
population of the Isles. The Irish annalists divide the
piratical bands, which, in the ninth and following centuries, infested Ireland, into two great tribes, styled by
these writers, *Fiongall*, or white foreigners, and *Dubh-
gall*, or black foreigners. These are believed to represent, the former the Norwegians, the latter the Danes;
and the distinction in the names given to them, is
supposed to have arisen from a diversity either in their
clothing or in the sails of their vessels. These tribes
had generally separate leaders; but they were occasionally united under one king; and, although both
bent, first on ravaging the Irish shores, and afterwards
on seizing portions of the Irish territories, they frequently turned their arms against each other. The
Gaelic title of *Righ Fhiongall*, or King of the Fion-

gall, so frequently applied to the Lords of the Isles, seems to prove that Olave the Red, from whom they were descended in the female line, was so styled, and that, consequently, his subjects in the Isles, in so far as they were not Celtic, were Fiongall or Norwegians. It has been remarked by one writer, whose opinion is entitled to weight,[1] that the names of places in the exterior Hebrides, or the Long Island, derived from the Scandinavian tongue, resemble the names of places in Orkney, Shetland, and Caithness. On the other hand, the corresponding names in the interior Hebrides are in a different dialect, resembling that of which the traces are to be found in the topography of Sutherland; and appear to have been imposed at a later period than the first-mentioned names. The probability is, however, that the difference alluded to is not greater than might be expected in the language of two branches of the same race, after a certain interval; and that the Scandinavian population of the Hebrides was, therefore, derived from two successive Norwegian colonies. This view is further confirmed by the fact that the Hebrides, although long subject to Norway, do not appear to have ever formed part of the possessions of the Danes.

Having thus traced, as briefly as possible, the origin of the inhabitants of the Western Highlands and Isles, as we find them early in the twelfth century, it remains, in the *second* place, to trace the rise, progress, and fall of the great family of de Insulis, or Macdonald, Lords of the Isles.

The origin of Somerled of Argyle, the undoubted founder of this noble race, is involved in considerable

---

[1] Chalmers' Caledonia, Vol. I., p. 266.

obscurity.   Of his father, Gillebrede, and his grandfather, Gilladomnan, we know little but the names.
According to the·seannachies or genealogists, both
Irish and Highland, Gilladomnan was the sixth in
descent from a certain Godfrey MacFergus, who is
called, in an Irish Chronicle, Toshach of the Isles, and·
who lived in the reign of Kenneth MacAlpin.   There
is a tradition that this Godfrey, or one of his race, was
expelled from the Isles by the Danes,[1] which, if correct, may apply to the conquest of Harald Harfager,
who, in all probability, dispossessed many of the native
chiefs.   But the Celtic genealogists do not stop short
with Godfrey MacFergus.   Through a long line of
ancestors, they trace the descent of that chief from the
celebrated Irish King, *Conn Chead Chath*, or Conn of
the Hundred Battles.   Such is the account of Somerled's origin, given by those who maintain his Scoto-Irish
descent.   Others have asserted that he was undoubtedly
a Scandinavian by descent in the male line.   His name
is certainly a Norse one;[2] but then, on the other hand,
the names of his father and grandfather are purely Celtic; whilst the intermarriages that must have taken place
between the two races in the Isles and adjacent coasts,
make it impossible to found any argument on the Christian name alone.   Somerled is mentioned more than once
in the Norse Sagas, but never in such a way as to enable
us to affirm, with certainty, what the opinion of the Scandinavian writers was as to his origin.   He appears to have

---

[1] MS. History of the Macdonalds, by Hugh Macdonald, a Seannáchie
of the end of the 17th century.

[2] The Norse *Somerled*, and the Gaelic *Somhairle*, are both rendered
into the English, *Samuel*.

been known to them as *Sumarlidi Haulldr*,[1] and the impression produced by the passages in which he is mentioned, is rather against his being considered a Norseman. It is possible, however, as he was certainly descended from a noted individual of the name of God- frey, that his ancestor may have been that Gofra Mac- Arailt, King of the Isles, who died in 989. But, on the whole, the uniformity of the Highland and Irish tradi- tions, which can be traced back at least four hundred years,[2] leads to the conclusion that the account first given of the origin of Somerled is correct.

It is from tradition alone, as it appears in some of the genealogical histories of the Macdonalds, that any par- ticulars of the early life of Somerled can be gathered; and it is obvious, that information derived from a source so liable to error, must be received with very great cau- tion. We are told that Gillibrede, the father of Somer- led, was expelled from his possessions, and that, with his son, he was forced to conceal himself, for a time, in a cave in the district of ·Morvern, whence he is known in tradition as *Gillibrede na'n Uaimh*, or Gillibrede of the Cave. From certain circumstances, obscurely hinted at, it would seem that Gillibrede, after the death of Malcolm Canmor, had, with the other Celtic inhabitants of Scot- land, supported Donald Bane, the brother of Malcolm, in his claim to the Scottish throne, to the exclusion of Ed-

---

[1] *Haulldr*, in its strict sense, implies, that the person who bore the epithet was a cultivator of the soil, and not of noble birth. But it was very commonly applied as a nickname to kings and nobles, so that no inference as to the rank or status of Somerled can be drawn from the use of the word in the present instance.

[2] Genealogical MS. (in Gaelic) of the 15th century, printed in Collectanea de Rebus Albanicis, Vol. I., p. 60.

gar, Malcolm's son. Consequently, on the final triumph of the Anglo-Saxon party, Gillibrede would naturally be exposed to their vengeance in exact proportion to his power, and to the assistance he had given to the other party. Of this chief we hear no more; nor are we informed of the extent of his possessions, or where they lay, but they are believed to have been on the mainland of Argyle. Somerled, when young, was, through an accident, which is minutely detailed by tradition, drawn from his obscurity, and placed at the head of the men of Morvern, collected at the time to resist a band of Norse pirates, who threatened to ravage the district. On this occasion Somerled, by his courage and skill, defeated these fierce marauders; and, soon after, following up this success, recovered his paternal inheritance, and made himself master of so large a portion of Argyle, that he thenceforth assumed the title of Lord or Regulus of Argyle, and became one of the most powerful chiefs in Scotland. There is every reason to believe that, by his talent and bravery, he had now raised himself to a higher rank than his father, or any of his immediate predecessors held. It appears by no means improbable, too, that Somerled, aware of his own power and resources, contemplated the conquest of a portion, at least, of the Isles, to which he may have laid claim through his remote ancestor, Godfrey. On these, or similar grounds, Olave the Red, King of Man and the Isles, was naturally desirous to disarm the enmity, and to secure the support of the powerful Lord of Argyle, whose marriage

Cir. A.D. with Ragnhildis, the daughter of Olave—the

1140. first authentic event in the life of Somerled—

seems to have answered this purpose. Of this marriage, which is lamented by the author of "The Chronicle of

Man," as the cause of the ruin of the whole kingdom of the Isles, the issue was three sons—Dugall, Reginald, and Angus.[1]

Olave the Red, after a peaceful reign of forty years, was murdered in the Isle of Man, by his nephews, the sons of Harald, who had been brought up in Dublin, and had made a claim to half the kingdom of the Isles. Godred the Black, who was in Norway at the time of his father's death, returned to the Isles without delay, and being received with joy by the Islanders as their King, apprehended and executed the murderers. Early in his reign, he was invited by the Ostmen of Dublin to rule over them, and was thus led into wars in Ireland, in which he was successful; but, on his return to Man, thinking that no one could resist his power, he conducted himself so tyrannically, that he speedily alienated the affections of many of the insular nobility;—one of the most powerful of these, Thorfin, the son of Ottar, addressed himself to Somerled, and demanded from him his son, Dugall, then a child, the nephew of Godred, whom he proposed to make King of the Isles. The ambitious Lord of Argyle readily entered into the views of Thorfin, who, with his partisans, carrying Dugall through all the Isles, except apparently Man itself, forced the inhabitants to acknowledge him as their king, and took hostages from them for their obedience. One of the chief islanders, Paul by name, escaping secretly, fled to the court of Godred, and made him aware of what had just taken place. Roused by the emergency, the king collected

A. D. 1154.

---

[1] I follow here the Orkneyinga Saga, p. 383, which is very explicit, and is a better authority than the Chronicle of Man. The latter adds a fourth son, *Olave*.

a large fleet, with which he proceeded against the rebels, who, under the guidance of Somerled, with a fleet of eighty galleys, did not decline the encounter.

A. D. 1156.

After a bloody but indecisive action, a treaty was entered into, by which Godred ceded to the sons of Somerled what were afterwards called, in Scottish geography, the South Isles, retaining for himself the North Isles and Man. The point of Ardnamurchan formed the division between the North and South Isles, so that, by this treaty, Bute, Arran, Isla, Jura, Mull, and several smaller islands, as well as the district of Kintyre (which, singularly enough, has always been reckoned among the South Isles),[1] although nominally ceded to the sons of Somerled, were, in reality, added to the possessions of that warlike chief, who naturally acted as guardian for his children during their minority. From this time, says the chronicler, may be dated the ruin of the Kingdom of the Isles. The allegiance of all the Isles to Norway seems still to have been preserved.

A. D. 1158.

Two years after this treaty, Somerled invaded Man with a fleet of fifty-three ships, and laid the whole island waste, after routing Godred in battle. Whether this invasion was in consequence of

[1] The origin of this was a stratagem of Magnus Barefoot. After that prince had invaded and conquered the Isles, he made an agreement with Malcolm Canmor, by which the latter was to leave Magnus and his successors in peaceable possession of all the Isles which could be circumnavigated. The King of Norway had himself drawn across the narrow isthmus between Kintyre and Knapdale, in a galley, by which he added the former district to the Isles. This anecdote has been doubted by some, but it appears in Magnus Berfaet's Saga, a contemporary work; and it is certain that, as late as the commencement of the seventeenth century, Kintyre was classed by the Scottish government as one of the South Isles.

any infringement of the treaty by Godred, or whether it arose from the insatiable ambition of Somerled, is uncertain; but the power of Godred was so much broken, that he was compelled to visit Norway to seek assistance against his rival; nor did he return to the Isles till after Somerled's death, from which it may be inferred that the latter had succeeded in extending his sway over the whole Isles.

Malcolm IV. was now King of Scotland. To this prince, Somerled had early made himself obnoxious, by espousing the cause of his nephews, the sons of Wymund or Malcolm MacHeth, a claimant of the earldom of Murray, whom it suited the Scottish government for the time to detain in prison as an impostor, but whose claim now seems, on minute inquiry, to have been well founded.[1] Owing to the additional power which he acquired from the late events in the Isles, Somerled was enabled, on one occasion, to bring his contest with the Scottish King to a close by a treaty, which was considered so important as to form an epoch from which royal charters were dated.[2] From some cause, which our historians do not sufficiently explain, this ambitious lord was, ere long, induced again to declare war against Malcolm, and, assembling a numerous army from Argyle, Ireland, and the Isles, he sailed up the Clyde with one hundred and sixty galleys, and landed his forces near Renfrew, threatening, as some of A. D. 1164. the chroniclers inform us, to make a conquest of the whole of Scotland. Here, according

[1] On the first appearance of Malcolm MacHeth, Somerled gave him his sister in marriage, which shows the opinion he entertained of the justice of Malcolm's claims.

[2] Sir James Dalrymple's Collections, p. 425.

to the usual accounts, Somerled was slain, with one of his sons,[1] and his great armament dispersed, with much loss, by a very inferior force of the Scots. But, from the well-known character of this celebrated chief, there seems great reason to believe that tradition is correct, when it states that he was assassinated in his tent by an individual in whom he placed confidence, and that his troops, thus deprived of their leader, returned in haste to the Isles. In their retreat, they, probably, suffered much from the Scots, who, if not privy to the assassination, must have soon learned the disaster that had befallen the invaders. From the same traditionary source we learn that the King of Scotland sent a boat, with the corpse of Somerled, to Icolmkill, at his own charge; but modern inquiries rather lead to the conclusion that he was interred at the Church of Sadale, in Kintyre, where Reginald, his son, afterwards founded a monastery. Somerled, according to tradition, was " a well-tempered man, in body shapely, of a fair piercing eye, of middle stature, and of quick discernment." [2]

Besides the three sons of his marriage with the daughter of Olave the Red, Somerled had other sons, who seemed to have shared with their brothers, according to the then prevalent custom of gavel-kind, the mainland possessions held by the Lord of Argyll; whilst the sons, descended of the House of Man, divided amongst them, in addition, the South Isles, as ceded by Godred in 1156. The Isle of Man, and any other conquests made by Somerled in the Isles, from 1158 to his death

[1] The son's name was Gillecolane (Gillecallum or Malcolm).— Hailes' Annals, ad annum 1164.
[2] Hugh Macdonald's MS.

in 1164, did not remain with his family, but fell again
under the authority of Godred the Black, their proper
ruler, with whose descendants they remained till the
final cession of the Isles to Scotland, a century later.
In the division of the South Isles, Mull, Coll, Tiree,
and Jura, seem to have fallen to the share of Dugall;
Isla and Kintyre to that of Reginald; and Bute (which,
from its position, was peculiarly exposed to the aggressions of the Scots) to Angus. Arran was, perhaps,
divided between the two latter, and may have been the
cause of the deadly quarrel which, we know, existed
between them; for, in 1192, the Chronicle of Man
mentions a battle between Reginald and Angus, in
which the latter obtained the victory. Eighteen years
later, we learn, on the same authority, that Angus was
killed, with his three sons, by the men of Skye; after
which, it is probable, that Argyle and the South Isles
were exclusively divided between Dugall and Reginald,
the latter of whom bestowed Bute and part of Kintyre
upon his son Roderick, or Ruari, who became the
founder of a distinct family, which afterwards became
very powerful in the Isles. Both Dugall and Reginald
were called *Kings* of the Isles at the same time that
Reginald, the son of Godred the Black, was styled
King of Man and the Isles; and, in the next generation, we find, in a Norse chronicle, mention of three
Kings of the Isles, of the race of Somerled, existing at
one time.[1] It is evident, therefore, that the word king,
as used by the Norwegians and their vassals in the
Isles, was not confined, as in Scotland, to one supreme

[1] Anecdotes of Olave the Black, edited by Johnston. This chronicle
informs us that the Sudureyan *Kings*, of the family of Somerled, were
very untrue to King Haco.

ruler, but that it had with them an additional meaning, corresponding either to prince of the blood-royal or to magnate. Many seannachies or genealogists, in later times, being ignorant of, or having overlooked this distinction, have, by means of the expression King of the Isles, been led to represent those whom they style the direct heirs or successors of Somerled, through his son Reginald, and who alone, according to them, bore the royal title, as holding a rank very different from that which they actually held.

It would occupy too much space here to enter minutely into the history of the immediate descendants of Somerled prior to the great expedition of Haco, King of Norway;—suffice it to say, that from King Dugall sprung the great House of *Argyle and Lorn,* patronymically Macdugall,[1] which, at the time of Haco's expedition, was represented by Dugall's grandson, Ewin, commonly called King Ewin, and sometimes, erroneously, King John. From King Reginald, on the other hand, sprang two great families, that of *Isla,* descended from his son Donald, and therefore patronymically styled Macdonald; and that of *Bute,* descended from his son Ruari, already mentioned, and therefore patronymically styled Macruari.[2] At the date of Haco's expedition, we find that the family of Isla was represented by Angus, the son of Donald (the Angus Mor of the Seannachies); that of Bute by Ruari himself and his sons, Allan and Dugall. It appears that most, if not all of the descendants of So-

---

[1] This family used generally the territorial surname of " *de Ergadia,*" or " of Argyle."

[2] Both the Macdonalds and Macruaries used the territorial surnames of " *de Yla,*" or " of Isla," and " *de Insulis,*" or " of the Isles."

merled, had, for a century after his death, a divided allegiance, holding part of their lands, those in the Isles, from the King of Norway; their mainland domains being, at the same time, held of the King of Scotland. The latter, whose power was now gradually increasing, could not be expected long to allow the Isles to remain dependent on Norway, without making an effort to conquer them. The first footing obtained by the Scots in the Isles was, apparently, soon after the death of Somerled, when the Steward of Scotland seized the Isle of Bute. That Island seems after this to have changed masters several times, and, along with Kintyre, to have been a subject of dispute between the Scots and Norwegians, whilst, in the course of these quarrels, the family of the Steward strengthened their claims, by marriage, in the following manner. We have seen that Angus MacSomerled (who is supposed to have been Lord of Bute), and his three sons, were killed in 1210; nor does it appear that Angus had any other male issue. James, one of these sons, left a daughter and heiress, Jane, afterwards married to Alexander, the son and heir of Walter, the High Steward of Scotland, who, in her right, claimed the Isle of Bute, and, perhaps, Arran also.[1] This claim was naturally resisted by Ruari, the son of Reginald, till the dispute was settled for a time by his expulsion,

---

[1] In the traditions of the Stewarts, this lady's grandfather is called Angus Mac*Rorie*, which, as I conceive, is an error for Angus Mac*Sorlie* —the latter being the way in which MacSomerled (spelt MacSomhairle) is pronounced in Gaelic. That there was, about this time, a matrimonial alliance between the house of Stewart and that of Isla, is probable from a dispensation in 1342, for the marriage of two individuals of these families, as being within the forbidden degrees. Andrew Stewart's "Hist. of the Stewarts," p. 433.

and the seizure of Bute and Arran by the Scots. Their success here encouraged the latter to further encroachments, and it is well known that Alexander II. died on the coast of Argyleshire, while leading an expedition against the Isles. Although this event suspended for a time the projects of the Scots, they were by no means forgotten, but, on the contrary, were resumed in the course of a few years. Early in the reign of Alexander III., Angus, the son of Donald, and Lord of Isla, was closely pursued by that King, because he would not consent to become a vassal of Scotland for the lands he held of Norway. The complaints of Ruari of Bute, and the other Islanders, to the Norwegian court, of the aggressions of the Scots, led to Haco's celebrated expedition, in which, without difficulty, he made himself master of such of the Isles as had been conquered by the Scots, and restored Bute to Ruari, who had long been in Norway, seeking assistance from him, and had accompanied him on this expedition. These triumphs were, however, of short duration. The Norwegians, not content with re-establishing their authority in the Isles, proceeded to ravage the neighbouring districts of Scotland, and, while thus occupied, at a late season of the year, suffered severely from storms, which, joined to a check they received at Largs, in an attempt to make a descent on Ayrshire, caused them to retire to the Orkneys, where Haco soon after died. Alexander III. immediately took advantage of this circumstance, and resumed his projects against the Isles with such success, that, on the death of Magnus, King of Man (a descendant of Godred the Black), Magnus of Norway, the successor of

A. D. 1255.

A. D. 1263.

A. D. 1265.

Haco, was induced to cede all the Western Isles to Scotland. One of the articles of the important treaty by which this cession was made, provided that a certain annual sum should be paid by Scotland to Norway, in consideration of the latter yielding up all claim to the Isles. Another declared that such of the subjects of Norway as were inclined to quit the Hebrides, should have full liberty to do so, with all their effects, whilst those who preferred remaining, were to become sub-jects of Scotland. To this latter class, the

A. D. 1266.

King of Norway, in fulfilment of his part of the treaty, addressed a mandate, enjoining them henceforth to serve and obey the King of Scotland, as their liege lord; and it was further arranged, that none of the Islanders were to be punished for their former adherence to the Norwegians.[1]

[1] The preceding portion of this introductory sketch has been drawn up with great pains, from the best authorities to which I have had an opportunity of referring; and much has been done to rectify the chronology. Want of space has prevented my quoting these authorities more minutely. I may here mention, generally, the authorities I allude to:—Caledonia, Vol. I., and the Roman authors there referred to; the early Scottish Chronicles, printed in the Appendix to Innes's Critical Essay, and elsewhere; the early Irish Chronicles, or Annals, printed in the Scriptores.Rerum Hibernicarum; the Scriptores Rerum Danicarum; the Orkneyinga Saga; Magnus Berfaet's Saga; Chronicle of Man; Anecdotes of Olave the Black; Expedition of King Haco in 1263; Rymer's Fœdera Angliae; the Saxon Chronicle; Collectanea de Rebus Albanicis; Dr. Macpherson's Dissertations; Mr. Dillon's Observations on the Norse Account of Haco's Expedition, in the Archaeologia Scotica, Vol. II.; Lord Hailes' (Sir David Dalrymple's) Annals; Duncan Stewart's History of the Stewarts, &c., &c. I must here acknowledge the valuable assistance which I have received from my colleague and friend, William F. Skene, Esq., not only in the researches which were rendered necessary by my undertaking the present

During these transactions, the position of the descendants of Somerled was rather singular. Ewin of Lorn, who, in 1249, had refused to join the Scots, attached himself, in 1263, to Alexander III.; but, at the same time, honourably resigned into the hands of Haco all that he held of the crown of Norway. On the other hand, Angus of Isla, who had previously been made to give hostages to Alexander, was, on the arrival of Haco in the Isles, forced to join the Norwegians in person. Ruari of Bute and his sons were devoted partisans of Haco. The treaty of cession seems to have been acted on, in a liberal manner, by the Scottish king. Ewin of Lorn was, of course, restored to the lands he had formerly held of Norway, and further rewarded for his services. Angus of Isla, having determined to remain in the Isles, became, according to the treaty, a vassal of Scotland for his lands there, and was allowed to retain, under a single king, all that he had formerly held under two. Lastly, the sons of Ruari, although forced to resign Bute, had lands assigned to them (on their agreeing to remain subjects of Scotland) in that portion of the Isles which had belonged to the King of Man. Hence this family came to be styed Macruaries of the North Isles; and, on the death of Dugall, called

A. D. 1268. *Rex Hebudum*, one of the brothers,[1] Allan, the survivor, united, in his person, the possessions of both, to which afterwards he appears to have added the Lordship of Garmoran, on the mainland. The Isles of Skye and Lewis were conferred upon the

---

work, but in all the historical inquiries which I have had occasion to make for several years past.

[1] Langebeck, Scriptores Rerum Danicarum, vol. III., p. 109.

Earl of Ross,[1] no part of these islands, or of Man, Arran, and Bute, being granted by Alexander III. to the descendants of Somerled. Of these descendants, there were, in 1285, three great noblemen, all holding extensive possessions in the Isles, as well as on the mainland, who attended in that Scottish Parliament by which the crown was settled on the Maiden of Norway. Their names were, Alexander de Ergadia of Lorn (son of Ewin of Lorn), Angus, the son of Donald, and Allan, the son of Ruari.[2] From the nature of the treaty in 1266, it is obvious that these individuals were vassals of the King of Scotland for all their possessions, and not merely for what they held on the mainland, as some have supposed. It is further clear, that, at this time, none of the three bore the title of Lord of the Isles, or could have been properly so considered; and it is equally certain, that the first individual whom we find assuming the style of Lord of the Isles, in its modern signification, possessed all those Isles, and very nearly all those mainland estates, which, in 1285, were divided among three powerful noblemen of the same blood. But of this hereafter. From the preceding remarks, it will readily be perceived that the boasted independence of the modern Lords of the Isles is without historical foundation. Prior to 1266, the Isles were subject to Norway; at that date, the treaty of cession transferred them to Scotland; and, ever since, they have remained subject to the latter crown, notwithstanding successive rebellions, instigated in every case by the government of England, in order to embarrass the Scots.

A. D. 1284.

[1] Robertson's Index to Missing Scottish Charters, p. 124, No. 26.
[2] Rymer's Fœdera, II. 266.

In the series of struggles for Scottish independence, which marked the close of the thirteenth and the opening of the fourteenth centuries, the Lords of Lorn, who were closely connected by marriage with the Comyn and Balliol party, naturally arrayed themselves in opposition to the claims of Bruce. On the other hand, the houses of Isla and of the North Isles supported, with all their power, the apparently desperate fortunes of King Robert I.;[1] and thus, when he came to be firmly seated on the throne, had earned the gratitude of that Prince, in the same proportion as the family of Lorn, by the inveteracy of their hostility, had provoked his resentment. On the forfeiture of Alexander, Lord of Lorn, and his son and heir John, their extensive territories were granted by Bruce to various of his supporters; and, amongst others, to Angus Oig, *i.e.*, Junior, of Isla, and to Roderick or Ruari MacAlan, the bastard brother and leader of the vassals of Christina, the daughter and heiress of Alan MacRuari of the North Isles.[2] The Isles of Mull (the possession of which had, for some time past, been disputed betwixt the Lords of Isla and Lorn), Jura, Coll, and Tiree, with the districts of Duror and Glenco, fell, in this way, to the share of Angus Oig. Lorn Proper, or the greatest part of it, was bestowed on Roderick MacAlan, to whom his sister Christina gave, at the same time, a large portion of her inheritance in Garmoran and the North Isles.[3] The Lordship of Lochaber, forfeited by one of the powerful family of Comyn, seems to have been divided between Angus Oig and Roderick. The former

---

[1] Barbour's Bruce; Fordun a Goodal, II., p. 234. Angus of Isla joined the party of Bruce as early as 1286; Tytler's Scotland, I. 65.

[2] Robertson's Index, p. 2, No. 51, 52, 54; p. 26, No. 23.

[3] Charter in Haddington's MS. Collections, Adv. Library.

likewise obtained, in this reign, the lands of Morvern[1] and Ardnamurchan, which seem previously to have been in the hands of the crown. But while Bruce thus rewarded his faithful adherents, he was too sensible of the weakness of Scotland on the side of the Isles, not to take precautionary measures against the possible defection of any of the great families on that coast, who might with ease admit an English force into the heart of the kingdom. He procured from Angus Oig, who was now, apparently, the principal crown vassal in Kintyre, the resignation of his lands in that district, which were immediately bestowed upon Robert, the son and heir of Walter the High Steward, and the Princess Marjory Bruce.[2] At the same time, the fortifications of the Castle of Tarbert, between Kintyre and Knapdale, the most important position on the coast of Argyleshire, were greatly enlarged and strengthened, and the custody of this commanding post was committed to a royal garrison.[3] Following out the same policy in other places, the keeping of the Castle of Dunstaffnage, the principal messuage of Lorn, was given by Bruce, not to Roderick MacAlan, the "High Chief of Lorn," but to an individual of the name of Campbell, who was placed there as a royal constable.[4]

Towards the end of Bruce's reign, Roderick MacAlan, of Lorn and the North Isles, was forfeited of all his possessions, for engaging in some of the plots which, at that period, occupied the attention

A. D. 1325.

---

[1] The district now called Morvern was, in former times, it would appear, known as Kenalban, or the promontory of Alban or Scotland.

[2] Robertson's Index, p. 26, No. 32.

[3] High Treasurer's Accounts, temp. Rob. I.

[4] Robertson's Index, p. 14.

and called forth the energies of that celebrated King.[1] On this occasion, it is probable that Angus Oig, whose loyalty never wavered, received further additions to his already extensive possessions; and before King Robert's death, the house of Isla was already the most powerful in Argyle and the Isles. Angus Oig and his munificent patron died about the same time; but John of Isla, the son and heir of the former, was far from exhibiting the same devoted loyalty to the House of Bruce which had characterised his father.

When the star of Edward Balliol was in the ascendant, John of the Isles was induced to join that party, owing, in some measure, to his prospect of losing many of the lands granted to his father by Robert Bruce, even if he should remain neuter in the struggle which was going on. To secure so important an adherent, Balliol, besides granting to him nearly the whole of the territories which Angus Oig had possessed at his death, gave, in addition, the lands of Kintyre and Knapdale, and the Isles of Skye and Lewis, which the expected forfeiture of the High Steward and his relations, and of the Earl of Ross, was to place at the disposal of the pseudo-King.[2] On the return of David II. from France, after the final discomfiture of Balliol and his supporters, John of the Isles was naturally exposed to the hostility of the Steward and the other nobles of the Scottish party, by whose advice he seems to have been forfeited, when many of his lands were granted to one of his relations, Angus Mac-Ian, progenitor of the house of Ardnamurchan.[3] This

A. D. 1335.

A. D. 1341.

[1] Robertson's Index, p. 28.
[2] Rymer's Fœdera, IV., 711.
[3] Ch. in Haddington's Collections, Adv. Library.

grant did not, however, take effect; and such was the resistance offered by John and his kinsman, Reginald or Ranald, son of Roderick MacAlan (who had been restored, in all probability, by Balliol, to the lands forfeited by his father), and so anxious was David at the time to bring the whole force of his kingdom together in his intended wars with England, that he A. D. 1344. at length pardoned both these powerful chiefs, and confirmed to them the following possessions :—To John, he gave the Isles of Isla, Gigha, Jura, Scarba, Colonsay, Mull, Coll, Tiree, and Lewis, and the districts of Morvern, Lochaber, Duror, and Glenco ; to Ranald, the Isles of Uist, Barra, Egg, and Rum, and the Lordship of Garmoran, being the original possessions of his family in the north.[1] By this arrangement, Kintyre, Knapdale, and Skye, reverted to their former owners, and Lorn remained in the hands of the Crown, whilst it is probable that Ardnamurchan was given as a compensation to Angus MacIan.

A. D. 1346. Soon after this time, Ranald MacRuari was killed at Perth, in a quarrel between him and the Earl of Ross, from whom he held the lands of Kintail. As he left no issue, his sister, Amie, the wife of John of Isla, became, in terms of the above-mentioned grant from David II., his heir; and her husband, uniting her possessions to his own, assumed henceforth the style of *Dominus Insularum*, or Lord of the Isles.[2]

---

[1] Robertson's Index, p. 100. The Lordship of Garmoran (also called Garbhchrioch) comprehends the districts of Moydert, Arasaig, Morar, and Knoydert.

[2] The first recorded instance of this style being used by John of Isla is in an indenture with the Lord of Lorn, 1354.—Appendix to "Hailes' Annals of Scotland," 2nd edition. This indenture, a very remarkable deed, does not appear either in the first or third edition of these annals.

Thus was formed the modern Lordship of the Isles, comprehending the territories of the Macdonalds of Isla, and the Macruaries of the North Isles, and a great part of those of the Macdugalls of Lorn; and although the representative of the latter family was nominally restored to the estates of his ancestors on the occasion of his marriage with a niece of the King,[1] yet he was obliged to leave the Lord of the Isles in possession of such portion of the Lorn estates as had been granted to the latter by David in 1344. The daughter and heiress of John de Ergadia, or Macdugall, the restored Lord of Lorn, carried Lorn Proper to her husband, Robert Stewart, founder of the Rosyth family, by whom the Lordship was sold to his brother, John Stewart of Innermeath, ancestor of the Stewarts, Lords of Lorn.[2]

After the reconciliation of David II. and John of Isla in 1334, we can trace various attempts, on the part of the English government, to withdraw the latter from his allegiance, all of which seem to have failed.[3] In the later years of David's reign, the Lord of the Isles was again in rebellion; nor was he reduced to obedience without much difficulty. The records of the period, however, show that his turbulence at this time was not the result of English intrigue, but connected with a general resistance, on the part of the Highlanders, to some of the fiscal measures of the Scottish government.[4] The second reconciliation of the Lord of the Isles with David II. took place in 1369, a year before the death of that King; and, from this time till his death, in the reign of Robert II., he conducted himself as a loyal and obedient

---

[1] Robertson's Index, p. 30.

[2] Inventory of Argyle Writs, title Lorn.

[3] Rymer's Fœdera, V., 530, 849. Rotuli Scotiæ, I., 677.

[4] Ancient Book of Record, quoted by Mr. Tytler, Vol. II., p. 169.

subject. Having thus given a brief sketch of the public history of John, first Lord of the Isles, under the reigns of David II. and Robert II., it now becomes necessary to allude to his private history during the same period.

He married, as we have mentioned, Amie Macruari, heiress of that family;[1] and his sons by this marriage were John, Godfrey, and Ranald. The eldest of these sons was dead before 1369, leaving issue, Angus, who did not long survive. Of the others we shall afterwards have occasion more particularly to speak. Notwithstanding that he had, in right of Amie his wife, succeeded to such extensive possessions, the Lord of the Isles divorced that lady,[2] and married, secondly, the Lady Margaret, daughter to Robert, High Steward of Scotland. Of this marriage there were likewise three sons—viz., Donald, John, and Alexander. We cannot fix precisely the date of this second marriage; but it must have taken place in the reign of David II., as Donald, the eldest son, was named as a hostage by his father in 1369. It is probable that the Lord of the Isles, and his father-in-law, the Steward, had come to a secret understanding before the marriage, on which they afterwards acted, when, at the death of David, the Steward ascended the throne by the title of Robert II. Certain it is, that, after that event, A. D. 1370. the destination of the Lordship of the Isles was altered, so as to cause it to descend to the grandchildren of the

[1] The dispensation for this marriage was dated in 1337; Andrew Stewart's History of the Stewarts, p. 446.

[2] It seems clear, from the unvarying tradition of the country, that the Lady Amie had given no grounds for this divorce. She dwelt on her own estates till her death; and is said to have built the Castles of Elanterim in Moydert, and Borve in Benbecula.

King.[1] Aware that his right to Garmoran and the
North Isles was annulled by the divorce of his first wife,
the Lord of the Isles, disregarding her claims, and trusting
to his influence with the King, his father-in-law, procured
a royal charter of the lands in question, in which her name
was not even mentioned.   Godfrey, the eldest son of the
Lord of the Isles, by his first wife, resisted these unjust
proceedings—maintaining his mother's prior claims, and
his own as her heir; but Ranald, his younger brother,
being more pliant, was rewarded by a grant of the
North Isles, Garmoran, and many other lands,
A. D. 1373.   to hold of John, Lord of the Isles, *and his
heirs*.[2] Such was the state of affairs in the Lordship of
the Isles at the death of the first Lord.   He
A. D. 1380.   died at his own castle of Ardtornish, in Morvern, and was buried in Iona, with great splendour, by
the ecclesiastics of the Isles,[3] whose attachment he had
obtained by liberal grants to the Church, and who
evinced their gratitude, by bestowing on him the appellation, which tradition has handed down to our days, of
" the good John of Isla." [4]

Donald, the eldest son of the second marriage,
became, on his father's death, second Lord of the
Isles, and in that capacity was, most undoubtedly, feudal
superior and actual chief of his brothers, whether of
the full or of the half blood.   He married Mary Leslie,

---

[1] This appears from various charters in the public records, soon
after the accession of Robert II.

[2] Reg. of Great Seal, Rot. III., No. 18.

[3] Macvurich's MS. in Gaelic, commonly, but erroneously, called
the Red Book of Clanranald.

[4] See Dean Monro's Genealogies, written in the sixteenth century.

who afterwards became Countess of Ross, and his contest with the Regent Duke of Albany, regarding that
Earldom, in the course of which the battle
A. D. 1411.
of Harlaw was fought, is too well known to
require repetition here. It is only necessary to remark,
that the whole array of the Lordship of the Isles
followed him on that occasion, and that he was not
weakened by any opposition, on the part of his elder
brothers or their descendants, which certainly might
have been looked for. Ranald, the youngest, but most
favoured son of the first marriage of the good John,
was, as the seannachies tell us, "old in the government of the Isles at his father's death." After that
event, he acted as tutor or guardian to his younger
brother, Donald, Lord of the Isles, to whom, on his
attaining majority, he delivered over the Lordship, in
presence of the vassals, "contrary to the opinion of
the men of the Isles,"[1] who, doubtless, considered Godfrey as their proper Lord. On the death of Ranald,
who did not long survive his father, his children, then
young, were dispossessed by their uncle Godfrey, who
assumed the style of Lord of Uist (which, with Garmoran, he actually possessed), but never questioned
the claims of Donald to the Lordship of the Isles.[2]
If the opinion of the Islanders was, at first, really in
favour of Godfrey, the liberality of Donald seems soon
to have reconciled them to the rule of the latter; at
least, there is no trace, after this time, of any opposition among them to Donald, or his descendants. As

[1] Macvurich's MS.

[2] Charter by Godfridus de Insula, Dominus de Uist, to the
monastery of Inchaffray, in 1388; dated, "apud castrum nostrum
de Elantyrim:" Chartulary of Inchaffray.

the claim of "Donald of Harlaw," to the Earldom of Ross, in right of his wife, was, after his death, virtually admitted by King James I., and as Donald himself was actually in possession of that Earldom, and acknowledged by the vassals in 1411, he may, without impropriety, be called the first Earl of Ross of his family. To his brothers of the full blood, he gave ample territories, as his vassals; and each of them became the founder of a powerful family. The eldest, John Mor, or John the Tanister, as he was called, was the progenitor of a numerous tribe, called the Clandonald of the South, or the Clan Ian Mhor of Isla and Kintyre, where their hereditary possessions lay. Alexander, or Allaster Carrach, the youngest of the brothers, was styled Lord of Lochaber; and from him descended the Macdonalds of Keppoch, or, as they are sometimes styled, the Clanranald of Lochaber. After the death of John, Lord of the Isles, we discover various indications that the intrigues of the English court with the Scottish Islanders had been resumed; and it is not altogether improbable, that it was a suspicion of these treasonable practices which caused the Regent, Robert of Albany, to oppose the pretensions of Donald, Lord of the Isles, to the Earldom of Ross.[1] But, although English emissaries were, on various occasions, despatched, not only to the Lord of the Isles himself, but to his brothers, Godfrey and John—and two of the brothers even appear to have visited the English court —we cannot, at this distance of time, ascertain how far these intrigues were carried. Donald, second Lord of

[1] Rymer's Fœdera, VIII., 146, 418, 527. Rotuli Scotiæ, II., 94, 155.

the Isles, had issue, by the heiress of Ross, Alexander,
Cir. A. D. his successor, and Angus, afterwards Bishop
1420. of the Isles; and, dying in Isla, he was
interred at Iona with the usual ceremonies.[1]

The history of Alexander, third Lord of the Isles,
and second Earl of Ross, of his line, is given, with
tolerable accuracy, by the writers of the period; as his
high rank, and his relationship to the sovereign, give
him a prominent place in the annals of the reign of
James I. The policy of this King was, in every respect,
opposed to that of the family of Albany; and, consequently, when the Earldom of Ross, which had been
procured by Duke Robert for his son, John, Earl of
A. D. 1424. Buchan, fell to the crown, by the death of
that nobleman,[2] King James at once restored
it to the heiress of line, the mother of the Lord of the
Isles. In the following year, Alexander, Lord of the
A. D. 1425. Isles, and Master of the Earldom of Ross,
sat upon the jury which condemned to death
Murdoch, Duke of Albany, his sons, and the aged Earl
of Lennox;[3] but he did not long retain the favour
which, at this time, he seems to have enjoyed. To
understand, however, the position in which the Lord of
the Isles was placed when we first find him at variance
with the King, it is necessary to turn, for a while, to the
history of some of the branches of the family of the Isles.

[1] Macvurich's MS.

[2] John Stewart, Earl of Buchan and Ross, was killed at the battle of
Verneuil in France, in 1424.

[3] Bower's Continuation of Fordun's Scotichronicon; Edit. Hearne,
IV., p. 1271. The historian styles him loosely *Earl* of Ross, in 1425.;
but, from a charter granted by him two years later, we find that his
proper style, at this time, was " *Magister* Comitatus Rossiæ."—Reg. of
Great Seal, XIII., 188.

It has been mentioned that Godfrey, Lord of Uist, on the death of his younger brother, Ranald, asserted successfully his claim to the North Isles and Garmoran, from which he had been unjustly excluded by his father. Both Godfrey and Ranald left male issue, who must naturally have been opposed to each other, like their fathers; but the meagre notices which we possess of the domestic feuds in the Highlands and Isles at this period, do not enable us to trace the progress of these dissensions. We may readily conceive, however, that, where so rich a prize was in dispute, much blood would be shed, and many atrocities committed. The issue of Godfrey, or the Siol Gorrie, as they were called, must, for a time, have acquired a superiority over the Clanranald—so the descendants of Ranald were styled; at least, under the year 1427, we find mention made, by a contemporary historian, of Alexander MacGorrie of Garmoran, described as a leader of two thousand men.[1] But, in addition to the causes of disturbance arising from the rival claims of two families so closely connected with the Lord of the Isles, there were other circumstances which tended to involve that nobleman in feuds which his disposition led him to settle by the sword, rather than by an appeal to the laws. A certain John Macarthur, of the family of Campbell, and a leader of note in the Highlands, seems to have revived about this time a claim which one of his ancestors had acquired to a portion of Garmoran and the North

---

[1] He is generally called by our historians, "MacRuari," which surname he seems to have assumed from his father's maternal ancestors; or, which is most probable, "MacRorie," as it is frequently written, may be an error for "MacGorrie." Hugh Macdonald states distinctly in his MS. that Gorrie had a son, Allaster.

Isles;[1] and it is not difficult to conjecture what reception such pretensions would meet with from the Lord of the Isles and his warlike vassals. The event, however, that seems to have had most effect in throwing the Highlands and Isles into confusion, was the murder of John, Lord of Isla and Kintyre, uncle to the Lord of the Isles, by an individual called James Campbell. The latter is said to have received a commission from the King to apprehend John of Isla; but it is added, that he exceeded his powers in putting that chief to death.[2] When we consider the lawless state in which even the more accessible parts of Scotland were found by King James, owing to the weakness and incapacity of the Regent Murdoch, Duke of Albany, we can easily conceive how the circumstances above alluded to should have raised disturbances in the Highlands and Isles, which it might require all the energy of the King to suppress.

A. D. 1427.

Determined to restore order, and to enforce the laws, James held a Parliament at Inverness, to which the Lord of the Isles, who is described as the principal disturber of the public peace, and the other great Highland chiefs, were summoned. On their arrival at Inverness, they were, to the number of forty, seized by a stratagem of the King, and committed to separate prisons. Some, whose crimes were most notorious, were immediately brought to trial, condemned, and executed; and of this number were Alexander

[1] Charter by Christina, daughter of Alan (MacRuari) to Arthur, son of Sir Arthur Campbell, knight, early in the fourteenth century, of the lands of Moydert, &c. This charter is quoted for the witnesses' names in a MS. History of the Macnaughtons in the Advocates' Library.

[2] Hugh Macdonald's MS.

MacGorrie of Garmoran, and John Macarthur. At
the same time, James Campbell was hanged for the
murder of John of Isla, as if to show the impartiality
of the Sovereign. Others, whose guilt was not at first
so apparent, were detained in prison for some time,
and then executed; but the greater number, and among
them the Lord of the Isles, were liberated without
more severe punishment than was implied in their
imprisonment for various periods, according to the magnitude of their offences.[1] The Lord of the Isles, by
his conduct after his liberation, showed that he felt
deeply the indignity he had suffered. The death of
his mother[2] had now made him Earl of Ross; and soon
after his return from prison, he summoned together his
vassals, both of Ross and the Isles; wasted
the Crown lands near Inverness, at the head
of a force of ten thousand men; and then burned the
town of Inverness to the ground. No sooner had
information of this inroad reached the King, than, with
his characteristic promptitude, he prepared to vindicate
his insulted authority. Leading in person some troops

A. D. 1429.

---

[1] Bower a Hearne, IV., pp. 1283-4. Chronicle of the Earls of
Ross, printed in the Miscellanea Scotica. Among the other chiefs
mentioned, are, " *Mak Makan,*" that is, MacMahon or Mathewson of
Lochalsh, leader of one thousand men ; and a certain " *Kenneth Moire,*"
whom I conjecture to have been the chief, for the time, of the Mackenzies, although omitted in the MS. histories of that family, probably
from his leaving no issue.

[2] In 1429, the Countess of Ross, being charged with encouraging
her son in his violent proceedings, was arrested and confined at Inch-
colm, in the Frith of Forth, where she is said to have remained *fourteen*
months a prisoner. Bower a Hearne, IV., p. 1226. This is hardly
reconcilable with a charter, dated 24th October, 1429, in which her son
styles himself *Earl* instead of *Master* of Ross. Sutherland additional
case, cap. v., p. 30.

hastily collected, he succeeded, by forced marches, in coming up with the rebels, who were then in Lochaber, at a time when he was least expected. On the appearance of the royal banner, the Clanchattan and Clanchameron, two potent tribes that supported the Earl of Ross, went over to the King, who, following up his advantage, attacked and routed the rebels, pursuing them so hotly that their leader was glad to sue for peace. James, however, sternly refused to enter into a negotiation with his rebellious subject, on any other footing than that of an unconditional surrender; and returned to his capital, after giving strict orders to his officers, that every effort should be made to apprehend the fugitive Earl. The latter, at length, driven to despair by the activity of his pursuers, adopted the resolution of throwing himself on the mercy of his Sovereign. Upon the eve of a solemn festival, this haughty nobleman presented himself before the King, who, and the Queen and Court, were assembled in the church of Holyrood. He was clothed only in his shirt and drawers; he held his naked sword by the point in his hand, and, with a countenance and manner in which destitution and misery were strongly exhibited, he fell upon his knees, and, surrendering his sword, implored the royal clemency. His life was spared, but he was committed to close ward in the Castle of Tantallon, under the charge of William Earl of Angus.[1]

A. D. 1431.   While the Earl of Ross was still in prison, the Royal forces which, under the Earls of Mar and Caithness, occupied Lochaber, in order to overawe the clans of the west, were surprised and routed by a body of the latter, under a leader named Donald Balloch. This

[1] Bower a Hearne, IV., p. 1286. Chronicle of the Earls of Ross.

chief was the cousin-german of the Earl of Ross; being
the son of that John of Isla who, as formerly mentioned, was murdered by James Campbell. The news
of the battle of Inverlochy, in which the Earl of
Caithness, and many of the royal troops, were killed,
and the Earl of Mar was severely wounded, was received with great indignation by the King, who immediately prepared to punish the aggressors. Having
procured from his Parliament a land tax, to defray the
expenses of the expedition, he soon made his appearance at the Royal Castle of Dunstaffnage, in Lorn,
with the avowed intention of proceeding to the Isles,
to inflict exemplary punishment on Donald Balloch and
his followers. That chief, after ravaging the lands
of the Clanchattan and Clanchameron, had quitted
Lochaber, and, on the approach of the King, fled to
Ireland.[1] The other leaders of the insurgents, dreading the determined character of James, came to meet
him at Dunstaffnage, eager to make their submission,
and to throw the whole blame of the insurrection upon
Donald Balloch, whose power, as they affirmed, they
had not dared to resist. By their means, a number of
the most noted robbers in the West Highlands and
Isles were seized and led to immediate execution; and
the peace of that part of the country secured
A. D. 1431. for some time to come, by the activity and
determination of the King.[2] On the return of James
to Edinburgh, a head, said to be that of Donald Balloch, was sent to him by Hugh Buy O'Neill, an Irish

---

[1] It may be noticed here that Donald Balloch inherited, through
his mother, Margery Bisset, the territory of the Glens in Antrim.

[2] Tytler's Scotland, III. 277-9. Buchanan, b. X., c. 33-36; Chronicle
of the Earls of Ross. Hugh Macdonald's MS.

chief of Ulster; and it was generally believed at the Scottish Court that the ringleader of the late insurrection was now no more. But, as Donald Balloch certainly survived King James many years, it is obvious that the sending of the head to Edinburgh was a stratagem devised by the crafty Islander, in order to check further pursuit. It is only necessary to mention further, in connection with this brief rebellion, that Alexander of Lochaber, uncle of the Earl of Ross, seems to have been deprived of his lands for assisting Donald Balloch; and that Ross, as superior of the lands, was compelled by the King to bestow them upon the captain of the Clanchattan, Malcolm Macintosh.

As Ross, after a captivity of about two years in the Castle of Tantallon, received in this year a free pardon in Parliament for all his crimes,[1] it is probable that he was not considered in any way answerable for the insurrection of Donald Balloch and its consequences. From this time, to the death of James I., he seems to have continued loyal, duly appreciating, as we may suppose, the lenity shown to him by a prince celebrated for the unbending rigour of his government. In the minority of James II., the Earl of Ross held the important office of Justiciar of Scotland, A. D. 1438. north of the Forth;[2] an office which he probably obtained from Archibald, Earl of Douglas and Duke of Touraine, Lieutenant-General of the kingdom. In what manner Ross exercised this office is uncertain; but it was, perhaps, under colour of it that he wreaked

[1] Bower a Hearne, IV., p. 1288.
[2] Charters in the Ch. Chest of Innes, A.D. 1438; the Ch. Chest of Urquhart of Cromarty, 1439; and the Chartulary of Aberdeen, 1442.

his vengeance on the chief of the Clanchameron, who had deserted him in 1427. The latter, in order to save his life, was now forced to fly to Ireland, where he remained for many years, whilst his forfeited lands were bestowed, by the Earl of Ross, upon John Garve Maclean, founder of the family of Coll.[1] The Clanchattan were more fortunate in making their peace with their offended superior, and most unaccountably succeeded in retaining the lands formerly possessed by Alexander of Lochaber, from Angus his son. The Earl of Ross being the most powerful nobleman in the north of Scotland, was necessarily in frequent communication with the Earl of Douglas and the other leading nobles of the realm, and thus became involved in their intrigues. His loyalty to the son of James I. yielded to the temptations held out to him; and, in 1445, he entered into a secret and treasonable league with the Earls of Douglas and Crawford.[2] The details of this instrument have not been preserved; but there is little doubt that the confederate nobles had agreed, as the first step in their designs, to the dethronement of James II. But, before any overt acts of treason were committed in consequence of this conspiracy, the Earl of Ross died at his castle of Dingwall.[3] By his countess, Elizabeth, daughter of Alexander Seton, Lord of Gordon and Huntly, Alexander, Earl of Ross and Lord of the Isles, had issue, John his successor. He had likewise two other legitimate

A. D. 1449.

---

[1] MS. Histories of the families of Lochiel and Coll. Hugh Macdonald's MS.

[2] 7th March, 1445, Sir James Balfour's Annals, I. 173.

[3] He was buried at the Chanonry of Ross, 8th May 1449. Chronicle of the Earls of Ross.

sons (but whether by the same mother or not is uncertain), Celestine, Lord of Lochalche, and Hugh, Lord of Sleat; of whom, and their descendants, we shall afterwards have occasion to speak.[1]

A. D. 1449. When John, Earl of Ross, succeeded to the titles and estates of his family, King James II. was actively employed in weakening the power and usurped authority of William, eighth Earl of Douglas, many of whose adherents, and, particularly, the Livingstons, with which family the young Earl of Ross was connected by marriage,[2] were seized and executed, for various treasonable acts committed by

---

[1] I call these sons legitimate, notwithstanding that Celestine is called "filius *naturalis*" by Earl Alexander (Ch. in Ch. Chest of Macintosh, 1447), and "frater *carnalis*" by Earl John (Reg. of Great Seal, VI., 116, 1463); and that Hugh is likewise called "frater *carnalis*" by Earl John (Ch. in Westfield Writs, in the possession of Alex. Dunbar, Esq., of Scrabster, 1470). They are, however, both called "frater," without any qualification, by Earl John (Reg. of Great Seal, VI. 116; XIII. 186). The history of Celestine and Hugh and their descendants, as given in the present work, sufficiently shows that they were considered legitimate, and that, consequently, the words "naturalis" and "carnalis," taken by themselves, and without the adjunct "*bastardus*," do not necessarily imply bastardy. It is probable that they were used to designate the issue of those handfast or left-handed marriages, which appear to have been so common in the Highlands and Isles. Both *naturalis* and *carnalis* are occasionally applied to individuals known to be legitimate in the strictest sense of the word. A contract of friendship between the Dunbars and Macintoshes, dated in 1492, contains this clause—" The said Alexander Dunbar of Westfield, and Duncan Macintosh, Captain of the Clanchattan, sall obserf and keip kyndes and brethirheid to uthers as *carnale brethire* suld do, for all the dayis of thair lyffis."—(Collectanea de Rebus Albanicis, I. 83). In this instance, *carnal* can have no meaning but one equivalent to *german*.

[2] Chronicle of the Reign of James II., commonly called the Auchinleck Chronicle, pp. 42–44.

them.   It was found expedient to deal more mildly
with the Earl of Douglas, the head of the party, on
account of his great power and vassalage ; but the
King, without absolutely depriving this nobleman of the
high office of Lieutenant-General of the kingdom—a
measure which might, at this moment, have excited an
extreme commotion—silently withdrew from him his
countenance and employment; surrounding himself, at
the same time, by the ablest and most energetic counsellors of the opposite party, whom he promoted to the chief
offices in the State.   Douglas, sensible that his dominion
was on the wane, determined to leave the country for a
season, and repair to Rome, on a visit to the
A. D. 1450.
Pope.   But, although he went abroad with
the apparent intention of remaining several years, he
left powerful friends at home, whose motions he directed,
and by whose assistance he entertained the hope of
once more possessing himself of the supreme power in
the State; and there seems the strongest probability
that he now secretly renewed that treasonable correspondence with the families of Ross and Crawford,
which has been already mentioned.[1]

Douglas' return, however, was hastened
A. D. 1451.
by disturbances at home, arising out of the
insolence and tyranny of his brother, Douglas of Balvany, to whom he had delegated his authority; which
compelled the King to conduct in person an armed
expedition into the lands of the delinquent.   On this
occasion the King made himself master of Lochmaben
Castle, and razed to the ground that of Douglas, which
had long been the centre of insubordination.   The Earl,

---

[1] Tytler's Scotland, IV., pp. 70–86.

alarmed at the news of this expedition, set out forth-
with on his return home. In the meantime his friends
and confederates were not idle in Scotland; and the
Earl of Ross, in particular, broke out into open rebellion, and seized the Royal castles of Inverness, Urquhart, and Ruthven in Badenoch.[1] This last place was
immediately demolished; Urquhart was committed to
the custody of Sir James Livingston, father-in-law to
the Earl of Ross, who, on the first news of the rebellion
of the latter, had escaped from Court to the Highlands;
whilst Inverness Castle was supplied with military stores
and strongly garrisoned. The King, it may be supposed,
was too much occupied in securing himself against the
great power and ambition of the Douglas party in the
southern counties, now rendered more confident by the
return of their chief from abroad, to be able to take
prompt measures against the Earl of Ross; at least,
none such are recorded in the chronicles which have
come down to us. But there can be no doubt that
James contemplated proceeding to the north, to chastise
the rebels there; for it was upon the refusal of Douglas
to renounce the league offensive and defensive, into
which he had entered with the Earls of Ross and
Crawford, that the monarch, in a sudden fit of passion,
assassinated, with his own hand, that nobleman, whose
inordinate ambition was considered the chief cause of
all these commotions. William, Earl of Douglas,
being thus cut off in the height of his power, was suc-

[1] It appears, from a contemporary chronicle, that Ross had some
private grievances to urge him into rebellion. Among other things,
he complained that the King, who caused him to marry Sir James
Livingston's daughter, had promised him, with that lady, a grant of
lands, which promise had not been kept. Auchinleck Chronicle,
p. 44.

ceeded by James, ninth Earl, his brother, who, after repeated rebellions, was finally encountered and defeated A.D. 1455. by the Earl of Angus, leader of the King's troops, at Arkinholme in Annandale. In this battle, Archibald, Earl of Moray, and Hugh, Earl of Ormond, brothers to the Earl of Douglas, were slain; whilst the Earl himself, with his only remaining brother, Sir John Douglas of Balvany, made his escape into the West Highlands. Here he was received by the Earl of Ross, who still remained faithful to his engagements, having, it would appear, hitherto escaped, by reason of the remoteness and inaccessibility of his territories, the vengeance which had fallen so heavily on his confederates, Douglas and Crawford. Ross immediately collected a fleet of one hundred galleys, with a force of five thousand men on board, and despatched this expedition, under the command of his kinsman, Donald Balloch of Isla, to attack the coast of Ayrshire, with the intention, probably, of encouraging the Douglas party again to draw together, should such a course appear expedient. Owing to the able measures of defence adopted by the King, this enterprise met with little success. Donald commenced hostilities at Innerkip in Ayrshire; but being unable to effect any object of importance, he proceeded to ravage the Cumrays and the Isle of Arran. Not above twenty persons, men, women, and children, were slain by the Islanders, although plunder to a considerable amount—including five or six hundred horses, ten thousand oxen and kine, and more than a thousand sheep and goats—was carried off. The Castle of Brodick in Arran was stormed and levelled with the ground; whilst one hundred bolls of meal, one hundred marks,[1]

[1] Cattle intended for winter consumption.

and one hundred marks of silver, were exacted as tribute from the Isle of Bute.[1] The expedition was concluded by an attack upon Lauder, Bishop of Argyle or Lismore, a prelate who had made himself obnoxious by affixing his seal to the instrument of forfeiture of the Douglases; and who was now attacked by the fierce Admiral of the Isles, and, after the slaughter of the greater part of his attendants, forced to take refuge in a sanctuary, which seems scarcely to have protected him from the fury of his enemies.[2]

The Earl of Douglas returned to England after the failure of the expedition under Donald Balloch; and Ross, finding himself alone in rebellion, became alarmed for the consequences, and, by a submissive message, entreated the forgiveness of the King; offering, as far as it was still left to him, to repair the wrongs A. D. 1456. he had inflicted. James at first refused to listen to the application; but, after a time, consented to extend to the humbled chief a period of probation, within which, if he should evince the reality of his repentance by some notable exploit, he was to be absolved from all the consequences of his rebellion, and reinstated in the Royal favour.[3] The Earl of Ross was, in 1457, one of the Wardens of the Marches,[4] an office of great trust and importance, but obviously intended to weaken his influence in the Highlands and Isles, by forcing him frequently to reside at a distance from the seat of his power;

---

[1] It would seem that the Castle of Rothsay was also besieged. Acts of Parliament, II. 109.

[2] Tytler's Scotland, IV., pp. 86-127; Auchinleck Chronicle, pp. 44, 51, 55; Acts of Parliament, II. 190.

[3] Tytler's Scotland, IV., p. 156.

[4] Rymer's Fœdera, XI., p. 397.

and as he was, at the same time, one of the nobles who
guaranteed a truce with England,[1] it would seem that
he had lost no time in effecting a reconciliation with the
King. Previous to the siege of Roxburgh, at which

A. D. 1460.

James II. was unfortunately killed, the Earl
of Ross joined the Royal army with a body of
three thousand of his vassals, well armed, in their peculiar fashion. In order to prove his fidelity and loyalty,
he offered, in case of an invasion of England, to precede
the rest of the army, whilst in the enemy's country, by
a thousand paces distance, so as to receive the first shock
of the English. Ross was well received, and ordered to
remain near the King's person; but, as there was at this
time no invasion of England, the courage and devotion
of himself and his troops were not put to the test proposed.[2]

A. D. 1461.

Soon after the unfortunate death of James
II., and the capture of Roxburgh Castle, a
Parliament met at Edinburgh, which was attended by,
amongst others, the Earl of Ross, and all the Island
chiefs.[3] Of this Parliament, however, no records now
exist. Apparently, Ross perceived that the new government was not strong enough to command his obedience,
and thought this a favourable opportunity to pursue his
schemes of personal aggrandisement, and for that purpose to renew his confederacy with the banished Douglases. This once powerful family now looked chiefly to
the English King for their restoration to rank and power;
and, therefore, used all their influence to draw the Earl

---

[1] Rymer's Fœdera, XI., p. 397.

[2] Tytler's Scotland, IV., p. 176; Buchanan, b. XI.

[3] Tytler's Scotland, IV., p. 186; Auchinleck Chronicle, p. 59
February 1461, new style.

of Ross into a league with Edward IV.[1] On the 19th of October, Ross, by the advice of his principal vassals and kinsmen, assembled in council at his castle of Ardtornish, granted a commission, in the style of an independent prince, to his trusty and well-beloved cousins, Ranald of the Isles, and Duncan, Archdean of the Isles, to confer with the deputies of the English King.[2] The Commissioners met at Westminster; and, after a negotiation, concluded a treaty, which embraced some extraordinary conditions. The basis of it was nothing less than the contemplated conquest of Scotland by the vassals of Ross and the auxiliaries to be furnished by Edward, with such assistance as the Earl of Douglas might be able to give. The Earl of Ross, Donald Balloch, and John, the son and heir of Donald, agreed, upon the payment to each of a stipulated sum of money, to become for ever the sworn vassals of England, along with all their retainers, and to assist Edward in his wars in Ireland as well as elsewhere. In the event of the entire subjugation of Scotland by the Earls of Ross and Douglas, the whole of the kingdom to the north of the Forth was to be divided equally between the two Earls and Donald Balloch; whilst Douglas was to be restored to the possession of those estates between the Forth and the Borders of England from which he was now excluded; and, upon such partition and restoration being carried

---

[1] The King of England despatched the banished Earl of Douglas, and his brother, Sir John Douglas of Balvany, to meet the Earl of Ross or his ambassadors, by a writ dated 22nd June, 1461. Rotuli Scotiæ, II., p. 402. Tytler's Scotland, IV., p. 192.

[2] The English deputies were, Lawrence, Bishop of Durham, the Earl of Worcester, the Prior of St. John's, Lord Wenlock, and Mr. Robert Stillington, Keeper of the Privy Seal.

into effect, the salaries payable to Ross and his associates as the wages of their defection, were to cease.
The stipulated salaries were, to the Earl, £200 sterling
annually in time of war, and one hundred merks in time
of peace; to Donald Balloch, £40, and to John, his
son, £20 in time of war, and, in time of peace, half
these sums respectively. This remarkable treaty is
dated at London, on the 13th of February, 1462.[1]

While the negotiations which ended in the above
treaty were still pending, the Earl of Ross raised the
standard of rebellion. He assembled a large force,
which was placed under the command of Angus, his
bastard son,[2] assisted by the experience of the veteran
Donald Balloch. Having made themselves masters of
the Castle of Inverness, these leaders proceeded to issue
proclamations, in the name of the Earl of Ross, to all
the inhabitants of the sheriffdoms and burghs of Inverness and Nairn, couched in such a manner as to show
that Ross, overrating the effects of his contemplated
league with England, already assumed the powers of a
king in the north. The sheriffdom of Inverness at this
time comprehended not only the modern county of
Inverness, but likewise those of Ross and Caithness;[3]
and it was, therefore, over the inhabitants of four of the

---

[1] Tytler's Scotland, IV., p. 194. Rotuli Scotiæ, II., p. 407. 1461,
old style.

[2] This is distinctly mentioned in the Summons of Forfeiture
against the Earl of Ross, in 1475. Acts of the Parliament of Scotland,
II., p. 108. It does not appear, although generally asserted by our
historians, that Ross took the field on this occasion in person; and,
indeed, the contrary may be inferred from the fact that his son acted
as his lieutenant, with the highest powers of that office.—Acts of Parl.,
ut supra.

[3] Reg. of Great Seal, XV. No. 63.

modern shires of Scotland that the Earl of Ross sought to exercise royal authority. His proclamations commanded them to obey his bastard son, as his lieutenant, under the pain of death, which the latter was fully authorised to inflict upon the refractory; to pay to him all the taxes usually paid to the Crown; and to refuse obedience to the officers of King James.[1] How this extraordinary rebellion was suppressed is uncertain. We know that Ross was summoned before Parliament for treason; and that, on his failing to appear, the process of forfeiture against him was suspended for a time. There is reason, also, to believe, that an army was actually in readiness to march against him; although, eventually, this course was rendered unnecessary, by submission on the part of Ross, or by some other measures, which, as yet, we have not been able to trace. It is certain, however, that the Earl did not, at this time, receive an unconditional pardon, although allowed to retain undisturbed possession of all his vast estates for about fifteen years after this period.

A. D. 1475. At length the treaty concluded between Edward IV. and the Earl of Ross, in 1462, came to light, when it was determined at once by the Scottish Government to proceed against Ross as an avowed traitor and rebel. Accordingly, that nobleman was summoned, at his Castle of Dingwall, to appear before the Parliament to be held in Edinburgh in December, in order to answer to various charges of treason.[2] Commission was given to Colin, Earl of

---

[1] Auchinleck Chronicle, p. 60.

[2] Acts of Parliament, II. 108. All his acts of rebellion, both in 1455 and 1461, were charged against him, as well as the league with England.

7

Argyle, to prosecute a decree of forfeiture against him;[1] and, on the appointed day, sentence was pronounced, Ross having failed to appear.[2] Nor was this an idle ceremony. As soon as the weather permitted, a formidable armament, comprehending both a fleet and a land force, was prepared to carry the sentence of Parliament into effect, and placed under the command of the Earls of Crawford and Athole. The extent of these preparations, and the persuasion of his friends, induced Ross to sue for pardon, through the medium of the Earl of Huntly. The Queen and the States of Parliament were likewise prevailed upon to intercede for the repentant noble, who appeared in person at Edinburgh, and, with much humility, and many expressions of contrition, surrendered himself to the Royal mercy. The King, with wonderful moderation, consented to pardon the offender; and, in the Parliament held at

A. D. 1476.

Edinburgh on the 1st of July, John of Isla was restored to his forfeited estates of the Earldom of Ross and Lordship of the Isles. He then came forward, and made a voluntary resignation to the Crown of the Earldom of Ross, the lands of Kintyre and Knapdale, and all the castles, &c., thereto belonging; and, in return for this concession, was created, by the King, a Baron Banrent and Peer of Parliament, by the title of Lord of the Isles. The Earldom of Ross was now inalienably annexed to the Crown, and a great blow was thus struck at the power and grandeur of a family which had so repeatedly disturbed the tranquillity of Scotland.[3]

[1] Argyle Writs.
[2] Acts of Parliament, *ubi supra.*
[3] Chronicle of the Earls of Ross.   Ferrerius (the continuator

By the favour of the King, the succession to the new title and the estates connected with it, was secured in favour of Angus and John, the bastard sons of the Lord of the Isles ;[1] and Angus, the elder of them, was soon afterwards married to a daughter of the Earl of Argyle. This Angus was early accustomed to rebellion, having·acted as lieutenant to his father, in the great insurrection of 1461. Neither the favour now shown to him by the King, nor his alliance with the Earl of Argyle, were sufficient to keep the natural violence of his temper within bounds; and circumstances soon enabled him to establish an ascendancy over his father. The sacrifices made by the latter in 1476, when he gave up the Earldom of Ross and the lands of Kintyre and Knapdale, were very unpopular among the chiefs descended of the family of the Isles, who further alleged that he had impaired his estate by improvident grants of land to the Macleans, Macleods, Macneills, and other tribes. Thus, the vassals of the Lordship of the Isles came to be divided into two factions—one comprehending the clans last mentioned, who adhered to the old lord—the other consisting of the various branches of the Clandonald, who made common cause with the turbulent heir of the Lordship.[2] In these circumstances

of Boece's History), p. 393 ; Acts of Parliament, II. p. 113 ; Tytler's Scotland, IV., p. 246.

[1] Acts of Parliament, II. 190, 15th July, 1476. John, the younger of the two sons, was dead before 16th December, 1478. Reg. of Great Seal, VIII. 120.

[2] Hugh Macdonald's MS. The proceedings of the Islanders in reference to Kintyre and Knapdale, caused the Lord of the Isles to be summoned again, on a charge of treason, in April, 1478 ; but he seems soon to have satisfied the Government of his innocence, and, at the same time, to have procured the pardon of his son. Acts of

Angus not only [behaved with great violence to his father, but he involved himself in various feuds, particularly with the Mackenzies. It appears that Kenneth After Mackenzie of Kintaill had repudiated his first A. D. 1480. wife, Lady Margaret of the Isles, sister to Angus; and the latter, supported no doubt by his kinsmen, determined to make his quarrel with Mackenzie a cover for attempting to regain possession of the Earldom of Ross, or a portion of it.[1] He invaded Ross, accordingly, with a body of his Island vassals; and, encountering the Mackenzies and their supporters at a place called Lagebread, he defeated them with considerable loss. The Earl of Athole is said, by tradition, to have commanded the troops opposed to Angus of the Isles on this occasion. After this event Angus became so bold, and the insurrection appeared so formidable, that the government is said to have employed the Earls of Crawford, Huntly, Argyle, and Athole, to reduce him to obedience. He seems to have been expelled from Ross, and thence to have gone back to the Isles, where the Earls of Argyle and Athole procured an interview between him and his father, the old Lord, thinking thereby to bring about a reconciliation. In this they were disappointed; and the breach was, ere long, further widened, by the result of a sea-fight between the contending factions in the Isles, in which the adherents of John were routed with great loss by Angus and his followers. This conflict was fought in a bay in the Isle of Mull, near Tobermory, and is still

Parliament, II. 115, 119. Reg. of Great Seal, VIII. 120. The son, however, did not long continue in obedience.

[1] MS. Histories of the Mackenzies.

known in tradition as the battle of the Bloody Bay.[1]
Some time after this event, the Earl of Athole, who
still remained in the west, crossed over privately to
Isla, and carried off the infant son of Angus, called
Donald Dubh, or the Black, whom he delivered into the
hands of Argyle.   The Islanders always maintained that
this boy was the son of the young Lord of the Isles
and of his wife, Argyle's daughter;[2] but the legitimacy
of the child was afterwards denied by the government,
when, as we shall see, the Islanders brought him forward as heir to the Lordship.   In the meantime,
Donald Dubh was considered as a captive of great consequence, and was carefully guarded by Argyle in the
Castle of Inchconnell in Lochow.   The rage of Angus
knew no bounds when he discovered by whom his child
had been carried off.   He summoned his adherents
together, and sailing to the neighbourhood of Inverlochy, there left his galleys, whilst, with a body of chosen
warriors, he made a swift and secret march into the
district of Athole, which he ravaged with fire and
sword.   His appearance was so unlooked for, that the
inhabitants were unable to make effectual resistance to
the Islesmen.   The Earl of Athole and his Countess
took refuge in the Chapel of St. Bride, to which sanctuary many of the country people likewise fled for refuge
with their most valuable effects.   The sanctuary, however, was violated by the vindictive Islander, who
returned to Lochaber, his followers loaded with plunder,
and leading with him, as prisoners, the Earl and Countess

---

[1] Hugh Macdonald's MS; MS. Histories of the Macleods and
Macleans; Martin's Western Isles.

[2] Macvurich's MS., &c., &c.

of Athole.[1]   In the voyage from Lochaber to Isla,
many of his war galleys were sunk, and much of his
sacrilegious plunder lost, in a dreadful storm which he
encountered.   Such was the effect this circumstance
produced upon the superstitious feelings of the turbulent heir of the Isles, that he soon liberated his prisoners,
without even procuring, in return, the release of his son,
which seems to have been originally his chief object in
the expedition; and he, moreover, performed an igno-
minious penance in the chapel which he had so lately
desecrated.[2]   His career was now drawing to a close.
Happening to be at Inverness soon afterwards, on his
Before · way, as tradition bears, to attack his old enemy,
A. D. 1490. Mackenzie, he was assassinated by an Irish
harper.[3]   Thus fell Angus, the son and heir of John,
last Lord of the Isles.   With all his violence, which
appears to have verged upon insanity, he was a favourite with those of his own name, who, perhaps, flattered
themselves that he was destined to regain all that had
been lost by his father.   The chronology of this portion of the history of the Isles is so very deficient, and

[1] Hugh Macdonald's MS.; Ferrerius, p. 383; Bishop Lesley's
History of Scotland, edit. 1830, p. 34; Tytler, IV., p. 195-6. The
"Raid" of Athole has hitherto been, owing to an error of Ferrerius,
dated in 1461, in place of about twenty years later. It has likewise
been erroneously ascribed to John, Earl of Ross. Neither the
Auchinleck Chronicle (a contemporary MS., embracing the year
1461), nor the summons of treason against the Earl of Ross in 1475,
make any allusion to this remarkable occurrence, which must, therefore, have happened after the latter date. The Highland traditions
uniformly ascribe it to Angus, and not to his father, in which they are
undoubtedly correct.

[2] Ferrerius, Lesley, and Tytler, *ubi supra*.

[3] Hugh Macdonald's and Macvurich's MS.

the materials for supplying this deficiency are so scanty, that the author has not yet been able to assign a precise date to any of the events above narrated, from the quarrels of Angus with his father to his death at Inverness. The order in which they occurred has been adopted, after careful consideration of all the documents and traditions which bear upon this part of the history; and it would appear that, whilst all these events happened after the year 1480, the latest of them (the death of Angus) must have occurred several years before 1490.

The aged Lord of the Isles now resumed possession of his estates, from which he had been for some time excluded by the unnatural violence of his eldest son, Angus; and as John, his remaining son, had died without issue, the rank of heir to the Lordship was now held by his nephew, Alexander of Lochalsh, son of his brother, Celestine. Some accounts say, that Lochalsh merely acted as guardian for the child Donald Dubh, who still remained a captive in Inchconnel; but this is hardly reconcilable with known facts.[1] He, apparently with the consent and approbation of his uncle, who seems now to have retired from active life, placed himself at the head of the vassals of the Isles, and, with their assistance, endeavoured, as it is said, to recover possession of the Earldom of Ross. As the districts of Lochalsh, Lochcarron, and Lochbroom, which Alexander inherited from his father, and which he now held as

---

[1] I allude particularly to a charter dated in 1492, and granted by John, Lord of the Isles, *and Alexander de Insulis, Lord of Lochalsh*, to John Maclean of Lochbuy, of the office of Bailliary of the south half of the Isle of Tiree; an office which formed no part of the patrimony of the house of Lochalsh. Lochbuy Ch. Chest.

a Crown fief, lay in the Earldom of Ross, his influence there was greater than that of Angus of the Isles had been. Yet the only Crown vassal of the Earldom who joined him, was Hugh Rose, younger of Kilravock, whose father, at this time, was Keeper, under the Earl of Huntly, of the Castle of Ardmanach in Ross.[1] In the year 1491, a large body of Western Highlanders, composed of the Clanranald of Garmoran, the Clanranald of Lochaber, and the Clanchameron, under Alexander of Lochalsh, advanced from Lochaber into Badenoch, where they were joined by the Clanchattan. The latter tribe, which possessed lands both under the Lord of the Isles and the Earl of Huntly, was led by Farquhar Macintosh, the son and heir of the captain of the Clanchattan. From Badenoch the confederates marched to Inverness, where Farquhar Macintosh stormed and took the Royal Castle, in which he established a garrison; and where the forces of the Highlanders were probably increased by the arrival of the young Baron of Kilravock and his followers. Proceeding to the north-east, the fertile lands belonging to Sir Alexander Urquhart, the Sheriff of Cromarty, were plundered, and a vast booty carried off by the Islanders and their associates.[2] It is probable that, at this time, Lochalsh had divided his force into two parts, one being sent home with the booty already acquired, whilst with the other he proceeded to Strathconnan, for the purpose of ravaging the lands of the Mackenzies. The latter clan, under their chief, Kenneth, having assembled their forces, surprised and routed the invaders, who had encamped near the river Connan, at a place called Park,

[1] Writs in Ch. Chest of Kilravock, ad tempus.
[2] Kilravock Writs and Acts of Lords of Council, ad tempus.

whence the conflict has received the name of Blairnepark. Alexander of Lochalsh was wounded, and, as
some say, taken prisoner in this battle, and his followers
were expelled from Ross.[1] The victors then proceeded
to ravage the lands of Ardmanach, and those belonging
to William Munro of Foulis—the former, because the
young Baron of Kilravock, whose father was governor
of that district, had assisted the other party; the latter,
probably because Munro, who joined neither party, was
suspected of secretly favouring Lochalsh. So many excesses were committed at this time by the Mackenzies,
that the Earl of Huntly, Lieutenant of the North, was
compelled (notwithstanding their services in repel-
ling the invasion of the Macdonalds) to act against
them as rebels and oppressors of the lieges.[2] Meanwhile, the origin of these commotions did not escape
the investigation of the government; and the result
was, the final forfeiture of the Lordship of the Isles,
and its annexation to the Crown.

It does not appear, from the documents which we
possess, how far the Lord of the Isles was himself implicated in the rebellious proceedings of his nephew.[3] It
may be that his inability to keep the wild tribes of the
West Highlands and Isles in proper subjection was his
chief crime; and that the object of the government, in
proceeding to his forfeiture, was, by breaking up the
confederacy of the Islanders, to strengthen indirectly the

[1] MS. Histories of Mackenzies; Sir Robert Gordon's History
of the family of Sutherland, p. 77; Hugh Macdonald's and Macvurich's MS.

[2] Kilravock Writs and Acts of Lords of Council, ad tempus.

[3] In 1481, the King of England appointed Commissioners to treat
with " the *Earl of Ross* and Donald Gorme."—Fœdera, XII. 140.

Royal authority in these remote districts.   The tenor of all the proceedings of James IV., connected with the final forfeiture of the Lordship of the Isles, leads to this conclusion.   These proceedings will be considered at more length in their proper place.   At present, we have only to record the fact, that, in the Parliament which A. D. 1493. sat in the month of May, 1493, John, fourth and last Lord of the Isles, was forfeited and deprived of his title and estates.[1]   In the month of January following, he appeared in presence of the King, and went through the form of making a voluntary surrender of his Lordship;[2] after which he appears to have remained for some time in the King's household, in the receipt of a pension.[3]   Finally, this aged nobleman retired to the Monastery of Paisley, a foundation which owed much to the pious liberality of himself and his ancestors.[4]   Here he died, about the year 1498; and was interred, at his own request, in the tomb of his royal ancestor, King Robert II.[5]

Having thus traced the history of the great Lords of the Isles from their origin to the final forfeiture of their estates, it will be proper, before concluding this introductory sketch, to notice briefly the vassal tribes that followed the banner of this powerful family.   These may be divided into two classes.   The first comprehends those clans which boasted a male descent from

---

[1] The records of this Parliament are very defective, nor is the Act of Forfeiture preserved; but some charters, granted soon afterwards, show that the forfeiture must have taken place at this time.

[2] Acts of Lords of Council.

[3] High Treasurer's Accounts, *ad annum* 1495.

[4] Chartulary of Paisley, pp. 125-6-7-8, 147, 156.

[5] Hugh Macdonald's MS.

the family itself; the second includes the clans of other surnames. Most of the tribes alluded to became, by the policy of James IV., after the final forfeiture of their ancient line of Lords, independent of any superior but the Crown. It therefore becomes important, with reference to the object of the present work, to trace the extent of the possessions of each clan, as well as its position, both geographically and politically, with respect to the others.

In the first class are included, the house of Lochalsh, the house of Sleat, the Clan Ian Vor of Isla and Kintyre, the Clan Ranald of Lochaber, the Siol Gorrie, the Clan Ranald of Garmoran, the Clan Ian Abrach of Glenco, the Clan Ian of Ardnamurchan, and the Clan Allaster of Kintyre.

I. The House of Lochalsh.

Celestine, or, as he is called in tradition, Gillespick, of the Isles, second son of Alexander, Lord of the Isles and Earl of Ross, was the first of this family. He died in 1473,[1] and was succeeded by his only son, Alexander, whose insurrection, in 1491, led, as we have seen, to the forfeiture of the Lordship of the Isles. Besides the lands of Lochalsh, Lochcarron, and Lochbroom, in Ross, and those of Fernacostrie, Creichmor, and others, in Sutherland, which they held of the Earl of Ross prior to 1476, and of the Crown afterwards, these chiefs were superiors, under the Lord of the Isles, of the lands of Lochiel in Lochaber.[2] In a charter of the year 1492, Alexander of Lochalsh styles himself likewise Lord of Lochiel. He was thus closely

[1] Macvurich's MS.
[2] Reg. of Great Seal, VI. 116; XIII. 203.

connected with the Clanchameron, to whose captain,
Ewin Alanson, heritable keeper of his Castle of Strone
in Lochcarron, he gave one of his sisters in marriage. [1]
By his mother, Fynvola, daughter of Lauchlan Bronach
Maclean of Dowart, the Lord of Lochalsh was also nearly
allied to the numerous and warlike Clan Gillean.

II. The House of Sleat.

This family, whose representative, Lord Macdonald,
is now the undoubted heir-male of John, last Earl of
Ross and Lord of the Isles, sprang from Hugh, third
son of Alexander, Earl of Ross. In addition to Sleat
in Sky, which he occupied, and from which he took his
style, Hugh was nominal proprietor, under his brother,
Earl John, of lands in Uist, Benbecula, and Garmoran, [2]
in the possession of which he was opposed by his relations, the Clanranald of Garmoran. [3] His first wife
was Fynvola, daughter of Alexander Macian of Ardnamurchan, by whom he had John, his heir, who died
without issue. By his second wife, a lady of the Clan
Gun, he had a son, Donald—called Gallach, from being
fostered by his mother's relations in Caithness—who
afterwards became the heir of the family, [4] and from
whom the present Lord Macdonald is descended.
Hugh of Sleat had several other sons, legitimate and
illegitimate, whom we shall have occasion afterwards to
notice. He appears to have survived the last forfeiture

[1] Hugh Macdonald's MS.

[2] Reg. of Great Seal, XIII. 185, 336, 337; XIV. 141.

[3] Hugh Macdonald's MS.

[4] Ibid. In 1460, Hugh of Sleat, with William Macleod of Harris,
and "the young gentlemen of the Isles," ravaged the Orkneys.
Macvurich's and Hugh Macdonald's MS. I have nowhere else seen

of his brother, the Lord of the Isles, and to have procured a confirmation from the Crown of the
A. D. 1495. lands which he previously held under his
brother. The descendants of Hugh, who increased
very rapidly in the sixteenth century, were known as
the Clan Huistein, or children of Hugh, and sometimes
as the Clandonald *north*. Their appellation of Clandonald arose probably from this circumstance, that six
successive chiefs of this clan, after John, the son of
Hugh, bore the name of Donald; and the addition
north, indicating their residence in Sky and North
Uist, was adopted to distinguish them from the Clan
Ian Vor of Isla and Kintyre, who were also called
Clandonald. Since the extinction of the direct line of
the family of the Isles in the middle of the sixteenth
century, Macdonald of Sleat has always been styled in
Gaelic, " MacDhonuill na'n Eilean," or, " Macdonald of
the Isles."[1]

III. The Clan Ian Vor.

The founder of this powerful branch of the family
of the Isles was John Mor, second son of "the
good John of Isla," and of Lady Margaret Stewart,
daughter of King Robert II. John Mor received,
from his brother, Donald, Lord of the Isles, large
grants of land in Isla and Kintyre; and he afterwards
Cir. A.D. increased his possessions, by his marriage
1400. with Marjory Bisset, heiress of the district
of the Glens in the county of Antrim.[2] The footing

any notice of this expedition, which seems to have been one of
considerable importance.

[1] President Forbes' Memorial, 1745.
[2] Hugh Macdonald's and Macvurich's MS.

which he thus obtained in Ulster was, in later times, improved by his successors. On the death of John, who, as above related, was murdered before 1427, by a certain James Campbell, he was succeeded by his eldest son, Donald, surnamed *Balloch*. This is the chief who defeated the Earls of Mar and Caithness at Inverlochy; and who, having, A. D. 1431. by a stratagem, escaped the vengeance of King James I., took afterwards so prominent a part in the rebellions of John, Earl of Ross and Lord of the Isles. His celebrity as a warrior, and the high rank he held, have led several historians into the error of calling him Donald, *Lord* of the Isles, a title which he never claimed. Donald Balloch, who had attained, before 1475, the rank of knighthood,[1] survived the events of that and the following year. It is probable A. D. 1476. that, at this time, his lands in Kintyre—being part of those resigned to the Crown—were either retained in the King's hands, or bestowed upon a new vassal, unconnected with the family of the Isles. To Sir Donald succeeded his son, John, who did not long survive, and was succeeded by his son, another John, surnamed *Cathanach*, or warlike,[2] who was at the head of the Clan Ian Vor, when the Lordship of the Isles was finally forfeited by James IV. At this time the undisputed possessions of John Cathanach in Scotland, comprehended a great part of Isla, and some of the neighbouring Isles; and he also maintained a claim of superiority over the remote district of Sunart, the origin of which has not been traced.[3] It is pro-

---

[1] Writ in Charter Chest of Cassilis, dated 8th October, 1475.
[2] Hugh Macdonald's and Macvurich's MS.
[3] Acts of Lords of Council, A.D. 1495.

bable, too, that he and his clan possessed, by force, and without legal title, a portion of Kintyre. The matrimonial alliances of John Mor and his successors, down to John Cathanach, were all contracted in Ulster; but, among those Scots who, during the fifteenth century, married daughters of the family, we find Roderick Mac-Alan of Moydert, chief of the Clanranald, Macdougall of Lorn', and Bannatyne of Kaimes. In addition to these notices of the Clan Ian Vor, it may be mentioned that, from Ranald Bane, a younger brother of Donald Balloch, sprang a race called the Clanranaldbane of Largie in Kintyre—whose chieftain, or *ceantigh*, in 1493, was Donald MacRanald Bane. This tribe, together with the Macallasters, Maceacherns, and Mackays, in Kintyre, and the Macneills of Gigha, became followers of the Clan Ian Vor, after the forfeiture of the Lord of the Isles. The Clan Ian Vor was known also as Clandonald, from its celebrated chief, Donald Balloch; whilst, to distinguish it from the race of Hugh of Sleat, the appellation Clandonald *south* was employed. The chiefs were usually styled Lords of Dunyveg (á castle in Isla) and the Glens.[1]

IV. The Clanranald of Lochaber.

Alexander de Insulis, commonly called Allaster Carrach, third son of John, Lord of the Isles, and Lady Margaret Stewart, was the first of this family. In an authentic deed of the year 1398, he is styled " Magnificus vir et potens, Alexander de Insulis dominus de

---

[1] John Mor himself is so styled in a writ of the year 1400; Rotuli Scotiæ, II. 155. He is frequently mentioned as an ally of the English, from 1389 to 1396; Fœdera, VII. 626, 639, 657, 716, 777, 824.

Lochaber."[1]   He was forfeited for joining the insurrection of the Islanders, under Donald Balloch, in 1431;[2] and his lands, or a great part of them, were bestowed upon the Macintoshes, from whom his successors were never able to wrest the feudal possession.   They continued, however, to dwell in that part of Lochaber called the Braes, sometimes as tenants of Macintosh, sometimes by force, and without any legal right whatever. From Allaster MacAngus, the grandson of Allaster Carrach, this tribe received the appellation of Sliochd Allaster VicAngus;[3] and from Ranald, the grandson of the second Allaster, it was afterwards named the Clanranald of Lochaber[4]—an appellation which, in the course of the sixteenth century, nearly superseded the former.   The chief, at the date of the forfeiture of the Lord of the Isles, was Donald, the elder brother of Allaster MacAngus.   The later chiefs of this family were known as the Macranalds of Garragach and Keppoch.   Their Gaelic title was "Mac Mhic Raonuill," i.e., Mac Vic Ranald, or the son of Ranald's son.[5]

V. The Siol Gorrie.

Of this tribe, whose ancestor was Godfrey, eldest son of John, Lord of the Isles, and Amie, the heiress of the Macruaries of Garmoran, little remains to be said.

---

[1] Chartulary of Moray, a record in which this chief is frequently mentioned.

[2] Hugh Macdonald's MS.

[3] Supplication, Ewin Cameron of Lochiel to the Committee of Estates, 1650.

[4] Acts of Parliament, III. 467.

[5] President Forbes' Memorial, 1745.

We have seen that Godfrey, under the style of Lord of Uist, dates a charter at *his* Castle of Elantirrim, in 1388;[1] and that, in 1427, his eldest son, Alexander or Allaster MacGorrie of Garmoran, was executed at Inverness by James I.[2] The latter had a son likewise named Allaster, who died in 1460, and who receives, from the seannachie that records his death, the title of Lord of North Uist.[3] From this time, although there were several descendants of Godfrey still in existence, the tribe fell into decay; the lands of Uist and Garmoran being granted by John, Earl of Ross, to his brother, Hugh of Sleat, who, notwithstanding his charter, was kept out of possession by the Clanranald.

VI. The Clanranald of Garmoran, comprehending the families of Moydert, Morar, Knoydert, and Glengarry.

The history of Ranald, younger son of John, Lord of the Isles, and of the heiress of Macruari, has been already noticed, and need not here be repeated.[4] His descendants came, in time, to form the most numerous tribe of the Clandonald. During the whole of the fifteenth century, they seem to have been engaged in feuds regarding the lands which they occupied—first, with the Siol Gorrie, and, after the decay of that tribe, with Hugh of Sleat, from whose successor they succeeded in acquiring a legal title to the disputed lands.[5] Allan MacRuari, great-grandson of Ranald, and chief of the Clanranald, was one of the principal supporters of Angus, the young Lord of the Isles, at the battle of

---

[1] Chartulary of Inchaffray. [2] Supra, p. 36.
[3] Macvurich's MS. [4] Supra, p. 29 to 31.
[5] Reg. of Great Seal, XIII. 336, 337 ; XIV. 337.

8

the Bloody Bay;[1] and he likewise followed Alexander
of Lochalsh, in his invasion of Ross and Cromarty, in
1491, receiving a large share of the booty taken upon
that occasion.[2]   The Clanranald, being very prolific,
were connected, by marriage, with almost every family
of note in the Isles and adjacent Highlands.   Contemporary with Allan MacRuari, were John Macranald of
Glengarry, Allan Macranald of Knoydert, and Angus
Macranald of Morar; being, next to himself, the leading
men in the tribe.   The possessions of the Clanranald
seem, at this time, to have comprehended nearly the
whole of Uist and Benbecula, the Lordship of Garmoran, and the north-west part of Lochaber; in addition
to which, the district of Sunart was claimed by Allan
MacRuari, as a tenant under John Cathanach of Isla.[3]
The style usually borne by the chief of this clan was
Macranald of Moydert, captain of the Clanranald;
and, in Gaelic, "Mac Mhic Ailein," *i.e.*, Mac Vic
Allan, or the son of Allan's son.   Glengarry had the
Gaelic style of "Mac Mhic Alasdair," *i.e.*, Mac Vic
Allaster, or the son of Alexander's son; and Knoydert
bore that of "Mac Ailein Mhic Ailein," *i.e.*, Mac
Allan Vic Allan, or, the son of Allan the son of Allan.

VII. The Clan Ian Abrach of Glenco.

The founder of this tribe was John, surnamed *Fraoch*,
natural son of Angus Og of Isla, and brother of John,
first Lord of the Isles.[4]   His mother is said to have
been a daughter of Dougall MacHenry, then the lead-

---

[1] Hugh Macdonald's MS.

[2] Acts of Lords of Council, A.D. 1494, et sequen.

[3] Ibid, A. D. 1495.   [4] Macvurich's MS.

.ing man in Glenco,[1] where John Fraoch afterwards settled as a vassal, under his brother, the Lord of the Isles, and where his descendants yet remain. The early history of this family is very obscure. One of them, probably from being fostered in Lochaber, acquired the surname of Abrach, which he transmitted to his posterity, who were known as the Clan Ian Abrach.[2] At the date of the last forfeiture of the Lord of the Isles, the head of this sept was an individual styled, in the records, " John of the Isles, *alias* Abrochson." [3]

VIII. THE CLAN IAN OF ARDNAMURCHAN.

The ancestor of this ancient branch of the Clandonald was John, surnamed *Sprangaich*, or the Bold, younger son of Angus Mor of Isla. Angus the son of this John appears to have acquired Ardnamurchan in the reign of David II. In 1495 his descendant and representative, John Macian of Ardnamurchan, disputed the possession of the adjacent district of Sunart, with Allan Macruari of Moydert, who claimed it as tenant of John Cathanach of Isla. This John Macian likewise possessed some lands in Isla, Jura, and Mull. The chiefs of this family seem always to have held a high rank among the vassals of the Isles, prior to the forfeiture, and to have been connected, by marriage, with all the leading families.[4]

---

[1] Hugh Macdonald's MS.

[2] Acts of Parliament, A.D. 1587 and 1594.

[3] Acts of Lords of Council.

[4] These particulars regarding the Macians of Ardnamurchan have been collected from the following sources:—Genealogical MS. of the fifteenth century, printed in Collectanea de Rebus Albanicis, Vol. I.; Dean Monro's Genealogies; Ch. in Haddington's Collections,

IX. The Clan Allaster of Kintyre.

The Clan Allaster derived its descent from Alexander, or Allaster, son of Donald of Isla, the grandson of Somerled.[1] The possessions of this tribe appear to have been, from the first, in Kintyre, and were never very extensive. Its chieftain, in 1493, appears to have been John Dubh Macallaster; for, upwards of twenty years later, we find mention of Angus Macallaster of the Loupe, who is called "John Dubh's son."[2] After the forfeiture of the Lordship of the Isles, this family attached itself, for about a century, to the more powerful Clan Ian Vor. Next to that of Loupe, the most important branch of the Macallasters, was the family of Tarbert, the head of which was Constable of the Castle of Tarbert on Loch Tyne side.

The second class of the vassals of the Isles includes those clans not descended from the family in the male line, and bearing different surnames. Of these the most important are, the Clan Gillean, or Macleans, the Clan Leod, the Clan Chameron, the Clan Chattan, the Clan Neill, the Mackinnons, Macquarries, Macfies of Colonsay, Maceacherns of Killelan; and Mackays of Ugadale.

I. The Clan Gillean.

At the date of the forfeiture of the Lordship of the

cir. 1342; Acts of Lords of Council, 1495 ; Reg. of Great Seal, XIII. 123 ; XIV. 307.

[1] Collectanea de Rebus Albanicis, I. 59.

[2] Reg. of the Privy Seal, A.D. 1515. A certain Charles Macallaster is mentioned as Stewart of Kintyre, A.D. 1481. Reg. of Great Seal, X. 9.

Isles, this great clan was divided into four branches, independent of each other; by which is meant that each held of the Lord of the Isles, and that no one of them was feudal superior of the others.

The first and most important branch, on account of the extent of its possessions, was that of Dowart. Lauchlan Maclean, surnamed Lubanach, the founder of the house of Dowart, married, in 1366, Margaret, daughter of the first marriage to John, first Lord of the Isles.[1] From John, and his successor, Donald, as Lords of the Isles, Lauchlan, and his son, Hector, received extensive possessions, both in the Isles and on the mainland.[2] The same Hector was a principal leader, under Donald of the Isles, at Harlaw, and lost his life in that battle. His great-grandson, another Hector, commanded the fleet of the Lord of the Isles at the battle of the Bloody Bay, where he was taken prisoner by the Clandonald.[3] He was the leader of his tribe at the time of the forfeiture in 1493, when his possessions appear to have comprehended a great part of the Isles of Mull and Tiree, with detached lands in the Isles of Isla, Jura, Scarba, &c., and in the districts of Morvern, Lochaber, and Knapdale. He was, moreover, heritable keeper of the following castles:—Dowart, in Mull; Carneburg, in the Treshinish Isles, off the north-west coast of Mull; Dunconnell, in Scarba; Dunkerd, in the Garveloch Isles, near Scarba; and Isleborg, the locality of which is uncertain. Maclean of Dowart has generally been considered as the chief of all the Macleans.

The second branch of the Macleans, in point of importance, was that of Lochbuy, sprung from Hector

[1] Dispens. quoted in A. Stewart's History of the Stewarts, p. 447.
[2] Reg. of Great Seal, XIII. 300.   [3] Hugh Macdonald's MS.

Reganach, brother of Lauchlan Lubanach.   Hector
was father of Murchard, whose great-grandson, John
Maclean of Lochbuy, was at the head of this sept in
1493.   The nominal possessions of the family at that
date comprehended lands in Mull, Tiree, Jura, Scarba,
and Morvern, with the lands of Lochiel in Lochaber,
and those of Duror and Glenco in Lorn.[1]   The lands
of Lochiel, originally possessed by the Clanchameron,
had been granted, on the forfeiture of the chief of that
clan, by Alexander, Earl of Ross, to John Maclean` of
Coll; and were afterwards, for some reason which does
not appear, conferred by John, Earl of Ross, upon
Maclean of Lochbuy.[2]   All the three families kept up
their claims to the lands in question; but. the Clanchameron were successful in retaining the prize; and
the Macleans, although they appealed to the sword,
had little benefit from their charters to Lochiel.   It is
uncertain whether the Lord of Lochbuy was more successful in enforcing his claims to Duror and Glenco;
but, with these exceptions, he seems to have possessed
the lands above-mentioned, free from interruption, up
to the time of which we write.   The house of Lochbuy
has always maintained that, of the two brothers, Lauchlan Lubanach and Hector Reganach, the latter was the
senior; but this is a point on which there is no certain
evidence.

The third branch of the Macleans was that of Coll,
descended, like Dowart, from Lauchlan Lubanach, who
was great-grandfather, it is said, of the fourth Laird of
Dowart and the first Laird of Coll, they being bro-

[1] Reg: of Great Seal, XIII. 114, 115, 116.

[2] Argyle Writs, A.D. 1461.

thers.[1] John Maclean, surnamed Garve, the first of Coll, received that island and the lands of Quinish in Mull, from Alexander, Earl of Ross, who afterwards, on the forfeiture of Cameron, gave to John Garve a charter of the lands of Lochiel. This led to feuds between the Macleans and the Camerons, which continued long, and in which much blood was shed; but the Clanchameron in the end maintained their ground. At one time John, the son and successor of John Garve, occupied Lochiel by force, and was at last killed at Corpach by the Camerons.[2] His infant son, John, born in Lochaber, was saved by the good offices of the MacGillonies—a tribe in Lochaber who generally followed the Clanchameron—and was afterwards known as John Abrach Maclean of Coll.[3] He was the representative of the family in 1493, and from him his successors adopted the patronymic, which is still applied to the Laird of Coll, of MacIan Abrach.

The fourth branch of the Macleans, which held its lands direct from the Lord of the Isles, was that of Ardgour, descended from Donald, another son of Lauchlan, third Laird of Dowart.[4] Ardgour, which formerly belonged to a tribe named MacMaster, was conferred upon Donald, either by Alexander, Earl of Ross, or by his son, Earl John. Eugene, or Ewin, Donald's son, held the office of Seneschal of the House-

---

[1] It is disputed which brother was the senior. Without going into any details, I may state, that such evidence as I have seen tends to support the claim of the family of Coll to seniority, and to the conclusion, that the first Laird of Coll, whose mother was a Macleod of Harris, was disinherited, to make way for his half brother, Lauchlan Oig, whose mother was a daughter of the Earl of Mar.

[2] MS. Histories of Macleans and Camerons.

[3] Writ in Ch. Chest of Coll, A.D. 1529. [4] MS. Hist. of Macleans.

hold to Earl John, in 1463 ;[1] and the Laird of Ardgour, in 1493, was Lauchlan MacEwin Maclean.

A tribe so numerous, and possessed of such extensive possessions as the Clan Gillean was, as might be expected, allied by marriage to all the principal families of the Isles; and its influence was, in this way, much increased.

II. THE CLAN LEOD.

This clan comprehended two leading tribes—the Siol Torquil, or Macleods of Lewis, and the Siol Tormod, or Macleods of Harris. Although descended, according to tradition, from one common progenitor, Leod (whence their collective appellation of Clanleod), the Siol Torquil and Siol Tormod were, in fact, two powerful clans, perfectly distinct and independent of each other. We commence with the Siol Torquil, as having been connected with the Lords of the Isles for a greater length of time than the other branch of the Clanleod.

At the accession of David II., the islands of Lewis and Sky belonged to the Earl of Ross.[2] We have already noticed the first claim of John of Isla (afterwards Lord of the Isles) to these islands, founded on a grant by Edward Balliol; and we have likewise seen that, when he made his peace with King David in 1344, this powerful chief had influence enough to retain Lewis, whilst Sky was restored to its former owner. From this time the Siol Torquil held Lewis as vassals of the house of Isla. In the same reign Torquil Macleod, chief of the tribe, had a royal grant of the lands of

[1] Reg. of Great Seal, VI. 67.
[2] Robertson's Index, p. 53, No. 20; p. 124, No. 26.

Assint, in Sutherland.[1] These lands were, early in the fifteenth century, given in vassalage by Roderick Macleod of the Lewis, to his younger son, Tormod, ancestor of the Macleods of Assint.[2] The head of the Siol Torquil, in 1493, was another Roderick, grandson of the former, whose eldest son was mortally wounded fighting for the old Lord of the Isles, at the battle of the Bloody Bay,[3] and died without issue. Torquil, the second son, became heir of the Lewis, and married Katherine, daughter of Colin, Earl of Argyle, which shows that his family was then considered as one of great power and influence in the Isles.[4] The possessions of the Siol Torquil were very extensive—comprehending the Isles of Lewis and Rasay, the district of Waterness, in Sky, and those of Assint, Cogeache, and Gerloch, on the mainland.

Malcolm, son of Tormod Macleod, and head of the Siol Tormod, had, from David II., a charter of the lands of Glenelg, which he and his successors always held of the Crown.[5] But the principal possessions of these chiefs were, before the forfeiture in 1493, held under the Lord of the Isles, by whose predecessors they were acquired in the following manner. Harris, an island, or rather peninsula, adjacent to Lewis, belonged at an early period to the Macruaries of Garmoran and the North Isles, under whom the chief of the Siol Tormod appears to have possessed it. From this family the superiority of the North Isles passed, as we have already seen, to the house of Isla, by marriage; and thus Harris came to form a part of the Lordship of the

[1] Robertson's Index, p. 100. [2] Latin Hist. of Macintoshes, MS.
[3] Hugh Macdonald's MS. [4] Reg. of Great Seal, XIII. 377.
[5] Robertson's Index, p. 100.

Isles. The Isle of Sky, in which the Siol Tormod had large tracts of land, formed originally part of the Earldom of Ross, and likewise came to the family of the Isles by marriage, along with the Earldom. When, however, Ross was annexed to the Crown in 1476, Sky did not, as formerly, go along with that territory, but was left with the Lord of the Isles as an integral part of his Lordship. The districts in Sky held by the Siol Tormod under this nobleman, were, Dunvegan, Duirinish, Bracadale, Lyndale, Trouterness, and Minga-nish—forming fully two-thirds of the island.[1] William Macleod of Harris, great-grandson of the above-mentioned Malcolm, was one of the supporters of John, Lord of the Isles, in the disputes between the latter and Angus, his undutiful son; and was killed, fighting against Angus and the chiefs of the Clandonald, at the battle of the Bloody Bay.[2] Alexander, commonly called Allaster *Crottach*, or humpbacked, son of William, was at the head of the Siol Tormod in 1493.

The Lords of Lewis and Harris held a high and equal rank among the vassals of the Isles, and were allied by marriage to all the principal clans. In reference to the tradition of their descent from a common ancestor, it deserves to be noticed that their armorial bearings were different—that of Lewis being a burning Mount, that of Harris a Castle.[3]

III. THE CLAN CHAMERON.

This tribe, as far back as we can trace, has had its seat in Lochaber, and appears to have been first connected

[1] Charter Chest of the family.
[2] Hugh Macdonald's MS. ; Hist. of Macleods of Harris, MS.
[3] Sir David Lindsay's Heraldry, Reg. Jac. V., and other Scottish Heraldic Works.

with the house of Isla in the reign of Robert Bruce, from whom Angus Og of Isla had a grant of Lochaber. There is reason to believe that the Clanchameron and Clanchattan had a common origin, and for some time followed one chief.[1] These tribes have, however, been separate ever since the middle of the fourteenth century, if not earlier. Tradition mentions Allan, surnamed MacOchtry, that is, the son of Uchtred, as the chief of the Camerons in the reign of Robert II., at which time a deadly feud subsisted between them and the Clanchattan, regarding the lands of Glenluy and Locharkaig, in Lochaber. From the same authority we learn that the Clanchameron and Clanchattan were the tribes between whom was fought the celebrated combat of thirty against thirty, in presence of King Robert III., at Perth.[2] Donald Dubh, probably grandson of Allan MacOchtry, led his clan at the battle of Harlaw. He and the captain of the Clanchattan, although they agreed in supporting James I., when that King was employed in reducing to obedience Alexander, Lord of the Isles, pursued their private quarrels without intermission. In the same year in which they deserted the Lord of the Isles and joined the Royal banner, these clans had a desperate encounter, in which both suffered great loss; but that of the Clanchameron was the most severe.[3] Donald Dubh was present with the Royal forces at the battle of Inverlochy; after which his lands were ravaged by the victorious Islanders under

A. D. 1396.

A. D. 1411.

A. D. 1429.

A. D. 1431.

---

[1] John Major's History of Scotland, p. 302.

[2] MS. History of Camerons, introductory to the life of Sir Ewin Cameron of Lochiel.

[3] Bower, John Major, and other Scottish historians, ad tempus.

Donald Balloch.   On the liberation of Alexander, Lord
of the Isles, that nobleman took the earliest opportunity
of revenging himself upon the Clanchameron, for their
desertion of him in 1429.   Donald Dubh was forced
to retire to Ireland, and his lands of Lochiel were
afterwards bestowed on John Garve Maclean of Coll.[1]
We have seen that John, Earl of Ross, granted the
same lands, at a later period, to John Maclean of
Lochbuy, and again to Celestine, Lord of Lochalsh.
It is natural to suppose that the Clanchameron, the
actual occupants of Lochiel, would resist these various
claims; and we know that John Maclean, the second
Laird of Coll, having held the estate for a time by force,
was at length killed by the Camerons, in Lochaber,
which checked for a time the pretensions of the Clan
Gillean.   But, as the whole of that powerful tribe were
now involved in the feud—some from a desire to revenge
the death of Coll, others from their obligations to support the claim of Lochbuy—the chief of the Camerons
was forced to strengthen himself by acknowledging the
claim of the Lord of Lochalsh.   The latter immediately
received Cameron as his vassal in Lochiel, and thus
became bound to maintain him in possession against all
who pretended to dispute his right to the estate.[2]   We
hear no more of the feud with the Macleans till after
the final forfeiture of the Lord of the Isles, when circumstances concurred to renew it with all its former
violence.   Allan, the son of the above-mentioned
Donald Dubh, after becoming a vassal of Celestine of
Lochalsh for his lands of Lochiel, was appointed heritable Keeper of Celestine's Castle of Strone in Loch-

[1] Hugh Macdonald's MS., and MS. History of the Camerons.
[2] Reg. of Great Seal, XII. 203.

carron.[1]   By a lady of the family of Keppoch,[2] Allan had
a son, Ewin, who was captain of the Clanchameron in
1493, and became afterwards a chief of great note.
Besides the lands of Lochiel, Glenluy, and Locharkaig,
the Clanchameron occupied Glennevis, Mammore, and
other lands in Lochaber.   The most important followers
of this tribe, at the end of the fifteenth century, were the
Camerons or Macsorlies of Glennevis, the Camerons or
Macgillonies of Strone, and the Camerons or Mac-
martins of Letterfinlay.   These septs were all ancient
families in Lochaber, and seem to have adopted the
surname of Cameron, although not descended of the
family.   The Macgillonies had taken the part of the
Macleans of Coll against the rest of the Clanchameron,
and suffered severely in consequence,[3] but were afterwards reconciled to the latter.   The chief of the Clanchameron was generally known in the Highlands by his
patronymical appellation of " Mac Dhonuill Duibh," *i.e.*,
MacConnel Duy, or the son of Black Donald.

IV. The Clan Chattan.

The original possessions of the Clan Chattan, who are
said by some to have had a common origin with the
Clanchameron, seem to have been in Lochaber.   From
this district, it is probable that the Clanchattan proceeded to settle in Badenoch, on the forfeiture of the
Comyns, in the reign of Robert Bruce.   Here the tribe
became very numerous, and was divided into several
branches; one of which, and the most important, the

---

[1] Reg. of Great Seal, XII. 203.

[2] Ibid. Her name was Mariot, daughter of Angus ; and her father
was the son and heir of Allaster Carrach of Lochaber.

[3] MS. History of the Macleans of Coll.

Macintoshes, kept up also a connection with Lochaber; while the other branches were entirely confined to Badenoch.   William Macintosh the chief of this clan, received, in 1336, a grant of the lands

A.D. 1336.
of Glenluy and Locharkaig in Lochaber, from John of Isla, afterwards Lord of the Isles.[1]   From this time a deadly feud prevailed between the Clan-chattan and Clanchameron regarding these lands, which lasted, with little intermission, for upwards of three hundred years.   In the fifteenth century Malcolm Macintosh, then the chief, was involved in another feud with the descendants of Alexander of the Isles, Lord of Lochaber, the origin of which has been noticed in the account of the Clanranald of Lochaber, given above.   This feud was kept up for more than two hundred years.   Although this Malcolm had, along with the captain of the Clanchameron, deserted Alexander, Lord of the Isles, in 1429, he afterwards contrived to make his peace with that nobleman, from

A. D. 1443-
1447.
whom he received a confirmation of his lands in Lochaber, and a grant of the office of Bailliary of that district.   Duncan, son of Malcolm, is styled, in 1467, Captain and Chief of the Clan-chattan.[2]   He was in great favour with John, Earl of Ross, whose sister, Flora, he married; and his eldest son was Ferquhard, who engaged, during his father's life, in the insurrection of Alexander of Lochalsh in 1491, as has been already noticed.   In addition to their lands in Lochaber, the captains of the Clanchattan had large possessions in Badenoch (in which district they

---

[1] Charter Chest of Macintosh, as quoted in the Latin MS. History of the family.

[2] Collectanea de Rebus Albanicis, Vol. I., p. 80.

resided), which, from the middle of the fifteenth century, were held under the Lords of Gordon and Earls of Huntly; so that their allegiance was divided between the latter and the Lords of the Isles.

V. THE CLAN NEILL.

This tribe, like the Macleods, consisted of two independent branches, carrying different armorial bearings, and having but little connection with each other, yet said to be descended from brothers. These were the Clan Neill of Barra, and the Clan Neill of Gigha.

Gilleonan, son of Roderick MacMurchard Macneill, had, from Alexander, Lord of the Isles, in A. D. 1427. 1427, a charter of the Isle of Barra, and of the lands of Boisdale in South Uist.[1] He was killed in Coll, by John Garve Maclean, with whom he disputed the possession of that island.[2] His son, or grandson, was at the battle of the Bloody Bay, and narrowly escaped falling into the hands of the victorious Clandonald on that occasion.[3] Another Gilleonan, probably grandson of the first, seems to have been chief of this sept in 1493.[4]

The first of the Macneills of Gigha of whom we have any certain account, is Hector MacTorquil Macneill, who was, in 1472, keeper of Castle Sweyn, in Knapdale, under the Lord of the Isles. Malcolm Macneill of Gigha, probably his son, was chief of this sept in 1493.[5]

It deserves to be noticed here, that, after the forfeiture of the Lordship of the Isles, Macneill of Barra

---

[1] Reg. of Great Seal, XIII. 188.
[2] MS. History of Macleans of Coll.   [3] Hugh Macdonald's MS.
[4] Gilleonan Macneill of Barra occurs in Record, A.D. 1515.
[5] Reg. of Great Seal, XIII. 203.   Ch. in Ch. Chest of Lochbuy.

followed Maclean of Dowart, while Macneill of Gigha followed Macdonald of Isla and Kintyre. When, therefore, in the course of the sixteenth century, the Macleans and Macdonalds came to be at deadly feud, and were constantly engaged in acts of hostility, the two septs of Macneills turned their swords against each other. This circumstance, joined to the difference in their armorial bearings, and to the fact that the Christian names used in the one family were, with a single exception (the name Neill), entirely unknown in the other, leads to the conclusion that the tradition of their common descent is erroneous.

VI. THE CLAN FINNON OR MACKINNONS.

A. D. 1354. The first authentic notice of this ancient tribe, is to be found in an indenture between the Lord of the Isles and the Lord of Lorn. The latter stipulates, in surrendering to the Lord of the Isles the Island of Mull and other lands, that the keeping of the Castle of Kerneburg, in the Treshinish Isles, is not to be given to any of the race of Clan Finnon.[1] This proves that the Mackinnons were then connected with Mull. They originally possessed the district of Griban in that island, but exchanged it for the district of Mishnish, being that part of Mull immediately to the north and west of Tobermory. They, likewise, possessed the lands of Strathordell in Sky, from which the chiefs usually took their style. Lauchlan Macfingon, or Mackinnon, chief of his clan, witnessed a charter by Donald, Lord of the Isles, in 1409.[2] The name of the

[1] Indenture printed in the Appendix to the second edition of Hailes' Annals of Scotland.

[2] Reg. of Great Seal, XIII. 300.

chief in 1493 is uncertain; but Neil Mackinnon of
Mishnish was at the head of the tribe in 1515.[1] After
the forfeiture of the Lordship of the Isles, this family
generally followed Maclean of Dowart; but occasionally acted with the Macdonalds of Sky against the
Macleods.

VII. The Clan Guarie or Macquarries.

The first of this ancient tribe of whom we have any
authentic notice, is John Macquarrie of Ulva, who died
in 1473.[2] He had a son, Dunslaff Macquarrie of
Ulva, who was chief of the Clan Guarie in 1493.
This family possessed the island of Ulva and some
adjacent lands in Mull, and followed Maclean of
Dowart after the forfeiture of the Lordship of the
Isles.

VIII. The Clan Duffie or Macfies of Colonsay.

Donald MacDuffie or Macfie of Colonsay witnessed
a charter of John, Earl of Ross, in 1463.[3] The name
of the chief of this sept in 1493 is uncertain. Murroch
Macfie of Colonsay is mentioned in 1531.[4] The Clan
Duffie, after the forfeiture of the Lordship of the Isles,
followed the Macdonalds of Isla.

IX. The Clan Eachern or Maceacherns of Killelan.

This was an ancient tribe in Kintyre, which, after
the forfeiture of the Lordship of the Isles, followed the

---

[1] Reg of Privy Seal, A.D. 1515.
[2] Reg. of Great Seal, XXXI. 159.
[3] Reg. of Great Seal, VI. 17.
[4] Acts of Parliament, ad annum 1531.

Macdonalds of Isla and Kintyre. Colin Maceachern of Killelan was head of this tribe in 1493.[1]

X. THE MACKAYS OF UGADALE IN KINTYRE.

Gilchrist MacImar Mackay had a grant of lands in Kintyre from King Robert Bruce.[2] From him were descended the Mackays of Ugadale, who, after the forfeiture of the Lord of the Isles, attached themselves to the Macdonalds of Isla. They seem to have had no connection with the Mackays of Strathnaver.[3]

Such were the principal clans in the Lordship of the Isles at the date of the last forfeiture, in 1493, including those descended of the house of the Isles, and those of other surnames. They formed a large and attached body of vassals while the Lordship existed; and they afterwards, as we shall presently see, made various unsuccessful attempts to procure the restoration of a title with which so many old recollections and traditions were connected.

We have no space to notice in detail the *Mackenzies*, *Munroes*, *Rosses*, *Dingwalls*, *Urquharts*, and *Roses of Kilravock*, who, as vassals of the Earldom of Ross, were connected for about half a century with the Lordship of the Isles. The forfeiture of the Earldom in 1476, made all these families independent of any superior but the Crown; and, after that time, the Clankenzie was the only one of them that exercised much influence in the Isles, which arose chiefly from the locality of its

---

[1] Reg. of Privy Seal, IV., p. 148.

[2] Ch. in Haddington's MS. Collections.

[3] See Genealogies printed in Collectanea de Rebus Albanicis, Vol. I., p. 54, from a MS. of the fifteenth century.

ancient possession of Kintaill, on the western coast of Ross, and adjacent to the Isle of Sky. Alexander Mackenzie of Kintaill received, in 1463, Strathgarve and many other lands, from John, Earl of Ross;[1] and he increased his possessions greatly by grants from the Crown, after the forfeiture of the Earldom. From this time the Clankenzie always opposed the Clandonald, and particularly such of the latter as possessed lands in Ross.[2] Kenneth, the son of Alexander, having divorced his wife, a daughter of the family of the Isles, was particularly exposed to the resentment of her relations. It was he who routed Alexander of Lochalsh and his followers, at Blairnepark, in 1491; and he died soon after. Kenneth Oig, his son by the divorced wife, succeeded him, and was chief of the clan in 1493. On his death, without issue, he was succeeded by his brother, John, whose mother was a daughter of the Lord Lovat.

Of the other families in the West Highlands whose history in the sixteenth century is mixed up with that of the Islanders, the principal are, the *Campbells*, the *Macdougalls*, and the *Stewarts of Appin*. Of the two last, it is only necessary to say that they were, in the end of the fifteenth century, vassals of the Earl of Argyle, in his Lordship of Lorn; and that their respective representatives, in 1493, were Alexander Macdougall of Dunolly, and Dougal Stewart of Appin. The former was descended from the old house of de Ergadia or Macdougall, Lords of Lorn; and the latter was the natural son of the last Stewart, Lord of Lorn, whose daughter carried that Lordship to the family of Argyle.

[1] Dr. George Mackenzie's MS. History of the Mackenzies.
[2] All the genealogical histories agree in this.

The ancient and distinguished family of Argyle, which was henceforth to exercise so great an influence over the West Highlands and Isles, owed much of its elevation to the same cause which first aggrandised the house of Isla. To the gratitude of Robert Bruce for his faithful services, Sir Neill Campbell of Lochawe was indebted for many grants out of the lands forfeited by the house of Lorn, the Comyns, and other supporters of the Balliol party. The marriage of this baron with Lady Mary, the sister of his sovereign, attached the Campbells still more closely to the dynasty of Bruce; and their fidelity was proved in the minority of David II. Early in the fifteenth century we find that Sir Duncan Campbell of Lochawe, afterwards first Lord Campbell, was accounted one of the most wealthy barons in Scotland.[1] Colin, first Earl of Argyle, Sir Duncan's grandson, acquired by marriage the extensive Lordship of Lorn,[2] and held for a long time the office of Chancellor of Scotland. In 1475 this nobleman was appointed to prosecute a decree of forfeiture against John, Earl of Ross, and Lord of the Isles;[3] and, in 1481, he received a grant of many lands in Knapdale, along with the keeping of Castle Sweyn, which had formerly been held by the Lord of the Isles.[4] One of the daughters of Colin, Earl of Argyle, was married to Angus, the young Lord of the Isles, and was believed by the Islanders to have been the mother of Angus' son, Donald Dubh,

---

[1] Rymer's Fœdera, X. 302.

[2] There are some doubts as to the precise mode in which Argyle acquired Lorn; for although he married one of the heiresses of line, the Lordship appears to have been entailed on heirs male. He soon, however, overcame all difficulties, and possessed the Lordship without opposition.

[3] Argyle Writs.   [4] Reg. of Great Seal, IX.

who, as we have seen, was imprisoned in the Castle of Inchconnell from his infancy. Another daughter of the Earl of Argyle was married to Torquil Macleod of the Lewis. Colin, first Earl, died in 1492, and was succeeded by his son Archibald, second Earl.[1] It is obvious that the mode in which the forfeited lands of the Isles were disposed of by James IV. could not but be a matter of deep interest to this potent family; which, by its talent and policy, soon acquired an influence in the West nearly equal to what had been enjoyed by the Lords of the Isles in the height of their power.[2]

[1] Histories of the family.

[2] The reader is requested to observe that, throughout this work, where a patronymic is printed thus—"*MacDonald*"—with a capital letter, it indicates that the individual mentioned was really the *Son of Donald*, or as the case may be. Where, on the other hand, a patronymic is printed without the capital letter, thus—"*Macdonald*"—it is merely a general surname, and does not indicate the precise parentage of the individual.

CHAP. I.

FROM THE FORFEITURE OF THE LORDSHIP OF THE ISLES IN
1493, TO THE DEATH OF KING JAMES IV. IN 1513.

In the preceding introduction, the history of the West
Highlands and Isles has been brought down to the period
when, by the forfeiture of John, last Lord of the Isles,
all the extensive possessions of that nobleman fell into
the hands of the Crown.   We now proceed to the proper
object of the present work—namely, the history of these
districts during the reigns of James IV. and the three
succeeding sovereigns of Scotland.   This portion of
Highland history has been selected for the following
reasons :—*First,* the Scottish historians of the sixteenth
century, and their followers, have passed it over in a
manner for which it is very difficult to account. *Secondly,*
the national records, and other well-known sources of
information, hitherto neglected as far as the Highlanders
were concerned, supply ample materials for removing
the obscurity which the negligence of former writers has,
for such a length of time, thrown over the subject.

The repeated rebellions of the Lords of the Isles,
notwithstanding their propinquity to the Crown, and the
pardons so frequently accorded to them, make it probable that, on the occasion of the last for-
A. D. 1493. feiture, it had been determined by the Govern-

ment to take all necessary measures to prevent in future any single family acquiring an undue preponderance in the Isles. This desirable result was sought at first by means devised in a spirit of great moderation, and which showed the wisdom of the counsellors of the young King. The aged Lord of the Isles himself was, as we have seen, treated with great mildness, although deprived of his title and estates.[1] Immediately after the forfeiture of this powerful baron, James IV. proceeded in person to the West Highlands, to receive the submission of the vassals of the Lordship.[2] In this the King judged wisely; for experience had shown that the personal presence of the sovereign was nowhere attended with more marked effects than in the Highland portion of his dominions; and that the inhabitants of these wild and almost inaccessible regions had so much respect for the royal dignity, that they would willingly render to the prince who should come in person to demand it, that obedience which the king's lieutenant, with a powerful army, might find himself unable to enforce. Alexander de Insulis of Lochalsh, John de Insulis of Isla, John Maclean of Lochbuy, and Duncan Macintosh, captain of the Clanchattan, were among the chiefs, formerly vassals of the Lord of the Isles, who came in this year to meet the King and make their submission to him. They appear to have received in return royal charters of all or most of the lands they had previously held under the Lord of the Isles, being thus made freeholders and independent of

---

[1] Introduction, p. 58.

[2] He granted a charter at Dunstaffnage, on the 18th August, and another at Mingarry, in Ardnamurchan, on the 25th October, 1493. Reg. of Great Seal, XIII. 200, 104.

any subject;[1] and the two former were in such favour with the King that they received the honour of knighthood.[2] Alexander of Lochalsh took the lead of the other Islanders, as having been the presumptive heir to the Lordship of the Isles previous to the forfeiture of his uncle; and he received from the King a promise to secure all the free tenants of the Isles in their present holdings,[3] an engagement which at first seems to have been strictly adhered to. It must be allowed, that on this occasion the King displayed great lenity, particularly towards the knight of Lochalsh, who, as we have seen, was the principal leader of the insurrection which was the immediate cause of the forfeiture of the Lordship of the Isles. Matters having been thus arranged, the King took his departure for the Lowlands, resolving to return next year and complete what had been so well begun.

As some of the more powerful vassals still delayed their submission, it became advisable that another expedition should be accompanied by such a display of military force as should effectually awe the disobedient. In the month of April the King was in the A. D. 1494. Isles, when he made preparations for a third visit, by repairing and garrisoning the Castle of Tarbert, one of the most important points on the west coast.

---

[1] The Charters to Macintosh and Lochbuy are to be found in the Reg. of Great Seal, XIII. 96, 114, 115, 116. That the others had charters likewise (although not now extant), is inferred from.the fact of their being knighted about this time, and from other circumstances.

[2] Acts of the Lords of Council, 5th July, 1494. Treasurer's Accounts, 24th August, 1494.

[3] This promise is distinctly mentioned in several charters of the year 1498. Reg. of Great Seal, XIII. 336, 337.

In the month of July he returned to Tarbert with a powerful force, so anxious was he to hasten the settlement of the Isles.[1]   He then proceeded to seize the Castle of Dunaverty in South Kintyre, in which he placed a garrison, provided, like that at Tarbert, with artillery and skilful gunners.   It will be recollected that the districts of Kintyre and Knapdale were, in 1476, expressly resigned by the Lord of the Isles, along with the Earldom of Ross, to the Crown.   A great portion of Kintyre had been held, under the Lord of the Isles, by Sir Donald de Insulis, surnamed Balloch of Isla, prior to this resignation, which deprived Sir Donald and his family of a very valuable possession.   Whether Sir John of Isla, the grandson and representative of Sir Donald had, at the time he received knighthood, on the first visit of James IV. to the Isles, any hopes of the restoration of Kintyre, cannot now be ascertained. But it is certain that he was deeply offended at the step now taken, of placing a garrison in the Castle of Dunaverty; and he secretly collected his followers, determined to take the first opportunity of expelling the Royal garrison and taking possession of the district of Kintyre. This opportunity was soon afforded to him.   The King, not expecting opposition from this quarter, was preparing to quit Kintyre, by sea, with his own personal attendants—the bulk of his followers having previously been sent away on some other expedition—when the chief of Isla, finding everything favourable for his attempt, stormed the castle, and hung the governor from the wall in the sight of the King and his fleet.[2]   James,

---

[1] Treasurer's Accounts, April and July, 1494.

[2] The Treasurer's Accounts, under August, 1494, show that Sir John of the Isles was summoned, at that time, to answer for treason " in

unable at the time to punish this daring rebel, took, nevertheless, such prompt measures for the vindication of his insulted authority, that ere long Sir John of Isla and four of his sons were apprehended in Isla by Macian of Ardnamurchan, and brought to Edinburgh. Here they were found guilty of high treason, and executed accordingly, on the Burrowmuir, their bodies being interred in the church of St. Anthony. Two surviving sons, who afterwards restored the fortunes of this family, fled to their Irish territory of the Glens, to escape the pursuit of Macian.[1] In the course of this year, likewise, two powerful chiefs, Roderick Macleod of the Lewis, and John Macian of Ardnamurchan, made their submission;[2] and the activity displayed by the latter against the rebellious Islesmen soon procured him a large share of the Royal favour.

In the following year, after extensive preparations for another expedition to the Isles, the King assembled an army at Glasgow;[3] and, on the 18th of May, we find him at the Castle of Mingarry in Ardnamurchan, being the second time, within two years, that he had held his court in this remote castle.[4] John Huchonson, or Hughson, of Sleat; Donald Angusson of Keppoch; Allan MacRuari of Moydert, chief of the

A. D. 1495.

Kintyre." The precise act of treason is learned from a tradition well known in the Western Highlands.

[1] These particulars regarding the punishment inflicted on the chief of Isla and his sons, are derived from the MS. of Macvurich and Hugh Macdonald; corroborated by a charter from the King to Macian, dated 24th March, 1499, and preserved among the Argyle papers, rewarding the latter for his services in apprehending Sir John, his sons, and accomplices.

[2] Reg. of Great Seal, June, 1494, XIII. 128, 123.

[3] Treasurer's Accts., 1494-5.   [4] Reg. of Great Seal, XIII. 179.

Clanranald; Hector Maclean of Dowart, Ewin Allanson
of Lochiel, captain of the Clanchameron; and Gilleonan Macneill of Barra, seem to have made their submission, in consequence of this expedition.[1] In this
year, too, Kenneth Oig Mackenzie of Kintaill, and
Farquhar Macintosh, son and heir of the captain of the
Clanchattan, were imprisoned, by the King, in the Castle
of Edinburgh. This may have been partly owing to
their lawless conduct in 1491; but was, more probably,
caused by a dread of their influence among the Islanders
—for the mothers of these powerful chiefs were each
the daughters of an Earl of Ross, Lord of the Isles.[2]
The measures now taken by the King were, soon after,
followed up by an important act of the Lords
A. D. 1496.
of Council, which merits particular notice.
This act provided, in reference to civil actions against
the Islanders—of which a considerable number were
then in preparation—that the chief of every clan should
be answerable for the due execution of summonses and
other writs against those of his own tribe, under the
penalty of being made liable himself to the party bringing the action.[3] This, although undoubtedly a strong
measure, was, in all probability, rendered necessary by
the disturbed state of the Isles after so many rebellions,
and could hardly fail to produce a beneficial effect; for,
in these wild and remote districts, the officers of the law
could not perform their necessary duties in safety, without the assistance of a large military force. At the
same time that this important regulation was made, five

---

[1] Reg. of Great Seal, 1495, XIII. 150, 300, 203, 188.

[2] MS. Histories of Mackenzies and Macintoshes.   See also Introduction to the present work, p. 83.

[3] Acts of the Lords of Council, VII., fo. 39.

chiefs of rank—viz., Hector Maclean of Dowart, John Macian of Ardnamurchan, Allan MacRuari of Moydert, Ewin Allanson of Lochiel, and Donald Angusson of Keppoch—appearing before the Lords of Council, bound themselves, " by the extension of their hands," to the Earl of Argyle, on behalf of the King, to abstain from mutual injuries and molestation, each under a penalty of five hundred pounds.[1] Such were the steps taken by the King and Council to introduce, at this time, law and order into the remote Highlands and Isles.

A. D. 1497. The active share taken by King James in supporting the pretensions of Perkin Warbeck withdrew his attention, for a time, from the state of the Western Isles, and seems to have given opportunity for a new insurrection—which, however, was suppressed without the necessity for another Royal expedition. Sir Alexander of Lochalsh—whether with the intention of claiming the Earldom of Ross, or of revenging himself on the Mackenzies for his former defeat at Blairnepark, is uncertain—invaded the more fertile districts of Ross in a hostile manner. He was encountered by the Mackenzies and Munroes, at a place called Drumchatt, where, after a sharp skirmish, he and his followers were again routed and driven out of Ross.[2] After this event, the knight of Lochalsh proceeded southward among the Isles, endeavouring to rouse the Islanders to arms in his behalf, but without success— owing, probably, to the terror produced by the execution of Sir John of Isla and his sons. Meantime, Macian of Ardnamurchan, judging this a proper opportunity of

---

[1] Acts of the Lords of Council, VII., fo. 39.

[2] Gordon's History of Sutherland, p. 77; Macvurich's MS.; Hugh Macdonald's MS.

doing an acceptable service to the King, surprised
Lochalsh in the island of Oransay, whither he had
retreated, and put him to death.   In this Macian was
assisted, according to tradition, by Alexander, the eldest
surviving son of John of Isla, with whom he had contrived to effect a reconciliation, and to whom he had
given his daughter in marriage.[1]   Sir Alexander of
Lochalsh left both sons and daughters, who afterwards
fell into the King's hands, and of whom we shall have
occasion to speak in the sequel.   About the same time
as the unsuccessful insurrection of which we have just
spoken, the chiefs of Mackenzie and Macintosh made
their escape from Edinburgh Castle; but, on their way
to the Highlands, they were treacherously seized at the
Torwood by the Laird of Buchanan.   Mackenzie having offered resistance was slain, and his head, along
with Macintosh, who was taken alive, was presented to
the King by Buchanan.   The latter was rewarded, and
Macintosh returned to his dungeon, where he remained
till after the battle of Flodden.[2]

In the summer of 1498, King James, still intent upon
preserving and extending his influence in the Isles, held
his court at a new castle he had caused to be erected
in South Kintyre, at the head of Loch Kilkerran,[3] now
called the Bay of Campbellton.   Alexander Macleod
of Harris, or Dunvegan, and Torquil Macleod, now
(by the death of his father Roderick) Lord of the Lewis,
paid their homage to the King on this occasion; and

---

[1] Macvurich's MS.; Hugh Macdonald's MS.

[2] MS. Histories of Mackenzies and Macintoshes.

[3] On the 15th June the King was at Stirling, and on the 28th of
that month, and the 3d and 5th of August, he dated charters "apud
novum castrum in Kintyre." Reg. of Great Seal.

some steps were taken to suppress the feud between
the Clanhuistein of Sleat and the Clanranald of Moydert, regarding the lands of Garmoran and Uist.[1] The
King soon afterwards returned to the Lowlands, leaving,
as he imagined, the Isles and West Highlands in a state
of tranquillity not likely soon to be disturbed. A few
months, however, sufficed to produce a wonderful change
in the relations between the King and his subjects in the
Isles. The cause of this change remains involved in
obscurity; but it must have been powerful, to induce so
sudden and total a departure from the lenient measures
hitherto pursued, and to cause the King to violate his
solemn promise, by revoking all the charters granted by
him to the vassals of the Isles during the last five years.[2]
The new line of policy was no sooner dertermined on than
followed up with the wonted vigour of the Sovereign.

We find him at Tarbert in the month of April,
A. D. 1499. when he gave commission to Archibald, Earl
of Argyle, and others, for letting on lease, for the term
of three years, the entire Lordship of the Isles as possessed by the last Lord, both in the Isles and on the
mainland, excepting only the island of Isla, and the
lands of North and South Kintyre.[3] Argyle received
also a commission of Lieutenandry, with the fullest
powers, over the Lordship of the Isles; and, some
months later, was appointed Keeper of the Castle of
Tarbert, and Bailie and Governor of the King's lands in
Knapdale.[4] Argyle was not, however, the only indivi-

---

[1] Reg. of Great Seal, XIII. 305, 336, 337, 338, 377.

[2] The King's general parliamentary revocation of all charters granted
in his minority could not affect those of the Islanders, which seem all
to have been granted after his attaining majority.

[3] Reg. of Privy. Seal, I., fo. 3.   [4] Ibid, fo. 122, 108.

dual who benefited by this change of measures. Alexander, Lord of Gordon, eldest son of the Earl
of Huntly, received a grant of numerous lands
in Lochaber, formerly belonging to the Lordship of the
Isles.[1] Upon Duncan Stewart of Appin, who was much
employed in the Royal service, were bestowed the lands
of Duror and Glenco during the King's pleasure.[2]
The important services of Macian of Ardnamurchan
(who alone of all the Islanders seems to have retained
the favour of his Sovereign), were likewise suitably
acknowledged.[3]

About this time, the feud which had so long subsisted
between the Macleans and Camerons, regarding the
lands of Lochiel,[4] broke out with renewed violence.
The Macleans carried off a large prey of cattle from the
lands of the Clanchameron in Lochaber—an injury which
the latter, doubtless, did not suffer long to pass unre-
quited. These broils were ended for the time, probably
by the influence of Argyle; and the Macleans, who
appear to have been the aggressors, received a temporary
respite under the Privy Seal.[5]

Meantime, all the necessary legal steps
were taken preparatory to the expulsion of
many of the vassals of the old Lordship of the Isles
from their possessions.[6] The imminent danger in
which they now found themselves, joined to the escape
from prison and appearance amongst them of Donald
Dubh, whom they regarded as their hereditary Lord,
forced the Islanders into a combination, which soon

A. D. 1500.

A. D. 1501.

---

[1] Reg. of Great Seal, XII. 422.   [2] Reg. of Privy Seal, I., fo. 99.
[3] Royal charter among the Argyle Writs, 29th March, 1499.
[4] Introduction, p. 70, 76.   [5] Reg. of Privy Seal, I., fo. 114, 115.
[6] Acts of the Lords of Council, XI., fo. 13.

became formidable. The claims of Donald Dubh to represent the family of the Isles have been already stated;[1] and, as they seem to have been, to a certain extent, acknowledged by those who had, from his birth, detained him in a rigorous confinement, it is not surprising that the feelings of the Islanders should have been enlisted in his favour. On his liberation from his dungeon in the Castle of Inchconnel, which he owed to the gallantry and fidelity of the men of Glenco;[2] Donald Dubh repaired to the Isle of Lewis, and put himself under the protection of its Lord, Torquil Macleod, by whom his cause was warmly embraced. This powerful chief having married Katherine, daughter of the first Earl of Argyle, his opinion as to the legitimacy of Donald Dubh—whose mother was, according to the universal belief of the Islanders, a sister of that lady—must have had great weight with the other Hebridean chiefs and their followers. The adherents of Donald, therefore, increased daily.

As the King was in constant communication with the Earl of Argyle, with Macian of Ardnamurchan, and Stewart of Appin,[3] he did not long remain in ignorance of the escape of Donald Dubh, and of its effect upon the discontented chiefs of the West Highlands and Isles. In order, probably, to check any insurrectionary movements in Lochaber and the neighbouring districts, the Earl of Huntly was sent to that quarter with instructions to collect the Crown rents by force, if necessary.[4] Torquil Macleod was charged, under the

---

[1] Introduction. p. 53.

[2] Macvurich's MS.; Hugh Macdonald's MS.

[3] Treasurer's Accounts, ad tempus.

[4] Reg. of Privy Seal, II., fo. 61.

penalty of treason, to deliver up the person of Donald, the *bastard* son of the late Angus of the Isles, who is described as being at Macleod's "rule and governance;" and having failed to obey this mandate, he was formally denounced a rebel, his lands being at the same time forfeited.[1] A commission was afterwards given to the Earl of Huntly, the Lord Lovat, and William Munro of Fowlis, to proceed to Lochaber and let the King's lands of Lochaber and Mamore, for the space of five years, to *true men.* At the same time the commissioners had strict injunctions to expel all *broken men* from these districts, which, in the state of affairs at that time, was equivalent to an order to expel the whole population. Similar directions were given relative to the lands forfeited by Macleod of Lewis.[2] The only ascertained result of this commission was a grant, during the King's pleasure, of the lands of Mamore to Duncan Stewart of Appin, who was then actively employed in the Isles.[3] Many efforts were made by the King to break up the confederacy of the Islanders. His exertions were principally directed to winning over Ewin Allanson of Lochiel, and Lauchlan Maclean of Dowart. But although these powerful chiefs entered into communication with their Sovereign, and one or both of them came to Court to follow up their negotiations,[4] yet, on their return to the Highlands, they seem to have lost sight of everything except the duty by which they fancied themselves bound to support the claims of the alleged heir of Innisgall.

A. D. 1502.

---

[1] Acts of the Lords of Council, XII., fo. 123.
[2] Reg. of Privy Seal, II., fo. 108.   [3] Ibid, fo. 84.
[4] Treasurer's Accounts. Reg. of Privy Seal, II., fo. 96.

A. D. 1503. At length the insurrection, which seems to have been for some time apprehended, broke out. It commenced by an irruption of the Islanders and western clans, under their new leader, Donald Dubh, into the district of Badenoch, which was plundered and wasted with fire and sword, about the time of the festival of Christmas, in 1503.[1] As Badenoch belonged to the Earl of Huntly, and was inhabited chiefly by the Clanchattan, who followed that nobleman in his attempts to reduce Lochaber to obedience, we can easily understand how the attacks of the insurgents came first to be directed against this district. The rebellion thus begun, soon became so formidable that the attention of Parliament was necessarily drawn to the most effectual means of suppressing it; nor was this found to be an easy task. The array of the whole king-

A. D. 1504. dom, north of Forth and Clyde, was called out; whilst the Earls of Argyle, Huntly,[2] Crawford, and Marischall, and the Lord Lovat, with other powerful barons, were charged to lead this force against the Islanders. Huntly undertook to seize and garrison the castles of Strone in Lochcarron, and Elandonan in Kintaill, as being "rycht necessar for the danting of the Ilis," provided the artillery and ammunition necessary for besieging them were sent, by sea, at his Majesty's charge. Letters were directed to be written to many of the principal chiefs in the Isles, enjoining them to concur with the other forces sent against the rebels, offering

---

[1] Acts of Parliament of Scotland, II. 263.

[2] Alexander, third Earl of Huntly, succeeded his father in 1502. He had, 14th August, 1503, a charter of the lands of Mamore in Lochaber, previously held by Stewart of Appin, during the King's pleasure. Reg. of Privy Seal, II., fo. 84, 107.

high rewards to such as should apprehend any of the insurgents, and denouncing the penalties of treason against such as should assist the latter. The state of the castles of Inverlochy, Dunaverty, and Lochkilkerran—the two first of which seem to have been ruinous, while the last was as yet unfinished—occupied likewise the attention of Parliament; and measures were adopted for invading the disturbed districts by sea as well as by land. Lauchlan Maclean of Dowart, and Ewin Allanson of Lochiel, who were the foremost to join Macleod of the Lewis in proclaiming Donald Dubh Lord of the Isles, were forfeited as traitors; but, in spite of all the efforts of Parliament, the insurrection continued for a while to gather strength. John Maclean of Lochbuy, Dunslaff Macquarrie of Ulva, Gilleonan Macneill of Barra, and Donald Macranaldbane of Largie, were summoned to answer for their treasonable support given to the rebels, who appear also to have sought assistance both from England and Ireland.[1]

The Government, at the same time that these warlike preparations were made, occupied itself in introducing various important changes in the distribution of the Isles and remote Highlands, with reference to the administration of justice, which had, for many years, been so little attended to, that the habits of the people had become very wild and disorderly. To remedy this evil, which had, in a great measure, arisen from the great extent of the ancient sheriffdoms, the following legal divisions of the Highlands and Isles were sanctioned by Act of Parliament. A Justiciar or Sheriff was to be appointed for the North Isles, and a similar functionary

---

[1] Acts of Parliament, II. 240, et sequen.—commencing in March, 1503-4.

for the South Isles. The court of the former was to be held at Inverness or Dingwall, and that of the latter at Tarbert or Lochkilkerran.[1] The inhabitants of Duror and Glenco, and all the Lordship of Lorn, were to attend the Justice Air or Circuit Court of Perth; those of Mamore and Lochaber, the Justice Air of Inverness. The Justice Air of Argyle Proper was to be held at Perth, if the King should desire; so that Highlanders and Lowlanders might have equal facility in obtaining justice. It was further enacted, that that part of Cowal which was not comprehended within the Earl of Argyle's heritable jurisdiction, should be included in the Justice Air of Dunbarton; that the Justice Air of Bute, Arran, Knapdale, Kintyre, and Mekill Cumray, might, at the King's pleasure, be holden either at Rothsay or at the burgh of Ayr; and that there should be appointed a Sheriff of Ross, whose courts were to be held, according to the exigency of the case, either at Tain or at Dingwall.[2]

Notwithstanding the labours of Parliament, and the great preparations made for suppressing the rebellion in the Isles, two years elapsed before it was finally quelled. Our information does not enable us to trace regularly the progress of the Royal forces; but a few detached notices have been preserved, which possess considerable interest. From them we learn that the southern division of the Royal army had its rendezvous at Dunbarton, in April, 1504; and that, from this place, artillery and warlike stores of all kinds, including "gun stanes," or stone bullets, were despatched

---

[1] A Sheriffdom of Tarbert had been nominally established, at least as early as 1480. Reg. of Great Seal, IX. 47.

[2] Acts of Parliament, II. 241, 249.

for the siege of Carneburg, a strong fort on a small isolated rock, near the west coast of Mull. In this year, likewise, the Earl of Arran had two commissions against the Isles; and the Earl of Argyle, Macian of Ardnamurchan, and Macleod of Harris or Dunvegan, were in constant communication with the King, who did not himself proceed to the Isles with this expedition. The northern division of the army was commanded by Huntly, who probably besieged and took the castles of Strone and Elandonan. Owing, however, to the obstacles presented by the great extent of country, both mainland and insular, which it was necessary to occupy for the effectual crushing of so formidable a rebellion, little progress could be made in one campaign. In the next

A. D. 1505.   year, the Isles were again invaded; from the south by the King in person, and from the north by Huntly, who made several prisoners, but none of them of high rank.[1] These persevering efforts, on the part of Government, had, at length, the effect of dissolving the confederacy of the Islanders, and procuring the submission of the chief leaders. Maclean of Dowart set this example; which was followed, after a time, by Maclean of Lochbuy, and Donald Macranaldbane of Largie.[2] The submission of Dowart implied that of Macneill of Barra, and Macquarrie of Ulva, two chiefs who, since the fall of the Lord of the Isles, had followed the banner of their powerful neighbours, the Macleans;

[1] Treasurer's Accounts, A.D. 1504-5. In these various expeditions the Royal navy was much employed under Sir Andrew Wood and Robert Barton; but we have no detail of the services of these distinguished officers in the Isles.

[2] Reg. of Privy Seal, III., fo. 1, 27; Treasurer's Accounts, ad tempus; Acts of Parl., II. 263, et sequen.; Acts of Lords of Council, XVIII., part I., fo. 40.

so that the force of the insurgents was now completely broken. Ranald Allanson, also, the heir of the chief of Clanranald, was now in high favour at Court, and seems, at this time, to have brought the feud of his family with the Clanhuistein of Sleat to a successful issue.[1] Tor-quil Macleod of the Lewis, and others, who probably despaired of pardon, still held out, and a third campaign was thus rendered necessary. Mac-leod was solemnly forfeited in Parliament for not appear-ing to stand his trial for high treason;[2] and, in order to execute this sentence, and to complete the dispersion of the rebels, the Earl of Huntly again proceeded to the North Isles. The Castle of Stornoway in Lewis was besieged and taken, and the whole island reduced to obedience; but the fate of its Lord is uncertain. Y Mackay of Strathnaver, who, with his clan, was of much service in this expedition, was rewarded by a liferent grant of the lands of Assint and Cogeach, forfeited by the rebel Macleod.[3] But although this tedious rebellion was at length suppressed, it does not appear that the projects of the Government for expelling the old inhabi-tants from the Lordship of the Isles, and substituting "true men" in their room, had made any sensible progress. On the contrary, the clans of the Isles and adjacent coasts continued to occupy, many of them, perhaps, contrary to law, their ancient posses-sions. Donald Dubh, the alleged heir of the Isles, for whose sake the Hebridean chiefs had made such sacrifices, again became a prisoner, and was committed

A. D. 1506.

---

[1] Reg. of Gr. Seal, XIV. 141 ; Reg. of Cr. Rentals, A.D. 1505.
[2] Acts of Parliament, II. 263.
[3] Treasurer's Accounts, A.D. 1506. Reg. of Great Seal, XIV. 464.

to the Castle of Edinburgh,[1] where he remained
until he made his escape a second time, nearly forty
years after this period, under the Regency of the Earl
of Arran. That event, as we shall see in the course of
the present work, caused the faithful Islanders once
more to rally round this unfortunate nobleman, the last
male in the direct line of his ancient house.

A.D. 1507-
1513.
During the late rebellion the fury of the
insurgents had been particularly directed
against the lands of the Clanchattan·as vassals of the
Earl of Huntly, and of the Stewarts of Appin, who followed the Earl of Argyle. The former clan were more
particularly obnoxious, as having, in order to save the
life of their captive chief,[2] shaken off all. connection
with the other vassals of the Isles, and as still
claiming extensive possessions in the heart of Lochaber.
The Stewarts of Appin, under the protection of the
Earl of Argyle, and by the favour of their Sovereign,
daily encroached upon the Lordship of the Isles from
the other side. It is not wonderful, then, that the
Clanchattan, whose lands of Glenluy and Locharkaig in Lochaber had been for some years forcibly
occupied by the Clanchameron without acknowledgment,[3] should have suffered severely from the plunder
and devastation of the lands of Badenoch by the
rebels; whilst Appin, and other lands possessed by the
Stewarts, likewise felt the effects of a Highland inroad.
The feuds which, in former times, would have continued for generations between the injured parties and

---

[1] Treasurer's Accounts, A.D. 1522-3.

[2] Farquhar Macintosh, captain of the Clanchattan, who had been
a State prisoner since the year 1495.

[3] Since 1497; Acts of the Lords of Council, XVII., fo. 76.

the aggressors were now, by the influence of the King and of the Earls of Huntly and Argyle, settled by decisions of the Lords of Council, or of arbiters chosen by the parties themselves.[1]

The King was not, however, content with merely causing the laws to be obeyed—a result which might be produced more by a dread of the Royal arms, than by a sense of the benefits likely to flow from the introduction of order. He laboured to introduce a knowledge of the laws of Scotland into the Highlands by means of Highlanders. There is yet extant a gift of Crown lands in the Isle of Sky, bestowed by James IV. upon an individual named Kenneth Williamson, to support him at the schools, with a view to his studying and making himself master of the laws of Scotland, and of afterwards practising as a lawyer within the bounds of the Isles,[2] Although during the remainder of this reign, justice seems to have been dispensed with impartiality in all parts of the kingdom, yet we have to regret that the unsettled state of Scotland, during the three long minorities which occurred between the death of James IV. and the close of the sixteenth century, afforded but too many opportunities to the turbulent clans of the Highlands to relapse into the same lawless state from which that monarch had so earnestly and so successfully endeavoured to reclaim them.

The Royal authority was now so well established, and the King himself was so popular among the Islanders, that from the suppression of the insurrection in 1506, to the disastrous battle of Flodden in 1513, the West

---

[1] Acts of the Lords of Council, XIX., fo. 174; XX., fo. 104, 189, 237; XXIV., fo. 152-7-9; Reg. of Great Seal, XVI. 1.

[2] Collectanea de Rebus Albanicis, I., p. 22.

Highlands and Isles seem to have been free from any serious disturbance. The appointment of the Earl of Huntly, whose services had been of such importance, to the heritable Sheriffship of Inverness, did much to extend the Royal authority in the North and West Highlands. That extensive jurisdiction embraced the shires of Inverness, Ross, and Caithness; and Huntly was now empowered to appoint deputies for certain specified divisions of his sheriffdom. These deputies were to hold their courts respectively at Kingussie, for the district of Badenoch; at Inverlochy, for that of Lochaber; at Tain or Dingwall, for Ross; and at Wick, for Caithness. In addition to this important office, Huntly was appointed Governor of the Castle of Inverness, with a large grant of lands for the support of a garrison. Power was given to him to add to the fortifications; and he was at the same time bound, on his own expenses, to build upon the Castlehill of Inverness a hall of stone and lime upon vaults. This hall was to be one hundred feet in length, thirty feet in breadth, and the same in height; it was to have a slated roof, and to it were to be attached a kitchen and a chapel of proper size.[1]   The same nobleman had previously obtained a grant of the site of the Castle of Inverlochy, where he was bound to build a "tower and strength with a barmekyn," which, however, had not been done—owing to the Earl's constant employment in the King's service—so late as the year 1511.[2]   From this period

[1] Reg. of Great Seal, XV. 63. The Sherriffship and Governorship were conferred upon Huntly by the same charter, dated 16th January, 1508-9.

[2] Reg. of Great Seal, XIV. 205; 22nd March, 1505-6. Reg. of Privy Seal, III., fo. 167; IV., fo. 134. As, at this time, the castle was un-

the great power formerly enjoyed by the Earls of Ross, Lords of the Isles, was transferred to Argyle and Huntly; the former having the chief rule in the South Isles and adjacent coasts, whilst the influence of the latter prevailed in the North Isles and Highlands.

The general effect of the vigorous government of James IV. was a decided improvement in the state of the Isles during the latter part of his reign, which was accompanied, however, by great changes in the relative position of many of the principal insular families.   These changes we shall proceed briefly to notice.   In the course of James' frequent expeditions to the West Highlands, the children of Sir Alexander de Insulis of Lochalsh, who were all young at their father's death, had fallen into his hands.   It appears that they were brought up in the Royal household, and we may presume that their education was carefully attended to.   Donald, the eldest son—called by the Highlanders Donald *Galda*, or the Foreigner, from his early residence in the Lowlands—speedily became a great favourite with the King.   He was allowed to inherit his father's estates, or a great part of them, and was frequently permitted to visit the Isles.[1]   This privilege he did not abuse during the life of James IV.; and, but for the untimely death of that monarch, he would, no doubt, have received still greater marks of favour.

The *Clanhuistein*, or family of Hugh of Sleat,

doubtedly ruinous, and as it was afterwards rebuilt, and continued for a long time to hold a garrison under the Earls of Huntly—the present ruins of Inverlochy Castle (as, indeed, might be inferred from the style of architecture employed) can lay claim to no higher antiquity than the earlier part of the sixteenth century.

[1] Treasurer's Accounts, A.D. 1507 to 1512.   Acts of the Lords of Council, XXIV., fo. 186.

was not so fortunate. John, the eldest son of Hugh, having no issue himself, and having probably quarrelled with his brothers, made over all his estates to the Clanranald, as well those estates which had been claimed and forcibly occupied by that clan, as those which had remained in his own hands.[1]   The rest of the Clanhuistein, on John's death, were thus left without legal rights to any landed property in the Isles; and being, moreover, viewed with jealousy by the Government, owing to their propinquity to the last Lord of the Isles, they were, in a manner, forced to become rebels.   Donald Gallach (supra, p. 60), their leader, was, with another of the brothers, murdered by their own bastard brother, Archibald, or Gillespick Dubh, an unprincipled and ambitious man, whose atrocities seem to have been winked at by the Government, on the ground, probably, that his brothers were declared rebels, whom it was desirable to exterminate.   This happened about the year 1506; and Archibald, the fratricide, having endeavoured to seize the lands of Sleat, was expelled from the North Isles by Ranald Allanson, the heir of Moydert, to whom Sleat had been made over by John Huchonson, the last legal possessor.   Taking refuge in the South Isles, where he joined himself to a band of pirates, Archibald, after a time, procured his own pardon, by delivering up to justice some of his lawless associates.[2]   He then returned to Sky, and, being a man of ability, seized the command of his tribe, and exercised the office of Bailie of the extensive district of Trouterness; his right

---

[1] Reg. of Great Seal, XIII. 336-7; XIV. 141. John Huchonson had no brothers-*german*.

[2] Hugh Macdonald's MS.; Reg. of Privy Seal, III., fo. 161. The pardon was granted at the intercession of Argyle.

to which, however acquired, was recognised by the Government in 1510.[1] Such was the position of the Clanhuistein in the end of James IV.'s reign.

The history of the principal house of the *Clan Ian Vor*, from the time of the execution of its chief, Sir John of Isla, and four of his sons, in or soon after the year 1494, until the accession of James V., is a perfect blank, as far as appears from the records. We know, indeed, that the surviving sons possessed, during this period, no heritage in Scotland;[2] and although tradition mentions that Alexander, the eldest, was reconciled to Macian of Ardnamurchan, and assisted that chief in putting to death Sir Alexander of Lochalsh, it seems probable that his general residence was on his Irish estate of the Glens, until after the battle of Flodden. A subordinate branch of this family, the *Clanranald-bane* of Largie, was engaged, as we have seen, in supporting the pretensions of Donald Dubh; but they made their submission, and received a pardon under the Privy Seal in 1505.[3]

The private history of the *Macdonalds of Lochaber*, or house of Keppoch, during this reign, is not devoid of interest. Donald Angusson, grandson of Allaster Carrach, the founder, was chief of this tribe in 1496. Being killed in a battle with Dougal Stewart, first of Appin, about the year 1498, he was succeeded by his son John. The latter made himself obnoxious to his clan, by delivering up to Macintosh, as Steward of Lochaber, one of the tribe who, having committed some crime, had fled to his chief for protection. John of

---

[1] Reg. of Privy Seal, IV., fo. 70 ; Hugh Macdonald's MS.
[2] Acts of the Lords of Council, XXIX., fo. 128.
[3] Reg. of Privy Seal, III., fo. 51.

Keppoch was, accordingly, deposed from the chiefship by the elders of his tribe, and a singular dispute arose as to his successor. The immediate descendants of Allaster Carrach supported the claims of Donald Glas MacAllaster, cousin-german and heir-male presumptive of John, the deposed chief. On the other hand, some of the subordinate, but long-established tribes in Lochaber, who had hitherto followed the descendants of Allaster Carrach, proposed to set up an individual of another branch of the family of the Isles as chief of that district of Lochaber in which Keppoch lies. This was Godfrey or Gorrie, who was brought for the purpose from Uist, and who claimed his descent from Godfrey, Lord of Uist, the eldest son, as we have shown, of John, first Lord of the Isles. The adherents of Donald Glas eventually succeeded in procuring his elevation to the command of the tribe; and it is not a little remarkable that from him sprung the later chiefs of Keppoch, who always numbered among their most attached vassals the descendants both of the deposed chief and of the unsuccessfnl competitor, Gorrie.[1] During the reign of James IV., this tribe continued to hold their lands in Lochaber as occupants merely, and without a legal claim to the heritage.

Previous to the year 1509, the *Clanranald of Moydert* appear to have been in high favour with their Sovereign; and we have already seen the successful

---

[1] These facts are well known to the descendants of the Keppoch family who still remain in the Braes of Lochaber. The tribe most active in setting up Gorrie was called *Sliochd Gillemhantich*, or the race of the Stutterer. The descendants of the deposed chief, some of whom still remain, are pointed out as *Sliochd a Bhrathair shean*, or the race of the elder brother.

issue of their feud with the Clanhuistein of. Sleat.
But in that year their chief, Allan MacRuari, if we
interpret rightly the studied obscurity of the Gaelic
historian, was tried, convicted, and executed in presence
of the King, at Blair in Athole, where his body lies
interred.[1]   His crime is not mentioned or even alluded
to by the seannachie; nor do the records give us any
assistance in tracing it. He was succeeded by his
eldest son, Ranald Allanson, who, in 1513, met with the
same fate as his father; and over the circumstances of
his death a similar obscurity is thrown by the delicate
hand of the Celtic narrator.   The execution of Ranald
took place at Perth, and he seems, like his father, to
have been tried in presence of the King.[2]   As a chief
this Ranald was much beloved by those under him; and
he is highly praised for his good qualities by the family
historian.

While the other branches of the family of the Isles
were suffering more or less from the measures adopted
by Government after the year 1493, the *Clanian of
Ardnamurchan*, owing to the line of policy followed by
their chief, John Macian, as formerly noticed, increased
greatly in power, but became proportionably obnoxious
to the other Islanders.   The *Clanian of Glenco* seemed
to share in the general misfortunes of their house.
Leaving the family of the Isles, and turning to the other
western clans, we find little to add to what has already
been written of them in the present chapter.

Towards the end of James IV.'s reign, the old
quarrel between the Macleans and the Clanchameron,
regarding the lands of Lochiel, which had once more

---

[1] Macvurich's MS.   [2] Ibid.

broken out, and another feud, carried on with much bitterness, between the Macleans of Dowart and Lochbuy, regarding their conterminous lands in Morvern and the Isle of Tiree, were checked or extinguished by the attentive care of the Sovereign.[1]   The estate of Lewis was, in 1511, restored to one of the old family—Malcolm, the brother of the attainted rebel, Torquil Macleod; one among many proofs that the attempt to introduce a new class of tenants into the Lordship of the Isles had proved unsuccessful.[2]   Hector Roy Mackenzie, progenitor of the house of Gerloch, had, since the death of Kenneth Oig Mackenzie of Kintaill, in 1497, and during the minority of John, the brother and heir of Kenneth, exercised the command of that clan, nominally as guardian to the young chief.   Under his rule the Clankenzie became involved in feuds with the Munroes and other clans; and Hector Roy himself became obnoxious to Government, as a disturber of the public peace.   His intentions towards the young Lord of Kintaill were considered very dubious; and the apprehensions of the latter and his friends having been roused, Hector was compelled by law to yield up the estate and the command of the tribe to the proper heir.[3]   Hector Roy, after a long and bloody feud, acquired from the Siol Vic Gillichallum or Macleods of Rasay (a branch of the family of Lewis), a small portion of the lands of

[1] Acts of the Lords of Council, XIX., fo. 214—XX. fo., 105.

[2] Reg. of Great Seal, XVII. 16. This charter was granted to the exclusion of Malcolm Macleod's nephew, John, the son of Torquil. See infra, ad annum 1528.

[3] Acts of the Lords of Council, XXII., fo. 142; Reg. of Great Seal, XV. 89; MS. History of Mackenzies, in the possession of Lauchlan Mackinnon, Esq., of Letterfearn.

Gerloch, which his successors used so as to become in time masters of the whole of that district.[1]

In spite of the apparent harshness of some of his measures, the bold and chivalrous character of the King had made, before the end of his reign, a deep impression upon his Highland subjects. So great, indeed, was the attachment they felt for him, that when he summoned the array of his kingdom to attend him on his last and fatal expedition, the natives of the distant Highlands and Isles repaired to his standard. with unwonted alacrity. The rashness of the Highland division of the Scottish army is said to have been one of the principal causes of the disastrous defeat at Flodden; and it is certain that the Highlanders sustained a very severe loss in the conflict. No Hebridean chief of note appears to have fallen; but the Earl of Argyle, and many of his clan, were among the slain.[2]

Tradition has preserved a curious anecdote connected with the Mackenzies, whose young chief, John of Kintaill, was taken prisoner at Flodden. It will be recollected that Kenneth Oig Mackenzie of Kintaill, while on his way to the Highlands, after making his escape from Edinburgh Castle, was killed in the Torwood, by the Laird of Buchanan.—(Supra, p. 93). The foster-brother of Kenneth Oig was a man of the district of Kenlochew, named Donald Dubh Mac Gillecrist Vic Gillereoch, who, with the rest of the clan, was at Flodden with his chief. In the retreat of the Scottish army, this Donald Dubh heard some one near him say—

---

[1] Letterfearn MS. Applecross's MS. History of Mackenzies of Gerloch, Adv. Lib. Jac. V., 4, 15; Vol. I., p. 103.

[2] Archaelogia Scotica, III. 324.

"Alas, Laird! thou hast fallen!" On inquiry he was told that it was the Laird of Buchanan who had sunk from wounds or exhaustion. The faithful Highlander, eager to revenge the death of his chief and foster-brother, drew his sword, and, saying, "If he hath not fallen, he shall fall," made straight to Buchanan, whom he killed on the spot.[1]

Soon after their return from this battle, the Islanders, taking advantage of the confusion occasioned by so great a calamity, hastened to stir up a new rebellion. They were led by Donald, now Sir Donald, of Lochalsh, who seems to have been knighted under the Royal banner in the field of Flodden; but the history of this insurrection, as it belongs to the reign of James V., will be found in the next chapter.

[1] MS. History of Mackenzies, in the possession of L. Mackinnon, Esq., of Letterfearn.

11

CHAP. II.

THE death of so active a monarch as James IV. in the prime of life, and the loss of so many of the chief nobility of the country as fell at the battle of Flodden Field, had the natural effect of throwing Scotland into a state of great confusion. This was aggravated by the evils usually attendant upon the minority of a sovereign in these rude times, and from which the nation, in the present instance, did not soon recover.

A. D. 1513. The Highlands and Isles had their full share of these evils. Scarcely had the Highland chiefs returned, when a new plot was set on foot for proclaiming a Lord of the Isles, in the person of Sir Donald of Lochalsh. That chief himself, in the month of November, 1513, with a large force of Highlanders, among whom were Alexander Macranald of Glengarry and Wiland Chisholm of Comer, expelled the garrison and seized the Castle of Urquhart on Loch Ness, plundering and laying waste, at the same time, the adjacent lands, which, with the castle, belonged to John the Grant of Freuchy.[1] About the same time,

[1] Laird of Grant. Acts of Lords of Council, XXX., fo. 205.

Lauchlan Maclean of Dowart seized the royal Castle of
Carneburgh, near Mull; and afterwards, with the assistance of Alexander Macleod of Dunvegan, made himself master of that of Dunskaich, in Sleat.   Sir Donald
was then proclaimed Lord of the Isles, and the numbers
of his adherents increased daily.   To resist this rebellion Colin, Earl of Argyle,[1] who, in anticipation of
some outrages ,among the Islanders, had taken bonds
of fidelity from his vassals and others who had attached
themselves to the late Earl, was charged by the Council
to convocate so many of the King's liege subjects as
should be thought necessary, and to proceed against
Maclean and his associates.[2]   An act of
A. D. 1514.
Council was then passed, appointing certain
individuals of influence in the north to take charge of
particular divisions of the northern shires, in the character of Lieutenants, for the time.   Among these,
Mackenzie of Kintaill and Munro of Foulis had charge
of Wester Ross.   Ewin Allanson and William Lauch-
lanson were the guardians of Lochaber.   At the same
time letters were written by the Council to all the
chief men of the mainland adjacent to the Isles charging them, in case the Islanders should land within their
territories with hostile intentions, to resist with their
utmost power; and warning those who might refuse to
obey these orders, that they should be held equally
guilty with the insular rebels.[3]   These measures were,

[1] Colin, third Earl, son and successor of Archibald, second Earl of
Argyle, who fell at Flodden.

[2] Acts of Lords of Council, XXVI., fo. 25.   Reg. of Privy Seal, V.,
fo. 12.   Registers of Dunbarton.   Protocol Book of Robert Watson,
Notary Public, fo. 23, 17th October, 1513.

[3] Acts of the Lords of Council, XXVI., fo. 29.

however, but feebly seconded; and, some time
A. D. 1515. afterwards, it became necessary for John,
Duke of Albany, Regent of the kingdom, to give commission to John Macian of Ardnamurchan to treat with
the less violent of the rebels, and to promise them the
Royal favour, and remission for their crimes, provided
they engaged to carry themselves in future as obedient
subjects, and to make restitution to those who had
suffered from their incursions.[1] This commission excepts
the principal rebels, and shows the strength of the party,
which was far from contemptible; embracing the Macleans of Dowart, the Macleods of Lewis and Harris, and
Alexander of Isla, besides the near relations and personal adherents of Sir Donald of Lochalsh, and several
of the smaller clans in the Isles, who could not safely
refuse to take part with their more powerful neighbours.
In the course of a short time, the powerful influence of
Argyle prevailed upon the insurgents to submit to the
Regent, and, upon assurance of protection, to come to
Court, and arrange in person the terms upon which
they were to be pardoned and restored to favour; and
considerable progress seems to have been made in a
pacification of the Isles in consequence of this treaty.[2]
Argyle and his followers took out a remission for
ravages committed by them in the Isle of Bute in the
course of the insurrection, and rendered necessary, it
may be supposed, from some of the rebels having there
found shelter and protection.[3] In the north, Mackenzie

---

[1] Reg. of Privy Seal, V., fo. 2.

[2] Reg. of Privy Seal, V., fo. 9, 12, 26, 35.

[3] Ibid., fo. 31. Discharge by the inhabitants of Bute to the
Earl of Argyle, dated 26th May, 1518. Charter Chest of Mountstuart.

of Kintaill, who had, without legal warrant, seized
the royal Castle of Dingwall for his own purposes, now
professed his readiness to deliver it up to any one
appointed by the Regent;[1] and everything seemed to
promise a speedy conclusion to these intestine disorders.

A. D. 1516.   Various disputes, which had arisen between
Sir Donald of Lochalsh and Macian of Ardnamurchan, were submitted to the decision of the proper
tribunals; and, by the influence of Government, mutual
obligations of redress were exchanged between these
chiefs, for the injuries done by each to the lands and
properties of the other in time past.[2]   The reconciliation of Sir Donald to the Regent was apparently so
cordial, and so much power was still left to him in the
Isles, that, on the 24th Sept., 1516, a summons was
despatched to the Earl of Argyle, and to "Monsieur de
Ylis," to join the Royal army, then about to proceed to
the Borders.[3]   Some months after this time, the latter
appears to have been in Inverness with no good intentions; for the Earl of Huntly was directed to watch his
motions;[4] and ere long he was again in open rebellion.
Sir Donald and his followers had joined with Alexander,
Lord Home, in the treasonable practices which brought
that nobleman's head to the block; and, after his death,
had given shelter to his proscribed followers.[5]   This

[1] Acts of the Lords of Council, XXVII., fo. 60.

[2] Acts of the Lords of Council, XXVII., fo. 162-3, 171, 180, 192,
205, 206, 207. Sir Donald appeared frequently before the Council at
this time, relying on a safe conduct. He was likewise engaged in a
lawsuit with Argyle.

[3] Treas. Accounts, ad tempus.   [4] Treas. Accounts, Jan. 19, 1516-17.

[5] Reg. of Privy Seal, V., fo. 101, XIII., fo. 46. Lord Home and his
brother William were beheaded for treason, 8th October, 1516. Tytler's
Scotland, V., 122.

fact, regarding which all our historians are silent, would seem to imply that Sir Donald was first excited to rebellion by the intrigues of English agents, and serves to account for the inveteracy of the Scottish government against him after this time.[1]

A. D. 1517.   Having given out to the Islesmen, that the Lieutenandry of the Isles, and various other offices belonging to the Crown, had been bestowed upon him by the Regent and Council, Sir Donald succeeded at first in raising a considerable body of men, with which he expelled Macian from Ardnamurchan, and took possession of the Castle of Mingarry. Although repeatedly charged, by order of the Council, to deliver up the castle and lands to the rightful owner, he not only refused, but, in defiance of the Government, he razed the Castle of Mingarry to the ground, and ravaged the whole district of Ardnamurchan with fire and sword. Meantime, his chief leaders found that he had deceived them, and that his intention was to lay waste, instead of protecting, the lands of which he professed to have received the control. They became disgusted, too, with his refusal to follow their advice, and with the reckless character of his proceedings (for the danger-ous consequences, either to himself or his followers, however obvious they might be, could not terrify him, or divert him from his insane projects), and, at length, taking the matter into their own hands, determined on apprehending him, and delivering him up to the Regent. Sir Donald, however, being made aware of their design, effected his escape; but his two brothers were made

---

[1] Regarding Home's intrigues with England, and the policy adopted by Lord Dacre, the English Minister, towards Scotland, see Tytler, V, 108, et sequen.

prisoners by Maclean of Dowart and Macleod of Dunvegan, who hastened to offer their submission, and palliate their own conduct. Such is the account of these transactions which we derive from the statement of Maclean and Macleod themselves;[1] and it appears to be so far correct, and to be deficient only in omitting the services of the Earl of Argyle, which, from other sources, are known to have contributed mainly to bring the affairs of the Isles to the present pass.[2]

Early in 1517, Argyle, with the Macleans of Dowart and Lochbuy, and Macleod of Harris, presented to the Council certain petitions and offers relating to the affairs of the Isles. Although these petitions were each separate and distinct, the tenor of the whole was uniform, and all advocated the suppression of Sir Donald's rebellion. The importance of these State papers is so great, and so much light is, by means of them, thrown upon the history and manners of the period, that they merit particular notice.

The petition of the Earl of Argyle, which was presented to the King and his Regent by the advice of the Lords of Council, demanded that the Earl should be invested with very high powers over the men of the Isles, "for the honour of the realm and the commonweal in time coming." *First*, he desired a commission of Lieutenandry over all the Isles and adjacent mainland, on the grounds of the vast expense he had previously incurred, of his ability to do good service in future, and of his having broken up the confederacy of

---

[1] Petition of Lauchlan Maclean of Dowart, and Alexander Macleod of Dunvegan, to the Regent and Council, recorded in Books of Council, XXIX., fo. 211.

[2] Petition of Argyle to the Regent and Council. Ibid, fo. 210.

the Islanders, which commission he obtained, with certain exceptions.[1] *Next*, he claimed and obtained authority to receive into the King's favour all the men of the Isles who should make their submission to him, and become bound for future good behaviour—to promise them remission for their former offences, and to engage for the restitution, not only of their heritage, but of such Crown lands as they previously held in lease, upon proper security being given for payment of the accustomed rents and duties, by the delivery of hostages and otherwise; the last condition being made imperative, "because the men of the Isles are fickle of mind, and set but little value upon their oaths and written obligations."[2]   Sir Donald of the Isles, his brothers, and the Clandonald, were, however, specially excepted from the benefit of this article.   The Earl likewise demanded and received express power to pursue and follow the rebels with fire and sword, to expel them from the Isles, and to use his best endeavours to possess himself of Sir Donald's Castle of Strone in Lochcarron.   Particular instructions were given to him to demand hostages from the Clan Ian Vor, or Clandonald of Isla, and their followers, who were now the principal supporters of Sir Donald; and, in the event of their refusal, to pursue them with the utmost severity; while, on the other hand, if they should submit, their leaders, the surviving sons of the late Sir John Cathanach

---

[1] The exceptions were those parts of Lochaber belonging to the Earl of Huntly, the Clanchattan, and Ewin Allanson; also the Isles of Bute and Arran. The duration of the commission was limited to three years, and further during the Regent's pleasure.

[2] This quotation is slightly but faithfully modernised, to make it more intelligible.

of Isla, were to receive Crown lands, in the Isles, to the annual value of one hundred merks, to enable them to live without plundering the King's lieges, and to keep good rule in time to come—they being now without heritage, owing to their father's forfeiture.[1]

The petition of Lauchlan Maclean of Dowart, contained the following demands:—*First*, a free remission of all offences to himself and his associates; and particularly to his "kin, men, servants, and part-takers," following—viz., Donald Maclean,[2] Gilleonan Macneill of Barra, Neill Mackinnon of Mishnish, Dunslaf Macquarrie of Ulva, and Lauchlan MacEwin of Ardgour— it being understood that Dowart was ready to make redress of all damages committed against the Earl of Argyle and Macian of Ardnamurchan, according to the decision of certain mutual friends. This remission was authorised by the Council to be granted to Maclean, upon hostages being given for future obedience. His next demands are somewhat startling, when his own previous conduct, and the history of his predecessors, are taken into consideration, and might well justify the charge of fickleness of mind brought against the Islanders by the Earl of Argyle. He desired, in the *second* place, that Sir Donald of Lochalsh, with his associates, should be proceeded against as traitors, and their lands forfeited, according to law, for their treason and perseverance in rebellion. In the *third* place, he demanded that Sir Donald's *two brothers*, then in his custody, should be "justified," *i.e.*, executed, according

---

[1] Acts of the Lords of Council, XXIX., fo. 128; Petition of Argyle, facing fo. 211; Reg. of Privy Seal, V., fo. 102.

[2] Uncle to Dowart, and his heir, failing issue male of Dowart's body. Reg. of Great Seal, XIII., 301.

to law, "for pleasure and profit to the King and Regent, and for stability of the country;" and further stated that he would act with double zeal in the King's service, as soon as he should perceive that the Government was serious in "*destroying the wicked blood of the Isles; for, as long as that blood reigns, the King shall never have the Isles in peace, whenever they find an opportunity to break loose, as is evident from daily experience.*"[1] For his good services done and to be done— and particularly for collecting, which he now undertook to do, the King's duties, in all places "within the point of Ardnamurchan"[2] (except those belonging to Macian, who was to answer for himself), Maclean demanded an heritable grant of one hundred, merk lands in Tiree and Mull, free from all duties. This, however, the Council would not give for a longer term than till the majority of the King, an arrangement with which he was obliged to rest satisfied in the meantime. He made various other demands, chiefly regarding his lands and possessions in the Isles; and, with some trifling exceptions, these were all acceded to.[3]

John Maclean of Lochbuy, and Alexander Macleod of Harris, demanded and received remissions for themselves, and their kinsmen and followers, upon giving hostages, as in the other cases. The latter likewise demanded an heritable grant of the lands of Trouterness, in Sky, which was refused; but he was continued King's tenant as formerly.[4]

---

[1] This quotation is likewise slightly but faithfully modernised.

[2] "Within" here means "south of."

[3] Acts of the Lords of Council, XXIX., fo. 128, et sequen. Petition of Dowart, facing fo. 211; Reg. of Privy Seal, V., fo. 100, 101.

[4] Ibid. See onwards, under the year 1528.

The Earl of Huntly having found some of the Clan-chattan rather unruly at this time, prevailed with the Council to give directions to Argyle, Dowart, and the others, to expel the Clanchattan from the bounds of Argyle's Lieutenandry, in case they should fly in that direction; and, likewise, to give their assistance in re-ducing them to obedience. On the other hand, Huntly became bound to act in the same manner towards Sir Donald of the Isles, or any other rebels who might be flying from the Earl of Argyle, into those Highland districts of which Huntly was Lieutenant.[1]

In regard to the execution of the two brothers of Sir Donald, urged by Maclean of Dowart, the Council were divided in opinion; the majority being in favour of capital punishment, while the others wished the matter to be left entirely to the Regent; and, although it cannot positively be affirmed, there is reason to think that the opinion of the majority prevailed.[2] When the arrangements of the Council were finally concluded, Maclean of Dowart appeared before them, and gave his solemn oath of allegiance to the King and Regent; binding himself, at the same time, to give his best assis-tance to Argyle, as Lieutenant in the Isles, for the good government of these districts, and as far as lay in his power to observe the public peace, and administer justice to all the King's lieges.[3] It seemed now scarcely possible that Sir Donald of the Isles, the principal rebel, should escape death or imprisonment; but he had

---

[1] Acts of the Lords of Council, XXVIII., fo. 77.; XXIX., fo. 128.

[2] Ibid, XXIX., fo. 128. The brothers of Sir Donald, whose names are not mentioned in the Record, certainly died without issue, as Sir Donald was succeeded by his sisters.

[3] Ibid, fo. 128.

still some powerful friends, by whose assistance he kept himself for some time longer out of the power of his enemies, and was even enabled to revenge himself upon one whom he had some reason to look upon as his hereditary enemy, and as the instigator of many of the measures taken against him.

John Macian of Ardnamurchan had, under James IV., distinguished himself, as we have seen, by the vigorous and unhesitating manner in which he supported Government; and, among his other services, he had apprehended Sir John of Isla, and put to death Sir Alexander of Lochalsh. His activity and talent procured him much favour and many lucrative employments in the Isles from that King, which were continued to him by the present Government; and, as he was well aware that his concern in the death of the two individuals just mentioned would never be forgotten by their children and kinsmen, and that vengeance was only delayed till a favourable opportunity, he was one of the first to join the Earl of Argyle upon his return to the Isles after the battle of Flodden; and he uniformly opposed, to the best of his ability, Sir Donald of Lochalsh and his party. His lands and possessions suffered severely in consequence; and his life was sought with the utmost eagerness, not only by Sir Donald himself, but by Alexander of Isla,[1] who, although Macian's son-in-law, had early joined the rebels, with all his followers, determined to revenge the death of his father and brethren. Some time after the submission of the Macleans and Macleod of Dunvegan, Sir Donald, assisted by

A. D. 1518.

---

[1] At least, such is the tradition; supported by Hugh Macdonald's and Macvurich's MS.

the Macleods of Lewis and Rasay, came southwards
to Ardnamurchan, where he met Alexander of Isla;
and, having united their forces, these chiefs proceeded
against Macian. They came upon the latter at a
place called Craiganairgid, or the Silver Craig in
Morvern, where he was defeated and slain, along with
two of his sons, John *Sunoirtich* and Angus, and a
great number of his men; whilst the rumour of this
success brought many to join the insurgents.[1] Measures
had formerly been commenced to have Sir Donald
forfeited in Parliament for high treason; and, upon the
Council being informed of the slaughter of the Macians,
Argyle advised that sentence of forfeiture should be
pronounced as soon as the necessary forms would
admit. In this, however, he met with some
opposition, which caused him to take a
solemn protest before Parliament, that neither he nor
his heirs should be liable for any mischiefs that might
in future arise from rebellions in the Isles; as, although
he held the office of Lieutenant, neither was his advice
taken as to the management of the districts committed
to his charge, nor had he received certain supplies of
men and money, formerly promised to him by the
Regent for carrying on the King's service in the Isles.[2]
This last statement fully accounts for the length of
time Sir Donald had been allowed to remain at large
after the defection of so many of his adherents; and it
is difficult to say how much longer this state of things

A. D. 1519.

---

[1] Macvurich's and Hugh Macdonald's MS. Macian was dead
some time before 18th August, 1519. Reg. of Privy Seal, V., fo.
139. In February, 1517-18, the Earls of Huntly and Argyle were
both directed to proceed against "Donald Ilis, rebel and traitor,
and his complices." Acts of Lords of Council, XXX., fo. 199.

[2] Acts of the Lords of Council, XXXII., fo. 122.

might have continued, had not his death, which took place some weeks after his success in Morvern, brought the rebellion, which had lasted with little intermission during upwards of five years, to a sudden close.[1] Sir Donald was the last male of the family of Lochalsh, and died without issue.

A. D. 1520-1527. For some years after this time the Isles remained in a state of comparative tranquillity, owing partly to the continued imprisonment of Donald Dubh, which deprived the Islanders of their natural leader. This interval of peace was employed by Argyle in extending his influence among the chiefs, with whom his commission of Lieutenancy brought him in contact. He received from Alexander Macranald of Glengarry and North Morar, a bond of man-rent or service ;[2] and this, it may be presumed, was not a solitary instance among the vassals of the Isles. The principal coadjutors of Argyle in these plans for the aggrandisement of his family and clan were his brothers, Sir John Campbell of Calder, and Archibald Campbell of Skipnish. Calder, whose patrimony lay in the district of Lorn, was particularly active; and, having acquired from Maclean of Lochbuy certain claims, hitherto ineffectual, which that chief had to the lands of Lochiel, Duror, and Glenco, he did not fail to make use of his opportunities. At first, he

---

[1] Macvurich and Hugh Macdonald, in their MS., both agree as to the fact of Sir Donald's death very soon after the slaughter of Macian; but they differ as to the place where he died; the former making it Carneburg, near Mull, the latter the Inch of Teinlipeil in Tyree.

[2] Crawford's MS. Collections, Advocates' Library, 5th February, 1519-20.

was violently resisted by the Camerons and Stewarts, the occupants of the lands in question, and suffered many injuries from them in the course of this dispute. But by transferring his title to these lands to his brother Argyle, and employing the influence of that nobleman, Calder succeeded in establishing a certain degree of authority over the unruly inhabitants, in a mode then of very frequent occurrence. Ewin Allanson of Lochiel, and Allan Stewart of Duror, were, by the arbitration of friends, ordered to pay to Calder a large sum of damages, and, likewise, to give to him, for themselves, their children, kin, and friends, their bond of man-rent and service against all manner of men, except the King and the Earl of Argyle. In consideration of these bonds of service, three-fourths of the damages awarded were remitted by Calder, who became bound also to give his bond of maintenance in return. Finally, if the said Ewin and Allan should do good service to Sir John in helping him to obtain and enjoy lands and possessions, they were to be rewarded by him therefor, at the discretion of the arbiters.[1] By such means was the influence of the house of Argyle extended and confirmed in the West Highlands.[2]

The first symptoms of renewed disorders in the Isles arose out of an occurrence which is familiar to most readers, as having formed the groundwork of a celebrated modern tragedy. Lauchlan Cattanach Maclean

---

[1] Acts of the Lords of Council, XXXVI., fo. 109; XXXVIII., fo. 190; Reg. of Privy Seal, VI., fo. 47; Reg. of Great Seal, XXII. 252.

[2] Argyle's commission of Lieutenandry over all the Isles and adjacent mainland (except Bute and Arran) was renewed 16th Nov., 1524; Reg. of Privy Seal, VII., fo. 102.

of Dowart had married Lady Elizabeth, daughter to
Archibald, second Earl of Argyle; and, either from the
circumstance of their union being unfruitful, or more
probably owing to some domestic quarrels, he determined
to get rid of his wife. Some accounts say that she had
twice attempted her husband's life; but, whatever the
cause may have been, Maclean, following the advice of
two of his vassals, who exercised a considerable influence
over him from the tie of fosterage, caused his lady to be
exposed on a rock, which was only visible at low water,
intending that she should be swept away by the return
of the tide. This rock lies between the island of Lismore and the coast of Mull, and is still known by the
name of the "Lady's Rock." From this perilous situation, the intended victim was rescued by a boat accidentally passing, and conveyed to her brother's house.[1]
Her relations, although much exasperated against Maclean, smothered their resentment for a time, but only to
break out afterwards with greater violence; for the
Laird of Dowart being in Edinburgh, was surprised,
when in bed, and assassinated by Sir John Campbell of
Calder, the lady's brother.[2] The Macleans instantly
took arms to revenge the death of their chief, and the
Campbells were not slow in preparing to follow up the
feud; but the Government interfered, and, for the
present, an appeal to arms was avoided.[3]

A. D. 1528.   The young King, now in his seventeenth
year, having made his escape from the thral-

---

[1] MS. History of Macleans.

[2] Diurnal of Occurrents in Scotland (printed by Bannatyne Club),
p. 8, ad annum 1523; Letter, Commissioners of Lord of the Isles to
Privy Council of England, August, 1545—quoted by Tytler, V. 233.

[3] Reg. of Privy Seal, VI., fo. 66.

dom in which he had so long been held by the Earl of
Angus and the Douglases, the policy of the Government seems to have undergone a considerable change.[1]
An important enactment regarding the Isles, one of the
first passed by the new Privy Council, points out the
means employed by Angus, during his usurpation, as it
may be called, of the supreme power, to secure adherents in that quarter of the kingdom.   This act bears,
that certain persons in the Lordship of the Isles had
obtained new titles to lands there, which might "turn
to the great skaith of his Majesty, both in respect to
his own proper lands and his casualties, without the same
be wisely considered and foreseen to be for the good of
his grace and realm."   Indeed, it would appear that,
during the frequent minorities of the Scottish Sovereigns
the dilapidation of the Crown lands was the chief resource
of a weak or unpopular Government, in order to maintain itself longer in power, by the support of those who
were thus permitted to prey upon the patrimonial
revenues of the King.   In the present instance all such
grants were declared null; and it was provided that, in
future, no lands should be bestowed in the West Highlands and Isles, but by the advice of the Privy Council and of the Earl of Argyle, the King's lieutenant
in the Isles: "because it is understood by the King,
that the said lands, or the most part thereof, are his own
proper lands, or in his hands, through forfeiture, escheit,
or non-entries."[2]

In this year, owing, perhaps, to the sudden change
of government, serious broils occurred both in the north

---

[1] Tytler, V., p. 221.

[2] Collectanea de Rebus Albanicis, I., p. 155.

and south Isles. The disturbances in the north arose
out of a feud between the Macdonalds and Macleods
of Harris, regarding the lands and office of Bailliary of
the extensive district of Trouterness, in the Isle of Sky.
To understand this feud properly, it will be necessary
to trace, with some care, the history of the district in
question. By a charter under the Great Seal, in August,
1498, the office of Bailliary, with two *unciates* of the
lands of Trouterness, was confirmed to Alexander
Macleod of Dunvegan, as having been formerly held
by him under the Lord of the Isles, and as being then
in the hands of the Crown, by the last forfeiture of that
nobleman.[1] Two months later, another charter passed
the Great Seal, granting the same office, and eight
merks of the lands, to Torquil Macleod of the Lewis,
on precisely similar grounds.[2] Both of these charters
seem to have been rendered null by the general revocation in 1498, or 1499, already alluded to.—(Supra,
p. 94.)   In 1505, the eighty merk lands of Trouterness
were let, by the commissioners of the Crown, for three
years, to Ranald Bane Allanson of Moydert, the Earl
of Huntly being surety for the payment of the rent by
the latter.[3]   In 1510, Archibald Dubh, the blood-
stained captain of the Clanhuistein, was acting as
Bailie of Trouterness, and a letter was directed under
the Privy Seal to the tenants of Trouterness in his
favour.[4]   Ranald Bane of Moydert was executed at Perth
in 1513; and Archibald Dubh soon afterwards met with
the fate he deserved, being killed by his nephews, the
sons of his murdered brothers.[5]   Macleod of Dunvegan,

---

[1] Reg. of Great Seal, XIII. 305.   [2] Ibid, XIII. 377.
[3] Reg. of Crown Rentals, ad tempus.
[4] Reg. of Privy Seal, IV., fo. 70.   [5] Huge Macdonald's MS.

who seems to have been principal Crown tenant of Trouterness some time before 1517, had his lease continued from that year until the majority of James V.—
(Supra, p. 122.)   Under the government of the Earl of
Angus, Dunvegan appears to have obtained also an heritable grant of the lands of Sleat and North Uist; and
thus became additionally exposed to the hostility of the
Clanhuistein of Sleat, who were now under the command of Donald Gruamach.[1]   The latter chief sought
the assistance of his uterine brother, John MacTorquil
Macleod (son of Torquil Macleod of the Lewis, forfeited in 1506, and nephew of Malcolm, the present
Lord of Lewis), a man like himself, without legal inheritance of any kind, in order to expel Dunvegan and
his clan from Trouterness.   In this they were successful, as well as in preventing him putting in force his
new charter to Sleat and North Uist.   Trouterness was
again occupied by the Clanhuistein, and John Mac-
Torquil, taking advantage of the opportunity afforded
by the death of his uncle, and the minority of the son
of the latter, and aided by Donald Gruamach and his
followers, seized the whole barony of Lewis, which,
with the command of the Siol Torquil, he held during
his life.[2]   Having thus briefly traced the origin of the
disturbances which, in this and the following years,
occurred in the North Isles, we shall now turn to the
commotions in the South Isles.

[1] Donald Gruamach (or grim-looking) was son of Donald Gallach,
and grandson of Hugh, Lord of Sleat. His mother was first married
to Torquil Macleod of the Lewis. Hugh Macdonald's MS.; Dean-
Munro's Genealogies.

[2] Acts of the Lords of Council, XXXIX., fo. 159; XLI., fo. 79.
Acts of Parliament, II. 333. Sir R. Gordon's History of the family of
Sutherland, p. 263.

The Clandonald of Isla, and their present chief, Alexander MacIan Cathanach, were probably among the number of those rewarded by the Earl of Angus with grants of the Crown lands. But the late Act of Council having declared all such grants null, the efforts of Argyle to enforce an act so favourable to himself, and a sense of the injustice with which they conceived themselves to have been treated, soon drove Alexander of Isla and his followers into insurrection. They were readily joined by the Macleans, who still panted for an opportunity to revenge the death of their late chief, and the combined clans made descents upon Roseneath, Craignish, and other lands belonging to the Campbells, which they ravaged with fire and sword, killing at the same time many of the inhabitants.[1] The partisans of Argyle retaliated, by laying waste great part of the Isles of Mull and Tyree, and the lands of Morvern.[2] The insurrection had proceeded to a great height in August of this year, when Sir John Campbell of Calder, on behalf of his brother, the Earl of Argyle, demanded from the Council powers of an extraordinary nature, to enable him to restore the peace of the country. He requested among other things, that all the substantial householders in the shires of Dunbarton and Renfrew, and the bailliaries of Carrick, Kyle, and Cunningham, might be commanded to meet Argyle at Lochransa, in Arran, with provisions for twenty days, and to assist him against the Islanders. The Council refused to issue this order at present, on account of the harvest; but they gave directions for a cannon, with two falconets and three barrels of gun-

A. D. 1529.

---

[1] Reg. of Privy Seal, IX., fo. 18.   [2] Ibid, IX., fo. 179.

powder, under the charge of two gunners, and as many carpenters, to be forwarded to Dunbarton, for the use of the Earl, in case he should find it necessary to besiege any of the " strengths " in the Isles.   At the same time, they determined upon sending a herald, " of wisdom and discretion," to Alexander of Isla, with directions, in the first instance, to summon him and his followers to lay down their arms, under pain of treason; and, if he found them disposed to be obedient, the hearld was then authorised to treat with that chief about his coming under protection, to wait upon the King and state his grievances in person, being prepared to give hostages (Lowlanders) for his obedience, and for his payment of the rents and duties of such lands as might be assigned to him by his Sovereign.[1]

This mission, which indicated considerable doubt of Argyle, was entrusted to a pursuivant named Robert Hart, who, in the course of a month, reported to the Council the result of his conference with Alexander of Isla; which proved so unsatisfactory that directions were immediately given to the Earl to proceed against the rebels, and reduce the Isles to obedience without delay.[2] Little progress was made, however, during the next six A. D. 1530.   months; but in the spring of 1530, preparations on a more extensive scale were commenced for concluding this service.   The tenants of the Isles, according to a roll of them placed in Argyle's hands, were to be summoned to come to the King's presence, upon the 24th of May, " to commune with his Majesty for good rule of the Isles."   They were likewise to be prohibited from giving any assistance to the rebels, or

----

[1] Acts of Lords of Council, XL., fo. 80.   [2] Ibid, fo. 117.

from convocating the King's lieges in arms, under the pain of treason; whilst the men of Carrick, Kyle, and Cunningham, of Renfrew and Dunbartonshires, of Balquhidder, Braidalbane, Rannoch, Apnadull, Athole, Menteith, Bute, and Arran, were to be charged, under high penalties, to join the King's lieutenant at such places as he should appoint, and to continue with him in the service for a month; and the burghs of Ayr, Irvine, Glasgow, Renfrew, and Dunbarton, were to send their boats with provisions for the army, for which payment was to be made. In case any of the Islesmen should be afraid to trust themselves in the low country, they were offered protections for their coming to the King, and for thirty days additional, to admit of their returning home safe.[1]

These preparations produced some effect. In the month of May, nine of the principal Islanders,[2] sent by the hands of Hector Maclean of Dowart, one of their number, offers of submission to the King, who immediately granted them a protection against the Earl of Argyle and any others, provided they would come to Edinburgh, or wherever the King should happen to be holding his court, before the 20th of June, and remain as long as his Majesty should require their attendance; it being always understood that the protection was to last for twenty days after their departure for the Highlands. As an additional security for their safety in coming and

---

[1] Acts of Lords of Council, XLI., fo. 77.

[2] These were, Hector Maclean of Dowart; John Maclean of Lochbuy; John Moydertach, Captain of the Clanranald; Alexander Macian of Ardnamurchan; Alexander Macleod of the Harris (or Dunvegan); the Laird of Coll (Maclean); John Macleod of the Lewis; and Donald Gruamach of Dunskaich (a castle in Sleat).

going, the King promised to take two of the following hostages from the Earl of Argyle:—Duncan Campbell of Glenurchy, Archibald Campbell of Auchinbreck, Archibald Campbell of Skipnish, and Duncan Campbell of Ilangerig, who were to be confined in Edinburgh Castle.[1] Colin, Earl of Argyle, dying in this year, was succeeded by his son Archibald, fourth Earl, who immediately took the oath of allegiance to the King, and was appointed to all the offices held by his father and grandfather.[2] Meantime, owing to the sickness and death of the late Earl, the King's service in the Isles had remained stationary; and, in the month of November, it was resolved that the King should proceed in person against the rebels in the following April, which term was afterwards altered to the 1st of June; and, in contemplation of the Royal expedition, various important arrangements were made. The array of Perth and Forfar, and of all Scotland south of these shires, was directed to meet the King at Ayr on the day appointed, with provisions for forty days, to accompany his Majesty to the Isles; whilst the array of the northern shires was ordered to meet James, Earl of Murray, natural brother to the King, and Lieutenant of the North, at Kintaill, or elsewhere, as he should appoint, and to proceed in the service according to his directions. Finally, a Parliament was summoned to meet at Edinburgh on the 24th of April, to pass sentence of forfeiture against the Islesmen who should then continue disobedient.[3]

---

[1] Acts of Lords of Council, XLI., fo. 79.   [2] Ibid, fo. 134.

[3] Ibid, fo. 118, 154; XLII., fo. 35, 40. It appears that a "gratitude" of £5,000, to be levied on beneficed clergy of upwards of £100 a-year income, was voted by the Churchmen in Parliament for this expedition. Ibid, XLI., fo. 154, and Treasurer's Accounts, ad tempus.

A. D. 1531.

Alexander of Isla hastened to open a communication with the King, as soon as he became aware of the magnitude of the preparations made for the Royal expedition; and, having received a protection and safeguard, he came to his Majesty at Stirling, made his submission, and was received into favour upon certain conditions, which shall be afterwards noticed. The same course was pursued by Hector Maclean of Dowart; and, as these chiefs had been the principal leaders of the insurgents, the rebellion might now be looked upon as nearly at an end;[1] at least the King's presence was no longer thought necessary—the management of the expedition being committed to the Earls of Argyle and Murray. Previous to their departure on this service, these noblemen gave in to the Council certain offers, of which the following is an abstract:—Argyle offered to pay the King's duties as tenant of Kintyre, whether the land lay waste or not, and both in peace and war, as his predecessors had done. He then engaged to proceed to the borders of the South Isles, and endeavour to prevail upon the inhabitants, by fair means, to take their lands on lease from the King's commissioners, and to pay the rents yearly to his Majesty's comptroller; and, in the event of their refusal, he pledged himself with his own kinsmen, friends, and followers, to compel them to obedience, *or else to destroy them, root and branch,* and quiet the Isles in that way, without creating any burden upon the rest of the country; and, at the same time, he requested that two of the King's household should accompany him, to observe his behaviour, and to see that he did not

---

[1] Acts of Lords of Council, XLII., fo. 144, 185 ; Reg. of Privy Seal, X., fo. 50, 58.

proceed to extremities, until all other means had failed.
On the ground of the experience of himself, and his clan
and friends, "in the danting of the Ilis," he demanded,
further, that the Council should be commanded to consult with him, and take his advice in their future proceedings with reference to the Islanders, and particularly in the punishment of the disobedient, and the
rewarding of those who should do the King good service.
Lastly, he desired a commission of lieutenandry over
the South Isles and Kintyre—a request which would
imply that James, when preparing to go in person to
the Isles, had revoked all former commissions.   Murray made similar offers, and preferred nearly similar
petitions regarding the North Isles, over which he had
been appointed lieutenant; but went a little further
than Argyle, in declaring his readiness to find security
for the regular payment of the King's rents, within the
districts committed to his charge; and he concluded by
a statement, that he undertook this service upon his
own expenses, from a desire to forward the King's
service, and to pacify the country, and that he expected
no remuneration unless his endeavours were successful.[1]
The two Earls then proceeded to their respective posts;
and, in the course of this summer, the insurrection was
totally suppressed—not so much by their exertions as
by the voluntary submission of the principal chiefs, who,
finding that the King would gladly avoid measures of
extreme severity, followed the example of Alexander of
Isla and Maclean of Dowart, and made their personal

---

[1] Acts of the Lords of Council, XLII., fo. 186.   Argyle, at this time,
at the King's request, resigned his heritable office of Chamberlain of
Kintyre, fo. 185.

submission to the Sovereign, by whom they were pardoned, upon giving security for their obedience in future.

The terms given to Alexander of Isla, who was considered the prime mover of this insurrection, will serve
to show the line of policy pursued by the Government at
this period for restoring order in the Isles.   This chief
having come to Stirling, and offered his service to the
King in the most humble manner, by written offers, and
having placed himself wholly at the King's disposal,
was restored to favour, upon the following conditions:—
He became bound to assist the Royal chamberlains in
collecting the rents and duties of the Crown lands in
the South Isles and Kintyre, and to procure for them
the assistance of all chieftains or heads of tribes in these
districts over whom he had any control, in proof of
their obedience to the Royal authority.   He also promised to set at liberty all prisoners whom he had in
custody belonging to Argyle's party, and to abstain
from meddling with the lands and possessions of others;
and, finally, he pledged himself to support and maintain
the Church in all her privileges, and to cause the rents
of ecclesiastical lands to be punctually paid.   For these
promised services, he received a new grant, during the
King's pleasure, of certain lands in the South Isles and
Kintyre, formerly allowed to him under the regency of
Alexander, Duke of Albany, and a remission to himself
and his followers for the offences committed by them
during the late rebellion.[1]   Such were the means adopted
by James V. to win the Islanders to good government;
and, as he was now sensible of the beneficial effects
attending a free personal intercourse between himself
and these warlike chiefs, he soon acquired as much

[1] Acts of Lords of Council, XLII., fo. 186.

influence in the Isles as had been enjoyed by his gallant and chivalrous sire. Of this, an instance occurred about this time which deserves particular attention, as throwing much light upon the conduct of the family of Argyle towards the clans in their vicinity.

Colin, third Earl of Argyle, had, during all the eventful changes of government in the minority of James V., contrived to retain the important office of lieutenant over the whole Lordship of the Isles, and to make this, in fact, an heritable office in his family. But a jealousy of the increasing power of the Campbells seems early to have been entertained by some of the Privy Councillors, and from them transferred to the young King. Nor is this much to be wondered at. These councillors must have known that, in forfeiting the ancient Lords of the Isles, James IV. contemplated not a mere change of family, but an entire alteration of system, which would give the Crown an efficient control over these territories. They must have observed with alarm the office of lieutenant in the Isles—which implied much more extensive powers ·than could legally be exercised by the feudal lord— becoming hereditary in a family already distinguished for its wealth and extensive vassalage. These feelings seem gradually to have ripened into a suspicion that many of the disturbances in the Isles were secretly fomented by the Royal lieutenant, in the hope of benefiting by the forfeitures which were expected to follow. The first indication of distrust on the part of the King and Council, was their sending a herald direct to the chief of Isla in 1529; and when, two years afterwards, that individual endeavoured to open a communication with Government, he did so, not through Argyle, but

by the instrumentality of a worthy burgess of Ayr.
The Earl of Murray was now associated with Argyle,
whose operations, as we have seen, were restricted to
the South Isles, while the King used every means to
encourage the Islanders to apply in person to himself.
When Archibald, fourth Earl of Argyle, proceeded
in 1531 to the Hebrides, he was much disappointed
that the submission of Alexander of Isla and Maclean
of Dowart, joined to their influence upon the lesser
clans who followed them, had left him so little to do;
and, as the remissions obtained by these chiefs placed
them beyond his power as long as they remained quiet,
he seized every opportunity of irritating them, so as to
cause them to break the peace, and enable him to
proceed against them. Failing in these designs, he
presented a complaint to the Council, alleging that
Alexander of Isla had been guilty of various crimes
against him and his followers, thinking in this way to
bring the other into discredit. Alexander being summoned to answer the charges preferred by the Earl,
made his appearance without hesitation, much to the
surprise of his accuser; whilst Argyle absented himself,
and did not even attempt to prove his allegations; and
it was even reported that he took this opportunity of
proceeding, in concert with the Earl of Murray, again
to the Isles, where his appearance was dreaded as the
signal for new devastations. The chief of Isla, meanwhile, after waiting long for the arrival of Argyle,
gave into the Council a written statement of a very
remarkable nature. He denied solemnly the crimes
laid to his charge; declaring that he had done nothing
since his restoration to favour, but by the Royal autho-
'rity, and offering anew to exert all his influence to

cause the King's rents in the South Isles and Kintyre to be paid to any person properly appointed to
receive them. He expressed his apprehension of the
reported invasion of the Isles in terms which led to
the conclusion that, if such a measure was really in
progress, the authority for it must have been obtained
by false or exaggerated statements. He offered, i
commission were given to himself, or any other chief
in whom the King reposed confidence, for calling out
the array of the Isles, in the event of war with England,
or in any part of the realm of Scotland, to bring more
fighting men into the field than Argyle, with all his
influence, could levy in the Isles. He offered, likewise,
in case Argyle should be disposed at any time to resist
the Royal authority, and provided the King's commands
to that effect were issued to his lieges in the Isles, to
cause the Earl to quit Argyle, and dwell in another part
of Scotland, where "*the King's grace might get reason
of him.*" He then undertook that, if any person in the
Isles offended the Earl, or any individual in the Lowlands, he should cause the culprit to appear before the
King, and either stand his trial for the offence, or redress
the wrong inflicted, in the same way that Lowlanders
were bound to do; consideration being had for the
disturbed state of the Isles, caused, as this statement
distinctly asserts, by the late Earl of Argyle, and his
brothers, Sir John Campbell of Calder and Archibald Campbell of Skipnish. Finally, he engaged
to perform all his Sovereign's commands, "for the
honour and weal of the realm, with all his power,
with the utmost diligence, and without dissimulation."[1]
The King, moved with the confidence reposed in him,

[1] Acts of Lords of Council, XLIII., fo. 64.

made such an examination into the complaints of the
Islanders as satisfied him that the family of Argyle had
been acting more for its own benefit than for the welfare
of the country. The Earl was summoned to appear
before his Sovereign, to give an account of the duties
and rental of the Isles received by him; [1] and James
was so much displeased with the result of his inquiry
into Argyle's proceedings, that he committed him to
prison soon after his arrival at Court. The conduct of
the Earl of Murray, too, seems to have given the King
great dissatisfaction. The Earl of Argyle was soon
liberated from prison; but he was, at the same time,
deprived of the offices he still held in the Isles; some
of which were bestowed on Alexander of Isla, who now
rose rapidly in the Royal favour. [2] Nor does Argyle
appear again to have regained his authority over the
Islanders till after the death of James V. Alexander
of Isla, soon after he had obtained this triumph over
Argyle, was sent to Ireland at the head of a
body of seven or eight thousand men. This
force was intended to create a diversion in favour of the
Scots, who were engaged in a war with England; and,
as they committed great devastations in Ulster,[3] it is
not improbable that their leader employed this favourable opportunity to add to his hereditary possessions in
that province. King James, at the same time, provided for the education of the eldest son of the chief

A. D. 1532.

---

[1] Treasurer's Accounts, 1st Nov., 1531.

[2] Original Letter in State Paper Office, dated Newcastle, 27th
December, 1531, from the Earl of Northumberland to Henry VIII.,
which alludes to "the sore imprisonment of the Earl of Argyle, and the
little estimation of the Earl of Murray," by the King of Scots.

[3] Original Letter, Northumberland to Henry, 3rd September, 1532.
Cotton. MS., Brit. Mus. Caligula, B. 1. 124.

of Isla, who was placed under the special charge of William Henderson, Dean of Holyrood.[1] By this two important objects were served. The mind of a future leader in the Isles, as this young man proved to be in after life, was improved and enlarged, whilst his presence in Edinburgh, under the eye of the sovereign, secured the obedience of his father.

A.D. 1532-1539.   But while he thus gained, by these and similar favours, the attachment of this particular family, James did not neglect the rest of the Islanders. He kept up his influence by a close correspondence with the different chiefs, and by frequent visits to the West Highlands;[2] so that, for several years, these districts were in a more complete state of obedience than at any former period. The petty feuds between the different clans were not yet entirely suppressed. We find traces, in the latter part of this reign, of the old quarrels between the Clanchameron and Clanchattan; between the former tribe and the Macleans; and between the two principal families of this last-mentioned clan, those of Dowart and Lochbuy.[3] But the general peace of the Western Highlands and Isles was not seriously disturbed till the year 1539, when a new attempt was made to restore the Lordship of the Isles and Earldom of Ross to one of the old family.

Many of the Islanders still regarded Donald Dubh, for whose sake their fathers had risen in rebellion in

---

[1] Treasurer's Accounts, 1531-1535.

[2] The Treasurer's Accounts show that, in September, 1532, the King was in Argyle and at Inverary. He was again in Argyle in September and October, 1534.

[3] Acts of the Lords of Council and Session, Lib. X., fo. 83; XI., fo. 181; XII., fo. 188.

1503, as the proper heir; but the lengthened captivity
of this hapless chief, joined to the doubts of his legitimacy, which were countenanced by the Government,
contributed to bring forward another claimant. This
was Donald Gorme of Sleat, the son and successor of
Donald Gruamach. The talents of the father had done
much to raise the Clandonald or Clanhuistein of Sleat
from the depressed state into which they had fallen,
owing to confiscations and internal dissensions; and the
power of the son was much increased by his marriage
with the heiress of John MacTorquil Macleod.—(Supra,
p. 131). That chief, the representative of an elder, though
forfeited branch of the family of Lewis, had, as we have
seen, obtained possession of the estates and leading of
his tribe; and although he did not hold these by any
legal title, the claims of his daughter, after his death,
were far from contemptible, especially when supported by
the influence of the Clandonald. A compromise seems
to have been entered into between Donald Gorme and
Ruari Macleod, the legal heir of the Lewis. Ruari
Macleod was allowed to enter into possession of the
estate of Lewis, as formerly held by Malcolm Macleod,
his father, and the last lawful possessor. In return for
such an important concession on the part of the chief
of Sleat, the other became bound to assist in putting
Donald Gorme in possession of Trouterness, against all
the efforts of the chief of Dunvegan and his tribe, the
Siol Tormod, who had again contrived to seize that
district. It is probable, too, that Macleod agreed to
co-operate with him in his endeavours to obtain the
Earldom of Ross and Lordship of the Isles, to which,
indeed, on the supposition of the illegitimacy of Donald
Dubh, and setting aside the forfeiture, Donald Gorme

was heir-male.   This was the foundation of a conspiracy which soon embraced a majority of the Island chiefs, and was only extinguished by the death of Donald Gorme, and the active measures adopted by the King. It is probable that Argyle's loss of influence may have led the Islanders to expect that their object was to be obtained by the favour of the Crown; but, if so, they were disappointed, and their disappointment caused them to attempt seizing by force, what they could not compass by other means.

In the month of May this year, Trouter-A. D. 1539. ness was invaded and laid waste by Donald Gorme and his allies of the Siol Torquil, as we find from a complaint made against them by Alexander Macleod of Dunvegan.[1]   From Sky, taking advantage of the absence of Mackenzie of Kintaill, who was opposed to his pretensions, Donald Gorme passed over into Ross-shire, where, after ravaging the district of Kinlochew, he proceeded to Kintaill, with the intention of surprising Mackenzie's Castle of Elandonan.   This fortress was, at the time, almost destitute of a garrison, and, had the insurgents succeeded in their attempt, a formidable rebellion in the Isles would have been the consequence. But their leader, trusting to the weakness of the garrison, and exposing himself rashly under the walls of the castle, received a wound in the foot from an arrow shot by the constable of the castle, which speedily proved fatal;   for, not observing that the arrow was barbed, the enraged chief pulled it hastily out of the wound, by which an artery was severed; and the medical skill of his followers could devise no means of checking the effusion of blood which necessarily fol-

[1] Books of Adjournal, 16th Dec., 1539.

lowed. They conveyed him to an islet out of reach of the castle, where a temporary hut was constructed, in which this ill-fated representative of the Lords of the Isles closed his short career. The spot where he died is still pointed out, and receives from the natives the name of "Larach tigh Mhic Dhonuill;" or, "The site of Macdonald's house." Discouraged by this event, the insurgents returned to Sky, after burning all the boats belonging to the Kintaill men they could find.[1]

A. D. 1540.   In the following year the King, who had, in all probability, been made aware of the intentions of the Islesmen, determined, although the insurrection was now apparently at an end, to take steps that would effectually put a stop to such schemes in future. Preparations, on a formidable scale, were made for a voyage by the King in person to the Isles. Twelve ships, well provided with artillery, were ordered to be ready by the 14th day of May, six of which were to be occupied by the Royal suite and the soldiers under the immediate command of the King. Of the remaining ships, three were appointed for the sole purpose of victualling the armament; whilst the others were assigned to Cardinal Beaton and the Earls of Huntly and Arran. The Cardinal commanded five hundred men of Fife and Angus; Huntly, besides gentlemen,

---

[1] Remission to Archibald Ilis, *alias* Archibald the Clerk, Alexander MacConnell Gallich, and many others, for their treasonable fire-raising and burning of boats at Elandonan, and for the heirship of Kenlochew and Trouterness, dated 22nd March, 1540-41 (Reg. of Privy Seal, XV., fo. 47). MS. Genealogies of the Macdonalds of Sleat, of the Mackenzies, and of the Macras. The constable of Elandonan was of the last-mentioned tribe. Donald Gorme left an infant son, also named Donald, who fell under the guardianship of his grand-uncle, the above-named " Archibald Ilis."

and thirty of the Royal household, led five hundred men of the northern shires; and Arran was followed by the like number of warriors of the western districts, exclusive of the gentlemen and twenty-four servants in his train. To complete the preparations, a skilful pilot, Alexander Lindsay, was appointed to attend the King, and report the nautical observations.

It was not till the end of May that this powerful fleet quitted the Frith of Forth; and James then sailed northwards, by the east coast of Scotland, until he came to the Orkney Isles, where he and his army landed, and were honourably entertained by Robert Maxwell, at that time Bishop of Orkney. Here, likewise, their stock of fresh provisions was renewed. From Orkney the expedition sailed to the coast of Sutherland, for the purpose of seizing Donald Mackay of Strathnaver, which was effected without difficulty. Thence the fleet proceeded to the Isle of Lewis, where Ruari Macleod, with his principal kinsmen, met the King, and were made to accompany him in his further progress. The west coast of the Isle of Sky was next visited; and Alexander Macleod of Dunvegan, lord of that part of the island, was constrained to embark in the Royal fleet. Coasting round by the north of Sky, the King then came to the district of Trouterness, so lately desolated by the chief of Sleat. Here various chieftains, claiming their descent from the ancient Lords of the Isles, came to meet their Sovereign—particularly John Moydertach, captain of the Clanranald, Alexander of Glengarry, and others of "MacConeyllis kin." These chieftains probably hoped to secure the Royal favour by coming to meet the King before the course of his voyage led him to their own districts. From Trouterness,

James proceeded, by the coast of Ross, to Kintaill, where he was joined by the chief of the Mackenzies; and then, sailing southwards by the Sound of Sleat, he visited, in succession, the Isles of Mull and Isla, and the districts of Kintyre and Knapdale, taking with him, on his departure, Hector Maclean of Dowart, and James Macdonald of Isla, the two principal leaders in the South Isles. He then landed himself at Dunbarton; but sent the fleet, with the captive chiefs on board, back to Edinburgh, by the route followed in coming to the Isles. It is not the least remarkable circumstance connected with this important expedition, that the Earl of Argyle had no prominent command, if, indeed, he was employed at all, which is very doubtful.

Having now all these chiefs in his power, James proceeded to make the necessary regulations for retaining them and their successors in a more settled obedience; and it need scarcely be observed that his projects were much facilitated by his having to deal with prisoners. The enactments made on this occasion have not been preserved; but it is known that several of the chiefs were liberated, upon giving hostages for their obedience; and the proceedings under the regency of Mary of Guise, prove that there must have been some general regulation made at this time for securing the peace of the Highlands and Isles, by means of taking hostages from the principal men. Some of the more turbulent chiefs were detained in confinement until some time after the King's death, and were then only liberated by a piece of State policy, on the part of the Regent Arran, as short-sighted as it proved futile.[1]

[1] The most complete account of this expedition and its immediate results, is to be found in Lesley s History of Scotland, p. 156. It is

The detaining some of the chiefs in prison, and the taking of hostages from the others, were not the only precautionary measures adopted by the King while the Highland chiefs were in his power. He placed garrisons, commanded by captains of his own appointment, in several of the most important fortresses. Of this branch of his policy, one marked instance has come down to us. Archibald Stewart, of the family of Bute, was made captain of the Castle of Dunyveg in Isla, belonging to James· Macdonald, the son and successor of that Alexander of Isla who had formerly stood so high in the King's favour; and, shortly before the King's death, he received a commission as Governor and Sheriff of Isla.[1] As James Macdonald had been educated under the King's eye, it may be conceived that, when his castle was made a Royal garrison, those of many of the other chiefs did not remain in the powers of their owners. The annexation of the Lordship of the Isles, with North and South Kintyre, inalienably to the Crown,[2] seemed to give the finishing blow to the hopes so long cherished by the Islanders; and everything promised an assurance of a more lengthened period of repose than the Isles had hitherto enjoyed.

singular that so important a measure is uniformly misdated, both by Lesley, Buchanan, Pitscottie, and all our early historians; some placing it in 1535, others in 1539. The extracts from the Treasurer's Accounts, printed in Pitcairn's Criminal Trials, I. 303*, give the true date, 1540, which has been adopted by Mr. Tytler. Pinkerton was the first to correct this error.

[1] Reg. of Privy Seal, XVI., fo. 1. Treasurer's Accounts, ad tempus. From the last source, it appears that the Castle of Duna-vertich in Kintyre, likewise belonging to James Macdonald, or at least commanding a territory occupied by him and his clan, was at this time held by a Royal garrison.

[2] Acts of Parliament, 3rd December, 1540

A. D. 1542. But this fair prospect was soon clouded by the untimely death of James V. in the flower of his age, and the succession of his infant daughter to the Crown. This event exposed the kingdom not only to foreign aggression, but to domestic feuds between the powerful factions that contended for the government of the young Queen. In the next chapter we shall see the effect of these struggles in retarding the civilisation of the Highlands and Isles.

CHAP. III.

IT is not the province of a work like the present to trace minutely the proceedings of the great parties which divided Scotland during the minority of Queen Mary. A brief outline of these proceedings, and of the extraordinary changes which a very short time produced in the line of conduct pursued by some of the leading nobility, will serve to show the position in which the Islanders and Western Highlanders were placed at this time.

A. D. 1542. The leading party in Scotland was that of the Catholic clergy, at the head of which was the able but unprincipled Cardinal Beaton. " Of this faction," says a recent author, " the guiding principles were a determined opposition to the progress of the Reformation, and a devotion to the Papal see ; friendship with France ; hostility to England ; and a resolution, which all must applaud, of preserving the ancient independence of their country."[1] The ranks of the opposite faction included all the supporters of the Reformation ; and at their head was the Earl of Arran, whose assumption of this authority was owing more to his high rank, as next heir to the Crown, than to any natural energy

[1] Tytler's Scotland, V., p. 310.

of character he possessed. This party was naturally disposed to a friendly intercourse with the English King; and thus increased the influence which late events had given to that monarch over the affairs of Scotland.

Immediately after the death of James V., King Henry formed the plan of uniting Scotland to England, by a marriage between the infant Queen and his own son, Edward, Prince of Wales. His influence with the Earl of Angus and the Douglases, who now, after a lengthened banishment, returned to their native land, and the opportunity afforded by the capture of so many Scottish prisoners of rank at Solway, seem to have offered a temptation too strong to be resisted by so ambitious a prince. The leading prisoners were allowed to visit Scotland, after coming under strict engagements to Henry, in reference to the proposed marriage, not only disgraceful to them, as men of honour and natives of Scotland, but calculated to subvert entirely the liberties of their country. The principal opposition to these schemes, which were conducted with great caution, proceeded from the Cardinal. This able statesman was not discouraged by the failure of an attempt to possess himself of the regency, although the immediate consequence was the ascendancy of the English faction, who had the Regent Arran completely under their influence.

A. D. 1543. In order to work upon the fears of Arran, and make him subservient to his designs, Beaton had procured the return from abroad of Mathew, Earl of Lennox, whom he proposed to set up in opposition to Arran, as a claimant for the regency. The claims of Lennox, indeed, to this high office, were of such a nature as, in the hands of an opponent like the Cardinal, could hardly fail to alarm the present Governor. But the violence and impetuosity of the English King, by rousing the Scottish nation to a sense of its danger, and of the designs entertained against its independence, principally contributed to a coalition between Arran and the Cardinal, which put an end to the treaty for the marriage of the Queen of Scots.[1]

Having gained his object of a union with Arran, the Cardinal began to neglect Lennox, whom he had hitherto flattered with hopes of the regency and of the hand of Mary of Guise, the Queen-mother. That nobleman, who had lately been instrumental in procuring a promise from the French King of assistance to the Cardinal's party, in the event of a war with England, was so deeply offended at Beaton's conduct that he at once threw himself into the arms of the English party. Just at this time, the Sieur de la Brosse, a French ambassador, accompanied by a small fleet, bearing military stores, fifty pieces of artillery, and ten thousand crowns, to be distributed among the friends of the Cardinal, arrived in the Frith of Clyde. On hearing of his arrival, the Earls of Lennox and Glencairn hastened to receive from the ambassador the gold of which he was the bearer, which they secured in the Castle of Dunbarton, leaving De la Brosse, who was ignorant of the sudden change in the politics of Lennox, to find out his mistake when too late.[2]

The Earls of Arran and Lennox, one of whom held, and the other claimed to hold, the highest office in the realm to which a subject could aspire, had displayed, during late events, a disgraceful versatility; and others

[1] Tytler's Scotland, V. 311-346.   This remarkable coalition, which was very suddenly brought about, took place on 3rd Sept., 1543.
[2] Ibid, 348-9.

of the Scottish nobility, having sold themselves to England, were now leagued to destroy the independence of their country. From such proofs of the want of public spirit and principle among so many of the great barons, we turn with pleasure to contemplate the dignified and patriotic conduct of the two most powerful noblemen in the Highlands, the Earls of Huntly and Argyle, who, emulating the example of their gallant ancestors, never lost sight of their duty to Scotland. They acknowledged the advantages that might result from the proposed matrimonial alliance, if made on equal terms; but when the rashness and violence of Henry disclosed prematurely his ambitious views, they did not hesitate to oppose, to the utmost of their power, the projects of the English party.[1] This conduct procured for Huntly and Argyle the honour of the enmity, both of Henry and of his hired partisans in Scotland, but entitled them, on the other hand, to the respect and confidence of all their true-hearted countrymen. During the various struggles which preceded the union of the Regent and the Cardinal, and when a civil war seemed inevitable, it became of the greatest importance to deprive the Cardinal of the assistance of such powerful adherents; and for the attainment of this object, the state of the West Highlands and Isles afforded, at this time, great facilities. Donald Dubh, the grandson of John, last Lord of the Isles, was now once more at liberty. It will be in the recollection of the reader, that this unfortunate chief, who seems really to have been legitimate, was stigmatised as a bastard; and that, with the exception of the short period of his rebellion against James IV., he had been a State pri-

[1] Tytler, ubi supra.

soner from his infancy. In what manner Donald Dubh
effected this, his second escape, is doubtful; but it is
certain that he owed his liberty to the grace of God,
and not to the goodwill of the Government.[1] Having
come to the Isles, he was received with enthusiasm by
the same clans that had formerly supported his claims;
and, with their assistance, he prepared to expel the Earls
of Argyle and Huntly from their acquisitions in the
Lordship of the Isles. As long, however, as the chiefs
and hostages imprisoned by James V. in 1540, remained
in the power of the Government, the Highlanders were
compelled to proceed with great caution. A truce was
agreed to between the Earl of Argyle and the self-
styled Lord of the Isles, which was to last till May-
day, 1543; and, in the meantime, both parties were
active in preparing for war.[2] In June of the same
year, we find that Argyle was occupied in the Highlands with the " Irishmen," who were rebelling against
him; and, at the same time, the presence of Huntly
was required in the north, probably from the same
cause.[3] About this time, too, it was suggested to the
Regent by the Earl of Glencairn—one of the most
active of the English party, and between whom and
Argyle their existed a violent private feud—that the
Highland chiefs and hostages left in prison by the late
King should be liberated, in order to enable the Lord
of the Isles to act with vigour against Argyle and
Huntly.[4] The suggestions of Glencairn were doubtless enforced by the arguments of Sadler, the English

---

[1] This appears from a document in the State Paper Office, quoted by
Mr. Tytler, V., p. 232, note.

[2] Sadler's State Papers, I. 192, 194.

[3] Ibid, 214.   [4] Ibid, 273.

ambassador, as the attention of the King of England had been early drawn to the state of the Highlands and Isles.[1] Thus prompted, the feeble and short-sighted Arran liberated all the Highland prisoners, taking bonds from them, as we learn from Sadler's correspondence, " that they should not make any stir or breach in their country, but at such time as he should appoint them. But how they will observe these bonds," continues the ambassador, " now since they be at liberty, it is hard to say; for they be noted such perilous persons, as it is thought it shall not ly in the Earl of Argyle's power to daunt them, nor yet in the Governor's to set that country in a stay and quietness a great while."[2]

Immediately upon the return of the liberated chiefs to their clans, Donald of the Isles assembled a force of eighteen hundred men, with which he invaded Argyle's territories, slew many of his vassals, and carried off a great quantity of cattle, with other plunder. This inroad had the desired effect of preventing the junction of Argyle with the Cardinal, by keeping the former at home in the month of August, when a collision between the Regent and the Cardinal, and their respective adherents, was daily expected.[3] The sudden conversion of Arran from a supporter to an opponent of the views of the English King, caused his ill-judged policy in liberating the Highland chiefs, and encouraging them to attack Argyle and Huntly, to recoil on himself. And although, in order to repair his fault, he afterwards made great offers to Donald of the Isles, with the view

---

[1] Letter of "John Elder, Clerk, a Redshank," to King Henry, in 1542, a most curious and interesting document, printed in the Collectanea de Rebus Albanicis, I. 23.

[2] Sadler, I. 267.   [3] Sadler, I. 266-7, 275.

of detaching him and his followers from the English party, his efforts totally failed of success.[1] Of all the vassals of the Isles, James Macdonald of Isla alone supported the Regent; and future events showed that the fidelity even of this chief could not altogether be relied on.

A. D. 1544. The Earl of Huntly and his vassals probably suffered, as well as Argyle, from the inroads of the western clans in 1543; but in the following year, a feud between the Clanranald of Moydert and the Frasers, still further interrupted the tranquillity of those districts of the Highlands placed under the control of Huntly, as Lieutenant of the North. The circumstances connected with this feud are as follows:— Allan MacRuari of Moydert, chief of the Clanranald from 1481 to 1509, was twice married; first, to a daughter of Macian of Ardnamurchan, by whom he had two sons, Ranald Bane and Alexander; secondly, and late in life, to a daughter of the Lord Lovat, by whom he had one son, likewise named Ranald, and known by the clan as Ranald Galda, or the stranger, from his being fostered by his mother's relations, the Frasers, at a great distance from Moydert. Ranald Bane Allanson of Moydert, chief of the Clanranald, being executed, as we have seen, in 1513, was succeeded by his son, Dougal MacRanald, or Ranaldson. This chief, having made himself detested in the clan by his cruelties, was assassinated by them; and the command of the tribe, with the large family estates, was, by their consent, given to Alexander or Allaster Allan-

---

[1] Letter from Commissioners of the Lord of the Isles, to the English Privy Council, dated in August, 1545, and preserved in the State Paper Office.

son, the uncle of Dougal, to the exclusion of the sons of the latter, who were then young.[1]   On the death of Allaster, which took place before 1530, his bastard son, John Moydertach, a man of uncommon talent and ability, was acknowledged by the whole clan as their chief; and he even succeeded in procuring charters to the estates.   These he possessed without interruption, till, with other chiefs, he was apprehended by James V. in the course of that King's voyage through the Isles in 1540, and placed in prison.   Lord Lovat and the Frasers then bestirred themselves for the interest of their kinsman Ranald Galda, and made such a representation on the subject, that the charters formerly granted to John Moydertach were revoked, and the lands granted to Ranald Galda, as the heir of his father, Allan MacRuari.[2]   The existence of prior legal heirs (the sons of Dougal) seems to have been carefully concealed; and, by the assistance of the Frasers, Ranald was actually put in possession of the estate which he held only as long as John Moydertach remained in prison; for, immediately on the return of that chief to the Highlands, he was joined by the whole of the Clanranald, including the sons of Dougal, and again acknowledged as their chief.   Ranald, who had lost favour with the clan by exhibiting a parsimonious disposition, was expelled from Moydert, and forced to

---

[1] Allan, the eldest son of Dougal, and the undoubted heir-male of the Clanranald, acquired the estate of Morar, which he transmitted to his descendants.   He and his successors were always styled, in Gaelic, "MacDhughail Mhorair," i. e., Macdougal of Morar, from their ancestor, Dougal MacRanald.

[2] Macvurich's MS. and Hugh Macdonald's MS., compared with the traditions of the country.   Reg. of the Great Seal, XXIV. 151; XXVII. 102.   Acts of the Lords of Council, XLI. 79; Lesley's History of Scotland, 157 : Treasurer's Accounts, A.D. 1542.

take refuge with Lord Lovat, who once more prepared to assert the rights of his kinsman. The Clanranald, however, did not wait to be attacked, but, assisted by Ranald MacDonald Glas of Keppoch and his tribe, and by the Clanchameron, under their veteran leader, Ewin Allanson of Lochiel, they carried the war into the enemy's country. The districts of Abertarf and Stratherrick, belonging to Lovat, and the lands of Urquhart and Glenmoriston, the property of the Grants, were speedily overrun by the insurgents, who likewise possessed themselves of the Castle of Urquhart on Lochness. Not content with the usual system of indiscriminate plunder which characterised a Highland inroad, they seemed to aim at a permanent occupation of the invaded territories; and such was their audacity that the Earl of Huntly was at length constrained to levy a numerous force in the northern counties, and proceed to crush this threatening insurrection before it should spread farther. Among those who attended Huntly on this expedition, were Lord Lovat and the Laird of Grant, at the head of their respective clans, and Ranald Galda, so lately expelled from Moydert, all of whom were deeply interested in the success of the enterprise.

At the approach of Huntly, the Highlanders retreated to their mountain fastnesses, leaving the country open to the Royal forces; so' that, without more delay than was rendered necessary by the rugged nature of the country, that nobleman penetrated as far as Inverlochy. Having, without opposition, put Ranald Galda in possession of Moydert, and restored to their proper owners the other lands that had been occupied by the rebels, Huntly set out on his return home, satisfied with what

he had done, although it does not appear that he had
succeeded in apprehending, at this time, any leader of
the insurgents.   On arriving at the mouth of Glenspean,
in Lochaber, a separation of Huntly's forces took place.
The Earl himself, the Laird of Grant, and the bulk of
the army, proceeded to Strathspey by the Braes of Lochaber and Badenoch, while Lovat, in spite of repeated re-
monstrances on the rashness of his conduct, marched with
his own vassals, amounting to four hundred men, by the
line of the great glen, that being not only the shortest road,
but passing, for a great part of the way, through his own
lands of Abertarf and Stratherrick.   He was likewise
accompanied, out of compliment, by Ranald Galda, and
a few followers of the latter.   The fears of those who
had remonstrated with Lovat were soon realised.   The
insurgent Highlanders, who had drawn together again,
upon receiving intelligence of Huntly's intention to return
home, and had kept a close watch upon the movements
of the Royal army, no sooner perceived the separation
of Lovat from the main body, than they determined to
intercept and cut him off.   Accordingly, Lovat, who
marched by the south side of Loch Lochy, was hardly
out of reach of assistance from Huntly, when he perceived a superior force of Highlanders marching up the
north side, in seven companies, with displayed banners,
and so far advanced as to leave no doubt of their intercepting him at the head of the lake.[1]   On this,

---

[1] The Diurnal of Occurrents, printed by the Bannatyne Club, p.
34, states that the Earl of *Bothwell* was riding to a "tryst," or appointment, made by him with Lovat and the captain of Clanranald,
in order to settle the differences between these chiefs; but that,
before he arrived, the parties had encountered, and the battle was
over. This is nowhere else alluded to, and it is difficult to under-

Lovat, who perceived the danger of his position, detached a portion of his force, under a favourite vassal, named Bean Clerach, to occupy a pass in the hills at a little distance, by which, in the event of the day turning against him, he hoped .to secure a retreat. With the rest of his followers, who now amounted to about three hundred, a great proportion of whom were gentlemen, and well armed, he moved forward to meet the enemy. The Clanranald and their supporters were superior in number, amounting probably to five hundred; but of these many were of the inferior sort, and ill supplied with arms.   Just after the commencement of the action, the Frasers were joined, to the great grief of their leader, by the Master of Lovat, a youth of great promise, lately returned from abroad. He had been expressly charged by his father not to join this expedition, and he accordingly remained at home for some time after its departure; but, roused by the taunts of his stepmother, who wished to get rid of him, the gallant youth chose twelve trusty followers, and set out in search of his father and clan, whom he met at the head of Loch Lochy, in time to join in the fray.

The contest began with the discharge of arrows at a distance; but when their shafts were spent both parties rushed to close combat, and, attacking each other furiously with their two-handed swords and axes, a dreadful slaughter ensued. Such was the heat of the weather, it being the month of July, that the combatants threw off their coats and fought in their shirts; whence the battle received the named of " Blar-na-leine," or " The

stand the interference of Bothwell in a matter under Huntly's immediate jurisdiction. Perhaps for *Bothwell* we should read *Huntly*.

14

Field of Shirts." At length the Frasers, after fighting
with the greatest bravery, were obliged to retire; but,
unfortunately, Bean Clerach and his detachment, having
missed their way, were unable to render any assistance
to their clansmen; and the pass which they should have
occupied being seized by the Clanranald, the Frasers,
thus hemmed in, were, after a desperate and unavailing
struggle, almost entirely cut to pieces. According to
their own historians, one gentleman alone (James Fraser
of Foyers, who was severely wounded and left for dead),
and four common men of their party, survived this bloody
field, which threatened the annihilation of the name of
Fraser in the north. The loss of the victors is commonly represented as much greater, in so far as only
eight of their number are said to have survived the conflict. But this is certainly one of those exaggerations
in which traditionary historians are so apt to indulge;
for none of the leaders of the Clanranald and their
allies fell in the action; and, indeed, in the following year
they were all actively engaged in supporting the pretensions of their new Lord, Donald of the Isles. This would
have been impossible had they suffered so severe a loss
as is alleged to have been inflicted on them in this action.
The bodies of Lord Lovat, his son the Master, and
Ranald Galda, who had all fought with the utmost
bravery, and only yielded to superior numbers, were, a
few days after the battle, removed by a train of mourn-
ing relatives, and interred at the Priory of Beauly in
the Aird.[1] Such was the famous clan battle of Blar-

---

[1] These particulars regarding the battle of Kinloch-lochy, and
the events which preceded it, have been gathered from a careful
examination of the following sources:—Reg. of Privy Seal, XX., fo.
72; XXI., fo. 3; XXII., fo. 27; XXIII., fo. 45. Reg. of Great Seal,

na-leine, or Kinloch-lochy, by which the Clanranald maintained in possession of the chiefship and estates of their tribe an individual of their own choice, in opposition to one supported by all the influence of the feudal law. It is not unworthy of notice that John Moydertach, himself an elected chief, afterwards transmitted to his descendants, without difficulty, the possessions that had been so hardly won.

The news of the disaster that had happened to Lord Lovat and his followers being carried to the Earl of Huntly, that nobleman appears again to have penetrated into Lochaber.[1] But, although he laid waste the lands of some of the rebels, and executed such of them as came into his power, he had no better success than formerly in apprehending any of the principal leaders, who evaded his pursuit by retiring to the most inaccessible districts. More important national concerns seem now to have occupied Huntly's attention; and his withdrawal from Lochaber was the signal for new insurrections; nor was it for nearly two years that he was enabled to check these disturbances, by the execution of two of the principal chiefs, as will appear in the sequel.

Among the other methods adopted by the King of

XXX. 263, 314. Lesley's History of Scotland, p. 184. Diurnal of Occurrents, p. 34. Gordon's History of the Family of Sutherland, p. 109. MS. History of the Frasers, Adv. Lib. Jac. 5th, 7, 29. MS. History of the Camerons. Buchanan's History of Scotland, ad tempus. In the letter, formerly mentioned, as written by the Commissioners of the Lord of the Isles, in August 1545, to the English Privy Council, it is stated that, "the last yeir, the capitane of Clanranald, *in his defence*, slew the Lord Lovat, his son-in-law, his three brethren, with thirteen scoir of men."—Tytler, V. 233.

[1] Lesley, p. 185.

England, in this year, to force the Scottish nation into
a renewal of the marriage treaty, he did not neglect
sending an expedition to harass Scotland on the side of
the Isles. The rupture of the treaty, although solely
caused by his own violent and ungovernable temper, had,
nevertheless, irritated him highly against the Scots, and
his wrath was marked by acts, such as the burning of
Edinburgh and Leith, and the laying waste of a great
portion of the southern counties, which only tended to
widen the breach, and secured no solid advantage to
England. The expedition against the west coast, which
was under the command of the Earl of Lennox, had a
similar result. In the month of August, a well-manned
fleet of ten or twelve sail left Bristol, having on board
Lennox, accompanied by Sir Rise Mansell and Sir
Peter Mewtas, Knights, and several other officers of
experience, naval and military, with two hundred hack-
butteers, two hundred archers, and two hundred pike-
men.[1]

On his arrival off the coast of Scotland, Lennox first
attacked and plundered the Isle of Arran, and razed
the Castle of Brodick to the ground. He then proceeded to Bute, of which island, with its Castle of
Rothesay, he made himself master with little difficulty.
These acquisitions, according to agreement, were
delivered to Sir Rise Mansell and Richard Broke, who
accompanied the expedition, and took formal possession
of them in the name of the King of England. Lennox
next sailed towards the Castle of Dunbarton, the seizure
of which, and its delivery to the English, was the principal object of the expedition; but here he met with

---

[1] Tytler, V., p. 371; Dr. Patrick Anderson's MS. History of Scotland,
Advocates' Library, II. 34.

an unexpected disappointment. When some months earlier, upon an open rupture with the Regent, and the success of the latter at Glasgow Muir, the Earl of Glencairn was forced to seek safety in flight, he joined the Earl of Lennox, who had for some time been assembling his forces at Dunbarton. The nature of the intrigues in which these noblemen were engaged, made it necessary for Lennox to proceed in person to England. On his departure, Glencairn, and several gentlemen of his train, were left in the Castle of Dunbarton, the governor of which was Stirling of Glorat, a retainer of Lennox. In the meantime, during the absence of the latter nobleman, Glencairn was tampered with by the Queen Dowager, and the result was a plot to entrap Lennox and make him prisoner when he should appear to take possession of the fortress. Having landed in the immediate vicinity of the castle with three hundred men, Lennox proceeded with a small retinue into the castle itself in order to receive it from the governor. But before the preliminary arrangements were completed, and just after the money was laid down, which was to bribe the governor to betray his trust, by admitting an English garrison, Lennox became alarmed at certain symptoms of disaffection which he perceived, and, leaving the money behind him, hastily quitted the castle. Joining the English troops that were in waiting outside, he effected a hurried retreat to his ships, but not before such a step had become absolutely necessary; for shortly after Lennox had quitted the town of Dunbarton, a body of four thousand Scots, sent expressly to apprehend him, entered it under the command of Sir George Douglas—this baron, and his brother, the Earl of Angus, so long the soul of the English faction in Scotland, being now, by the reckless proceedings of Henry, converted into enemies.[1]

The expedition now returned to Bute, their leader deeply mortified by his failure at Dunbarton, and still further irritated from his fleet being fired at in its passage by the Earl of Argyle, who, with a large body of his vassals, and some pieces of artillery, had taken post at the Castle of Dunoon. Before leaving Dunbarton, Lennox had received an addition to his strength, consisting of seven score Highlanders, from the more remote districts of his own Earldom, under the command of Walter Macfarlane of Tarbet. These troops, we are told, spoke both Irish and English. They were light footmen, well armed with coats of mail, with bows and arrows, and with two-handed swords, and were of much service in the future operations. Being arrived at Bute, Lennox and his officers, after holding a council of war, determined to attack the Earl of Argyle at Dunoon. The latter with seven hundred men attempted to oppose the landing of the English troops, which was, notwithstanding, effected under a heavy fire from the ships. Argyle was forced to retire after a skirmish in which he lost eighty men, many of them gentlemen; and the village of Dunoon was then burnt, and the church, into which the country people had removed their goods and ornaments, was plundered of everything it contained. At nightfall, the invaders returned safely to their ships, Argyle sustaining further loss in a fruitless effort to harass their retreat. Four or five days afterwards, Lennox with five hundred men landed in another part of Argyle, and remaining on shore for a day, laid waste

---

[1] Tytler, V. 372; Anderson, II. 34, 35.

the surrounding country. Such were the dispositions made on this occasion by the skilful soldiers who accompanied Lennox, that Argyle, although at the head of two thousand men, was obliged to witness these devastations without being able to bring the invaders to an encounter. After this, Lennox invaded Kintyre, belonging to James Macdonald of Isla (who, at this time, supported Argyle), and burnt many places in that district, carrying off, at the same time, great numbers of cattle and much property. As he was highly incensed against the Earl of Glencairn, he did not spare the lands of that nobleman, but gave them up to fire and sword. And so great was the terror which this armament created in Kyle, Carrick, Cunningham, and Galloway, that many gentlemen of these districts, seeing no other mode of escape, placed themselves under Lennox's protection.[1]

While engaged in this expedition, Lennox, following his instructions, had entered into communication with the Islanders, from several of whom he took bonds of service.[2] Their anxiety to destroy the power of the Earl of Argyle, and to procure for their Lord the restoration of the ancient possessions of his family, disposed them to enter readily into the views of Lennox and the English King. Nor did they neglect the present opportunity of testifying their hostility to the Scots, by extending their ravages on every side, particularly on the lands

[1] Tytler, V. 373; Anderson, II. 35, 36.

[2] Reg. of Privy Seal, XX., fo. 86. According to Macvurich, "Donald Dubh, the true heir of Innisgall (the Isles) and Ross, came, after his release from captivity, to the Isles, and convened the men thereof, and he and the Earl of Lennox agreed to raise a great army for the purpose of taking possession."

of those who supported Argyle and Huntly. Finding, however, that he could, at present, make no permanent impression, the Earl of Lennox, with his English troops, returned to Bristol. He then sent Sir Peter Mewtas, and Thomas Bishop, a Scottish gentleman, to inform the King, now occupied with the siege of Boulogne, of all his proceedings. In his despatches he expressed much indignation against the Earl of Glencairn and his son; and the King was, no doubt, deeply chagrined at the failure of the attempt to secure the Castle of Dunbarton.[1] But, on the whole, the tidings sent to Boulogne were well received, probably because the alliance with the Islesmen, of which Lennox had now laid the foundation, promised to afford unwonted facilities for a future invasion of Scotland. Accordingly, as soon as Henry returned to England, he sent for Lennox to Court, and the intrigues against Scotland were resumed.[2]

A. D. 1545. Early in the following year was fought the battle of Ancrum Muir, in which the English, under Sir Ralph Evre and Sir Brian Latoun, were defeated by the Scots, under the Earl of Angus. Neill Macneill of Gigha, one of the Island chiefs, was certainly present, on the English side, at this battle;[3] but whether he was with the English as an ambassador from the Lord of the Isles, or fought in their ranks at the head of a body of auxiliaries, remains for the present uncertain.

Meantime, the Earl of Lennox—through a confiden-

---

[1] Tytler, V. 373; Anderson, II. 36.

[2] Anderson, ubi supra.

[3] Reg. of Privy Seal, XXVII., fo. 36.

tial vassal, Patrick Colquhoun, whose influence in the
Isles was considerable, from his having held for many
years the office of King's Chamberlain there[1]—exerted
himself successfully to confirm the Islanders in their
intention of transferring their alliance from the Scottish
to the English Crown.   These treasonable practices,
however secretly conducted, did not escape the notice
of the Scottish Government.   In the month of June
this year, a proclamation was issued by the Regent
Arran and his Privy Council, against "Donald, alleging himself of the Isles, and other Highlandmen, his
part-takers."   This document bears that the Council
had been frequently informed of the "invasions" made
by Donald and his supporters upon the Queen's lieges,
both in the Isles and on the mainland; which invasions
were not made by the power of the Islesmen alone, but
by the assistance of the King of England, with whom
they were leagued; such proceedings showing their
intention, as far as in them lay, to bring the whole Isles
and a great part of the mainland, under the obedience
of the King of England, in contempt of the authority of
the Scottish Crown.   Proclamation was therefore made,
charging Donald of the Isles and his followers to
desist in future from their rebellious and treasonable
proceedings; and, in the event of their continuing
obstinate, they were threatened with utter ruin and
destruction, from an invasion by "the whole body of
the realm of Scotland, with the succours lately come from
France."[2]   As no attention was paid to this proclamation by the Islesmen, and as it served rather to throw

---

[1] Reg. of Privy Seal, IX., fo. 48.

[2] Reg. of Privy Council, ad tempus.

them more decidedly into the arms of England, by
showing that they had no time to lose, the Government
was compelled to resort to measures of greater severity.
Processes of treason were immediately commenced
against the principal rebels, and followed up with as
much rapidity as the forms and sessions of the Parliament permitted.[1]   While these were in progress, a
commission was granted, on the 28th of July, by
Donald, Lord of the Isles and Earl of Ross, with the
advice and consent of his Barons and Council of the
Isles, of whom seventeen are named, to two commissioners, or rather plenipotentiaries, for treating, under
the directions of the Earl of Lennox, with the English
King.[2]   On the 5th of August, the Lords and Barons
of the Isles were at Knockfergus in Ireland, with a force
of four thousand men, and a hundred and eighty galleys;
when, in presence of two commissioners, sent by the
Earl of Lennox, and of the constable, mayor, and
magistrates of that town, they took the oath of allegiance to the King of England, "at the command of the
said Earl of Lennox."   In all the documents illustra-

---

[1] Treasurer's Accounts, ad tempus; Acts of Parliament, II., 453.

[2] The original document is preserved in the State Paper Office, and
is quoted in Tytler, V. 397.   The Barons and Council of the Isles
named were, Hector Maclean, Lord of Doward; John MacAllaster,
captain of Clanranald; Rorie Macleod of Lewis; Alexander Macleod,
of Dunvegan; Murdoch Maclean of Lochbuy; Angus Macdonald,
brother-german to James Macdonald; Allan Maclean of Torlusk,
brother-german to the Lord Maclean; Archibald Macdonald, captain
of Clanhuistein; Alexander Macian of Ardnamurchan; John Maclean
of Coll; Gilliganan Macneill of Barray; Ewin Mackinnon of Strag-
huordill; John Macquarrie of Ulva; John Maclean of Ardgour;
Alexander Ranaldson of Glengarry; Angus Ranaldson of Knoydert;
and Donald Maclean of Kengarloch.

tive of these proceedings, we find that Lennox was acknowledged by the Islesmen as the true Regent and second person of the realm of Scotland; and while, at his command, they gave their allegiance to the English King, they, at the same time, bound themselves, in particular, to forward Henry's views in regard to the marriage of the Princess of Scotland, and, in all other affairs, to act under the directions of Lennox.[1] The name of James Macdonald of Isla, whose lands of Kintyre had been so lately ravaged by Lennox, does not occur among the Barons of the Isles who accompanied their Lord to Knockfergus. It appears also that, in the month of April, he had even received a reward from Arran for his services against the English.[2] Yet now, his brother, Angus Macdonald, was one of the foremost in support of Lennox; and his own conduct, in the course of a few months, justifies the suspicion that already this powerful chief contemplated joining the rest of the Islanders.

The troops that accompanied the Lord of the Isles to Ireland are described, in the original despatches from the Irish Privy Council, giving Henry notice of their arrival, as being "three thousand of them very tall men, clothed, for the most part, in habergeons of mail, armed with long swords and long bows, but with few guns; the other thousand, tall maryners, that rowed in the galleys." An equal number of warriors had been left behind, to keep in check the Earls of Huntly and Argyle, forming a total force of eight thousand men now in arms, under the command of a leader who had passed

---

[1] Documents preserved in State Paper Office.

[2] Reg. of Great Seal, XXIX. 118.

most of his life in prison, deprived of all power and influence.   It cannot be doubted that many of the Islanders acted on this occasion from a feeling of attachment to the representative of the family of the Isles, as well as from a deed-rooted hostility to the house of Argyle.   But it is equally clear—and unfortunately harmonises too well with the venal conduct of many of the Scottish nobility of the period, to admit of question —that English gold must have had a great effect in producing unanimity among tribes so many of which were at deadly feud.[1]

From Knockfergus, the plenipotentiaries of the Island Lord proceeded to the English Court, bearing letters of recommendation from their master, both to the King and Privy Council.[2]   By the last of these letters, it appears that the Lord of the Isles had already received from Henry the sum of one thousand crowns, and the promise of an annual pension of two thousand.   After certain articles proposed by the Islesmen, together with their oath of allegiance, had been given in by the commissioners to the Privy Council, and the opinion of the Earl of Lennox had been taken as to the best mode of procedure, the following conditions were agreed to on

[1] Anderson, in his MS. History of Scotland, says that the Islesmen *elected* Donald for their Lord, as being the chiefest and nearest of blood; and adds, that, besides a pension from the King of England, he was to receive "certaine rich apparel of cloth of gold and silver from the said Earl" of Lennox.—II., p. 47.

[2] The plenipotentiaries were Ruari MacAllaster (brother to the captain of the Clanranald), Dean of Morvern, who was supported by the Islesmen, in opposition to Roderick Maclean, put forward by the Regent to the vacant Bishopric of the Isles (Keith's Bishops, p. 175); and Patrick Maclean (brother to Maclean of Dowart), Justiciar of the Isles, and Bailie of Icolmkill.

the 4th of September :—The pension of two thousand crowns was confirmed to the Lord of the Isles by letters patent; and Henry engaged that that nobleman and his followers should be included in any treaty made between England and Scotland. On the other hand, the Lord of the Isles became bound, with all his adherents, to serve the King of England truly and faithfully, to the annoyance of the Regent of Scotland and his partisans. He engaged to make no agreement with the Earls of Huntly or Argyle, or with any of the Scots, to the prejudice of the King of England; but, on the contrary, to continue steadfast in his opposition to them and in his allegiance to Henry. It was arranged that the Earl of Lennox, with a body of two thousand Irish, under the Earl of Ormond and Ossory, should lead an expedition against Scotland from the west, in which he was to be assisted by the Lord of the Isles with eight thousand men. As long as Lennox should remain in the country of the Earl of Argyle, the whole eight thousand men were to be placed at his disposal; but, in the event of his proceeding to another part of Scotland—and a march to Stirling was seriously contemplated—it was provided that only six thousand of the Islanders should follow him, while the remaining two thousand should be employed in occupying the attention of the Earl of Argyle. Lastly, three thousand of the Islesmen were to receive pay from the King of England for two months.[1]

In conformity with these arrangements, instructions were given to the Earl of Ormond to levy two thousand Irish foot for the expedition against Scotland; and the

---

[1] Original in State Paper Office.

other necessary preparations for an armament of such
importance were actively carried on by the Irish Privy
Council. But at this moment, the Earl of Hertford,
who was about to invade Scotland from the Border,
required the presence of Lennox in his camp; and the
western invasion was necessarily postponed till the ter-
mination of the campaign.[1] This delay caused, in the
end, the total failure of the expedition. The Lord of
the Isles, after waiting for some time in vain, expecting
the arrival of Lennox, and naturally anxious about the
safety of the vassals he had left behind, returned with
his forces to Scotland. Meantime, dissensions had
arisen among his barons as to the division of the English pay received for three thousand of their men;
and their quarrels ran so high that the army seems to
have been broken up, whilst the chiefs retired each to
his own castle.[2] At length, the Earl of Lennox arrived
in Ireland, where he received this mortifying intelligence; but although now uncertain what support he
might receive from the Islanders, he determined on
proceeding to Scotland as soon as the Irish armament
should be ready, in order that the great exertions of the
Privy Council of Ireland might not be rendered altogether useless. Immediately after the arrival of Lennox in Dublin, Patrick Colquhoun had been despatched

[1] Tytler, V. 398.

[2] Macvurich. His words (translated) are—" A ship came from England with a supply of money to carry on the war, which landed at
Mull; and the money was given to Maclean of Dowart to be distributed
among the commanders of the army; which they not receiving in
proportion as it should have been distributed amongst them, caused
the army to disperse." That Maclean acted a very prominent part in
the intrigues with England is corroborated by the documents in the
State Paper Office.

with some light vessels to the Isles. The object of his mission was to ascertain whether the Lord of the Isles still continued firm in his allegiance to Henry; and, in the event of this point being satisfactorily ascertained, to assist in bringing the forces of the Isles together in time to co-operate with the expedition from Ireland.[1] Having received information that a good opportunity now offered for possessing himself of Dunbarton Castle, which was still a favourite object with Henry, Lennox likewise despatched his brother, the ex-Bishop of Caithness, to practise on the fidelity of the Constable; and soon afterwards followed himself, sailing from Dublin on the 17th of November, with a formidable squadron, carrying on board two thousand Irish soldiers, under the command of the Earl of Ormond. So complete an armament, according to the opinion expressed by the Irish Privy Council, had not left the shores of Ireland for the last two hundred years.[2]

Stirling of Glorat, the Constable of Dunbarton, received the Bishop of Caithness with distinction; yet, as he had already refused to deliver the fortress to Lennox, he now declared that he would hold it out against all, till his mistress, the Queen, should be of age to demand it herself. He was closely besieged by Arran, Huntly, and Argyle, who had been alarmed by the admission of the Bishop into the castle; but the strength of the place defied their utmost efforts. Finding that force would not succeed, Cardinal Beaton and Huntly began to tamper both with the Bishop and the Constable, and succeeded

---

[1] Letter from Irish Privy Council to the King, dated 19th November, 1545. Letter Anth. St. Leger to the English Privy Council, 10th October, 1545. State Paper Office.

[2] Tytler, V. 407.

in corrupting them. Caithness, bribed by the promise
of his restoration to the see he had lost, proved false to
his brother; and Stirling, for a high reward, was induced
to deliver the fortress, in that age deemed impregnable,
into the hands of the Regent. Lennox and Ormond,
probably informed on their passage both of this disastrous event and of further dissensions among the Islesmen, do not seem even to have attempted a descent ;
at least, their farther proceedings are wrapped in obscurity.[1]

Donald, Lord of the Isles, appears to have accompanied Lennox on his return to Ireland, and to have
died soon after, of a fever, at Drogheda.[2] "His fune-
ral in Ireland," says an author, formerly quoted, "to
the honour of the Earl of Lennox, stood the King of
England in four hundred pounds sterling."[3] The
honours paid to the remains of their departed chief were
well calculated to gratify the prejudices of the Islesmen, who have always been, and to this day are, distinguished by a passion for magnificent interments.
Lennox, who was again projecting an invasion of Scotland, lost no time in despatching messengers to the Isles
with tidings of the death and burial of the late Lord ;
but some difficulty appears to have existed regarding
his successor. He had left one bastard son, whom, in
his dying moments, he commended to the care of the
King of England ; but it does not appear that any claim

---

[1] Tytler, V. 407-8.

[2] "Macdonald" (after the dispersion of his army and the failure
of Lennox's expedition) "went to Ireland to raise men; but he died
on his way to Dublin, at Drogheda, of a fever, without issue, either
sons or daughters."—Macvurich's MS. The documents in the State
Paper Office prove, however, that he left one son, a bastard.

[3] Anderson, II. 48.

was made on behalf of this individual to the succession. The family of Sleat, in which the male representation of the Earls of Ross and Lords of the Isles now centred, was, at this time, almost deprived of power. Its chief was a minor, the son of that Donald Gorme killed before the Castle of Elandonan in 1539; and, in addition to this source of weakness, the title of the family to their estates was disputed by the Macleods of Harris, who found this a good opportunity for reviving their former claims. At length the Islanders chose for their leader James Macdonald of Isla, whose patriotism seems to have evaporated on his perceiving a possibility of obtaining the pension of two thousand crowns promised to his predecessor. His pretensions to the Lordship of the Isles were certainly inferior to those of the chief of Sleat; but his power, as an individual, was much greater. He was, however, from various causes, opposed by many who had been among the firmest supporters of Donald Dubh; particularly the numerous and powerful Clangillean (with the exception of one prominent individual of that tribe), the Macleods, both of Lewis and Harris, and the lesser clans of the Macneills of Barra, the Mackinnons, and Macquarries. All these now endeavoured, and with success, to effect their reconciliation with the Regent.[1]

A. D. 1546.   On the 10th of February, the messengers of Lennox returned to Dublin bearing letters from James Macdonald—"which now declareth himself Lord of the Isles, by the consent of the nobility of the Insulans, as the bearers affirm"—to the Irish Privy Council. Along with the messengers came an accredited envoy

---

[1] Reg. of Privy Seal, XIX., fo. 27, 74.

15

of the new Lord, who was despatched, at the special request of the latter, to submit certain proposals, on his part, to the King of England.[1] These proposals bore that the Earl of Lennox, or any other person properly authorised, should be sent with an army to the Isle of Sandy, beside Kintyre, on or about St. Patrick's Day. Here the Lord of the Isles engaged to join him with the utmost power of his kinsmen and allies—namely, Allan Maclean of Gigha and Torlusk (brother to Maclean of Dowart, and celebrated in tradition, as a warrior, by the name of *Alein na'n Sop*), the Clanranald, Clanchameron, Clankayn,[2] and his own surname, the Clandonald north and south. But he required twenty days notice of the arrival of the expedition, and two or three ships to assist in bringing his forces together at the place of rendezvous. In return, he desired from the King a bond for a yearly pension of the same amount as that granted to his late " chief and maister, Donald, Lord of the Yllis, quhom God assoilyie; the quhilk deit in his said Grace's service."[3] To these offers it does not appear that Henry made any reply, his attention being probably engrossed by the events connected with the

[1] Letter, Privy Council of Ireland to that of England, 10th February, 1545–46. State Paper Office. James had no claim whatever to the Earldom of Ross, nor does he seem to have preferred any.

[2] Clankayn is an error for Clanayn or Clan Ian of Ardnamurchan.

[3] Letter, James Macdonald of Dunyveg and the Glens, and "appeirand ayr of the Ylis," dated at Ardnamurchan, 24th January, 1545-6, to the Lord Deputy and Privy Council of Ireland. State Paper Office. At the same time, Ewin Allanson of Lochiel wrote to the Lord Deputy, promising his services to the English King, and saying he had marched to the Lowlands and taken a prey both from Huntly and Argyle. He also required support, and recommended James, whom he styles "narrest of ayr to the hous of the Yllis," as a brave young man, with great strength of kinsmen.—Ibid.

progress of the Reformation in Scotland, and the plots for getting rid of Cardinal Beaton, who was assassinated in the Castle of St. Andrew's, on the 28th of May.[1]

About this time the Earl of Huntly, by the instrumentality of William Macintosh, captain of the Clanchattan, apprehended two of the principal Highland chiefs—Ewin Allanson of Lochiel, captain of the Clanchameron, and Ranald MacDonald Glas of Keppoch. These chiefs were not only concerned in the slaughter of Lord Lovat and the Frasers at Kinloch-lochy, but had supported, to the utmost of their power, all the rebellions hatched by the Earl of Lennox. They were imprisoned, for a short time, in the Castle of Ruthven in Badenoch, and afterwards tried for high treason at Elgin. Being found guilty by a jury composed of landed gentlemen, they were beheaded; while several of their followers, who were apprehended along with them, were hanged. The heads of the two leaders were then set over the gates of the town.[2] This severity seems to have had a salutary effect in disposing the rest of the rebellious Highlanders to submission. In the course of this year the processes of treason, which, some time before, had been instituted against the Islesmen, were dropped, and, by degrees, a general pacification of the remote Highlands and Isles seems to have been accomplished, whilst the authority of the Government was once more nominally established in these districts.[3]

[1] Tytler, V. 409, 427.

[2] Lesley, p. 185. Gordon's History of Sutherland, p. 110. MS. History of the Camerons.

[3] Acts of Parl. II., 469, 4th August, 1546. Reg. of Privy Seal, XX., fo. 86, 94; XXI., fo. 3, 8. Even John Moydertach succeeded, at length, in obtaining pardon in 1548.—Ibid, XXII., fo. 27.

James Macdonald of Isla, whose desertion of the party he had formerly acted with, and assumption of the title of Lord of the Isles, may be supposed to have made him particularly obnoxious to the Regent, was fortunate enough to escape the punishment he deserved. He had probably succeeded in concealing the full extent of his treasonable practices; but he had, nevertheless, committed himself so far as to incur the hostility of the Earl of Argyle. Their disputes, however, were settled by the mediation of the Regent;[1] and Macdonald, dropping his title of Lord of the Isles, seems ever after to have acted the part of a patriotic Scotsman and obedient subject. After this time we find no trace in the records of any attempt on the part of the Islesmen to restore the ancient dynasty of the Isles. The different branches of the family of the Isles, and the other tribes inhabiting the Lordship, became gradually more estranged from each other, and more desirous each to extend its own power at the expense of its neighbours. So far, this was the result contemplated by James IV. and his counsellors in their proceedings after 1493; but it is not to be supposed that they desired, or would have encouraged, the great increase which was eventually made to the power of the Earls of Argyle, through the individual weakness and dissensions of the Islanders.

A. D. 1547.   In the Scottish army which assembled under the Regent Arran in 1547, to oppose the progress of the Protector Somerset, and which sustained so severe a defeat at Pinky, a considerable number of Highlanders and Islanders were present, many of them

---

[1] Record of Privy Council, 18th June, 1546. Treasurer's Accounts, ad tempus.

being under the Earl of Argyle.[1]   But although some
of those who had formerly supported the English now
fought on the other side, not a few of the western clans
had failed, on this occasion, to obey the summons of the
Regent.   Of these, the most prominent were the tribes
concerned in the slaughter of the Lord Lovat and the
Frasers in 1544; who, being still considered as outlaws,
did not venture to trust themselves out of their mountain fastnesses.   The Macleods of Lewis were likewise
absent;[2] but, indeed, it is matter of surprise, not that some
of the Islanders failed to attend, but that any of them
should have been trusted to fight against their recent
allies—and that, too, under leaders so obnoxious to them
as the Earls of Huntly and Argyle.   The necessity,
after the disastrous result of the battle of Pinky, of preventing divisions among the Scots themselves, seems to
have induced Arran, in the course of the year 1548, to
pardon those Highlanders who still remained outlaws,
on easier terms than they could otherwise have expected.

Although the Regency of Arran continued till the
year 1554—when he resigned his office in favour of Mary
of Guise, the Queen Dowager—yet during the latter
years of his government, he acted, in a great measure,
under the advice of that able and energetic Princess.
She soon perceived the necessity of restoring the control which the possession of hostages, or the imprisonment of the most turbulent of the chiefs themselves, as
in the last years of the reign of James V., was calculated
to give to the Government over the Highlands in general.
All the late insurrections in the Isles, she was aware,
had followed immediately upon the liberation of those

---

[1] Pitscottie's History, ad tempus.
[2] Reg. of Privy Seal, XXII., fo. 27 ; XXVII., fo. 125.

hostages and chiefs, to which Arran, in his anxiety to
harass his political opponents, had so unadvisedly
consented. The efforts of the Queen Dowager were
therefore directed to the re-establishment of the policy
of James V.; and, for this purpose, the Regent, by her
advice, summoned all the chiefs of the Highland clans
to meet him in Aberdeen, on the 17th of June,
A. D. 1552. 1552, where he proposed to hold Justice
Courts, in the course of a progress through the kingdom,
undertaken "rather," as Lesley says, "for staying of
troubles in tymes to cum than for rigorous punishment
of any offences bypast."[1]   He held similar courts at
Inverness in the month of July. Most of the clans
appear to have submitted to the conditions imposed upon
them; but the Clanranald, under John Moydertach, and
the Clanchameron, under Ewin Beg Donaldson, held
out.   On this a commission was given to the Earls of
Huntly and Argyle against these clans; and we find
that, in the month of August, the latter nobleman was
in the district of Lochaber, in pursuance of his instructions.   In the course of the following month, Argyle
had entered into communication with John Moydertach,
who contrived to excuse his disobedience in such a way
as to procure a cessation of all proceedings against him
till the following February.   The Earl undertook that
this chief should make his personal appearance in
presence of the Privy Council before that time; and, in
the event of his failure, was enjoined to make war upon
him, according to his original instructions.[2]   The proceedings against the Clanchameron, which were entrusted

[1] Lesley's History, p. 243.
[2] Record of Privy Council, 17th October, 1552.   Treasurer's
Accounts, July and September, 1552.

menced against Ruari Macleod of the Lewis.[1]   In June following, a commission was given to the Earls of Argyle and Athole over the Isles; and, soon afterwards, Macleod gave in to the Privy Council, through the Earl of Argyle, certain offers, of which, eventually, the Regent approved so far as, in the month of September, to grant him a respite.[2]   Meanwhile, the Earl of Athole, who had proceeded against John Moydertach, the captain of the Clanranald, succeeded so well that he prevailed upon that restless chief, with two of his sons, and certain of his kinsmen, to come before the Regent, and submit themselves to her clemency.   Mary of Guise, pleased with their submission, pardoned them their past offences; but ordered them, in the meantime, to remain, some at Perth, and others at the Castle of Methven, till her will should be further declared to them. After remaining, however, in these places for a short time, the Highlanders made their escape to their native mountains; giving the Regent a lesson, as a Scottish annalist quaintly observes, "to hold the fox better by the ear while she had him in her hands."[3]   This result of her mistaken lenity only roused the Regent to greater exertions, and determined her to proceed next year in person to the North, to hold Justice Courts for the punishment of the great offenders, and thus to prevent

A. D. 1556.   misrule in time coming.   Accordingly, in the month of July, 1556, Mary of Guise arrived at Inverness, accompanied by the Earls of Huntly, Argyle,

---

[1] Treasurer's Accounts, ad tempus.   The nature of the treason is not specified.

[2] Record of Privy Council, Hadd. Coll. ; Reg. of Privy Seal, XXVII., fo. 125.

[3] Balfour's Annals, I., p. 304; Lesley's History, pp. 253-4.

Athole, and Marischall, and the Bishops of Ross and Orkney, with others of the Privy Council. Here courts were held, and offenders were visited with the most severe punishment—the chiefs of clans being obliged to apprehend and present to justice the criminals of their own tribes, according to the wise regulations laid down by James V., which, during the late wars, had fallen into desuetude.[1] As John Moydertach is not mentioned at all by Bishop Lesley in his account of this progress of the Queen Regent to the north, it seems probable that this arch-rebel had escaped the punishment which awaited him, by flying to the more remote Isles. There can, however, be little doubt that the Regent would soon have made her authority felt, even by those Islanders most removed from the seat of justice, had not her attention been, after this time, exclusively occupied by the progress of the Reformation in Scotland, and the measures which, unfortunately for herself, that princess was induced to pursue in opposition to the reformers.

Although the Reformation was undoubtedly one of the most important events in Scottish history, yet its progress is to be traced almost exclusively in the history of the Lowlands; at least, the history of the Highlands and Isles presents little that is interesting on this subject. It is not to be supposed, however, that the great Highland barons were slow to follow the example of their Lowland neighbours in seizing the lands and revenues of the church. On the contrary, the deplorable state in which the Highlands and Isles were found to be, in a religious point of view, at the commencement of the seventeenth century, was evidently owing to this cause.

[1] Lesley's History, pp. 256-7.

But in such proceedings the bulk of the Highland population, if we except the vassals of the Earl of Argyle, seem to have taken little interest; and many of them long continued to adhere, as a portion still do, to the worship of their fathers. On the death of Archibald, fourth Earl of Argyle, who had all along supported the measures of the Queen Regent, the weight of this great Highland family was thrown into the opposite scale, by his son and successor Archibald, the fifth Earl, who soon distinguished himself as one of the most able among the Lords of the Congregation. To weaken the influence of this powerful nobleman, the Regent endeavoured to sow dissensions between him and the Islanders, whose jealousy of the family of Argyle was well known. To embroil the Earl with James Macdonald of Isla—at this time the most powerful of the Islanders, and who, some years before, had allied himself to the family of Argyle, by marrying Lady Agnes Campbell, sister to the late Earl—became now a favourite object with the Queen Regent. We have seen that Huntly, when punished by her for his negligence in the pursuit of John Moydertach, had been compelled to relinquish a grant he had obtained from the Earl of Arran of the wardship and marriage of Mary Macleod, the wealthy heiress of Dunvegan. Huntly had endeavoured, while in disgrace, to dispose of this grant to the Earl of Argyle;[1] but his plans were frustrated by the vigilance of the Queen Regent, who now bestowed the disposal of the heiress upon James Macdonald.[2] In his anxiety to possess himself of this prize, Macdonald did not hesitate

A. D. 1558.

A. D. 1559.

---

[1] Gen. Reg. of Deeds, I., fo. 231.   [2] Ibid. IV., fo. 319.

to take part against Argyle; but the latter speedily counteracted the influence of the Regent; and we find that, in October, 1559, "James Macdonald, whom the Regent heretofore stirred against the Earl of Argyle," was actually on his way to join the Lords of the Congregation, with seven hundred foot soldiers.[1]

A. D. 1560.   In the following year, the Queen Regent died in the Castle of Edinburgh, partly of an old complaint, and partly of grief at the opposition which she had latterly encountered, and which, on her deathbed, she had sagacity enough to attribute to the right cause—namely, her following the counsels of foreigners, instead of ruling by the advice of the Privy Council of the realm. This princess was much regretted, and with reason; for we are informed by Bishop Lesley, that, "in the time that she was Regent, she kept good justice, and was well obeyed over all the parts of Scotland; as also in Orkney and the Isles." [2]

[1] Sir R. Sadler's State Papers, I., pp. 431, 517.
[2] Lesley's History, p. 289.

CHAP. IV.

FROM THE RETURN OF QUEEN MARY TO SCOTLAND, TO THE ACTUAL ASSUMPTION OF THE GOVERNMENT BY JAMES THE SIXTH. —1561–1585.

DURING the space of twenty-four years, which elapsed between the return of Queen Mary from France, in 1561, and the actual assumption of the Government by her son, in the nineteenth year of his age, in 1585, the general history of the Highlands and Isles possesses little interest. Repeated failures seem to have made the western clans sensible of the impossibility of re-establishing, in any shape, the old Lordship of the Isles; and they gradually learned to prefer holding their lands under the sovereign directly, to being the vassals of any subject, however powerful. Having now no longer a common object, they became, by degrees, more estranged from each other, whilst each chief laboured either to extend his own possessions, or to defend himself from the aggressions of his more powerful neighbours. It thus happened that, without any insurrection of a general nature, there were yet, during the interval of which we speak, many serious disturbances in the Highlands and Isles, which called for the interference of Government. Taking these disturbances in chronological order, the first that calls for notice is a dispute between Maclean of Dowart and Maclean of Coll, which is chiefly remarkable as indicating the progress of the feudal system in the Isles. Dowart, who was generally acknowledged as chief of his clan, insisted that Coll should follow and serve him in all his private quarrels, like the other gentlemen of the tribe. Coll, however, who held all his lands direct from the Crown, declined to follow this haughty chief, claiming the privileges of a free baron, who owed no service but to the sovereign as his feudal superior. Irritated at the independent tone assumed by Coll, and determined to assert what he conceived to be his just claims, the Lord of Dowart, taking advantage of the other's temporary absence, caused A. D. 1561. his lands to be ravaged and his tenants to be imprisoned. Such, indeed, was the tyranny exercised by Dowart over his weaker neighbour, that the family of Coll, from being in a prosperous condition, was reduced, in a short time, to the brink of ruin. Nor was it till after the lapse of several years, that the sufferer by these violent and illegal proceedings succeeded in drawing the attention of the Privy Council to his situation; so great was the power and influence of his oppressor. The decision of that tribunal was, as might have been expected, adverse to the claims of Dowart; who was ordered to make reparation to Coll for the injuries done to the property and tenants of the latter; and, likewise, to refrain from molesting him or his followers in future.[1] At a later period we shall find that the feud between these families was only suspended, not concluded, by this decision of the Privy Council.

The next dispute worthy of notice which occurred in

---

[1] Record of Privy Council, 1563-1567, fo. 46.

the Isles, was between the Macleans on the one part, and the Macdonalds of Isla and Kintyre on the other. This affair demands our attention, not so much on account of its origin, which was merely a quarrel as to the right of occupancy of certain Crown lands in Isla, as because it was the commencement of a long and bloody feud between these tribes, in which both suffered severely, and which led eventually to the utter ruin of that powerful branch of the Clandonald. Of the early details of this feud, which was aggravated by previous disputes regarding the island of Gigha, little is found in the usual sources of information. The Isles of Mull, Cir. A. D. 1562. Tiree, and Coll, were invaded by the Clandonald of Isla, assisted by its kindred tribe, the Clandonald of Sleat;[1] and it may be supposed that the Macleans and their allies were not backward in similar hostilities. It is uncertain which tribe was the original aggressor; but from the tenor of certain A. D. 1564. proceedings before the Privy Council, it appears probable that the Macleans were to blame—a fact which, indeed, is distinctly asserted by a historian, himself a Privy Councillor in the reign of James VI. According to this writer, the Rinns of Isla (the lands in dispute) were actually occupied by the Macleans, who claimed to hold these lands as Crown tenants; but the decision of the Privy Council established that James Macdonald of Isla was really the Crown tenant, and that the Macleans, if they continued to remain on the lands, must hold them of Macdonald, under the same conditions of personal and other services as the rest of Macdonald's vassals in Isla held their lands.[2] Such a

[1] Reg. of Privy Seal, XXXI., fo. 48.
[2] Sir R. Gordon, p. 188. Record of Privy Council, April, 1564.

decision must have been, no doubt, very galling to a powerful and high-spirited tribe like the Macleans; and we can scarcely be surprised at the deep-rooted hostility which so long prevailed between them and the Clandonald, when we consider the point of honour which was involved in their dispute. Such was the inveteracy with which the rival chiefs pursued their quarrel, even after the matter had been brought before the Privy A. D. 1565. Council, that, in 1565, they were compelled to find sureties each to the amount of ten thousand pounds, for their abstinence from mutual hostilities.[1] It deserves to be remarked, that Archibald, fifth Earl of Argyle, was one of the sureties for each chief, he being connected, by marriage, with both; as it proves that this nobleman did not contemplate extending his power and influence in the same unscrupulous manner that some of his successors afterwards did, at the expense • both of the Macdonalds and Macleans.

In this year, the Clandonald of Isla and Kintyre suffered a severe blow, by the loss of its chief, James Macdonald of Dunyveg and the Glens, under whose guidance the tribe had become the most powerful and prosperous of any in the Western Isles. As it was in Ireland that this leader lost his life, the present seems a proper opportunity for noticing the rise and progress of a powerful Hebridean colony in Ulster, connected with and dependent upon the Clandonald of Isla and Kintyre. It has been mentioned in the Introduction (supra, p. 61), that John Mor of Isla, founder of this branch of the family of the Isles, acquired a footing in Ulster, by his marriage with Mary or Marjory Bisset,

---

[1] Record of Privy Council, January and March, 1565.

heiress of the Glens, in the county of Antrim, being the district comprehended between the rivers Inver and Boyse.   The three immediate successors of John Mor strengthened themselves in their Irish inheritance by intermarriages with the families of O'Donnell, O'Neill of Claneboy, and Savage of the Arde ; and also by set- tling several cadets of their own house as tenants in the territory of the Glens.[1]   In their endeavours to main- tain and to extend their Irish possessions, the Clandonald were not only involved in frequent feuds with the Irish of Ulster, but were occasionally brought into hostile contact with the English forces.   On St. Patrick's day, in the year 1501, the Irish historians inform us, that there was fought a battle between the O'Neills and certain Scots or *Albani;* in which conflict, the latter lost a son of the Laird of *Aig,* of the family of the MacDonnells, the three sons of Coll MacAlexander, and about sixty common soldiers.[2]   In 1521, while the Earl of Surrey was Lord Lieutenant of Ireland, Hugh O'Donnell, Lord of Tirconnell, in offering his submis- sion to that nobleman, engaged, amongst other services, to join the Lord Lieutenant with his own men of Tir- connell, and likewise to hire a great number of Scottish Islanders, or Redshanks, to act against the Irish rebels.[3] On these conditions his submission was received; but, when called upon soon after to fulfil his engagements, the Lord of Tirconnell broke his word, and preferred leading his followers to attack the territories of O'Neill,

[1] Irish Genealogies; Harleian MS., British Museum, No. $\frac{2218}{8}$ and $\frac{1425}{103}$.

[2] Sir James Ware's Annals of Ireland; Edit. (in English) Dublin, 1705, p. 43.

[3] Ware's Annals, p. 70.

then exposed by the absence of that chief, who, with a
large body of men, was in the camp of the Lord Lieutenant.[1]   In the following year, the Earl of Ormond,
who had succeeded Surrey as Viceroy, dreading the
defection of many of the chiefs in the north of Ireland,
and desirous at the same time to repress the rapine
and piracies committed by the Scottish Islanders,
applied to Cardinal Wolsey for five or six vessels to
scour the channel between Scotland and Ireland, and
so prove a check both to Scots and Irish.[2]   Ten years
later, when Alexander Macdonald of Isla was sent to
Ulster, at the head of seven thousand men, by James
V., for the purpose of harassing the English in that
province (supra, p. 142), he seems to have profited by his
opportunities to add considerably to his Irish estates;
at least, by some genealogists this chief is styled
Lord of the Glens and *Route*[3]—the latter district lies
between the rivers Boyse and Ban, being the ancient
inheritance of the MacQuillans.   In 1545, we have seen
that the self-styled Lord of the Isles led four thousand
of his vassals to Ireland, intended to act in concert with
an English force under the Earl of Lennox, against
the French party in Scotland.   At this time, James
Macdonald of Isla alone, of all the islanders, supported
the French party; but on the death of the Lord of the
Isles, he assumed that title, and entered into friendly
communication with the Irish Privy Council early in
1546 (supra, pp. 157, 177).   Three years afterwards,
and when James Macdonald had made his peace with
the Regent of Scotland, a body of Scots was sent into

[1] Ware's Annals, p. 170.   [2] Ibid, p. 75.

[3] Said Irish Genealogies in Brit. Mus.

Ulster, to aid the Irish rebels against the English. This rebellion was quelled by the good conduct of Andrew Brereton, leader of some English troops, who, with only thirty-five horse, attacked and cut to pieces two hundred of the Scots.[1] Notwithstanding this check, we find the Hebrideans again infesting Ulster, and assisting the Irish rebels, in the year 1551, under the Viceroyalty of Sir James Crofts. The Viceroy having arrived at Knockfergus, sent a detachment, commanded by an officer named Bagnall, against the Scots, who, under their leaders, James Macdonald and his brother Coll, had taken post in the Isle of Rachlin. Bagnall met with very bad success: one of his ships was wrecked, whilst many of his men were slain, and himself taken prisoner by the Macdonalds. He was afterwards liberated in exchange for another brother of the chief of Isla, who had, on a former occasion, fallen into the hands of the English.[2]

Soon after this, the Chancellor of Ireland, in a letter to the Duke of Northumberland, mentions that both Hugh Macneill Oig, Captain of Claneboy, and Shane O'Neill, son of the Earl of Tyrone, were in league with the Scots. He adds that, "When the Scots doe come, the most part of Clanneboy, Mac-Quillan's and O'Cahan's countries, must be at their commandement;" and, when alluding to the Dufferin or White's country, he states that John White, the last proprietor, had been deceitfully murdered by "M'Ranill Boye, his son, a Scott," who had ever since kept possession of that territory by force.[3] In 1555, the

---

[1] Ware's Annals, p. 120.   [2] Ware's Annals, p, 124.

[2] Harleian MS., Brit Mus., No. $\frac{2}{3}$. Letter dated 6th May, 1552.

Lord Anthony St. Leger being Viceroy, the Hebridean
Scots attempted to take the town of Knockfergus; but
their design having been detected, the garrison was
enabled to frustrate it.[1] In the same year, in a dispute
between Manus O'Donnell, Earl of Tirconnell, and
his son Calvagh, the latter went to Scotland and procured a body of troops from "Gillespick MacCalain"
(Archibald, fourth Earl of Argyle).[2] Returning with
these auxiliaries to Ulster, in November, he entered
Tirconnell, and, seizing his father, placed him in prison,
where the old chief lingered till his death, nor were
the Scottish troops dismissed till the subsequent May.
In the meantime, they appèar to have had a skirmish
with their former ally, the Captain of Claneboy, in
which the latter, a man much esteemed among his
own kindred, was slain.[3]   Thomas Radcliff, Earl of
Sussex, being appointed Lord Lieutenant of Ireland,
landed at Dublin on Whitsunday, 1556.   He was
accompanied, among others, by Sir Henry Sidney,
as Treasurer of Ireland, who carried with him from
England the sum of twenty-five thousand pounds, destined to be applied towards the charges of an expedition against the Scottish Islanders, who invaded the
northern parts of Ulster, and against a few of the Irish
rebels. Early in July, the Lord Lieutenant having
mustered his forces, marched to the north against
the Islanders; and, on the eighteenth of that month,

---

[1] Ware's Annals, p. 137.

[2] Ibid, p. 137. In the accounts of the Lord High Treasurer of
Scotland for October, 1555, there occurs a payment to a messenger
bearing a letter from the Queen Regent, "to charge the Erle of Ergile
nocht to pas in Ireland."

[3] Ibid, p. 137.

engaged and defeated them. Of the Scots, more than two thousand were slain, and a great many taken prisoners.[1] Notwithstanding this victory, Sussex was obliged, in the following year, owing to the continued incursions of the Scots, to procure an enactment making it high treason for any Scots to come into Ireland, or for any of the natives to receive them. It was also declared, that any intermarriage by a native of Ireland with a Scot, without the Lord Lieutenant's permission, should be punished as a felony.[2] In the month of August, 1557, Sussex again marched to the north against the Scots, who were under the command of James Macdonald of Isla. The Islanders, however, shunned an encounter with the English forces, who ravaged the country at their pleasure. In the course of this expedition, the Lord Lieutenant received under his protection Richard MacQuillan, who had been expelled from his country of the Route by the Scots. At the same time, too, he knighted and adorned with a golden sword and silver gilt spurs, Alexander Mac-Ranald Buy, one of the Macdonalds, who had distinguished himself by his services against his kinsmen.[3] This individual was probably destined by the Viceroy to become exclusively a subject of England; and then, by supplanting James Macdonald in the latter's inheritance of the Glens, to prevent the inconvenience that had arisen from a powerful Scottish subject having influence in a province already sufficiently disinclined

---

[1] Ware's Annals, p. 139.   [2] Ibid, p. 142.

[3] Ibid, p. 142. Sir Alexander MacRanald Buy received also the more substantial favour of a grant of the greater part of the barony of Dunluce, with the monastery of Glenarm, and the lands belonging thereto, which, however, he seems to have been unable to retain for any length of time.

to the English yoke. In a State paper of some importance, titled, " Opinion touching Ireland," and·addressed
to the Lord Lieutenant by Dowdall, Archbishop of
Armagh, in July, 1558, the Primate strongly urges the
expulsion of the·Hebridean Scots from Ulster, by procuring their Irish neighbours, O'Donnell, O'Neill,
O'Cahan, and others, to unite against them.   He
argues, also, that the power of the Scots in Ireland proceeded chiefly from the Irish chiefs engaging them as
auxiliaries in their private quarrels—a practice to the
suppression of which the Archbishop earnestly draws
the attention of the Lord Lieutenant.[1] Sussex, however, seems to have decided on a more direct method of
checking the incursions of the Islanders.   With this
view, having received reinforcements from England, he
sailed from Dundalk towards the Isle of Rachlin, where
some of the Scots then were. Notwithstanding the loss
of one of his vessels, with some of the citizens of Dublin
on board, which was wrecked on the coast of Rachlin, he
himself, with the rest of his troops, landed, and having
killed all who offered resistance, laid the island waste.
Thence he sailed to Kintyre, where he committed great
ravages, as well as in Arran and the Cumbraes.   It
was his intention to have done more mischief to the
Scots at this time, but a storm arising, he was forced
to sail for Ireland, and landed at Knockfergus: before
he returned from that place to Dublin, he plundered
and burnt several villages inhabited by the Scots in the
county of Antrim.[2] About this time a body of the
Islanders went from Ulster into Connaught, to assist
some families of the Bourkes against Richard, Earl
of Clanricarde; but that noblemen encountered and

---

[1] Harleian MS., Brit. Mus., No. ⁴⁵/₁.   [2] Ware's Annals, p. 145.

routed the confederates with great slaughter.[1]   In
spite of these reverses, the Macdonalds still maintained
their footing in Ulster; and we find that in 1560 the
Earl of Sussex entered into an indenture with Sorley
Buy Macdonald, on behalf of his brother James, the
head of the family.   The Scot demanded to have, by
lease from the Queen of England, not only the Glens,
which he claimed as his ancient inheritance, but the Route,
from which the MacQuillans had been expelled.   Sorley
Buy was offered as a resident substitute for his brother in
these lands, and engaged to pay certain stipulated duties,
as well as to furnish twenty-four horse and sixty foot to
all hosts of the Lord Lieutenant.   Sussex, on his part,
undertook to bring these demands favourably under the
notice of Queen Elizabeth.[2]   The demands of the
Scots regarding the possession of the Route having
apparently been rejected, they soon relapsed into their
former state of hostility against the Irish Government;
and such of their own tribe as had submitted to the
Lord Lieutenant, were encouraged to act against them.[3]
After the recall of the Earl of Sussex, and while Sir
Henry Sydney was Lord Deputy, Sorley Buy Macdonald found himself so hard pressed by his enemies,
that, leaving his men under the command of his brother,
Alexander Oig, he proceeded to Scotland, to hasten
the departure of succours from that country.   In the
end of 1565 he returned to Ireland, accompanied by
his brother, James Macdonald of Isla, and a consider-

[1] Ware's Annals, p. 145.

[2] Cotton MS., Brit. Mus., Titus B., XIII. 19.   State paper, signed
" W. Cecill," dated 2nd April, 1560, and preserved among the Denmylne
MS. Adv. Lib.

[3] See various letters proving this fact, and dated about the year 1562,
among the Cotton MS., Brit. Mus., Vesp. F. XII.

able body of men. Soon after landing, they were surprised by a party of the O'Neills, under the celebrated Shane O'Neill, Earl of Tyrone; and in the conflict which ensued, the Scots were defeated with considerable slaughter. James Macdonald was mortally wounded, and his brother Angus was slain; while Sorley Buy fell into the hands of the victor, with many of his followers.[1] O'Neill had recently, after repeated rebellions, made his submission to the English Government, and was thus induced to turn his arms against his former associates, the Scots of the Glens. But soon afterwards, becoming once more a rebel, and having sustained a defeat from the English forces, this powerful chief became alarmed at the extent of the preparations against him, and was compelled to take refuge with the very Islanders he had so lately attacked as enemies. By liberating Sorley Buy and his other prisoners, he hoped to secure their good offices with their kinsmen; and he then proceeded to Claneboy, where Alexander Oig Macdonald, the brother of Sorley Buy, lay, at the head of six hundred Scots, and threw himself on the protection of that leader. At first O'Neill was well received, a great entertainment being prepared for him; but, in the middle of the feast, a dispute arose in consequence of some rash expressions of O'Neill's secretary, which were defended by O'Neill himself. Some of the Scots, eager to revenge the death of their late chief, took advantage of this circumstance, and, rushing into

---

[1] Ware's Annals (Reg. Elizab.), pp. 8, 10. Camden's Britannia, by Gough, III., p. 626. Leland's Ireland, II., p. 230. Crawford's MS. Collections, Adv. Lib., quoting a deed from the Dunstaffnage Papers, which shows that the Earl of Argyle proposed to intercede for the liberation of Sorley Buy.

the tent with drawn dirks, despatched both O'Neill and his secretary; and the head of the former, being carried to Dublin by Captain Piers, an English officer, was set on the top of the castle, by order of the Lord Deputy.[1] O'Neill was succeeded by one of his tribe, named Torlogh Luineach, who made war upon the Scots, and killed Alexander Oig Macdonald in the year following the death of Shane O'Neill.[2]

From the above sketch of the history of the Clandonald of Isla, with reference to its possessions in Ulster, it seems evident that the power of the tribe, as compared with that of the Macleans and other great clans in the Isles, must have been seriously weakend, owing to its late losses in Ireland. Indeed, after the death of James Macdonald, this family never regained its former power; and the son of that chief lived to see its almost total destruction.

In the same year in which the chief of Isla made his last and fatal expedition to Ulster, the Earl of Argyle, and many of his vassals, were involved in the rebellion of the Duke of Chatelherault and the Earl of Murray, arising out of the opposition made by these noblemen to the marriage of Mary, Queen of Scots, with the Lord Darnley. Murray retired to Argyleshire in the month of August, where he was joined by the Earl of Argyle, and the men of Breadalbane, Lorn, and Argyle Proper. Commission was given to the Earl of Athole to proceed against the rebels; and the Royal forces were summoned

[1] Ware's Annals (Reg. Elizab.), p. 11. Cliffe's Irish Rebellions, p. XVII.; Leland's Ireland, II., p. 243-4. Act of Attainder of O'Neill's memory by the Irish Parliament, 11th Eliz. Sess. 3. Captain Piers is said, by Leland, to have incited the Scots to this assassination.

[2] Ware's Annals (Reg Elizab.), p. 11. Leland, II., p. 244.

by proclamation, to meet the Commissioner in Lorn, on the 20th of September. Among other chiefs specially required to meet the Earl of Athole in Lorn, we find Ruari Macleod of the Lewis, Tormod Macleod of Harris, Donald Gormeson of Sleat, and Kenneth Mackenzie of Kintaill. The march of the rebels to the Lowlands, and the subsequent flight of their leaders to England, when they found the adherents of the King and Queen too strong for them, speedily put an end to this bloodless insurrection, without the necessity of an invasion of Lorn by the Royal forces. The country suffered for some time by that stoppage of communication between the West Highlands and the Lowlands which was the inevitable consequence of a rebellion in Argyle. But the insurgent chiefs having made their peace with the Government early in 1566, a proclamation was soon afterwards issued, removing all restrictions on the trade in cattle and other commodities.[1]

Towards the end of Queen Mary's reign, a violent dispute broke out among the Camerons, in which Donald Dubh (patronymically styled MacDonald Vic Ewin), the chief of that clan, was put to death by some of his own kinsmen.[2] He had for some time been at feud with the family of Glennevis; but the chief instruments of his death seem to have been his uncles, Ewin, founder of the house of Erracht, and John, founder of that of Kinlochiel, younger sons of Ewin Allanson, the

---

[1] Sir Walter Scott's History of Scotland, II., p. 99. Record of Privy Council, July, 1565, to April, 1566. Treasurer's Accounts, 27th August, 1565. Collectanea de Rebus Albanicis, I. 151.

[2] Reg. of Privy Seal, XXXVI. 32. Record of Privy Council, November, 1564, February, 1576-7. Pitcairn's Criminal Trials, Vol. I., 33. MS. History of Camerons.

A. D. 1567. captain of the Clanchameron, who, along with Macdonald of Keppoch, was executed by the Earl of Huntly in 1547 (supra, p. 179). On the death of Donald Dubh, the estate of Lochiel seems to have devolved upon his infant nephew, Allan, son and heir of Donald's younger brother, John Dubh; but Allan being a minor, his granduncles usurped the estate, under pretence of acting as his guardians. The friends of the young chief appear, however, to have considered his life in danger if he should remain in Lochaber; and, accordingly, provided for his safety by removing him to the care of his maternal relations, the Macleans of Dowart.[1] In the meantime, the government of the Clanchameron remained in the hands of Erracht and Kinlochiel, of whom we shall have further occasion to speak in a future part of this work.

In this reign the Earl of Argyle contrived to extend his influence into the North Isles, and over two of the most powerful tribes in that quarter, the Clandonald of Sky and North Uist, and the Clanleod of Harris, Dunvegan, and Glenelg. The mode in which this object was attained is so characteristic of the policy of the house of Argyle that it seems to merit some detail, in reference to the rapid increase of the power of that noble family.

William Macleod of Harris, chief of the "Siol Tormod," was the undisputed proprietor of the estates of Harris, Dunvegan, and Glenelg, under a particular destination, which, on his death in 1553, caused these

---

[1] MS. History of the Camerons. This authority errs in calling Allan the son of *Donald*, for the contemporary records style him, in numerous instances, *MacIanduy*. Occasionally, no doubt, he appears as *MacConnellduy*; but this is evidently the well-known style of the chief of the Camerons, derived from a remote ancestor.

extensive possessions to descend to his daughter and heiress, Mary.[1]   He was, at the same time, nominal proprietor of Sleat, Trouterness, and North Uist, the possession of which, we have seen, the Siol Tormod had unsuccessfully disputed with the Clandonald.   On the death of William Macleod, his claim to the last mentioned estates was inherited by his brother and heir male, Donald.[2]   The Siol Tormod was now placed in a position which, though quite intelligible on the principles of feudal law, was totally opposed to the Celtic customs that still prevailed, to a great extent, throughout the Highlands and Isles.   A female and a minor was the legal proprietrix of the ancient possessions of the tribe, which, by her marriage, might be conveyed to another and a hostile family; whilst her uncle, the natural leader of the clan according to ancient. custom, was left without any means to keep up the dignity of a chief, or to support the clan against its enemies.   His claims on the estates possessed by the Clandonald were worse than nugatory, as they threatened to involve him in a feud with that powerful and warlike tribe, in case he should take any steps to enforce them.   In these circumstances, Donald Macleod seized, apparently with the consent of his clan, the estates which legally belonged to his niece, the heiress; and thus, in practice, the feudal law was made to yield to ancient and inveterate custom.   Donald did not enjoy these estates long, being murdered in Trouterness by a relation of his own, John Oig Macleod, who, failing Tormod, the only remaining brother of Donald, would have become the

---

[1] Reg. of Great Seal, XIII., No. 305; XXVI. 446.

[2] Collectanea de Rebus Albanicis, I. 445.

heir male of the family.[1] John Oig next plotted the destruction of Tormod, who was at the time a student in the University of Glasgow; but in this he was foiled by the interposition of the Earl of Argyle. He contrived, notwithstanding, to retain possession of the estates of the heiress, and of the command of the clan, till his death in 1559.[2] In the meantime, the feudal rights of the wardship, relief, and marriage of the heiress of Harris, were eagerly sought after by various powerful individuals. They were first bestowed, in 1553, by the Regent Arran, upon the Earl of Huntly, who afterwards proposed to sell his interest in the heiress and her property, to the fourth Earl of Argyle, for a large sum of money.[3] But Huntly, having fallen into disgrace with the Queen Regent, as formerly mentioned, was compelled to relinquish his bargain with Argyle, and to resign into her hands the claims he had acquired from Arran to the guardianship of Mary Macleod.[4] The Regent, while endeavouring, in 1559, to secure the assistance of James Macdonald of Isla against the Protestants, of whom the fifth Earl of Argyle was one of the principal leaders, committed the feudal guardianship of the young heiress to that chief.[5] In 1562, we find that the person of the young lady had, by some accident, come into the custody of Kenneth Mackenzie of Kintaill, who, having refused to give her up to her lawful guardian, James Macdonald, was at length compelled to deliver her to Queen Mary, with whom she remained for some years as a maid of

[1] MS. History of Macleods.   [2] Ibid.

[3] Collectanea de Rebus Albanicis, I. 137, 138.

[4] Ibid, 141; Anderson's History of Scotland, MS. Adv. Lib., II. 174.

[5] Sadler's State Papers, II. 431.

honour, being, no doubt, one of the Queen's celebrated
Maries.[1] Macdonald seems now to have made over
his claims to Argyle, who finally exercised the right of
guardianship, by giving Mary Macleod in marriage to
his kinsman, Duncan Campbell, younger of Auchinbreck.[2] But, previous to the marriage, the Earl, sensible of the difficulty which would attend any attempt to
put an individual of his clan in possession of the territories of the Siol Tormod, even although he had the law
in his favour, entered into the following arrangements,
the most judicious that could be devised for making
the most of his position at the time. His first agreement was with Tormod Macleod, who had been for
some years in actual possession of Harris and the other
estates of the heiress, and had already given to the
Earl (for the good offices of the latter) his bond of
service for himself and his clan.[3] It was arranged that
Macleod should renounce, in favour of Argyle, all claim
he had to the lands of the Clandonald; that he should
likewise pay the sum of one thousand merks towards the
dowery of his niece. Argyle, on the other hand, engaged
to procure from Mary Macleod, and any husband she
might marry, a complete surrender of her title to the
lands of Harris, Dunvegan, and Glenelg; and to obtain
for Tormod a Crown charter of that estate.[4] His
next agreement was with Donald MacDonald Gorme
of Sleat: and in consideration of that chief paying five
hundred merks towards the dowery of Mary Macleod,

---

[1] Collectanea de Rebus Albanicis, I. 143-4.

[2] Ibid, p. 151, and Histories of both families.

[3] A contract to this effect, dated in 1559, will be found in the
Collectanea de Rebus Albanicis, I. 91.

[4] Ibid, I. 145. The contract is dated 24th February, 1566-7.

and of his likewise giving his bond of service for himself and his clan to Argyle, the latter engaged to make
him his vassal in the lands of Trouterness, Sleat, and
North Uist, to which the Macdonalds had at present no
legal claim.[1]   Argyle's agreement with Tormod Macleod
was actually carried into effect;[2] but circumstances
seem to have interfered with the final completion of
his contract with Macdonald.   It is evident, however,
that, although in the case of the Siol Tormod, at this
time, ancient custom prevented the feudal law of succession from being carried into effect in its full extent,
yet the Earl of Argyle did not surrender his legal claims
without indemnifying himself amply for the sacrifice.

   The important events which marked the close of the
reign of Queen Mary and the commencement of that
of her son, must, in a great measure, have withdrawn
the attention of the Scottish government from the
administration of justice throughout the realm.   This
neglect was soon followed by its necessary consequence—
an increase in the number of private feuds as well as
in the rancour with which these disputes were conducted.[3]   As soon, however, as the Regent Murray
found himself firmly seated in the government, he pro-

----

   [1] Collectanea de Rebus Albanicis, I. 147.   The contract is dated
4th March, 1566-7.

   [2] Reg. of Great Seal, XXXIII. 9.   MS. History of Macleods, quoting
a Royal charter to Tormod, dated 4th August, 1579.

   [3] On 28th April, 1567, Queen Mary (then at the Castle of Dunbar) granted a commission of Lieutenandry to the Earl of Argyle
against Hector Maclean of Dowart and his clan, who had, since the
death of James Macdonald of Dunyveg, ravaged with fire and sword
the Isle of Gigha, being part of the jointure lands of Lady Agnes
Campbell, Macdonald's widow.   Analecta· Scotica, p. 393.   Reg. of
Great Seal, XXXI. 47.

ceeded to check all such disorders with that vigour which distinguished his character.[1]   In June,

1569, the Regent and his Privy Council sat at Inverness, and laboured to put an end to the feuds of the Highlanders. Among other feuds which attracted Murray's notice at this time, was one between the Clanchattan and the Macdonalds of Keppoch, the origin of which has been traced in the Introduction, and which had been aggravated, in the early part of the last reign, by the apprehension and execution of Ranald Mac-Donald Glas of Keppoch. It will be recollected that this chief, having been concerned in the attack upon Lord Lovat, and the slaughter of the Frasers, was, along with Ewin Allanson of Lochiel, apprehended in 1547, by William Macintosh, captain of the Clanchattan, and delivered to the Earl of Huntly, by whom both these leaders were executed (supra, p. 179). Notwithstanding the great obstacle thus thrown in the way of an accommodation between the Clanchattan and the Macdonalds, the Regent succeeded in procuring from Launchlan Macintosh, now the head of the former tribe, a promise that he would grant to Ranald MacRanald of Keppoch such titles to the lands occupied by the latter and his clan, as to the Regent should seem fair and equitable.[2] This long-protracted feud was now in a fair way of being brought to an amicable conclusion, but for the assassination of the Earl of Murray, which

---

[1] In a Parliament, held at Edinburgh, in 1516, the Lords of the Articles were required to report, "by what meane all Scotland be brocht to universal obedience, and how *John Moydart* and *Mackay* may be dantonit." Vol. III. p. 43-4. The particulars of the rebellious conduct of these chiefs do not appear.

[2] Record of Privy Council, ad tempus.

had the effect of throwing the country into still greater confusion than that from which he had already succeeded in rescuing it.

In August of this year, Donald Gormeson or Macdonald of Sky, and Colin Mackenzie of Kintaill, were forced, in the presence of the Regent and Privy Council at Perth, to settle, under Murray's mediation, certain quarrels in which they and their clans had been for some time involved. The principal argument used by the Regent to force these chiefs to an accommodation, was a threat that the whole influence of Government would instantly be employed to crush the party who should refuse his mediation, or, having accepted it, should fail to implement the conditions imposed upon him.[1] One cause of feud between the Clandonald of Sky and the Clankenzie, was the death of Donald Gormeson's father, in his abortive attempt to seize Mackenzie's Castle of Elandonan in Kintaill, in the latter part of the reign of James V. (supra, p. 146). But the dissensions of these powerful tribes had of late been aggravated by their connection in different ways with the Siol Torquil, or Macleods of Lewis. To understand the respective positions of the clans alluded to, it will be necessary to glance briefly at the later history of that last mentioned—viz., the Siol Torquil. Roderick or Ruari Macleod, the Baron of Lewis, and heir male of his ancient house, was first married to Janet, daughter of John Mackenzie of Kintaill. The alleged issue of this marriage was a son, Torquil—afterwards, from his residence among his mother's relations in Strathconnan, surnamed *Connanach*. The Lady of

---

[1] Record of Privy Council, ad tempus.

Lewis, however, having eloped with John Macgille-challum of Rasay, chieftain of a powerful branch of the Siol Torquil, was divorced by her husband, who, at the same time, disowned and disinherited Torquil Connanach, alleging that the latter was not his son, but the son of the Breve or Celtic Judge of the Lewis.[1] Ruari Macleod married, secondly, in 1541, Barbara Stewart, daughter of Andrew, Lord Avandale; and by this lady had a son, likewise named Torquil, and surnamed *Oighre,* or the Heir, to distinguish him from Torquil Connanach.[2] The latter being supported by the Mackenzies, a feud between the two clans was the result. Nor did the quarrel, thus begun, end but with the total destruction of the family of Lewis. Some time in or before the year 1566, Torquil Oighre, a young chief of great promise, was, with many of his attendants, drowned in a tempest, when sailing from Lewis to Sky. As he left no male issue, this event gave fresh spirit to the supporters of

---

[1] MS, History of the Mackenzies, in the possession of L. Mackin-non of Letterfearn, Esq. Dr. George Mackenzie's MS. History of the Mackenzies. Sir R. Gordon's History of Sutherland, p. 267. That Ruari Macleod's wife, contrary to the MS. Histories above cited, was a *daughter,* instead of a *sister,* of John Mackenzie of Kintaill, is proved by a decreet arbitral in 1554, in which Torquil Connanach is called the *oy* of John Mackenzie.—Acts and Decreets of Session, X., fo. 201.

[2] Reg. of Privy Seal, XV., fo. 77. Sir R. Gordon, p. 267. MS. Histories above cited. As Barbara Stewart is found to have been alive and styled Lady Lewis, in 1566—and Torquil Connanach is mentioned as engaged in active life prior to 1554 (Acts and Decreets of Session, X., fo. 201), and had a son grown up in 1585 (Privy Seal, LIII., fo. 40)—it is clear, contrary to the assertion of Sir Robert Gordon and the other writers above quoted, that Barbara Stewart must have been the *second,* and not the *first* wife of Ruari Macleod.

Torquil Comnanach, and to that individual himself, who
had now married a daughter of the Laird of Glengarry.

A recent massacre of the Macleods of Rasay contributed, at this time, to weaken the Siol Torquil, and to
irritate the Mackenzies more against them. The following are the circumstances under which tradition
states the massacre to have taken place. It has been
mentioned that John Macgillechallum of Rasay, called
"*Ian na Tuaidh*," or John with the Axe, carried off the
first wife of his chief, Ruari Macleod of Lewis. By this
lady, who was a daughter of John Mackenzie of Kintaill (and whom, after her divorce from her first husband,
he appears to have married), Rasay had issue several
sons and a daughter. The latter was married to Allaster
Roy, a grandson of Hector or Eachan Roy, the first of
the Mackenzies of Gerloch.[1] On the death of his first
wife, Rasay married a relation of his own, being the sister
of Ruari MacAllan Macleod—surnamed "Nimhneach,"
i.e., venomous, or bitterly hostile—head of that portion
of the Siol Vic Gillechallum which dwelt in Gerloch. Of
this marriage there was likewise issue. Rasay had given
offence to his clan by marrying his daughter to a Mackenzie of the house of Gerloch, with which the Siol Vic
Gillechallum had been long at deadly feud. Taking
advantage of the discontent of the tribe, Ruari MacAllan
plotted the destruction of his *ceantighe*, and of the sons
of the latter's first marriage; so that the lands of Rasay
might come to the eldest son of the second marriage,
who was his own nephew. Having contrived to assemble
the Laird of Rasay, his sons by the first marriage, and

---

[1] MS. History of Mackenzies of Gerloch, and Letterfearn MS.

several of his nearest relations, at the Island of Isay in
Waterness, as if to consult on matters of importance,
the relentless MacAllan proceeded to carry his blood-
thirsty design into execution.   After a feast, which
concluded the business of the day, he left the apartment; and, causing Rasay and the others to be sent for
singly, he had each of them assassinated on coming to
his presence.   Not one of the party escaped; but
although Ruari MacAllan's nephew was now nearest
heir, he did not succeed in retaining possession of
Rasay.   That estate, by the assistance of the Mackenzies, became the property of Malcolm or Gillecallum
Garve MacAllaster Macleod, who was residing with his
fosterfather at the time of the massacre of his relations;
and was, during his minority, placed by that faithful
guardian under the protection of Campbell of Calder.
Meantime, the Mackenzies of Gerloch pursued Ruari
MacAllan, in revenge for the murder of the sons of
Rasay's first marriage, whose mother was a Mackenzie,
and whose sister had married into that family, as above
mentioned.[1]   This occurred about the time that the
disputes of Ruari Macleod of Lewis and Colin Mackenzie of Kintaill, who supported Torquil Connanach,
had run very high, and must, of course, have had the
effect of aggravating the feud.   Ruari Macleod now
sought the assistance of Donald Gormeson, a chief
whose previous quarrel with the Mackenzies made
him more ready to oppose them upon this occasion; and who appears, with the sanction of the
chief of the Siol Torquil, to have taken steps to procure

[1] Letterfearn MS. I have nowhere else seen this massacre alluded
to.

his own recognition as heir of the line of Lewis.[1]   In all these disputes, Neill Angusson Macleod of Assint, and the blood-stained Ruari MacAllan, were among the leading partisans of the chiefs of Lewis and Sleat; whilst Torquil Connanach Macleod, and John Mackenzie of Gerloch, were the most active on the other side.[2]   Such was the feud which was now quelled by the influence of the Regent Murray so effectually as to prevent its renewal at any future time, so far as the Macdonalds of Sky and the Mackenzies were concerned.

A. D. 1570-1572.   After the assassination of Murray, the Earls of Lennox and Mar were successively Regents of Scotland.   These noblemen, however, held the sovereign power for so short a space, and were so much occupied in defending themselves and their supporters against the Queen's party, which was still very strong, that neither of them had leisure or opportunity to follow out any particular system with regard to the administration of justice, or the maintenance of internal tranquillity.   The Earl of Mar was succeeded by the celebrated James, Earl of Morton; who, although an unprincipled man, and avaricious to excess, ruled with much vigour and an appearance of justice.

During the feud between the Clandonald and other supporters of Ruari Macleod, and the Clankenzie, as supporters of Torquil Connanach, which we have lately noticed, the old chief of Lewis had been seized by his

[1] Protest in Ch. Chest of Dunvegan, dated 22nd August, 1566, taken by Donald MacDonald Gorme, claiming to be heir of Lewis, on the ground of an alleged confession of Hucheoun, the Breve of the Lewis, that Torquil Connanach was son to the said Breve.

[2] Acts and Decreets of Session, X., fo. 201 ; Record of Privy Council, August, 1569.

alleged son, who detained him four years in captivity.
Being brought, while a prisoner, before the Earl of
Mar, then Regent, and his Privy Council, he was compelled to resign his estate into the hands of the Crown,
taking a new destination of it to himself in liferent, and,
after his death, to Torquil Connanach, as his son and
heir-apparent. On his liberation, the first act of Ruari
Macleod was to revoke all that he had done when a
captive, on the ground of coercion, and of the undutiful
conduct of Torquil.[1] Fresh dissensions followed this
revocation; and, at length, both father and son were
summoned to Edinburgh, where, in presence
A. D. 1576. of the Regent Morton and the Privy Council,
they agreed to bury in oblivion their mutual animosities.
Torquil Connanach was again recognised as heir-
apparent of the Lewis; and, in that character, received
from his father the district of Cogeache, and various
other lands, for his support during the life of the latter.[2]
It will afterwards appear that this reconciliation did not
endure for any great length of time.

About the same time, a petty quarrel arose between
the Earls of Argyle and Athole, which might have been
attended with very serious consequences, from the
manner in which these noblemen took it up. The
circumstances connected with this dispute were as
follow. Colin, sixth Earl of Argyle, who had succeeded his brother in 1575, claimed, in virtue of his
heritable office of Justice-General, that a Commission
of Justiciary, formerly given by Queen Mary to the
Earl of Athole, over his own territory of Athole,

---

[1] Reg. of Great Seal, XXXIII. 32. Instrument of Revocation by
Ruari Macleod, dated 2nd June, 1572, in Ch. Chest of Dunvegan.

[2] Gen. Reg. of Deeds, XV., fo. 186.

should be annulled.[1] This was opposed by the latter,
who not only refused to give up for trial two of the
Athole Stewarts, against whom Argyle alleged various
crimes, but took an opportunity of seizing two of the
Camerons, charged with the murder of the late chief of
that clan. These men he committed to prison, and
detained there, although claimed by Argyle as his
dependants.[2] Disdaining to yield to each other, the
rival Earls summoned together their vassals in arms,
and prepared to decide this ignoble dispute by the
sword. The Regent, before the parties could come to
blows, interfered; and, by a very judicious exercise of
the Royal authority, compelled them to disband their
forces.[3] But Argyle and Athole, having secret information that Morton meditated a charge of treason
against them, so as to make their late discord profitable
to himself, forgot their private animosities, and united
against the common enemy. The Regent, who feared
their joint power, was forced unwillingly to abandon
his project; and a blow was thus struck at his influence,
which from this time gradually waned, until, at length,
A. D. 1578. he was deprived of the Regency.[4] The
Government was now nominally assumed by
the King, who was in the twelfth year of his age; but,
for the next seven years, the chief power of the State
was engrossed by the profligate Captain James Stewart,
upon whom, in 1581, the Earldom of Arran was conferred.

[1] Record of Privy Council, Feb., 1575-6.
[2] Ibid., 31st July, 1576; 2nd and 26th February, and 1st March,
1576-7.
[3] Ibid., 23rd June, 1576, to 20th January, 1576-7.
[4] Robertson's History of Scotland, II. 225; Historie of King James
the Sext, p. 159-60.

Early in 1578, we find the Earl of Argyle—who, since his rupture with the Regent Morton, had avoided the Court, and dwelt in his own country—accused of levying his vassals, nominally with a view to punish some disturbers of the public peace, but really, as was alleged, to wreak his vengeance upon the Laird of Glengarry. How the latter chief came to offend the powerful Earl of Argyle does not appear; but upon his petition to the Privy Council, proclamation was made, prohibiting the Earl from assembling any of the lieges in arms, and from attacking Glengarry, under the pain of treason. At the same time, the tutor of Lovat, Colin Mackenzie of Kintaill, and several other powerful chiefs, were directed to assist Glengarry with all their force against the Earl. A similar direction was given generally to the inhabitants of the Earldoms of Ross and Murray, and the Lordships of Badenoch and Balquhidder; and Maclean of Dowart and Mackinnon of Strathordell were prohibited from giving assistance to the Earl of Argyle.[1] These decided measures seem to have checked the Earl's proceedings, for the matter is not again alluded to in the record.

About this time various other complaints were made against Argyle for oppressive and illegal conduct; particularly by John, son and heir to James Macdonald of Castle Camus in Sky, and John Maclean, uncle to Lauchlan Maclean of Dowart, who were both kept prisoners in Argyle's Castle of Inchconnell in Lochow, without warrant; and by Lauchlan Maclean, the young chief of Dowart, whose Isle of Loyng was invaded and plundered by a party of Campbells sent by Argyle,

---

[1] Record of Privy Council, ad tempus.

under the command of Dougal Macconachy of Inveraw.[1]
It is difficult to account for this Earl of Argyle pursuing
a line of conduct so opposed to the policy of his predecessors.   After his being made Lord High Chancellor
of Scotland, in August, 1579, he seems to have paid
more regard to the laws.

The powerful family of the Macleans had now for
their chief a young man of an active and energetic
spirit, under whom this tribe exercised a great influence
in the Isles.   Circumstances had early familiarised
Lauchlan Mor (as this young chief, from his great
stature, was styled) with scenes of blood and rapine.
During his minority, the family estates had been held
by Hector Maclean, son of Alein na'n Sop (supra,
p. 178), who pretended to administer them as guardian
for his kinsman, Lauchlan, but, in reality, plotted the
destruction of the latter, intending to seize the estates
afterwards for himself.   Even after Lauchlan Maclean,
who is said to have received a good education in the
Lowlands, had attained majority and taken possession
of his estates, his quondam guardian was suspected of a
design upon his life.   This was, however, frustrated by
the activity of Lauchlan, who apprehended Hector, and
imprisoned him for a considerable time in the Castle of
Dowart.   Thence he transported him to the Isle of
Coll (the Macleans of that island having, on a renewal
of the old feud, been expelled by the young Lord of
Dowart), where the unfortunate Hector was beheaded,
by order of his nephew, without trial or warrant.[2]
Under a chief disposed to act in so violent and illegal

[1] Record of Privy Council, 1576 to 1579.

[2] Record of Privy Council, 10th and 12th April, 1579.

a manner the Macleans could not long avoid a collision with the Macdonalds of Isla regarding the disputed district in that island.   We find, accordingly, that the King and Council, upon information of mutual hostilities already committed by the followers of these chiefs, commanded Lauchlan Maclean of Dowart, and Angus Macdonald of Dunyveg, to subscribe, within a certain limited period, assurances of indemnity to each other, under the penalty of treason.[1] This led to a temporary suspension of hostilities between the two clans, and to the marriage of Macdonald with the sister of Maclean; but their friendship, although thus cemented, was not destined to be of long duration.

A. D. 1579.

Some time after these disturbances in the South Isles, a serious feud broke out between Donald MacAngus of Glengarry and Colin Mackenzie of Kintaill.   The former chief had inherited one half of the districts of Lochalsh, Lochcarron, and Lochbroom, from his grandmother, Margaret, one of the sisters and co-heiresses of Sir Donald Macdonald of Lochalsh, who, as formerly mentioned, died about the year 1518.[2]   The predecessors of Kintaill had acquired the other half of these districts by purchase, from Dingwall of Kildun, the son of the other co-heiress of Sir Donald.[3]   The vicinity of these lands to the other possessions of the Mackenzies had probably tempted some of that tribe to make aggressions upon Glengarry's portion.   Their intrusion was fiercely resented by that chief, who, in order the better to maintain his rights,

A. D. 1581.

---

[1] Record of Privy Council, 12th January, 1578-9.

[2] Supra, p. 126. Vindication of the Clanranald of Glengarry, pp. 9-12.

[3] Reg. of Privy Seal, XVII., fo. 92.

took up his residence, for a time, in Lochcarron, and placed a garrison of his followers in the Castle of Strone, in that district. The breach between the two clans gradually became wider; and, in the course of their dissensions, Glengarry himself, and many of his followers, fell into the hands of a party of the Mackenzies, headed by Ruari Mackenzie of Redcastle, brother to the Lord of Kintaill. Glengarry's life was spared; but he was detained in captivity for a considerable time, and only procured his release by yielding the Castle of Lochcarron to the Mackenzies. The other prisoners, however, including several of Glengarry's near relations, A. D. 1582. were put to death, with many circumstances of cruelty and indignity. After his liberation Glengarry complained to the Privy Council, who, investigating the matter, caused the Castle of Strone to be placed under the temporary custody of the Earl of Argyle, and detained Mackenzie of Kintaill at Edinburgh, in what was called open ward, to answer to such charges as might be brought against him.[1]

A. D. 1585. The dissensions among the Macleods of Lewis, which had been quieted under the Regency of Morton, were now again renewed with greater violence than before. The old chief had recently married, for his third wife, a sister of Lauchlan Maclean of Dowart, and, by that lady, was father of two sons—the elder named Torquil Dubh, and the younger, Tormod. He had likewise five bastard sons,

---

[1] Record of Privy Council, 10th August and 2nd December, 1582; 11th January and 8th March, 1582-3. In connection with this feud, Colin Mackenzie of Kintaill was confined in the Castle of Blackness in May, 1586. Ibid. ad tempus; and Treasurer's Accounts in June, 1586.

all come to man's estate; three of whom, Donald, Ruari
Oig, and Neill, joined with their father when that chief
once more disinherited Torquil Connanach, and named
Torquil Dubh as his heir. The other bastards, Tormod *Uigach* and Murdoch, attached themselves to
Torquil Connanach; and these elements of discord in
the tribe soon produced their natural results. Tormod
Uigach was slain by his brother,Donald, who, again, was
seized by Murdoch, and delivered to Torquil Connanach
with a view to his punishment. Donald, however, contrived to escape his threatened doom, and, in his turn,
seized Murdoch, who was then imprisoned by old Ruari
in his Castle of Stornoway in the Lewis. Torquil Connanach took arms to relieve Murdoch from durance,
and justified himself for his hostility to his father, by
alleging that his own life was in danger from the latter.
Having besieged the Castle of Stornoway, and taken it,
after a short siege, he not only liberated his bastard
brother, Murdoch, but again made his father a prisoner,
after killing a number of his men. He likewise carried
off all the charters and writings of the family, which, on
a future occasion, he delivered to Mackenzie of Kintaill.
Before leaving the Lewis, Torquil Connanach sent for
his eldest son, John, a youth who had been brought
up under the charge of the Earl of Huntly, and made
him keeper of the Castle of Stornoway, in which the
old chief, his grandfather, was left as a prisoner. John
Macleod continued in possession of the castle and of
the island for some time, until he was attacked and
killed by his bastard uncle, Ruari Oig. The old man
was once more liberated and restored to his estate,
"which," says our authority, "he did possesse during
the rest of his troublesome days." On hearing of the

death of his son, Torquil Connanach, by the advice of the Mackenzies, apprehended and executed, at Dingwall, his bastard brother, Donald, who was believed to have been privy to the designs of Ruari Oig.[1] Thus was the Siol Torquil weakened by private dissensions, and exposed to fall a prey, as it did soon afterwards, to the growing power of the Mackenzies.

As the Scottish Islanders still continued to exercise a considerable influence in the North of Ireland, it will be proper, before concluding the present chapter, to take a retrospective view of the events in Ulster in which they were chiefly concerned since the death of James Macdonald and Shane O'Neill. The children of James Macdonald being young at his death, the Irish estates of the family were seized by their uncle, Sorley Buy, who, during his brother's life, had merely been manager under the latter. Sorley Buy was a man of conduct and courage, and speedily extended his influence over the adjacent territories of the Route and Claneboy— being generally successful in his enterprises, whether against the native Irish or the forces of the English Government.[2] In September, 1575, while Sir Henry Sidney, then Lord Deputy of Ireland, was at Drogheda, in the course of a progress from Dublin to the north, he received intelligence of a desperate attack made by Sorley Buy upon the garrison of Knockfergus. The

---

[1] Sir R. Gordon's History of Sutherland, p. 268; Reg. of Privy Seal, LIII. 40; Letterfearn MS.

[2] A full and interesting account of Sorley Buy's wars with the Mac-Quillans and O'Neills in the year 1569, is given in an ancient MS., cited by the Rev. Dr. Drummond in the notes to his poem called "The Giant's Causeway." See also Hamilton's Letters on Antrim, for feuds between the Clandonald and the MacQuillans.

principal object of this attempt was to carry off the
cattle which had been collected there, to be under the
protection of the garrison; and although the Scot was
repulsed without effecting his object, the garrison suffered
severely in the conflict.   In the following month Sidney
set out on his journey towards Knockfergus.   In his
report of the state of Ulster, he describes the districts
of Duffreyn and Claneboy as totally waste and void of
inhabitants, whilst the Glens and Route, possessed by
the Scots under Sorley Buy, were full of corn and
cattle; and that leader is represented as being then
very haughty, owing to his late victories.   The Lord
Deputy not being in a condition to reduce Sorley Buy,
at this time, by force of arms, arranged with him that
he should abstain from hostilities until certain petitions
given in by him should be considered by the English
Queen.   In these petitions, Sorley Buy not only claimed
to be recognised as proprietor of the Glens, but also
desired to be confirmed in his possession of the Route.
As it was now evident that Sorley Buy totally disre-
garded the claims of his nephew, Angus, the son of
James Macdonald,[1] to the Glens, and was labouring
exclusively for his own advancement, James' widow,
who, since his death, had married the celebrated Torlogh
Luineach O'Neill, afterwards Earl of Tyrone, addressed
herself to the Lord Deputy, with a view to counteract
the intrigues of Sorley Buy.   This lady came to

---

[1] This Angus Macdonald of Dunyveg and the Glens, is first mentioned
in a Scottish Chronicle, A.D. 1573, as under:—" Upoun the 23d. day
of Aprile, the great O'NEILL (Torlogh Luineach, step-father of Angus)
come in to Edinburgh, and gave in ane complent aganis *Angus MacConeill*,
becaus he wald not be subdewit to the Erle of Ergyle." Diurnal of
Occurrents, printed by Ban. Club, p. 330.

Armagh to wait upon Sir Henry Sidney, by whom she is described as " one very well spoken, of great modesty, good nurture, parentage, and disposition, being aunt to the Earl of Argyle." Knowing the aversion of the English Queen to have Scottish subjects as proprietors in Ireland, she passed over the claims of her eldest son, but desired to have the Glens granted to her second son, who would swear to be her Majesty's liegeman and a dutiful subject. She engaged, also, that her son would dwell upon the property himself, and yield what rent and service her Majesty could reasonably demand; and that he would defend it against Sorley Buy and his followers. Her offers, as well as those of Sorley Buy, were transmitted by Sidney to the English Privy Council; and he, at the same time, expressed his opinion that the Route should be restored to its former proprietors, the MacQuillans. He recommended, also, that the Queen should write to the Regent of Scotland, effectually to keep the Scots at home; " who, from that region, and, namely, the oute Isles, dayly swarm hither, to the great annoyance of the north part of this realme." [1]

In the following year Sidney received offers from Torlogh Luineach, bearing, that if the Lord Deputy would make war upon the Scots, and do but one day's service upon them, Torlogh would repudiate his wife, and do his best to expel her countrymen out of Ireland. Being aware that O'Neill's principal strength consisted in the Scots, as he was hated by his Irish followers, Sidney distrusted the promises of this crafty chief, and con-

---

[1] Letters of Sir Henry Sidney to the English Government, 28th September, and 15th November, 1575. Cotton MS., Brit. Mus., Titus, B. X.

tented himself with recommending a new application to the Scottish Regent, to check the incursions of the Islanders into Ireland.[1] In 1579, we find it reported that O'Neill had invited over great numbers of Scots, with evil intentions, on his part, against the Government.[2] The English ministers were now forced to turn their serious attention to the progress of the Scots in Ulster; and, being informed that the Earl of Desmond, then in rebellion, had applied to O'Neill for assistance, they immediately despatched Captain Piers, an officer of experience, to treat with Torlogh Luineach and prevent his joining the rebels. The secret instructions given to this envoy, and signed by Burleigh and Walsingham, two of the ablest ministers of the English Queen, afford the strongest proof of the power to which the intruding Islanders had attained. After conferring with O'Neill as to the rebellion of Desmond, Piers was instructed to ascertain, with caution, how far the former was inclined to break with the Scots, or, at least, to agree to their being both limited in number, and confined to their inheritance of the Glens. He was to pretend that his sole motive in this proposition was to benefit "the ancient lords and captains of the land of Ireland," several of whom were expelled from their possessions and deprived of their wealth by the Scots, who grew rich "by spoiling of the land of Ireland." The envoy was then directed to explain to the Irish families who suffered most from the Scots and were pressing for their expulsion, the reasons which prevented the Queen from following that course; and he was charged, at the

[1] Letters of Sir Henry Sidney to the English Government, 17th March, 1576-7.

[2] Harleian MS., 7/988.

same time, to obtain their approval of a limitation of the number of the Scots to four hundred. Finally, he was to sound the Scots themselves, to ascertain how they felt disposed towards the projected limitation of their numbers, and diminution of their territories.[1] The effect of the mission of Captain Piers, in so far as regards the Scots, is uncertain. We find that, in 1585, Angus Macdonald, his brother Donald Gorme, and his mother, the Lady Tyrone, were engaged in a negotiation with Sir John Perrot, then Lord Deputy of Ireland, on the basis of certain conditions proposed by the latter. Before, however, this treaty was concluded, Macdonald and his mother were summoned to the Scottish court;[2] and the increasing difficulties in which this chief was soon after involved, threw his Irish estates entirely into the hands of Sorley Buy, from whom Angus never was able to recover them.

The history of Sorley Buy and his sons—who, from this time, became Irish subjects, and threw off, for many years, any connection with Scotland—may here be summed up in a few words, as far as regards their possessions in Ulster. In 1585, Sir John Perrot took Sorley Buy's fortress of Dunluce, and expelled him and his followers from the Route. In the following year, however, Sorley Buy recovered the castle, and slew the Governor, Cary, who made a gallant defence; but the Lord Deputy having sent against him an officer of

---

[1] Instructions, dated at Westminster, 26th May, 1580. Harleian MS., $\frac{7004}{104}$. "Plot for the better inhabiting of Clandeboy, the Route, and the Glens, upon an offer made by certain inhabitants of the said countries."—Ibid, $\frac{7004}{104}$.

[2] Letter, Sir John Perrot to Lord Burghley, 24th April, 1585. Harleian MS., $\frac{7004}{113}$.

experience, named Merryman, the Scot was defeated with
great loss—two of his brothers and his son, Alexander,
being among the slain.   Merryman then plundered the
lands possessed by Sorley Buy, from which he carried
off no less than fifty thousand head of cattle, in which
the wealth of that chief consisted.   To such distress
was Sorley Buy reduced by this blow, that he surrendered Dunluce, went to Dublin, and made his public
submission in the cathedral of that city, offering, at the
same time, an humble petition for mercy.   Being afterwards admitted into the Deputy's apartment, as soon
as he saw the picture of Queen Elizabeth which hung
there, the wily Scot threw away his sword, and more
than once prostrated himself before it, and devoted
himself to her Majesty's service.   He was then received
into favour, and obtained letters of naturalisation; and,
on his abjuring all allegiance to any foreign prince, was
rewarded by considerable grants of land.   He had a
grant of four districts, called *Tuoghes*—viz. : the district between the rivers Boyse and Ban, and the territories of Dunseverig, Loghill, and Ballamonyn, with the
government of Dunluce Castle, to be held by him and
the heirs male of his body under the Kings of England.   He was bound to restrain his followers from
ravaging, and to furnish, in time of war, twelve horsemen and forty footmen to the Royal army; paying, also, a
certain number of cattle and hawks annually to the King.
His eldest son, Sir James MacSorley Buy or Macdonnell of Dunluce, joined in the Earl of Tyrone's rebellion
in the year 1597, and was present at the battle of the
Blackwater.   In the same year, by means of an ambuscade, he took prisoner the Governor of Carrickfergus,
whom he caused to be beheaded on a stone at the head

of the glen. In 1599 he was still in rebellion, and had four hundred foot and a hundred horse under arms; but on the accession of King James to the throne of England, he cheerfully submitted to and became a strenuous supporter of the government of that monarch. Sorley Buy's second son, Sir Ranald MacSorley, or Macdonnell, had considerable grants of land in the county of Antrim from James VI., after the year 1603. He is described as having been "a singular promoter and patron of civility in the north of Ireland." In 1618 he was created Viscount of Dunluce, and afterwards advanced to the dignity of Earl of Antrim. Ranald, his son, succeeded as second Earl, and for his services against the Irish rebels in 1641, was created in 1643 Marquis of Antrim.[1]

To return to Angus Macdonald of Isla. Soon after his arrival in Scotland, an act of Privy Council was passed, bearing that he having declared himself the King's obedient subject, was on that account, and through some pretended quarrels, menaced with invasion by his neighbours. All the lieges, therefore, were, by proclamation, strictly charged to assist him against his enemies, under high penalties. At the same time, Lauchlan Maclean of Dowart, Donald Gormeson of Sleat, Ruari Macleod of the Lewis, and Tormod Macleod of Harris, were summoned to appear before the King and Council, to give their advice regarding the good rule and quietness of the Highlands and Isles.[2] There is reason to believe that the quarrels alluded to

---

[1] Camden's Britannia (by Gough), III., pp. 626, 627; Playfair's Brit. Fam. Antiq., IV., p. 39; O'Sullivan, p. 147; Hamilton's Letters on Antrim.

[2] Record of Privy Council, ad tempus.

arose out of the old feud between the Macdonalds and
Macleans, aggravated in all probability by some im-
prudent grant conferred by the influence of Arran
upon Angus Macdonald, of lands disputed between the
two clans. The Privy Council might have succeeded,
as on former occasions, in quelling this feud, but a
concurrence of unfortunate events tended to plunge
these clans and their supporters into scenes of blood
and strife, which retarded for a length of time the
civilisation and improvement of the Isles.

About this time, Allan MacIan Duy, the young
chief of the Camerons, who, on the murder of his uncle,
had been carried for safety when an infant to the
Isle of Mull (supra, p. 203), returned to take the command of his tribe. During his minority and absence,
the clan had been ruled by his granduncles, Ewin
Cameron of Erracht, and John Cameron of Kinlochiel;
but they having made themselves obnoxious by their insolence and tyranny, Donald MacEwin Beg, bastard son
of a former chief, was brought forward by a party in the
clan to oppose them. The Laird of Macintosh, taking
advantage of these dissensions, invaded the lands of the
Clanchameron, and forced Erracht and Kinlochiel to
agree to a treaty regarding the disputed lands of Glenluy and Locharkaig, which was considered very disad-
vantageous to the Camerons. So strong was the feeling displayed by the clan when the terms of this treaty
became known, that Erracht and Kinlochiel were forced
to repudiate it, and to prepare for an immediate attack
upon the Clanchattan. To strengthen themselves in
the proposed expedition, they sought a reconciliation
with the bastard, Donald MacEwin, with whom and his
party they had a meeting at the Castle of Inverlochy.

Here, Ewin of Erracht was barbarously murdered by some of his opponents, and John of Kinlochiel was forced to leave Lochaber. He was afterwards, at the instigation of the bastard, apprehended by the Earl of Argyle, and executed at the Castle of Dunstaffnage. Allan MacIan Duy was now recalled to Lochaber, where, by false reports of the evil intentions entertained against him by the bastard, he was induced to consent to the death of the latter. This was so much resented by the clan, with whom Donald MacEwin had been a great favourite, that Lochiel was under the necessity of quitting Lochaber for a time until the affair should be forgotten. Having, while resident in Appin, nearly lost his life through an unlucky broil, in which a son of Campbell of Glenurchy was killed, the Clanchameron became impatient for his return ; and, accordingly, about the year 1585, Allan MacIan Duy of Lochiel again entered upon the command of his clan.[1]

The fall of the odious favourite, the Earl of Arran—brought about, at length, by the united efforts of the nobility—opened a new era in the reign of James VI. That prince was now in his nineteenth year ; and from this time he took upon himself more of the cares of Government than could have been expected at his age. His mode of governing, and his efforts to improve the Highlands and Isles, will be fully illustrated in the succeeding chapters.

[1] MS. History of Camerons.

CHAP. V.

FROM THE ASSUMPTION OF THE GOVERNMENT BY JAMES
VI. TO THE SUPPRESSION OF THE REBELLION OF THE
CATHOLIC EARLS.—1585-1595.

A. D. 1585.   AFTER the young King had taken the government into his own hands, he was soon called
upon to interfere in the feud between the Macdonalds
and Macleans, which owing to an unfortunate accident,
now raged with greater fury than ever.   The immediate
cause of these renewed disorders, which speedily involved
several other clans, was as follows.   Donald Gorme
Mor of Sleat, being on a voyage from Sky, with a retinue
befitting his rank, to visit his kinsman, Angus Macdonald
of Dunyveg, in the island of Isla, was forced by stress
of weather to take shelter in that part of Jura belonging to Maclean of Dowart.   At the same time, two
gentlemen of Donald Gorme's clan,[1] with whom he had
lately quarrelled, were by the same storm driven into
a neighbouring harbour.   On learning that their chief

---

[1] Their names were Huistein MacGillespick Clerach, and Macdonald
Terreagh.   Gordon's History of Sutherland, p. 187.   Donald Gorme
Mor was the son of Donald Gormeson, and the fifth in descent from
Hugh of Sleat,

lay so near them, these vassals secretly carried off by night a number of cattle from Maclean's lands, and took to sea, in the expectation that Donald Gorme and his party would be blamed by the Macleans for the robbery and suffer accordingly. Their malicious design, unfortunately, took effect, for in the course of the following night the men of Sky were attacked by a superior body of the Macleans, and, as they apprehended no danger, fell an easy prey to the assailants. Sixty of the Macdonalds were slain, and their chief only escaped the same fate from the circumstance of his accidentally sleeping on board his galley on the night of the attack. He immediately returned to Sky, much exasperated at what he had every reason to believe such an unprovoked attack, and vowing vengeance against the Macleans; feelings which quickly spread amongst all the branches of the Macdonalds and their allies. Violent measures of retaliation were immediately resorted to, and carried to such an extent that, in the month of September, we find the King himself writing to Macleod of Harris, and earnestly requesting that chief to assist Maclean of Dowart against the Clandonald, who had already done much injury to Maclean and his followers, and threatened to do more.[1] Meantime, Angus Macdonald of Dunyveg, having gone to Sky to consult with Donald Gorme, determined on his return, against the advice of his followers, to visit Maclean at his Castle of Dowart, and endeavour to effect an amicable arrangement of all their disputes. In taking this step, Macdonald calculated on his private influence with Maclean, whose sister he had married some years before; but he was doomed to be

---

[1] Original Letter in Charter Chest of Dunvegan, dated 18th September, 1585.

disappointed. His brothers, Ranald and Coll, strongly dissuaded him from his purpose, and finding him obstinate, refused to accompany him. Their fears were justified by the result. Angus and his followers were at first well received by Maclean; but the present was too good an opportunity of personal aggran-

A. D. 1586.   disement to be lost by the latter, whose violent character has already been noticed. On the day after their arrival, Macdonald and his train—with the exception of Ranald MacColl, Angus' cousin, who was left at liberty—were perfidiously seized and thrown into prison by their host.[1] Here Macdonald was detained in close captivity, until, to preserve his life, he agreed to renounce, in favour of Maclean, the lands of the Rinns of Isla, so long disputed between the two families. For the performance of this agreement he was obliged to give his son James, then a boy, and his brother Ranald, as hostages; whereupon he was set at liberty with his attendants. He then returned to his own Castle of Dunyveg, more than ever exasperated against his brother-in-law, and determined to obtain full revenge for the injuries inflicted both on himself and on his kinsman, Donald Gorme.

[1] "Trew it is, that thir Ilandish men ar of nature verie prowd, suspicious, avaricious, full of decept and evill inventioun each aganis his nychtbour, be what way soever he may circumvin him. Besydis all this, thay ar sa crewall in taking of revenge that nather have they regard to person, eage, tyme, or caus; sa ar they generallie all sa far addictit to thair awin tyrannicall opinions that, in all respects, they exceid in creweltie the maist barbarous people that ever hes bene sen the begynning of the warld."—Historie of King James the Sext, p. 217. The author of the work in which the above severe reflections on the character and disposition of the Islanders occur, seems, from a passage in Sir R. Gordon's History of Sutherland, p. 188, to have been one "John Colwin."

Some time afterwards, Maclean came to Isla to receive performance of the promises made by Macdonald regarding the Rinns of Isla, bringing with him his nephew, James Macdonald, one of the hostages, the other being left behind in the Castle of Dowart. Maclean took post at the ruinous fort of Elan Loch Gorme in the Rinns of Isla, and had not been long in this place when he received an invitation from Macdonald to come to the latter's house at Mullintrea, which was more convenient and better stored with provisions than the fort of Loch Gorme. Such, however, was the distrust felt by Maclean of this invitation, that it was only after solemn and repeated protestations by Macdonald that no hostility was meditated, that he was at length prevailed upon to comply with the request. Maclean accordingly came to Mullintrea, with eighty-six of his clan and servants, in the month of July, 1586, and was sumptuously entertained on his arrival. In the meantime, the Macdonalds being secretly collected together to the number of three or four hundred men, surrounded the houses in which Maclean and his followers were lodged, and made them all prisoners, with the exception of two, to whom they refused quarter. One of these was a Maclean of rank and influence in the tribe, renowned for his valour and manhood; the other was Macdonald Terreagh, one of those vassals of Donald Gorme who were the original cause of the slaughter in Jura, and who, since that time, had attached himself to the Macleans. The house in which these two men were was burned to the ground, with its inmates, by the Macdonalds.

When the report of the seizure of Maclean and his followers came to Mull, Allan Maclean, a near relation of the chief, caused a false rumour to be spread abroad that Ranald MacJames, the hostage left behind at Dowart, had been put to death. His object in this was to induce Angus Macdonald to kill Maclean and his clansmen; in which event, Allan would have succeeded to the management of the estate, as guardian to Maclean's children, who were then very young. And although this device did not succeed, as was intended, in procuring the death of Maclean, yet it had this effect, that Coll MacJames, under the impression that his brother Ranald had really been executed, let loose his vengeance against the rest of the unfortunate prisoners. Two of these were executed every day, until at last Maclean himself alone survived of all those who had been seized by the Macdonalds at Mullintrea; and Maclean's life was only saved by an accident that happened to Angus Macdonald as he was mounting his horse to witness the execution of his rival. These atrocities at length reached the ears of the King, who employed the chiefs of the Campbells who governed the Earldom of Argyle during the minority of the seventh Earl, to mediate between the contending clans. By their influence, Macdonald agreed—on receiving a promise of pardon for his crimes,[1] and on eight hostages A. D. 1587. of rank[2] being placed in his hands by Maclean, for the performance of certain conditions, which

---

[1] A remission was granted to him accordingly.—Record of Privy Council, 16th April, 1587.

[2] These hostages were—Hector Maclean, Dowart's eldest son; Alexander, brother of William Macleod of Dunvegan; Lauchlan and Neill, sons of Lauchlan Mackinnon of Strathordell; John and Murdo, sons of Ruari MacNeill of Barra; Allan, son of Ewin Maclean of Ardgour; and Donald, son of Hector Maclean, Constable of Carneburg.—Record of Privy Council, 16th April, 1587.

the latter was forced to subscribe—to consent to the liberation of his opponent. After this, Macdonald went to Ireland to attend to his affairs in that country, when Dowart, regardless of the safety of his hostages and of his own promises, roused his clan to arms, and invaded Isla, a great part of which he wasted with fire and sword. On Macdonald's return to the Isles, he disdained to punish the hostages; but collected a large force of his vassals and friends, with which he invaded the Isles of Mull and Tiree, and put to death all the inhabitants that fell into his hands, as well as the domestic animals of every description. "Finally," says Sir Robert Gordon, "he came to the very Benmore in Mull, and there killed and chased the Clanlean at his pleasure, and so revenged himself fully of the injuries done to him and his tribe." While Macdonald was thus employed, Maclean ravaged and plundered a great part of Kintyre; and "thus for a while they did continually vex one another with slaughters and outrages, to the destruction almost of their countries and people."[1]

It may easily be conceived that the effects of this deadly feud were not confined to the Clandonald of Isla and the Clanlean. Besides the Macdonalds of Isla and Sky, who were more particularly involved, there were numbered, among the opponents of the Macleans, the Clanranald, the Clanian of Ardnamurchan, the Clanleod of Lewis, the Macneills of Gigha, the Macallasters of

---

[1] Sir R. Gordon's History of Sutherland, p. 186, et sequen.— Historie of King James the Sext (printed for the Bannatyne Club), p. 221. The latter authority is more favourable to the Macleans than Sir R. Gordon, but is not so well supported by the evidence preserved in the records.

Loup, the Macfies of Colonsay, and other tribes of lesser note. On the other hand, among the partisans of the Macleans we find the Clanleod of Harris, the Macneills of Barra, the Mackinnons, and Macquarries.[1] The disastrous consequences of a dispute between two powerful clans in the South Isles came thus to be felt throughout the whole extent of the Hebrides; and it became necessary for the Government to take immediate steps for the suppression of such alarming disorders. After having sanctioned the delivery of hostages by Maclean to Macdonald, and promised the latter a pardon for the atrocities of which he had been guilty, the King and Council now turned round and issued a proclamation, ordering the hostages to be given up to the young Earl of Argyle, or his guardians, to be conveyed by them to his Majesty, and kept where he should appoint, till the final settlement of the matters in dispute between the Clandonald and Clanlean. The heads of both these tribes, and their principal supporters and allies, were charged to remain quiet, and abstain from all conventions or gathering in arms, and from all attacks upon each other; so as not to hinder or disturb his Majesty in his attempts to bring about a settlement of their various disputes.[2]

The King, at the same time, wrote with his own hand a pressing letter to the Earl of Huntly, desiring that nobleman to exert himself to prevent the north Islanders

---

[1] Ibid, LVII., fo. 75; LIX., fo. 87. Record of Privy Council, ad tempus. In May, 1587, Angus MacJames, Lord of Kintyre (Macdonald of Isla), and Donald Gorme of Sleat, entered into an alliance, offensive and defensive, with Lauchlan Macintosh, captain of the Clanchattan.—Collectanea de Rebus Albanicis, I., p. 97.

[2] Record of Privy Council, 16th April, 1587.

from gathering in arms, or committing acts of hostility against each other; and stating that it was his Majesty's intention to take "some speciall paines" in the affairs of the Isles, as he had lately done in those of the Borders.[1] In pursuance of this policy, a very important Act of Parliament was passed, for maintaining good order both on the Borders and in the Highlands and Isles. The plan on which this Act, commonly called the "General Band," or "Bond," chiefly proceeded, was, to make it imperative on all landlords, bailies, and chiefs of clans, to find sureties to a large amount, proportioned to their wealth and the number of their vassals or clansmen, for the peaceable and orderly behaviour of those under them. It was provided that, if a superior, after having found the required sureties, should fail to make immediate reparation of any injuries committed by persons for whom he was bound to answer, the injured party might proceed at law against the sureties for the amount of the damage sustained. Besides being compelled in such cases to reimburse his sureties, the superior was to incur a heavy fine to the Crown. This important statute likewise contained many useful provisions for facilitating the administration of justice in these rude districts.[2]

To return to the disturbances in the South Isles. Macdonald having failed to liberate the hostages according to the proclamation above mentioned, was outlawed; whilst Maclean, having declared himself an obedient subject, was received into favour.[3] So innate,

---

[1] History of the Gordons, by W. R. (MS. Adv. Lib.), in which the letter, dated 20th April, 1587, is quoted verbatim, p. 229.

[2] Acts of Scottish Parliament, latest edition, III. 461-467.

[3] Reg of Privy Seal, LVI., fo. 75 ; LVII. 35.

however, was the disposition of this chief to violence
and rapine, that in a very short time he lost the advantages he had gained, and subjected himself to a process
of forfeiture. It has been mentioned that the Clanian
of Ardnamurchan supported their relations, the Clandonald, in the feud with the Macleans, by which they
naturally incurred the resentment of the chief of Dowart.

An opportunity now presented itself to Mac-
A. D. 1588.   lean to be revenged on the Macians, of which
he did not hesitate to avail himself. John Macian of
Ardnamurchan, the chief of his tribe, had, before the
breaking out of the late feud, been a suitor for the
hand of Maclean's mother. This lady was a daughter
of one of the Earls of Argyle, and her high birth and
connections, together with a large jointure, made the
alliance a very desirable one for Macian. Dowart, who
had hitherto opposed the match, now changed his policy,
and gave his consent to the proposed alliance, in order
to get Macian into his power. That chief was easily
persuaded to proceed to the Isle of Mull, with a retinue
of the principal gentlemen of his tribe, in order that his
marriage with the mother of Maclean might be celebrated with becoming splendour. The ceremony having
been performed at Torlusk, one of Maclean's houses in
Mull, with the usual forms observed on like occasions
in the Isles, Macian and his bride retired to their own
chamber; whilst the gentlemen of the Clanian and
their servants, after receiving all the rites of hospitality
from the Macleans, were lodged by themselves in a
barn near to the principal mansion. Here, in the dead
of the night, they were assaulted by a large armed party
of those who had so lately entertained them in friendship, and massacred without compassion. Not satisfied

with this barbarity, the chief of Dowart, and some of his followers, proceeded to the nuptial chamber, in order to complete their bloody purpose, by the murder of the bridegroom. Macian having been roused by the shrieks and groans of his unfortunate kinsmen, stood upon his defence, but would inevitably have fallen a sacrifice to the fury of his enemies, had it not been for the lamentable cries and earnest entreaties of his wife, for whose sake his life was spared. He, and two of his clan, who, by some fortunate accident, had escaped the fate of their companions, were then thrown into a dungeon, where, it is said, that Macian himself was put to daily torture by the Macleans.[1]

Soon after this occurrence, the Florida, one of the large vessels of the Spanish Armada, was driven by a storm into the harbour of Tobermory in Mull.[2] On hearing of the arrival of this vessel, Maclean of Dowart repaired to the spot, and, as the price of such assistance as the Spaniards required and he could give, in refitting and victualling the ship, he procured the temporary assistance of a hundred Spanish soldiers in his private feuds. With this force, and a number of his own clan, Dowart first proceeded to ravage and plunder the Isles of Rum and Eig—then occupied, particularly the latter, by the Clanranald—and the Isles of Cauna and Muck, belonging to the Clanian. In this expedition he is said to have burned the whole inhabitants of these Isles, sparing neither sex nor age. He then, with his foreign auxili-

---

[1] Sir R. Gordon's History of Sutherland, p. 191 ; Record of Privy Council, 18th June, 1578.

[2] Here the Florida was afterwards blown up by a plot of Maclean ; for which offence he took out a remission, 20th March, 1588-9.—Reg. of Privy Seal.

aries, proceeded to the mainland, and laid close siege
to Macian's Castle of Mingarry, in Ardnamurchan, for
three days, laying waste all the lands in the vicinity with
fire and sword.   At length he was forced to return to
Mull, without obtaining possession of the castle, by the
approach of a superior force, composed probably of
some of the neighbouring clans, ordered by the Privy
Council to proceed against him.[1]   Meantime, the Macdonalds, in the prosecution of this feud, ravaged the
lands of the Macleans with fire and sword, being assisted,
it is said, by a band of English mercenaries.[2]   Tired
at last of these fruitless barbarities, the hostile clans
came to an agreement, by which the eight hostages formerly placed by Maclean in the hands of the chief of
Isla, were exchanged for Macian and the other prisoners
taken by the Macleans.[3]

It seems now to have been determined on
A. D. 1589. by the King and Council, to take effectual
measures for reducing to obedience the unruly chiefs
whose contentions had caused so much bloodshed in the
Isles.   Instead, however, of resorting to force, and thus
compelling them and their followers to submission, a
less manly course, although one, perhaps, more suited to
the disposition of the sovereign, was followed on this
occasion.   Remissions, under the Privy Seal, were
granted to the Macleans and Macdonalds, and their principal adherents, for all the crimes committed by them
during their late feud;[4] and, by these and similar means,

---

[1] Record of Privy Council, 3rd January, 1588-9 ; Pitcairn's Criminal
Trials, I. 228-9.

[2] Criminal Trials, I. 226-7.

[3] Sir R. Gordon's History of Sutherland, p. 192.

[4] Reg. of Privy Seal, LVII., fo. 75 ; LIX., fo. 87.

Lauchlan Maclean of Dowart, Angus Macdonald of Isla, and Donald Gorme Macdonald of Sleat, were at length induced to come to Edinburgh, on the pretence of consulting with the King and Council for the good rule of the country. While there, by a breach of faith on the part of the Government which no circumstances can excuse, and which only proves the weakness of the executive at this period, the three island chiefs were seized and imprisoned in the castle. After some time, Maclean and Angus Macdonald were brought to trial for the crimes already pardoned by the remissions under the Privy Seal; one of the principal charges against them being their treasonable hiring of Spanish and English soldiers to fight in their private quarrels. Both these chiefs, however, refused to plead or to go to a jury; but submitted themselves absolutely to the King's mercy, placing their lives and lands at his disposal.[1]

A. D. 1591.

In considering the measures pursued by the King, after this time, towards the chiefs who had been guilty of such barbarities, and were now so completely in his power, we must always keep in view the pecuniary embarrassments of James VI., which were now, and continued afterwards to be, very great. The Crown revenues from land had been much impaired by the improvident grants made to grasping and avaricious courtiers during the minorities of James and his mother; whilst the carelessness and extravagance of the young King, after he had assumed the government, soon involved him in the greatest difficulties. In such

---

[1] History of the Family of Sutherland, p. 192. Historie of King James the Sext, p. 222. Criminal Trials, I. 224, et sequen.

circumstances the irregular payment, or rather the withholding altogether of the Crown rents in the Isles, the inevitable result of the desolating feuds which we have noticed, must have occupied much of the attention of the King and his advisers. The cupidity of the monarch seems also to have been excited by exaggerated reports of the value of the fisheries on the west coast, and of the facility with which this branch of the national industry might be prosecuted. Hence, during the whole of his reign, the measures adopted for the improvement of the Highlands and Isles, although praiseworthy in themselves, and apparently well calculated to attain the object in view, were impeded by the eagerness of the King to fill his coffers from the new sources of wealth which he persuaded himself he had discovered. In his anxiety to realise these golden visions he frequently overlooked the just claims of the natives of the Highlands, and was too eager to enforce against them the penalty of forfeiture, which, under various severe acts of Parliament, they frequently incurred. At other times he acted with more apparent lenity; but, in these cases, the offenders generally paid a large sum for pardon; so that they who by their crimes had justly deserved death, were frequently permitted to return to their own estates, with but feeble security for their future peaceable behaviour.

Under such a system of Government, it cannot surprise us to find that Macdonald and Maclean were, upon paying each a fine to the King, and subscribing and finding surety for their performance of certain conditions imposed upon them, permitted to return home with new pardons for all their offences. These pardons, however, were only to remain in force in the event of their fulfilling the stipulated conditions in every point; the King reserving to himself the power of pronouncing sentence of death and forfeiture in the event of their disobedience. The terms granted to Maclean were more favourable than those granted to his rival, a difference arising, in all probability, from the influence of the Earl of Glencairn, whose daughter Maclean had married; for before Macdonald was liberated, he had to place in the hands of the Council his two sons and one of his nearest relations, as hostages for his appearance before the Council on a certain fixed day; and even if he should then appear his hostages were to be detained until Donald Gorme of Sleat (who was liberated at the same time) should give hostages from amongst his own kinsmen for the performance of the conditions prescribed to him. Maclean, on the other hand, was not burdened with giving hostages before his liberation, but merely promised to present them within a certain time after his release. In order to enable the Council better to ascertain their obedience, these three chiefs were further bound to return to their confinement in the Castle of Edinburgh whenever they should be summoned, upon twenty days' warning.[1] The amount of the fines imposed upon Macdonald of Isla and Maclean, in the shape of arrears of their feu-duties and Crown rents in the Isles, and for which they had to find security, cannot be easily ascertained. One author calls it "a small pecuniall sum,"[2] whilst another maintains that each of them was fined in the sum of twenty thousand pounds.[3] The fine imposed upon Mac-

[1] Record of Privy Council, 8th June, 1592.
[2] Sir R. Gordon's History of Sutherland, p. 192.
[3] Johnston's Hist. of Scotland, MS., Advocates' Library, fo. 600.

donald of Sleat, likewise under the denomination of arrears of Crown rents and feudal casualties for his lands, was four thousand pounds.[1]   Finally, John Campbell of Calder, guardian to the young Earl of Argyle, bound himself as surety for the Macdonalds; and John Campbell of Ardkinlass promised to answer for the obedience of Maclean.   These arrangements were concluded, and the Islanders liberated in consequence, in the summer of 1591.   It deserves to be noticed that, before their liberation, the Macdonalds were compelled, on the application of Bowes, the English ambassador, to find sureties for their good behaviour towards the Government of Ireland; whilst Maclean offered, through Bowes, to the Queen of England his services in Ireland against the chiefs of Isla and Sleat, as well as against O'Rourk, an Irish rebel.[2]

A. D. 1592.   In the month of February following, the Earl of Murray, commonly called "The Bonny Earl," was murdered at his own house of Donibirsel, in Fife, by a party of the Gordons, under the command of his deadly foe, the Earl of Huntly, who had received a commission to apprehend Murray as being concerned in some of the numerous treasonable attempts of Francis Stuart, Earl of Bothwell, to seize the King's person. There is no doubt that, in putting this nobleman to death, Huntly exceeded the powers contained in his commission; and the lenity with which he was treated by the Government afterwards caused many complaints and murmurs all over Scotland, particularly among the relations of the murdered Earl, of whom Lord Ochiltree and the Earl of Athole were the most active.[3]

---

[1] Harleian MS., No. 4648, p. 37.   [2] Ibid.
[3] Moysie's Memoirs, pp. 88-92.

These murmurs gradually assumed the shape of suspicions that the Chancellor Maitland, and perhaps the King himself,[1] had plotted the death of "The Bonny Earl;" suspicions which were justified, in some measure, by their having employed, on such a delicate service, a declared enemy of Murray, instead of a neutral person who had no private revenge to gratify. In the same month John Campbell of Calder was assassinated in Lorn.[2] It has not hitherto been remarked by any of the historians of the period, that the murder of Calder was in any way connected with that of the Earl of Murray; but a late discovery has made it appear that both crimes were the result of the same conspiracy. It is now certain that the Chancellor Maitland did actually join in this conspiracy, which likewise involved many of the barons and chiefs in the West Highlands. In order, however, to trace the origin and ramifications of this extraordinary plot, which was only partially carried into effect by the slaughter of Murray and Calder, it is necessary to glance at the history of the house of Argyle since the death of Colin, the sixth Earl, Chancellor and Justice-General of Scotland.

This powerful nobleman died in the month of September, 1584. By his last will and testament he commended his eldest son, Archibald, then a minor, with his whole kin and friends, to the maintenance and protection of the King, in consideration of the faithful services of his predecessors and of his own loyalty. The principal charge of the young Earl and his vast

---

[1] Moysie's Memoirs, p. 91; Anderson's MS. History of Scotland, Advocates' Library, III., fo. 246.

[2] Anderson's History of Scotland, III., fo. 246; Pitcairn's Criminal Trials, I. 391.

estates was left to his mother, the Countess of Argyle, who was to have the advice and assistance of the six following persons—viz., Duncan Campbell of Glenurchy; Dougal Campbell of Auchinbreck; John Campbell of Calder; Sir James Campbell of Ardkinlass, Comptroller to the King; Archibald Campbell of Lochnell; and Neill Campbell, Bishop of Argyle. As the will provided that no matter of importance, such as the granting of leases, could be carried into effect without the signatures of Calder, Ardkinlass, and the Bishop, their influence in the affairs of the Earldom speedily eclipsed that of the other counsellors.[1] Ardkinlass, too, procured, through his interest at Court, a grant of the valuable feudal right of the ward and marriage of the young Earl;[2] and the King having, in compliance with the request of the late Earl, promised to maintain and protect his family and clan, and signified his approval of the arrangements made for the management of the Earldom of Argyle,[3] the whole power of the Earldom was thrown into the hands of Ardkinlass and his associates, Calder and the Bishop. Lochnell, conceiving himself entitled to the principal guardianship as nearest heir, took offence at his exclusion from power; and his hostile feelings against those who had usurped the place he thought himself entitled to hold were secretly fostered by Duncan Campbell of Glenurchy, a man whose ambition and grasping character would not allow him to be satisfied with anything less than the entire control of the clan during the minority of his chief. After a time, it became necessary that

---

[1] Commissary Register of Edinburgh, Lib. XV. Will, dated 5th and 8th September, 1584.

[2] Reg. of Privy Seal, LI., fo. 64.   [3] Ibid, LI., fo. 77.

the young Earl, on attaining the age of pupilarity, should nominate his own guardians, when a new struggle took place between the two factions of the Campbells. Lochnell and Glenurchy proposed to associate with themselves, as guardians, the Earl of Montrose, Campbell of Loudoun, heritable Sheriff of Ayr, and Mr. John Graham, advocate. Ardkinlass and Calder, on the other hand, proposed, and succeeded in procuring, their own appointment, together with the Earl of Mar, the Master of Glammis, and Mr. George Erskine, advocate, Mar's brother. Jealousies now arose between Ardkinlass and Calder, which led to each of these barons attempting, without success, to procure the assassination of the other; and upon the death of the former in 1591, his feelings of hostility to Calder were transmitted to his son and successor. John Campbell, the new laird of Ardkinlass, was a man of a weak and vacillating disposition, who was very soon deprived by Calder of the influence which, as heir to his father, he had hoped to exercise in the Earldom of Argyle—a serious addition to the causes of enmity already subsisting between these barons.[1] All the real power of the Earldom now centred in the person of Calder, who was supported by many of the nobility connected with the family of Argyle, and particularly by the Earl of Murray.

A feud had, for a considerable period, subsisted between the families of Huntly and Murray, originating in their rival claims to the rich and fertile Earldom of Murray, of which one of the Earls of Huntly had been

---

[1] Confessions of Margaret Campbell, widow of John Oig Campbell of Cabrachan, dated 5th October, 1595, corroborated by the Confessions of John Campbell of Ardkinlass, dated 21st May, 1594.

deprived, when it was bestowed, by Queen Mary, upon her brother, the Lord James Stuart, afterwards Regent of Scotland. In these disputes the Earls of Argyle had uniformly supported the claims of the Regent Murray and his heirs, and had thus incurred the enmity of Huntly and the Gordons.[1] In the year 1590, various circumstances concurred to embitter this hereditary feud; and it became an important object with the Earl of Huntly to deprive his adversary of the support which he received from John Campbell of Calder, the administrator of the Earldom of Argyle.[2] Huntly was thus drawn into communication with Lochnell and Glenurchy, whose animosity against Calder has been already noticed; and the result of this communication was a conspiracy, by which it was contemplated, through the most atrocious acts, to gratify the revenge both of Huntly and of the discontented barons of Argyle. The conspirators were bound, in the most solemn manner, to compass, by every means in

[1] Dame Annas Keyth, Countess of Murray, widow of the Regent, was second wife of Colin the sixth, and mother of Archibald the seventh Earl of Argyle.

[2] On 1st November, 1590, the Earls of Athole and Murray, Lord Lovat, John Grant of Freuchie, John Campbell of Calder, Thomas Stewart of Grantullie, Patrick Grant of Rothiemurchus,
Sutherland of Duffus, and Archibald Grant of Bellintone, entered into an alliance, offensive and defensive, evidently directed against the Earl of Huntly.—Contract in Charter Chest of Grant of Monymusk. On the other hand, Huntly, on 6th March, 1590-1, entered into an indenture with Allan Cameron of Lochiel, by which the latter became bound to assist Huntly against all his enemies, and particularly against the Clanchattan and the Grants; whilst the Earl agreed to reward Lochiel to his entire satisfaction, and promised to make no agreement with his opponents without including Lochiel. MS. History of Camerons.

their power, the destruction of James, Earl of Murray;
Archibald, Earl of Argyle; Colin Campbell of Lundy,
his only brother and heir apparent; and John Campbell
of Calder.   In order to strengthen themselves against
the enemies whom the execution of their criminal projects would certainly raise in every part of the nation,
they drew into the plot John, Lord Thirlestane, Chancellor of Scotland, at that time a great supporter of the
Earl of Huntly; and John, Lord Maxwell, who claimed
the title of Earl of Morton.   Lauchlan Maclean of
Dowart—whose ancestor had been assassinated by Calder's grandfather, and who was likewise hostile to Calder from the latter having taken up the cause of the
Macdonalds of Isla—was easily induced to join the conspiracy;[1] as were likewise John Stewart of Appin, who
was connected by marriage with the house of Lochnell,
and Duncan Macdougall of Dunolly, with others of
lesser note.   The burden of putting to death the individuals whose lives were aimed at, was laid upon the
Highlanders; and, in return for their services, Huntly,
the Chancellor, and Maxwell, were to defend them from
the consequences.   Besides this, Huntly and the Lowland conspirators were to exert their utmost endeavours
to procure for Lochnell the peaceable possession of the
Earldom of Argyle; which being accomplished, Lochnell agreed to reward certain of his associates in the following manner.   To the Chancellor, he was to give the
lands of Pincarton in Stirlingshire belonging to the
Earl of Argyle; to Glenurchy, the barony of Lochow

---

[1] It will be recollected that, in 1591, Ardkinlass became surety for
the payment of the arrears due by Maclean to the Crown. Supra,
p. 244.

and the lands of Benderaloch; to Stewart of Appin, the Earl of Argyle's part of the Lordship of Lorn; and to Macdougall, the lands of Loyng.

The manner in which the Earl of Murray's death was brought about has been already noticed. It cannot now be doubted that the Chancellor and Huntly procured the employment of the latter to apprehend Murray, with the express design of cutting off that unfortunate nobleman. This plan likewise afforded a greater chance of attaining the object in view, and with less risk than if the original device of employing Highland assassins to shoot him while hunting in his woods of Doune had been followed. It now remains to point out the progress of the unhallowed conspiracy we have described, in another important point—the death of Campbell of Calder. Glenurchy, knowing the feelings of personal animosity cherished by Ardkinlass against Calder, easily prevailed upon the former to agree to the assassination of their common enemy, with whom Glenurchy himself had now an additional cause of quarrel, arising from the protection given by Calder to some of the Clangregor, who were at feud with Glenurchy. But although himself the principal mover in this branch of the plot, Glenurchy contrived to shift the execution of it on his associate, who was, as yet, ignorant of the intentions of the conspirators against the Earl of Argyle, and only sought to gratify his own revenge against Calder.[1] After various unsuccessful attempts, Ardkinlass procured, through the agency of John Oig Campbell of Cabrachan, a brother of Lochnell, the services of a man named MacEllar, by whom Calder was assassinated.

[1] Confessions of Margaret Campbell and of Ardkinlass, above cited— copies of which are in the author's possession.

The deed was committed with a hackbut supplied by
Ardkinlass; and the fatal shot was fired at night,
through one of the windows of the house of Knepoch
in Lorn, at the unsuspecting Calder, who fell pierced
through the heart with three bullets.[1]   The assassin
eluded pursuit for a season by the connivance of Macdougall of Dunolly, one of the conspirators.   Although
some time elapsed after the perpetration of this murder
before the share which Ardkinlass had in it was certainly known, yet he was generally suspected, owing
to his hereditary feud with Calder; and he was, in consequence, threatened with the vengeance of the young
Earl of Argyle, who already began to display a spirit
beyond his years.[2]   In these circumstances Glenurchy
ventured to communicate to Ardkinlass the plan for
getting rid of the Earl and his brother, and for assisting
Lochnell to seize the Earldom of Argyle.   For his
assistance in carrying into effect this part of the conspiracy, there was promised to Ardkinlass, when the
plot should be brought to a successful issue, a grant of
the lands of Boquhan and part of Roseneath.   Becoming terrified as to the consequences of the crime
already committed, Ardkinlass refused, although repeatedly urged, to become a party to any designs against
the life of the Earl, proposing to make his peace with
Argyle by disclosing the full extent of the plot.   There
is reason to believe that the conspirators, notwithstanding the refusal of Ardkinlass to join them, continued
for some time their machinations for the murder of the

[1] Letters of Treason against Ardkinlass, dated 6th April; and Commission for his Trial, to the Bishop of Dunkeld and other special
Justices, dated 29th March, 1596.

[2] Record of Privy Seal, June 9, 1592.

Earl; and that, during a severe illness with which he was attacked at Stirling, soon after his marriage, in the year 1594, some of his household were bribed to poison him—if indeed the disease itself was not caused in the first instance by poison. Argyle, however, escaped all the attempts of his enemies, and lived to exercise, for many years, an overpowering influence in the affairs of the Highlands and Isles. As a curious specimen of the manners of the times, it deserves to be noticed, that Ardkinlass endeavoured, and seriously expected, to convert, by means of witchcraft, the hostility of his' chief into friendship; and that he seems to have been much disappointed when this miserable resource failed him. It does not appear by what accident or indiscretion the discovery was first made; but at length, John Oig Campbell and MacEllar, the subordinate instruments in the murder of Calder, being charged with the crime, were apprehended and thrown into prison. John Oig being put to the torture by the boots, confessed his own share and that of Ardkinlass and Macdougall in the affair. These two chiefs A. D. 1593. were in consequence apprehended and detained in prison for some time; but by the same powerful agency which smothered inquiry into the Earl of Huntly's conduct with regard to the slaughter of Murray, they were at length liberated without punishment; although, at one time, a special commission had actually been issued for the trial of Ardkinlass. The inferior agents, John Oig Campbell and MacEllar, were both executed; nor could all the influence of Calder's relations or friends obtain the punishment of any of the higher parties.[1] In the month of May, 1594, Ardkin-

---

[1] Confessions above cited. MS. History of Campbells of Calder.

lass, despairing otherwise of procuring a reconciliation with Argyle, and moved, as he affirmed, in conscience, made a confession of all that he knew, not only of the plots against Calder's life, but of the great contract, as it was called, which contemplated the destruction likewise of the Earls of Murray and Argyle. This confession was afterwards corroborated by the evidence of Margaret Campbell (the widow of John Oig), through whom Ardkinlass had consulted the witches. The many minute particulars in the statements of Ardkinlass and this woman leave no doubt of the existence of that remarkable conspiracy, the history of which we have endeavoured to elucidate. The general impression, and the outcry against Lord Chancellor Thirlestane at the time, for his accession to the Earl of Murray's death, may serve as a corroboration of the statements made by Ardkinlass and others. Lastly, an additional proof of the undue influence used on this occasion to impede the course of justice, may be found in the fact, that Glenurchy was allowed to clear himself of all concern in the plots attributed to him by his own unsupported and extrajudicial denial.[1] It seems to have been considered proper to keep the Earl of Argyle in ignorance of the designs entertained against his life, in so far, at least, as Lochnell and Glenurchy were concerned. This concealment, as we shall presently see, gave Lochnell

---

Moysie's Memoirs, p. 162. Criminal Trials, I., pp. 363, 391; II., p. 129. Historie of King James the Sext, p. 248.

[1] A copy of this singular writing, dated and signed at the Castle of Carrick, in Cowal, before the Earl of Mar, Hew Campbell of Loudoun, and Mr. George Erskine, 28th June, 1594, is in the author's possession. Glenurchy offered to abide his trial, which he well knew the Chancellor and Huntly were deeply interested in preventing.

another opportunity of attempting to advance himself to the Earldom.

The murder of the Earl of Murray was the cause of serious commotions in many parts of the North Highlands, whilst that of Calder had a similar effect in the west. In the north, the Macintoshes and Grants, who were of Murray's faction, eagerly endeavoured to revenge his death by hostile inroads into various parts of Huntly's estates. Huntly retaliated, by causing the Clanchameron to invade and plunder Badenoch, where the principal part of the Clanchattan's lands lay; and by sending the Clanranald of Lochaber, under Keppoch, their chief, to waste and spoil the lands of Strathspey belonging to the Grants.[1] In this way a great portion of the Highlands was thrown into confusion by the instigation of those who should have been the foremost to preserve order. Alexander MacRanald of Keppoch seized the Castle of Inverness for Huntly; but was afterwards forced by Macintosh to evacuate it for want of provisions before September, 1593, with the loss of one of his sons, and of an officer named Gothred or Gorrie Dubh, who were taken and hung; and Macintosh then concluded an agreement with the Magistrates of Inverness for holding the town against Huntly.[2] He likewise entered into a league with Argyle in this year;[3] and Huntly, fearful of losing all the influence which, as Lords of Badenoch, he and his predecessors exercised over the Clanchattan, began now to court the Macphersons, and to sow jealousies between them and the

---

[1] Sir R. Gordon's History of Sutherland, p. 217; MS. History of Camerons; Latin History of Macintoshes; MS. History of Gordons, by W. R., p. 183.
[2] Latin History of Macintoshes.   [3] Ibid.

Macintoshes. The Macphersons readily entered into Huntly's views; and, under his protection, became in time powerful enough to disclaim any dependence upon Macintosh as captain and chief of the Clanchattan, and even to dispute, although without success, the right of that chief to the high station which his family had held for centuries. In Argyle, besides the dissensions in the clan Campbell, the assassination of Calder caused a feud between the Stewarts of Appin and the Campbells of Calder's house, the effects of which were long felt. Nor was it only on the mainland that the consequences of the events we have narrated were perceived. The three island chiefs who had been liberated on security for their performance of certain conditions, and for their future good behaviour, by the efforts of the Barons of Calder and Ardkinlass, felt themselves in a great measure freed by late events from the reponsibility under which they lay. They not only failed to perform the' conditions imposed upon them; but, on the contrary, distinguished themselves by open and avowed disobedience to the Government. They were, therefore, summoned to appear before the Privy Council on the 14th day of July, in order to fulfil these conditions; and, in the event of their non-appearance on that day, the pardons granted to them were to be declared null, and immediate steps threatened to be taken for the forfeiture of their lands and goods, and the execution of the hostages given by Angus Macdonald—Maclean never having presented hostages, according to his promise.[1] These proceedings of the Privy Council were ratified by the Parliament held in June, 1592,

---

[1] Record of Privy Council, 8th June, 1592.

when the three estates promised to assist his Majesty
with their "bodies, counsel, and whole force to make
his authority be obeyed by his subjects, and to cause
the treasonable and barbarous rebels of the Hielandis
and Ilis to be punished and repressed, as they have
worthily deserved."[1] In pursuance of this engagement, there were produced in Parliament, a year afterwards, summonses of treason duly executed against
Angus Macdonald of Dunyveg and the Glens, Donald
Gorme of Sleat, John MacIan of Ardnamurchan, and
others their associates, for certain crimes of treason and
lese-majesty committed by them.[2] For the present,
however, the proceedings against the Earls of Huntly,
Angus, and Erroll, and the other Catholics who were
accused of plotting with Philip of Spain for the restoration of the Catholic religion in Scotland, prevented
the King from prosecuting his plans for the improvement of the Isles with the necessary vigour.

A. D. 1594.   In June, 1594, the three Catholic Earls,
along with Sir Patrick Gordon of Auchin-
doun, were forfeited by Parliament; and a similar
sentence was, at the same time, pronounced against
Maclean of Dowart and Macdonald of Dunyveg, who
still remained contumacious.[3] Huntly and his associates having drawn together in arms, and forcibly
liberated some Catholics imprisoned by the magistrates
of Aberdeen, commission was given by the King to the

---

[1] Acts of Parl. of Scotland, III. 561.

[2] Ibid, IV. 4.

[3] Johnston's MS. History of Scotland, fo. 620. Birrel's Diary.
Moysie's Memoirs, p. 118. Historie of King James the Sext, p.
330. The forfeiture of Macdonald of Sleat is asserted by some
writers, whilst others are silent regarding it.

young Earl of Argyle (now in his eighteenth year), the Earl of Athole, and the Lord Forbes, to march against the rebels, and reduce them to obedience. It may be remarked that both Argyle and Athole had Huntly at feud for the slaughter of the Earl of Murray, for which cause it is probable they were selected on this occasion. Argyle having raised an army of six or seven thousand men, partly among his own vassals, and partly among other clans—particularly the Macleans, Macneills, Macgregors, Macintoshes, and Grants—marched into Badenoch, and laid siege to the Castle of Ruthven, which was gallantly held out for Huntly by the Macphersons. Failing in his endeavours to possess himself of this strength, he then proceeded through the hills towards Strathbogie, with the intention of carrying fire and sword through Huntly's lands in that quarter. On his arrival near Glenlivat, Argyle found that Huntly and Erroll were in the vicinity with fourteen or fifteen hundred men.[1] This force was principally cavalry; but there were also Highlanders in Huntly's army, particularly of the Clanchameron and Clanranald of Lochaber, and the Macphersons. Trusting to the superiority of his numbers, the Earl of Argyle did not avoid a combat, although advised to do so until joined by Lord Forbes, who was at no great distance with eleven hundred men. But he acted upon the defensive, and took up a strong position, which he thought his opponents would find it impracticable to force. Huntly and Erroll, however,

---

[1] Argyle himself "had in his company to the number of sax thowsand men, weill provided with muscatis, bowis, arrowis, and twa-handit swordis; of the quhilk nomber there ware fyftene hundreth muscateirs and hagbutters."—Historie of King James the Sext, p. 338.

were followed by a number of gallant gentlemen, well mounted and armed, and not to be deterred by the mere strength of a position from attacking even a superior force of comparatively undisciplined Highlanders. They were further encouraged to make the attempt by a communication received from Archibald Campbell of Lochnell, commander of one of the divisions of Argyle's army. This ambitious baron—whose previous machinations for the destruction of his chief and his own advancement to the Earldom had not yet come to the knowledge of Argyle—thought the present an excellent opportunity of accomplishing his long-cherished views. He therefore sent a private message to Huntly, desiring him to attack the Highlanders, and promising, in the course of the engagement, to aid him with the division under his command. He likewise suggested that some pieces of artillery which accompanied Huntly's army should be fired at Argyle's banner; hoping thus both to get rid of that nobleman by an apparent chance shot, and to discourage the faithful Highlanders, who were many of them unacquainted with the use of artillery.[1] The advice of Lochnell was followed; but the result was unexpected. As Huntly approached to the attack of the position occupied by the Highlanders, the guns were fired with fatal effect at the yellow standard of Argyle. The Earl himself escaped, in a miraculous manner, without hurt, whilst the deadly missiles struck down in their progress his treacherous kinsman Lochnell (who, by an extraordinary chance, thus fell a sacrifice to his own villanous stratagem), a brother of the latter, and a gallant warrior of the Macneills, son of the chief of Barra.

[1] Calderwood's MS. Church History, Advocates' Lib., XI. 422.

During the confusion caused by this incident Huntly commenced the attack, and, after a severe conflict, and sustaining a heavy loss, succeeded in routing Argyle's forces, who, from the strength of their position, and the mountainous nature of the country, which impeded pursuit, escaped with a loss comparatively trifling. The conduct of Lauchlan Maclean of Dowart, who was one of Argyle's officers in this action, would, if imitated by the other leaders, have converted the defeat into a victory. That chief acted the part of a brave and skilful soldier, keeping his men in their ranks, and employing with good effect all the advantages of his position. It was his division which inflicted the principal loss on the rebels; and, at the close of the action, he retired in good order with those under his command.[1] It is said that, after the battle, he offered, if Argyle would give him five hundred men in addition to his own clan, to bring the Earl of Huntly prisoner into Argyle's camp. This proposal was rejected; but having come to the ears of Huntly incensed him greatly against Maclean, whose son afterwards, according to tradition, lost a large estate in Lochaber through the animosity of that powerful nobleman.[2]

The triumph of the Popish Earls for their success at Glenlivat was but of short duration. The King, who was at Dundee when the Earl of Argyle himself brought intelligence of his discomfiture, lost no time in proceeding to the disturbed districts with a force sufficient to

---

[1] For various accounts of the battle of Glenlivat, and the circumstances connected with it, see Sir R. Gordon's History of Sutherland, p. 226; Anderson's MS. History of Scotland, III., fo. 265; MS. History of Gordons, by W. R.; Moysie's Memoirs, pp. 119, 120; Historie of King James the Sext, p. 338; Calderwood, ubi supra.

[2] MS. History of Macleans.

awe the malcontents, who did not venture to appear in the field against the Royal banner. The Castles of Strathbogie and Slaines, belonging to Huntly and Erroll, and other fortresses belonging to the insurgents, were demolished; whilst the barons and gentlemen who followed the banners of these noblemen were forfeited, and their estates divided among the royalists. In order to escape the penalties of treason loudly denounced against them by the Presbyterians, who now formed the bulk of the nation, Huntly and Erroll were compelled to fly abroad, whilst Angus lurked as a fugitive in the wilds of Douglasdale.[1] Indeed, were it not that James wished to avoid irritating the English Catholics, and thus impeding his ascent to the throne of England on the death of Queen Elizabeth, the Scottish Catholic Earls would, in the excited state of the nation at that time, have been brought to the block. But the King was noways anxious himself to proceed to such extremities. In the meantime, the Duke of Lennox and the Earl of Argyle were employed to reduce Huntly's vassals to obedience; and, in pursuance of his commission, the latter sent deputies to Huntly's lands. These deputies were at the Castle of Auchindoun in November, 1595, when, among others, Alexander MacRanald of Keppoch, an old vassal of the Earl of Huntly in Lochaber, gave his bond of service to the Earl of Argyle, and delivered to the deputies one of his sons as a hostage for his obedience; in return for which he claimed protection and maintenance from Argyle in all the lands and possessions to which he laid claim.[2] It is probable that similar steps were taken

A. D. 1595.

---

[1] Moysie's Memoirs, p. 120-122.
[2] Collectanea de Rebus Albanicis, I., p. 200.

with Allan Cameron of Lochiel and the other western
Highlanders who had assisted Huntly at the battle of
Glenlivat.

During the brief rebellion we have just noticed, two
powerful chiefs in the Isles, Donald Gorme Macdonald
of Sleat, and Roderick Macleod of Harris (the well
known Ruari Mor of tradition), employed themselves
in another direction. They led, each of them, five
hundred Hebridean warriors to the shores of Ulster, to
assist Red Hugh O'Donnell, the chief of his ancient
race, who was at this time in rebellion against the Queen
of England. Landing in Lough Foyle, between Kinel
Conel and Kinel Owen, and being informed that
O'Donnell was then besieging Enniskillen, they sent a
messenger to him to notify their arrival, and to announce
that, if he did not come to meet them as he had promised,
they would instantly return to their own country. On
receiving this intelligence, O'Donnell immediately left
Enniskillen with a few attendants, in order to welcome
his allies, the bulk of his army being left to continue
the siege. He met the Islanders accordingly, and
entertained them for three days and three nights; after
which, Donald Gorme bade him farewell and returned
to the Isles, leaving his brother in command of his clansmen. Macleod of Harris remained in person with his
followers.[1] Before the Scots had been long in Ireland,
we find Hugh, Earl of Tyrone, promising to the Lord
Lieutenant to do his best to cause O'Donnell dismiss
immediately the Scottish auxiliaries.[2] In the following
year, however, Tyrone himself was joined with O'Don-

---

[1] Life of Red Hugh O'Donnell, written in Irish, by Peregrine
O'Clery, and translated by the late Edward O'Reilly, Esq.

[2] Harleain M.S., $\frac{7004}{110}$; Leland's Ireland, II. 329.

nell; and, on the application of the English ambassador in Scotland, Macdonald of Sleat and Macdonald of Dunyveg were charged by the Privy Council not to assist the Irish rebels.[1]

[1] Record of Privy Council, 18th June, 1595.

CHAP. VI.

FROM THE SUPPRESSION OF THE REBELLION OF THE CATHOLIC EARLS, TO THE DEPARTURE OF KING JAMES VI. FOR ENGLAND.—1595—1603.

A. D. 1595.

THE rebellion of the Catholic noblemen being now suppressed, the King found himself more at leisure to attend to the improvement of the Isles, and the expected increase to the Royal revenue from that portion of his dominions. Early in 1596, James Macdonald—who had remained as a hostage for his father, Angus Macdonald of Dunyveg, during the last four years—received a licence to visit his father and his clan, in the hope that he might prevail on the former to make his submission and fulfil the conditions formerly prescribed to him.[1] That chief, and others of similar rank in the Isles, still delayed to enter into the views of their sovereign and his councillors, although some of them were in treaty with the Lords of Exchequer. In order, therefore, to compel their submission, and avoid further delay in a matter of such importance to the revenue, the King, by the advice both of the Privy Council and of the Estates of Parliament then sitting,

A. D. 1596.

---

[1] Notes from Exchequer Rolls, in Haddington's MS. Collections, Advocates' Library.

resolved to proceed against the Islanders in person. A proclamation to this effect was accordingly issued in the month of May, by which all Earls, Lords, Barons, and freeholders, worth above three hundred merks of yearly rent, and the whole burgesses of the realm, were summoned to meet his Majesty at Dunbarton, on the first day of August, well armed, and with forty days' provisions, and likewise provided with vessels to carry them to the Isles. Disobedience to this summons was to infer loss of life, lands, and goods.[1] The effects of this proclamation were soon evident. Maclean and Macdonald of Sleat immediately repaired to Court, and, upon making their submission, and satisfying the demands of the Exchequer, by agreeing to augment their rents, and to make certain other concessions required of them, were received into favour, and restored against the acts of forfeiture under which they had lain for two years.[2] Roderick Macleod of Harris, and Donald (MacAngus) Macranald of Glengarry, made their submission about the same time.[3] The Lewis was now held by Torquil Dubh Macleod, whose title was disputed by his elder brother, Torquil Connanach. The origin of this dispute has been traced in a former chapter; and it seems about this time to have broken

[1] Record of Privy Council, 22nd May, 1596; Acts of Parliament, IV. 97.

[2] Record of Privy Council, 15th June, 1596; Reg. of Privy Seal, LXIX., fo. 17, 152; Original Papers in General Register House, connected with the submission of Donald Gorme. At this time the Lords of Exchequer recognised Donald Gorme as the heir of Hugh of Sleat, his grandfather's great-grandfather. Ibid, and MS. Advocates' Library, M. 6, 15.

[3] Balcarras Papers, Advocates' Library, Vol. VI., No. 70; Reg. of Privy Seal, LXVIII., fo. 127.

out with renewed violence. As each of the claimants, however, professed his willingness to agree to the terms proposed by the Exchequer—hoping thus to obtain a recognition of his right as heir of the estate—the Siol Torquil was withdrawn from the list of disobedient clans.[1] Of all the great chiefs in the Isles, Angus Macdonald of Dunyveg alone remained contumacious. The displeasure of the King was marked, in the first instance, by his granting to Maclean a lease of the Rinns of Isla, so long disputed between that chief and the Macdonalds.[2] At the same time preparations continued to be made for the expedition to the Isles, which, through the submission of most of the other tribes, dwindled down into an expedition against the Clandonald of Kintyre and Isla. As the time for proceeding to the Isles drew near, the King found that it would be more convenient and less dangerous for him to remain at some place near the Highland coasts, until it should be reported by his Lieutenant and Commissioner, whether or not his Majesty's presence was necessary. The person chosen to lead the expedition on this occasion was Sir William Stewart of Houston, Knight, Commendator of Pittenweem, who received, accordingly, in the month of June, a commission of lieutenandry and justiciary, with the fullest powers.[3] One of the principal points to which his attention was directed, was to obtain possession of and garrison the principal castles in the West Highlands and Isles;[4] a step the necessity for which seems in most cases to have been obviated by the submission of the chiefs previous to the setting out of the expedition. A

[1] Balcarras Papers, ubi supra.
[2] Sir R. Gordon's History of Sutherland, p. 237.
[3] Record of Privy Council, 30th June, 1596.
[4] Balcarras Papers, ubi supra.

difficulty in procuring the necessary funds seems to have delayed the expedition much beyond the day originally fixed. Early in August, we find that the necessary forces for accompanying the Lieutenant were not yet raised. A proclamation was now issued, which, in consideration of the near approach of harvest, and other weighty causes, allowed those called out by the first proclamation to compound for their personal service in the following manner. Each county might escape the burden of personal service, by sending twenty horsemen and thirty footmen to meet the King at Dunbarton, on the 20th August, or else pay the King £24 for every horseman and £12 for every footman that might be wanting of these numbers. The whole burghs of the realm were allowed to compound, by sending 500 men, one-third armed with muskets, one-third with pikes and corselets, and the remaining third with hackbuts and headpieces; or by paying £12 for every man of the 500 that should fail to appear. The burghs were likewise charged to furnish three ships of middling size, well supplied with ammunition. The inhabitants of the shires of Berwick, Roxburgh, and Selkirk, and the burghs in these shires, were specially exempted from this service against the Isles, so that they might attend to the peace of the Borders. The inhabitants of Inverness-shire, and the town of Inverness, were licensed to remain at home on this occasion; but were directed to hold themselves in readiness for similar service in the spring of the following year. Finally, the whole inhabitants of the sheriffdoms of Tarbert and Bute were peremptorily ordered to give their personal service, and were not permitted to compound either in men or money.

[1] Record of Privy Council, 2nd August, 1596.

Another proclamation authorised the Commendator of Pittenween to levy soldiers for the service in the Isles to the amount of one thousand men, and to appoint officers over them.[1] A third proclamation charged the Islesmen to remain quiet at home; assuring them, notwithstanding false reports to the contrary, that his Majesty did not intend to proceed to extremities against any of them, except such as continued in open and avowed rebellion. They were further assured that such sinister reports of his Majesty's intentions could only proceed from wicked persons, who envied their future "happie estate and felicitie, as the success" (of his Majesty's experiments), "with God's grace, sall evidentlie declare, in sic sorte, as, within few yeirs, they sall be able to compare their estate to the maist happie estate that has occurrit in man's memorie."[2]

Want of money, however, and a growing dislike, on the part of the people, to these harassing raids, as they were called, to which every slight disturbance in the kingdom made them liable, and of which an unusual number had occurred during the present reign, still further delayed this long talked of expedition. Towards the end of September, among other measures for raising money, it was proposed to borrow four thousand pounds from the Duke of Lennox. That nobleman was further requested to go in person to the Lennox, and cause two hundred of his vassals to accompany the Lieutenant to Kintyre. The Earl of Argyle likewise was earnestly required to give his concurrence to the Lieutenant, and to send two hundred men to Kintyre, under his kinsman, Campbell of Auchinbreck. A let-

---

[1] Record of Privy Council, 3rd August, 1596.   [2] Ibid.

ter was also written by the King to James Macdonald of
Dunluce (son of Sorley Buy Macdonald, and consequently cousin of Angus Macdonald, against whom all
these preparations were directed), promising him high
reward if he gave such assistance to the Lieutenant in
this service as should be required of him.[1] Early in
October, Lord Blantyre, High Treasurer, was in the
west, superintending the progress made by the Commendator of Pittenweem in the preparations for the expedition to Kintyre; and, from a letter addressed by the
Treasurer to the Secretary of State, it appears that the
sum of seven thousand merks was still wanting to enable the expedition to sail.[2] On the 22nd of October, the
Lieutenant was still in Glasgow, from which, however,
he had despatched some of his forces to Kintyre, to
ascertain whether Angus Macdonald meant to oppose
the Royal troops.[3] In the meantime, James Macdonald
had returned to Edinburgh; and, appearing before the
Privy Council, in the name and by the authority of his
father, made submission both for his father and himself
to the King's will, promising that they would fulfil whatever conditions should be prescribed to them by his
Majesty, to the uttermost of their power. For himself
he likewise promised to remain with the King, and on
no account to proceed to the Isles without licence.[4]
This submission came too late to prevent the Lieutenant,
who had heard a report that the Clandonald were
gathering in arms, from proceeding to Kintyre, where
he held a court on the first of November. Here Angus
Macdonald and his followers came to make their per-

[1] Balcarras Papers, No. $\frac{7.3}{1}$.   [2] Ibid, No. $\frac{7.3}{2}$.
[3] Ibid, No. 74.
[4] Record of Privy Council, 8th October, 1596.

sonal submission to the King's representative. A roll was made of the tenants of Kintyre, of the lands occupied by them individually, and of the waste and unoccupied lands; and, on his departure, the Lieutenant took with him hostages from the principal chieftains in the district.[1] These he presented to the Privy Council, by which all his proceedings were approved.[2] It appears, by a letter from James Macdonald of Dunluce to the King, that Angus Macdonald had made to him, before the Lieutenant's arrival in person, great promises if he would aid in expelling the King's troops from Kintyre.[3] All these offers were, however, refused by the wary Lord of Dunluce; and Angus Macdonald, deprived of support, was obliged to submit as the other chiefs had done. While Macdonald of Isla thus found his life and fortunes once more at the disposal of the King, his former antagonist, Maclean of Dowart, was nearly losing the advantages he had gained by a more timely submission. Taking advantage of the death of Hector Maclean of Coll, and the minority of Lauchlan, the son and successor of that baron, he had renewed the ancient feud between the families of Dowart and Coll, by seizing, without any just cause, the castle and island of Coll, and the other estates of that family, from which he expelled all their adherents. Lauchlan Maclean of Coll having now reached majority, appealed to the Privy Council against this oppression and injustice

---

[1] Original Record of this Court, preserved in General Register House. From this document, it appears that, out of 139 merk lands in North Kintyre, 36½ were waste; and out of 205 merk lands in South Kintyre, 45 were waste.

[2] Record of Privy Council, 11th November, 1596.

[3] Original Letter in Balcarras Papers, dated 26th October, 1596.

on the part of Dowart; and the result was an order on
the latter to deliver up, not only the Castle of Brekach
in Coll, but all his own castles and fortalices, to Sir
William Stewart, King's Lieutenant of the Isles, or such
as he should appoint to receive them, upon twenty-four
hours' warning.   He was further required to restore to
Coll, within thirty days, all the lands of which he had
so unjustly deprived him, and to abstain from molesting
him or his tenants; a penalty of ten thousand merks
being imposed upon Dowart if he should fail in any of
these particulars.[1]

In the North Isles, the Macleods of Lewis were once
more involved in those dissensions which eventually
ruined this ancient clan.   The Isle of Lewis was still
held by Torquil Dubh, while the mainland estates of
the family remained with Torquil Connanach, whose
claim to the whole, however, had been recently acknowledged by Government.[2]   The latter had lost both his
sons; and, having married his eldest daughter to Ruari
Mackenzie, brother of the Lord of Kintaill, now threw
himself entirely into the hands of the Mackenzies, to
whom, in the end, he conveyed the barony of Lewis,
as far as writings could accomplish this object.[3]   His
competitor, Torquil Dubh, had married a sister of
Macleod of Harris, and, strengthened by this alliance,
proceeded to ravage the lands of Cogeache and Lochbroom; and openly announced his intention of keeping
by force what he had hitherto possessed.   As this young
chief was very popular with his clan, and was followed
by seven or eight hundred men, he was enabled to set

---

[1] Record of Privy Council, 11th November, 1596.
[2] Reg. of Privy Seal, LXVIII., fo. 298.
[3] Sir R. Gordon's History of Sutherland, p. 274.

his rival for some time at defiance in spite of the power of the Mackenzies. At length his enemies, who seem to have been taken by surprise by the vigorous measures of Torquil Dubh, made a complaint against him to the Privy Council, of which body, unfortunately for him, the Lord of Kintaill was a member. In this complaint the "Usurper of the Lewis" was represented as having been guilty of barbarous and unheard of cruelty, sparing neither man, woman, nor child, in his destructive progress, and recklessly slaying all the cattle he could find, so as to lay the lands in question absolutely waste.[1] Being summoned to answer to this charge, Torquil Dubh naturally enough hesitated to trust himself in the power of a court where one of his enemies had so much influence. He was therefore denounced a rebel; and being soon afterwards treacherously seized, along with several of his followers, in the Lewis, by the Breve or Celtic judge of the island (who acted at the instigation of Mackenzie and Torquil Connanach), they were delivered into the hands of Mackenzie, by whom, without further ceremony, they were beheaded in the month of July, 1597. Instead of benefiting the conspirators, by smoothing the way for the succession of Torquil Connanach to the Lewis, this severity only irritated the remaining adherents of Torquil Dubh, amongst whom the most conspicuous was his bastard brother Neill. As Torquil Dubh had left three young sons—whose cause was supported not only by their uncle, Neill, who now took

A. D. 1597.

---

[1] Record of Privy Council, 11th February, 1596-7. Letter, Kenneth Mackenzie of Kintaill to the King, dated 3rd January, 1596-7; copied by Dr. George Mackenzie into his MS. History of the family.

the command of the Isle of Lewis, but by the Macleans and Macleods of Harris—the final success of the Mackenzies, and of the competitor whose claims they supported, appeared nearly as distant as before.[1] At this time, too, the Mackenzies attempted to seize the whole lands of Gerloch, which led to a renewal of the ancient feud between them and the Siol Vic Gillechallum of Rasay and Gerloch.[2] The chief effect of these perpetual dissensions was to hurry the adoption of the crude but well meant plans of the King for the improvement of the Highlands and Isles.

Angus Macdonald of Dunyveg, whose late submission to the King's Lieutenant has been noticed, came to Edinburgh early in this year to hear the King's will declared as to the particular terms on which he was to receive a pardon. Two plans seem to have been suggested for curbing the power of this restless chief. One was to deprive him, by his own consent, of all his possessions in Isla, and to confine him and his tribe within Kintyre, making provision at the same time for a Royal garrison, or some equivalent check, in the latter district.[3] The other proposal, which was that attempted to be carried into effect, was to deprive him of his lands in Kintyre and of any claim he might have to the Rinns of Isla, thus confining him and his clan to the other parts of Isla.[4] In order to test his sincerity, Macdonald was required, before anything could be done in his favour—*First*, To find security for the arrears of his Crown rents, which had been allowed to

---

[1] Sir R. Gordon's History of Sutherland, p. 270.   [2] Ibid, p. 277.

[3] Balcarras Papers, No. 77.

[4] Letter, Mr. John Skene to Secretary Lindsay, 28th April, 1597.— Balcarras Papers.

accumulate to a serious amount; *Next*, To remove his clan and dependers from Kintyre and the Rinns of Isla; and, *Lastly*, To deliver his Castle of Dunyveg in Isla, before the 20th of May, to the person whom the King should send to receive it.[1] These preliminary conditions he subscribed and promised to observe, and was thereupon liberated, to give him an opportunity of fulfilling them.[2] His son, Sir James Macdonald of Knockrinsay (who had lately received the honour of knighthood), remained at Court, as a sort of hostage for his father; soon after whose departure a claim of an unexpected nature was made by James Macdonald of Dunluce to all the estates formerly held by Angus Macdonald. In the letter which, as we have seen, the Lord of Dunluce addressed to the King at the time of Sir William Stewart's expedition to Kintyre, after magnifying his own services, and indulging in much of that fulsome flattery to the monarch which characterised this reign, he hinted at his own claims as heir to the lands of Kintyre and Isla, held by his cousin Angus, on the ground, as he alleged, of the illegitimacy of the latter (supra, p. 269). Having received from the King answers of a favourable tenor, Dunluce readily accepted an invitation to visit the Court of Scotland; and he and his train, on their arrival at Edinburgh, were received with great distinction. Dunluce himself is described by several Scottish writers of the period as a man of handsome appearance and dignified manners; and, although ignorant of the Lowland tongue, he speedily became a great favourite at the Scottish Court. While

---

[1] Balcarras Papers, VI., No. 77.

[2] Letter to Secretary Lindsay above quoted. Haddington's Collections.

in Edinburgh, his claim to the estates of Kintyre and Isla was formally brought before the Privy Council; but as it was founded on an erroneous allegation— namely, the bastardy of Angus Macdonald—it was speedily dismissed by the advisers of the Crown. At the very moment when. Dunluce's claim was read in council, the Earl of Argyle, who professed to espouse the cause of Angus Macdonald, happened to enter the council chamber and take his seat; and it was remarked that Dunluce made no sign of respect to that powerful nobleman. To make up in some measure for his disappointment, he received from the King the honour of knighthood, as an *eques auratus*, by the style of Sir James Macdonald of Dunluce, together with a grant of thirty merk lands in Kintyre; and on his departure from Edinburgh, he was saluted with a volley from the Castle guns.[1]

Towards the end of this year, Maclean of Dowart and Macdonald of Isla, having patched up a hollow truce, made preparations for proceeding together, with a force of two or three thousand of their vassals, into Ulster, under pretence of assisting the Queen of England against Hugh Earl of Tyrone, whose rebellion at this time presented a formidable appearance. The Irish Privy Council viewed this union between two chiefs of such power, whose enmity had so lately borne the most implacable character, as proceeding either from the intrigues of the Earl of Huntly, who, as a Catholic, bore no good will to Queen Elizabeth, or from a plot

[1] Said Letter to Secretary Lindsay. Reg. of Privy Seal, LXIX., fo. 101. Birrel's Diary, ad tempus. MS. History of Scotland, (Anon.), Advocates' Library. Anderson's MS. History of Scotland, III., fo. 282.

laid by Tyrone himself, who, they conceived, calculated on the Islanders as his friends from the moment they should arrive in Ulster.[1]   When we consider, however, the position in which Macdonald now stood at home, and that Dunluce, who had so lately attempted a grievous injury, and one not to be forgiven, against him, was one of Tyrone's supporters at this time—while we may feel unable to account for the alliance between Macdonald and Maclean, we can have no difficulty in believing that the former was sincere in his intention of supporting the Queen in this struggle; for his services, if really useful, would not only conduce to forward his interests with King James, at whose mercy he now lay, but would also give him a title, on the suppression of Tyrone's rebellion, and the expected forfeiture of his adherents, to claim restoration to those Irish estates formerly wrested from him by his uncle, Sorley Buy, the father of Sir James Macdonald of Dunluce.   It is probable that the representations of the English ambassador at the Scottish Court caused the projected expedition of the Islanders to be given up; for we do not find, from the writers on Irish history, that the warriors whose arrival the Privy Council of Ireland seemed to expect with so much alarm, ever quitted their native shores.

In the Parliament held at Edinburgh in December, 1597, an act was passed of a most important nature, in reference to the Highlands and Isles; and the effects of it were soon apparent.   The preamble of this act bears, that the inhabitants of the Highlands and Isles had not only neglected to pay the yearly rents, and to perform the services due from their lands to the Crown,

[1] Summary Report of the State of Ireland, 5th November, 1597. Cotton MS., Titus, B. XIII.

but that they had likewise, through their "barbarous inhumanity," made the Highlands and Isles, naturally so valuable from the fertility of the soil and the richness of the fisheries, altogether unprofitable either to themselves or to their fellow-countrymen. The natives of these districts are further described as neither cultivating any "civil or honest society" among themselves, nor admitting others to traffic with them in safety. It was, therefore, by this act, made imperative upon all landlords, chieftains, leaders of clans, principal householders, heritors, and others possessing, or pretending right to, any lands in the Highlands and Isles, to produce their various title-deeds before the Lords of Exchequer upon the 15th day of May, 1598. They were further enjoined, at the same time, to find security for the regular payment of their rents to the Crown, and for the peaceable and orderly behaviour of themselves and of those for whom, by the law, they were bound to answer, particularly in regard to those individuals desirous of trading in the Highlands and Isles. The penal part of this act, however, was the most important. Disobedience to any of the injunctions above detailed was made, by a very harsh exercise of the highest powers of Parliament, to infer absolute forfeiture of all the titles, real or pretended, which any of the recusants might possess to lands in the Highlands and Isles.[1] Taking into consideration both the loss of title-deeds — which, in the unsettled state of the country, must have been a very common occurrence—and the difficulty which many even of the most powerful chiefs could not fail to experience in finding the requisite bail for their peaceable and orderly behaviour, as well as that of

---

[1] Acts of Parliament, IV. 138; Collect. de Rebus Albanicis, I. 158.

their vassals and tenants—it is evident that this act
was prepared with a view to place at the disposal of
the Crown, in a summary manner, many large tracts
of land; affording thus an immediate opportunity to
the King to commence his favourite plans for the
improvement of the Highlands and Isles. It is not
much to the credit of James that the State papers
relating to these projects show clearly that they sprung,
as has been already hinted at, not from the higher
motives which have made some monarchs the benefactors of mankind, but from the necessity of replen-
ishing an exchequer which had been drained chiefly
by his private extravagance, and by his excessive liberality to unworthy favourites. Another act of Parliament for the erection of three Royal burghs—one of
them in Kintyre, the second in Lochaber, and the third
in the Lewis—received, at this time, the sanction of
the legislature.[1] The state of the country for many
years did not permit this design to be carried into full
effect; but the suggestions now made seem eventually
to have led to the erection of Campbellton, Fortwilliam,
and Stornoway, the first only of which was made a
Royal burgh. In order to secure good advice to the
King, in regard to the establishment of these burghs
and his other projected improvements, a council of ten
was appointed, whose special attention was to be directed
to the affairs of the Highlands and Isles, and without
the advice of five of whom nothing could be done
therein. The chief of these counsellors were, Mr. John
Lindsay of Balcarras, Secretary of State, and Sir William
Stewart, Commendator of Pittenweem.[2] Some mem-

---

[1] Acts of Parliament, IV. 139; Collect. de Rebus Albanicis, I. 159.
[2] Record of Privy Council, 4th May, 1598.

bers of this council came soon to have a deep personal interest in the improvement of the Isles; but their united exertions failed, after a great loss both of men and means, to produce any permanent advantage.

The first mentioned of these acts was not suffered to remain a dead letter. The record of the proceedings in Exchequer, on the 15th of May, 1598, has not come down to us; so that it is by no means easy to ascertain how many chiefs or proprietors failed to appear. This much is certain, that the Isles of Lewis and Harris, and the lands of Dunvegan and Glenelg, were declared to be at the King's disposal. The three last estates belonged to Ruari Macleod of Harris by unexceptionable titles; but it is probable that he incurred the penalties of the act, from thinking it unnecessary to appear. The abilities of this chief enabled him, although with much difficulty, and after the lapse of many years, to ward off the effects of this summary process of forfeiture. The Macleods of Lewis were less fortunate. Their island, the largest of the Hebrides, and the district of Trouterness in Sky, in which Macdonald of Sleat had but lately been received as King's tenant, were granted to a company of Lowland adventurers—the object of whose association was to colonise and improve their acquisitions in the Hebrides according to the plans suggested by the King. The principal adventurers were—the Duke of Lennox; Patrick, Commendator of Lindores; William, Commendator of Pittenweem; Sir James Anstruther, younger, of that Ilk; Sir James Sandilands of Slamanno; James Leirmonth of Balcolmy; James Spens of Wormestoun; John Forret of Fingask; David Home, younger, of Wedderburne; and Captain William Murray. By the terms of

a contract between these individuals and the Government, ratified by Parliament, they were, in consideration
of the great expenses to be incurred by them, and the
improvements which they were expected to make, freed
from any payment of rent for seven years.   At the end
of this time, an annual grain-rent of one hundred and
forty chalders of bear, for the lands and Isles of Lewis,
Rona-Lewis, and Ilanshand, was to commence; whilst,
for the lands of Trouterness, they were to pay yearly a
money rent of four hundred merks, being twenty merks
more than the rent stipulated to be paid by Macdonald
of Sleat when he procured a lease of Trouterness in
1596.[1]   About the same time the lands of Harris, Dunvegan, and Glenelg, were granted to the same parties;[2]
but as the efforts of the Lowlanders were first directed
to the colonising of the Lewis, and were ultimately unsuccessful even in that island, all the other lands seem
to have escaped the experiments to which the Lewis was
subjected, and, on the final discomfiture of the adventurers, to have returned to the old proprietors.

The proceedings of the Government in this matter,
it must be allowed, were too precipitate.   Had the Lewis
alone been granted to a Lowland company, the dissensions of the natives made success very probable; and
the only serious opposition to be calculated upon was
that which the Lord of Kintaill might be expected to
offer.   But when grants were likewise made to these

---

[1] Acts of Parliament, IV. 160.   The contract was dated 28th June,
1598.

[2] Reg. of Privy Seal, LXXIX., fo. 252.   Allan Cameron of
Lochiel appears also to have incurred forfeiture of his lands at this
time, which afterwards gave him much trouble.   MS. History of
Camerons.

Lowlanders of the estates belonging to Macleod of Harris, and of a large district occupied, under a very recent lease, by Macdonald of Sleat, a powerful party was at once created in the North Isles, whose interest it clearly was to frustrate and discourage the adventurers by every means in their power. These chiefs could not fail to perceive that the success of the adventurers in the Lewis would enable the latter to seize, with greater facility, all the other lands to which Parliament had given them a claim. That they should deprecate such an event was perfectly natural; and it will appear, accordingly, that the enterprise of the Lowlanders at length failed, owing to the obstacles secretly but perseveringly thrown in their way by the three great northern chiefs, Macleod of Harris, Macdonald of Sleat, and Mackenzie of Kintaill. Meantime, however, the preparations of the adventurers for their settlement in the Lewis were carried on with great spirit and at no small expense.[1]

Whilst such measures were in progress for the civilisation of the North Isles, the state of the South Isles again called loudly for the interference of Government. Angus Macdonald of Dunyveg had been liberated early in 1597, as we have seen, in order to test his sincerity, by his performance of certain conditions (supra, p. 273). A considerable time having elapsed without the fulfilment of these conditions, his son, Sir James Macdonald, was permitted to go from Court to visit him in Kintyre—it being supposed that the influence of Sir James would insure his father's obedience. The result of this step did not, however, answer the expectations of those who advised it. The reader will

---

[1] Anderson's MS. History of Scotland, III., fo. 295.

remember that, when Sir William Stewart was preparing to invade Kintyre, in November, 1596, Angus Macdonald had sent his son to make his submission to the King and Council. At that time, under the impression that his son might obtain better terms than himself, Angus had made over to the latter all his estates, stipulating only for a proper maintenance for himself and his wife during their lives.[1] This, as being the act of a man already deprived by forfeiture of all his former rights, was of course not recognised by the Privy Council; and it is probable that Angus soon repented the facility with which he had stripped himself of his possessions, when he found that this act was productive of no direct benefit to himself or his tribe. The transaction, however, was not forgot by Sir James, who, led away by evil advisers, as well as by the natural violence of his temper, and presuming on the favour with which he had been treated at Court, now endeavoured to take the estate into his own hands, and deprive his father of all influence. A quarrel among the Macallasters of Loupe favoured his designs, and seems to have suggested to him the idea of procuring his father's death, as if by accident. The young Laird of Loupe, Gorrie Macallaster, who had succeeded to the estate when a minor, had lately, since he was come of age, a serious dispute with his tutor or guardian, in the course of which he killed the latter. The sons of the tutor took refuge with their chief, Angus Macdonald of Dunyveg; whilst the Laird of Loupe, who eagerly sought their lives, procured the support of Sir James Macdonald on the arrival of the latter in Kintyre. Understanding that the

---

[1] Record of Privy Council, 8th October, 1596.

tutor's sons were with Angus Macdonald, at his house
of Askomull in Kintyre, Sir James and his associates,
to the number of two or three hundred armed men,
surrounded the house in the dead of night, and on the
refusal of the Macallasters to surrender themselves
prisoners, the house was immediately set on fire.
Although perfectly aware that his father and mother
were in the house, Sir James savagely refused to let
the fire be extinguished; and at length his father,
endeavouring to make his escape, was made prisoner,
after being severely burnt and suffering many indigni-
ties from Sir James' servants. He was then carried
to Smerbie in Kintyre, and confined there in irons for
several months. The other inmates of the house likewise fell into the hands of Sir James, and were treated
with various degrees of severity; but he does not appear
to have caused any of them to be put to death.[1] Sir
James now took the command of his clan, and neglect-
ing his promises to the King, conducted himself with
such violence in his new capacity, that in the month of
June, 1598, it became necessary to issue a proclamation
for another Royal expedition or raid to Kintyre. The
burden of this expedition was placed on the shires of
Dunbarton, Bute, and Renfrew; the bailliaries of Carrick
and Cunningham, the Lower Ward of Clydesdale, and
the burghs of Dunbarton, Glasgow, Ayr, Irvine, Renfrew, Rothesay, and Paisley. The King was to meet
the array of these shires and burghs at Dunbarton on
the 20th of August, and to proceed in person at their
head to Kintyre.[2] Early in August, Sir James Macdonald had contrived to procure from the King a letter

[1] Pitcairn's Criminal Trials, III., p. 5.
[2] Record of Privy Council, 30th June, 1598.

approving of his late proceedings in Kintyre, and particularly of his apprehension of his father;[1] but it was not, therefore, thought advisable to give up the expedition to Kintyre.   On the contrary, a new proclamation was issued at this time, the chief object of which was to remove the doubts generally entertained as to the King's intention of going in person on this expedition; and his Majesty even went so far as to name the particular vessel in which he was to sail, and to give directions for its being properly manned and furnished for the voyage.[2]   When the time came, however, for the departure of the expedition, the doubts of the lieges were justified, by the appointment of the Duke of Lennox as Lieutenant over the Isles.   In the Duke's commission it was specially provided that it should not be in his power to show favour to any of the Islanders, unless by the advice of his Majesty, and of the councillors formerly named for the affairs of the Isles.[3]   This change in his Majesty's intentions seems to have been caused by news received, in the course of the month of August, of a conflict between the Macdonalds and Macleans, in which the chief of the latter was slain.   Even after all the preparations which were made, and the nomination of the Duke of Lennox to be Lieutenant of the Isles, it is doubtful if the expedition ever left Dunbarton; and, indeed, the approach of harvest had probably prevented a sufficient force from assembling at that town. The immediate cause of the conflict between the Macdonalds and Macleans was as follows.

Sir Lauchlan Maclean of Dowart had succeeded in

---

[1] Criminal Trials, III., p. 9.
[2] Record of Privy Council, 5th and 6th August.
[3] Ibid, 25th August.

procuring from the King a grant of part of the island
of Isla, forfeited by his old rival Angus Macdonald.
Taking advantage of the dissensions of the Clandonald,
and calculating on the youth and inexperience of his
nephew, Sir James, he levied his vassals and proceeded
to Isla, in order to expel the Macdonalds, and put
himself in possession of his new acquisitions in the
island. Sir James Macdonald was not, however, disposed to yield to the pretensions of Maclean, and had
already collected a number of his clan in Isla to oppose
his uncle's proceedings. The mutual friends of both
parties, desiring to spare the effusion of blood, laboured
to effect a mediation between them. A meeting was
accordingly agreed to be held at Lochgruinart, in Isla,
to arrange their differences, to which place the rival
chiefs repaired, each with a considerable number of
their followers, but the Macdonalds were inferior in
force. To the pressing entreaties of the mediators, Sir
James Macdonald yielded so far as to offer his uncle
the half of the island for his life (denying at the same
time the validity of the title on which Maclean founded
his pretensions), provided he would agree to hold it,
as his predecessors had held the Rinns of Isla, for their
personal service to the Clandonald. Moreover, Sir
James offered to refer their disputes to the decision of
any impartial persons Maclean might choose to name ;
and, in case of their differing, to the decision of the
King. But Maclean, much against the opinion of his
friends, who advised him to accept these offers, would
hear of nothing but an absolute surrender, on the part
of Sir James, of all title or claim to the island. Upon
this, both parties resolved to settle the dispute by the
sword. They encountered at the head of Lochgruinart,

and a desperate conflict ensued. Sir James in the beginning of the action caused his vanguard to make a detour, as if they intended a retreat, but really with the object of gaining the top of an eminence near at hand, which Sir Lauchlan was also desirous to possess. By this stratagem Sir James succeeded in gaining the height first, from which he charged the Macleans with great vigour, and, forcing their van back upon their main body, threw the whole into confusion, and finally routed them. Sir Lauchlan Maclean, with fourscore of his kinsmen and two hundred common soldiers, were killed; and his son, Lauchlan Barrach Maclean, being dangerously wounded, made his escape with difficulty, with the survivors, to their boats. Sir James Macdonald was himself severely wounded, and, for a time, his recovery was doubtful; whilst thirty of his followers were killed and sixty wounded.[1] According to the family history of the Macleans, Hector, the son and successor of Sir Lauchlan, obtained a commission of fire and sword, as it was called, against Sir James Macdonald and his tribe. He and his clan then invaded Isla, accompanied by Macleod of Dunvegan, Cameron of Lochiel, Mackinnon and Macneill of Barra, with their followers. They encountered the Macdonalds at a place called Bern Bige, attacked and defeated them, and afterwards ravaged the whole island, in

---

[1] Sir R. Gordon's History of Sutherland, p. 237. The MS. History of the Macleans gives a somewhat different account of this affair, throwing the chief blame upon the Macdonalds. Anderson's History of Scotland and Birrel's Diary agree in the censure of Sir James Macdonald; but the information of Sir R. Gordon seems to have been more minute, and probably therefore more correct than that of the other authorities. The battle of Lochgruinart was fought on the 5th August, 1598.

revenge for the slaughter of the Macleans at Loch-gruinart. As, however, no commission appears in any of the records of the time, it would rather seem that the revenge taken by the Clanlean and their confederates proceeded from their own private councils, and had not the sanction of the Government in any shape.[1] It is not a little remarkable that, a year after the battle of Lochgruinart, we find Sir James Macdonald treating with the King's Comptroller regarding the lands of Isla and Kintyre, and making offers which were approved of by the Privy Council. When along with this, we consider the still more remarkable fact that the indict-ment on which Sir James was condemned to death in the year 1609, makes no allusion to the slaughter of Sir Lauchlan Maclean and his kinsmen, it is impossible to avoid the conclusion that Maclean was the aggressor, and that Macdonald was considered by the authorities as having fought in self-defence.

A new commission of Lieutenandry over the whole Isles and Highlands of Inverness-shire, was A. D. 1599. in July, 1599, granted to the Duke of Lennox and the Earl of Huntly, the latter of whom had lately been restored to favour. A special charge was given to both Lieutenants to assist, by every means, and with all their forces and power, the " gentle-men venturers and enterprisers of the conquest of the Lewis, towards the perfect settling and establishing of that island under their obedience." The preamble of this commission gives a shocking picture of the state of the Islanders at this time, charging them with the grossest impiety and the most atrocious barbarities.

---

[1] This is corroborated by the MS. History of the Camerons.

One clause, however, points out, although unintention-
ally, the offence which appeared most heinous in the
eyes of a needy monarch and his grasping courtiers, and
leaves some room to suppose that the rest of the preamble may have been exaggerated, to give more colour
to.the harsh measures now in progress.   The words of
this clause are—" And besides all their other crimes,
they rebelliously withhold from his Majesty a great part
of the patrimony and proper rent of the Crown, deprive
the country of the benefit which might redound thereto,
by the trade of fishing, and of other commodities which
these bounds render.   And now, at last, a great part of
them have banded, conspired, and daily practise, by
force and policy, in their barbarous and rebellious form,
to disappoint his Majesty's service in the Lewis."   A
council of northern Earls and Barons was appointed by
the Commission, by whose advice the Lieutenants were
to be guided in the execution of their office.   This
Commission was plainly intended to assist the Lowland
adventurers in their enterprise against the Lewis; and
it deserves to be noticed, that it gave express power to
the Lieutenants to punish with military execution, not
only the avowed opponents of the enterprise, but those
who should be found to impede it indirectly.   It is
uncertain to what extent this Commission was acted
upon.[1]

   In the month of August, Sir James Macdonald
appeared in presence of the King's Comptroller at
Falkland, and made certain offers, embracing, as he
affirmed, the most certain method of establishing the
Royal authority within the bounds of Kintyre and Isla.

---

[1] Record of Privy Council, 9th July, 1599.

He offered to cause his whole tribe and dependers evacuate Kintyre, leaving those lands wholly at the King's disposal; and he, at the same time, engaged for himself and his clan, not only to refrain from molesting the new tenants who should be placed in that district, but, on the contrary, to support and defend them to the utmost of his power. He also agreed that the Castle of Dunyveg in Isla should be placed in the hands of a governor and garrison appointed by the King, and that sixty merk lands in its vicinity (from which he offered to remove the present tenants) should be assigned for the maintenance of the garrison. Sir James then required the remaining lands of Isla (estimated to extend to three hundred merk lands) to be granted to him in heritage for the annual feu-duty of £2 for every merk land, or £600 in all, the title-deeds to contain the same clauses as those granted to the Islesmen by James IV. Besides this rent, he offered to pay to his father, wherever the King should appoint the residence of the latter, a yearly pension of one thousand merks, or about six hundred and seventy pounds. For the performance of all these offers he proposed to give his brother as a hostage, and to support him in a becoming manner as long as he should continue in captivity. These offers being submitted by the Comptroller to the Privy Council, received the approbation of that tribunal; and the Comptroller was authorised to treat with Sir James Macdonald for his performance of them in every point, and regarding the heritable grant of the lands of Isla sought by the latter.[1] Much obscurity rests upon the causes which prevented this matter from being brought

---

[1] Record of Privy Council, 6th September, 1599.

to a satisfactory conclusion. There is reason to believe that the influence of the Earl of Argyle and John Campbell of Calder was already, if not earlier, secretly used in thwarting the endeavours of Sir James Macdonald to reconcile himself and his clan to the Government. It is not to be supposed that this chief, unless under the influence of interested advisers, would have abandoned, as he seems very soon to have done, the favourable position in which he was now placed. That Argyle and Calder were deeply interested will afterwards appear; and the marriage of Sir James Macdonald to Calder's sister, which took place about this time, must have, at first, disposed him to receive with unsuspecting confidence the counsels of that crafty baron. It would appear that Argyle took the part of Angus Macdonald, Sir James's father, in order to embarrass Sir James as much as possible in his arrangements with the Government. Calder, on the other hand, by professing to support his brother-in-law, seems to have urged the young chief to acts of violence which led to his ruin. Certain it is, that, in after life, Sir James blamed Argyle and Calder as the prime movers of all the severities exercised against him and his clan. It was the opinion, too, of one of the contemporary officers of state for Scotland—a man of much sagacity and experience—that the frequent insurrections in the South Isles which occurred in the first fifteen years of the seventeenth century were encouraged, if not originated, by Argyle and the Campbells for their own purposes.[1] In the following pages undoubted evidence will be found of such underhand proceedings,

---

[1] Letter, Sir Alexander Hay to Mr. John Murray of Lochmaben, then in London, dated 21st December, 1615; Denmylne MS., Advocates' Library.

on the part of the Earl of Argyle, in one of the most prominent of these insurrections.

Leaving for a while the affairs of the South Isles, which gradually become more interesting, we proceed to trace the progress of the Lowland adventurers who proposed to colonise the Lewis. Their contract with Government was ratified, as we have seen, by Parliament in June, 1598, and their preparations were commenced without loss of time. It seems probable that they went no further in that year than merely preparing for their expedition; but, in October of the following year, fortified, in some measure, by the commission granted in July to the Duke of Lennox and the Earl of Huntly, they actually proceeded to the Lewis with a force of five or six hundred hired soldiers, besides gentlemen volunteers, and artificers of all sorts. The late season of the year at which the adventurers arrived in the island was very injurious to them; for the cold weather, and want of proper shelter and provisions, caused many, soon after their arrival, to die of the flux.[1] None of the authorities of the period mention why the expedition should not have sailed at least six months earlier than it did; and we are, therefore, led to conclude that the delay was caused either by actual opposition of a formidable nature being threatened, or by reports circulated by Mackenzie and the other hostile chiefs that such opposition was intended.[2] Under all these disadvantages the colonists commenced building in a convenient place, and at length completed what Sir Robert Gordon calls "a pretty town," where

---

[1] Moysie's Memoirs, p. 165.

[2] This is confirmed by a passage in Anderson's MS. History of Scotland, III., fo. 295.

they encamped. The natives of the island, under Neill and Murdoch, the two surviving bastard sons of Ruari Macleod, the last undisputed Lord of Lewis, made considerable opposition, to which they were probably incited by Mackenzie. Leirmonth of Balcolmy, being on his way from the Lewis to Fife with his own vessel, was intercepted near the Orkneys by Murdoch Macleod, who is said to have received his instructions from the Lord of Kintaill. Many of his crew were slain, and he himself was detained a prisoner in the Lewis for six months, after which he was liberated by his captor on promise of a ransom. This, however, the unfortunate Laird of Balcolmy never lived to pay, having died in the Orkneys on his way home of disease brought on by the harsh treatment he had suffered in his captivity. About this time, luckily for the adventurers, Neill Macleod quarrelled with his brother, who had not only a principal share in the execution of Torquil Dubh Macleod a few years before, but continued to support the treacherous Breve and his kin, the Clan Vic Gilvore, as they were called, by whom Torquil Dubh had been apprehended and delivered to Mackenzie. In following up this dispute, Neill apprehended his brother and several of the Breve's kindred, and immediately put all his prisoners, his brother excepted, to death. The adventurers, hearing of this, offered to Neill Macleod that, if he would deliver his brother up to them, as one of the chief obstructors of their enterprise, they would both give to himself a portion of the island, and assist him further to revenge the death of Torquil Dubh. The Islander accepted these terms, delivered up his brother Murdoch to the colonists, and went with them to Edinburgh, taking along with

A. D. 1600.

him the heads, ten or twelve in number, of those of the
Clan Vic Gilvore, whom he had lately put to death.
On this occasion Neill received a pardon for his
offences; and the colonists returned to the Lewis, their
prospects much improved by their alliance with the most
powerful man in the island.   In the meantime, Murdoch
Macleod was executed at St. Andrews; and, in consequence of some confessions made by him, and of complaints by the adventurers, the Lord of Kintaill was
apprehended, and committed prisoner to Edinburgh
Castle.   This artful chief, however, contrived to escape
without a trial by the help of his friend the Lord
Chancellor; nor did the risk he had run cause him at
all to relax in his endeavours to frustrate the colonisa-
tion of the Lewis, as we shall presently have occasion
to see.[1]

The commission of lieutenandry lately granted to the
Duke of Lennox and the Earl, now Marquis, of Huntly
over the North Highlands and Isles, had failed to produce any effect, owing, no doubt, to the difficulty of
bringing a feudal army from the rest of Scotland together
in the harvest months.   It is evident, too, that the
Lowland militia were becoming impatient of the frequent calls upon them to suppress petty insurrections
in the Isles.   These difficulties suggested to the King,
for the third time, the project of going in person to the
Isles, as experience had shown that this was the best
way to overcome the growing dislike, on the part of the
people, to so oppressive a feature of the feudal system.
The fighting men of a great part of Scotland were

[1] Sir R. Gordon's History of Sutherland, p. 270-1. Moysie's
Memoirs, p. 165. Dr. George Mackenzie's History of the Mackenzies.
Letterfearn MS.

accordingly summoned, by proclamation, dated the 2nd of April, to meet his Majesty, part of them at Dunbarton, on the 10th of July, and the remainder at Kintyre, two days later. The boatmen of the Clyde and adjacent coasts were ordered to have their vessels ready by that time, to convey the army, with its Royal leader, to the scene of operations.[1] In the course of two months, however, it was found out that the burghs already ordered to send their quotas to the expedition, could not furnish a sufficient number of ships or men *to insure his Majesty's safety*, and a new proclamation was issued affecting all the burghs of the realm.[2] Even this last summons failed either to bring together a sufficient force, or to overcome the natural timidity of the monarch; for a third proclamation, in the month of July, announced the total abandonment of the intended expedition, on the alleged ground of the inability of the lieges, from poverty, to equip themselves properly for the service.[3] The ridicule attending this renewed exhibition of his pusillanimity seems effectually to have deterred James from again proposing an expedition "in proper person" to the Isles.

A. D. 1601.   The next year witnessed another abortive attempt to reduce the Isles and adjacent Highlands to obedience by means of commissions of lieutenandry. The Lieutenants named were Lennox and Huntly. The commissions now granted to these noblemen differed materially from those they had received in 1599; for, besides that the South or Argyleshire Isles were included and placed under the immediate charge of Lennox, whilst the North Isles (excepting

---

[1] Record of Privy Council, 2nd April, 1600.
[2] Ibid, 6th June, 1600.   [3] Ibid, 14th July, 1600.

the Lewis) were committed to the guardianship of Huntly, it was provided that the Lieutenants should try what their own private power and resources could effect in the first instance. Should it then become necessary to call out more than their own vassals, they were required, in doing so, to take the advice of the same counsellors nominated in their former commissions. The Lieutenants were also enjoined, as before, to assist the colonists, so that the latter might be the better able to pay their rent to the King, which would *greatly augment* his Majesty's rents. The powers given to the Lieutenants were very ample, enabling them to summon, and, in case of resistance, to take by force all such castles and fortalices as they should consider necessary to the success of their proceedings; and to pursue the rebellious Islesmen, and the Highlanders of the mainland who should take part with them, with fire and sword. Pardons were, at the same time, promised for all slaughters that might happen to be committed by them or their followers in carrying their commissions into effect. To encourage these powerful noblemen to enter with energy on the duties imposed upon them, it was declared that, if they accomplished the pacification of the Isles, taking proper security for the payment of his Majesty's rents, they should be deemed worthy of a great reward. And if all this were effected by their own power and resources, without any military service or other burden upon the country at large, an immediate recompense was promised to them.[1] Notwithstanding the inducements held out, there appears no trace of any active steps taken by Lennox or Huntly towards the subjection of the rebellious Islesmen.

[1] Record of Privy Council, 16th June, 1601.

The attention of the Government, was at this time occupied, apart from the civilisation of the Lewis and Kintyre and the general measures proposed for the improvement of the Isles, by a sudden quarrel, followed by much bloodshed and various desolating inroads, between the two great chiefs in the Isle of Sky, Donald Gorme Macdonald of Sleat, and Ruari Macleod of Dunvegan. Donald Gorme had married Macleod's sister; but; owing to some jealousy, or other cause of displeasure conceived against her, he repudiated that lady. Macleod, being informed of this, was highly offended, and sent a message to Donald Gorme, desiring him to take back his wife. This the latter refused; and, on the contrary, set about procuring a legal divorce, in which he succeeded, and immediately afterwards married a sister of Kenneth Mackenzie of Kintaill. Macleod, in the first transports of his resentment at this indignity, assembled his clan and carried fire and sword through Macdonald's district of Trouterness, in Sky. The Clandonald, in revenge, invaded Harris, which island they laid waste in a similar manner, killing many of the inhabitants, and carrying off the cattle. This retaliation roused the Macleods to make a foray upon Macdonald's estate of North Uist; and, accordingly, they sailed from Sky towards that Island; and, on arriving there, the chief sent his kinsman, Donald Glas Macleod, with forty men, to lay waste the island, and to bring off from the church of Kiltrynad the cattle and effects of the country people, which, on the alarm being given, had been placed there for safety. In the execution of these orders Donald Glas was encountered by a celebrated warrior of the Clandonald, nearly related to their chief, called Donald MacIan Vic James, who had only twelve men with him. The Macdonalds behaved with so much gallantry on this occasion, that they routed their opponents, and rescued the cattle, Donald Glas and many of his men being killed. The chief of Dunvegan, seeing the ill success of this detachment, and suspecting that a larger force was at hand, returned home, meditating future vengeance. These spoliations and incursions were carried on with so much inveteracy, that both clans were brought to the brink of ruin; and many of the natives of the districts thus devastated were forced to sustain themselves by killing and eating their horses, dogs, and cats.

At length, in the year 1601, while Ruari Macleod was absent, seeking assistance from the Earl of Argyle against his enemies, the Macdonalds invaded Macleod's lands in Sky in considerable numbers, wishing to force on a battle. The Macleods, under Alexander, the brother of their chief, took post on the shoulder of Benquhillin (a very high and rugged mountain or ridge of hills in Sky), and did not decline the contest. After a fierce and obstinate combat, in which both parties fought with great bravery, the Macleods were overthrown. Their leader, with thirty of their choicest warriors, fell into the hands of the victors; and two of the chief's immediate relations, and many others, were slain.[1] The Privy Council now interfered to prevent further mischief. The Marquis of Huntly, and the Earl of Argyle, and all others, were prohibited from giving assistance to either of the contending parties; whilst the chiefs themselves were ordered to disband their forces and to quit the island in the meantime. Macleod was enjoined to give himself up to the Earl of

[1] Sir R. Gordon's History of Sutherland, p. 244.

Argyle, and Macdonald to surrender himself to Huntly; and both were strictly charged, under the penalty of treason, to remain with these noblemen till the controversy between them should be settled by the King and Council.[1]   A reconciliation was at length effected between these chiefs, by the mediation of Angus Macdonald of Isla, Maclean of Coll, and other friends; after which, the prisoners taken at the battle of Benquhillin were released, and ever after these clans refrained from open hostility, and submitted their disputes to the decision of the law.[2]   There is great reason to believe that this reconciliation was hastened by their dread of the progress of the colonists of the Lewis, after the latter had strengthened themselves by their alliance with Neill Macleod, the bastard.

The settlement of the Lewis now met with a severe and unexpected check.   The leaders of the adventurers who returned to the island with Neill Macleod, after procuring his pardon, and delivering up his brother Murdoch to justice, were the Commendator of Pittenweem, the lairds of Wormestoun, Fingask, Balcolmy, and Airdrie.   Their situation at this time was so promising, that they were induced to limit the exemption from rent, which by their contract was to last for seven years, to two years from the commencement of their undertaking.[3]   Soon after their return, however, some injury done by Spens of Wormestoun to Neill Macleod embroiled them once more with the latter.   Wormestoun laid a plot to entrap Macleod, but that leader having

---

[1] Record of Privy Council, 29th June, 11th and 22nd August, 1601.

[2] Sir R. Gordon's History of Sutherland, p. 245.

[3] Record of Privy Council, 26th March, 1607.

a similar design against Wormestoun, was upon his guard, and as soon as a party sent to apprehend him were at a sufficient distance from their camp, he attacked and routed them, with the loss of sixty of their number.[1] Mackenzie of Kintaill, who, since the agreement made between Neill Macleod and the colonists, had almost despaired of frustrating the enterprise, was no sooner informed of this quarrel than he hastened to profit by it. He had detained in captivity, for several years, Tormod, the younger brother of Torquil Dubh, and only surviving legitimate son of old Ruari Macleod of the Lewis. Although ordered by the Privy Council, in April, 1600, to produce his prisoner before them, he had evaded compliance, and still detained Tormod Macleod in custody without a warrant. Suddenly changing his plan, on hearing of the quarrel between Neill and the adventurers, Mackenzie restored this young man to liberty, and sent him into the Lewis, promising him, secretly, great assistance if he would attack the settlers in concert with his uncle. On his arrival in the island, Tormod was received with open arms by Neill Macleod and all the old followers of the family of Lewis, by whom he was at once acknowledged as their lord and master. Encouraged by the support he received from his clan and the other natives of Lewis, and guided by the advice and experience of Neill Macleod, who had so long been their leader, the young chief attacked the camp of the adventurers, forced it, burned the fort, killed many of their men, and at length forced the principal gentlemen to capitulate with him on the following conditions:—*First*, They were

<hr />

[1] Sir R. Gordon's History of Sutherland, p. 271 ; Letterfearn MS.

to obtain from the King a remission to the Macleods for all their bypast offences; *Secondly*, They promised never to return to the Lewis, and agreed to give up their title to that island to Tormod Macleod; *Lastly*, For the performance of these conditions they were obliged to leave Sir James Spens, and his son-in-law, Thomas Monypenny of Kinkell, as hostages.[1] In order to obtain the liberation of the hostages, who were detained for eight months by the Islanders, a remission was readily granted,[2] and it is probable that the adventurers pretended to surrender their legal rights by a formal deed; but when their object was attained by the release of these gentlemen, no further attention was paid to the capitulation. Notwithstanding their promise never to return, they seem only to have waited till their hostages were out of danger before taking immediate steps for a reconquest of the island and its restless inhabitants. Accordingly, in the month of July proclamation was made, summoning the fighting men in most of the northern counties to meet a Royal lieutenant, probably the Marquis of Huntly, at Inverness, on the 20th of September, then to proceed against the rebels of the Lewis.[3] On the approach of harvest, however, this proclamation was recalled, and "the raid of the Lewis was delayed till the spring of the following year."[4]

A. D. 1602.

The feud between the Mackenzies and the Clanranald of Glengarry, regarding their lands in Wester

---

[1] Sir R. Gordon's History of Sutherland, p. 272; Dr. George Mackenzie's MS. History of the Mackenzies; Letterfearn MS.

[2] Dr. George Mackenzie's MS.

[3] Record of Privy Council, 17th July, 1602.

[4] Ibid, 15th September, 1602.

Ross, was now renewed with great violence. On this occasion Glengarry appears to have been the aggressor; a position in which he was placed, partly by the craft of his opponents, partly by his own ignorance of the laws. The result was, that the Lord of Kintaill procured a commission of fire and sword against Glengarry and his men, by virtue of which he invaded the district of North Morar, belonging to Glengarry, which he devastated in the cruel manner then practised, and carried off all the cattle.[1] The Macdonalds did not fail to retaliate by predatory excursions, in one of which they plundered the district of Applecross, which had always before been considered as a sanctuary. On another occasion, a large body of Macdonalds had landed on the coast of Lochalsh, vowing to burn and destroy all Mackenzie's lands as far as Easter Ross; but their leader, Allaster MacGorrie, in whom they had great confidence, having separated himself with but few attendants from his main body, was surprised by some of Mackenzie's followers and killed.

This loss so disheartened the Macdonalds that they returned home without performing any action of consequence. Meantime, the Lord of Kintaill went to Mull to visit Maclean, by whose means he hoped to prevent the Macdonalds of Isla from giving assistance to their relations in the north. In his absence, Angus Macdonald, the young chief of Glengarry, desirous to revenge the death of his kinsman, MacGorrie, had collected all his followers, and proceeding northwards to Lochcarron (in which the Macdonalds now only held the Castle of Strone, with a small garrison), he loaded

---

[1] Sir R. Gordon's History of Sutherland, p. 248; Record of Privy Council, 9th September, 1602.

his boats with the plunder of that district, after burning all the houses within reach, and killing many of the inhabitants. The inhabitants of Kintaill and Lochalsh having been drawn together in the absence of their chief, and encouraged by the example of his lady, posted themselves at the narrow strait or kyle which separates Sky from the mainland, intending to annoy the Macdonalds as much as possible on their return. Night had fallen before the Macdonalds made their appearance; and some of Mackenzie's vassals, taking advantage of the darkness, rowed out in two boats towards a large galley of the enemy, which was then passing the kyle. Being allowed to approach within a very short distance, they suddenly attacked the Macdonalds with a volley of musketry and arrows. The latter, in their alarm crowding to one side of the galley, already heavily laden with their plunder, it overset, and the whole crew were precipitated into the water. Such of them as contrived to reach the shore were immediately despatched by the Kintaill men; and among the slain was the young chief of Glengarry himself, whose boat it was that the Mackenzies had happened to attack. The rest of the Macdonalds, hearing the alarm, and discovering their loss, returned on their own route as far as Strathordell in Sky, where they left their boats; and, proceeding on foot through the island to Sleat, they crossed from that district to Morar. Finding that Mackenzie was not yet returned from Mull, they sent a large party to take post in an island near which he must pass, so that they might have an opportunity of intercepting him, and thus revenging the death of their young chief. This party was only one night in the island when the chief of

Kintaill came past in Maclean's great galley, commanded by the captain of Carneburg. At this time it was low ebb, and the boats of the Macdonalds were aground; but in order to detain them as long as possible, the captain, suspecting whose vessels they were, pretended that he was going to land on the island. The stratagem took effect; for the Macdonalds, not to deter him from landing, retired from the shore and concealed themselves among the rocks; when suddenly he hoisted his sails, and bore away from the island, and was soon out of reach of pursuit. When Mackenzie came to Kintaill, he observed a number of dead bodies lying on the shore, and was soon informed of the success which his vassals had met with. He then collected his men, and laid siege to the Castle of Strone, which was in a short time surrendered to him, on which he caused it to be blown up, that it might no longer be a stronghold against him and his successors. After this, the Clanranald of Glengarry, under Allan Macranald of Lundie, made an irruption into Brae Ross, and plundered the lands of Kilchrist and other adjacent lands belonging to the Mackenzies. This foray was signalised by the merciless burning of a whole congregation in the church of Kilchrist, while Glengarry's piper marched round the building, mocking the cries of the unfortunate inmates with the well-known pibroch, which has been known, ever since, under the name of Kilchrist, as the family tune of the Clanranald of Glengarry.[1] Some of the Macdonalds chiefly concerned in this outrage were afterwards killed by the Mackenzies; but it is somewhat startling to reflect that

A. D. 1603.

[1] Letterfearn MS.; Sir R. Gordon's History of Sutherland, p. 248; Reg. of Privy Seal, XCIV. 142.

this terrible instance of private vengeance should have occurred in the commencement of the seventeenth century without, so far as we can trace, any public notice being taken of such an enormity. Eventually, the disputes between the chiefs of Glengarry and Kintaill were amicably settled by an arrangement which gave the Ross-shire lands, so long the subject of dispute, entirely to Mackenzie; and the hard terms to which Glengarry was obliged to submit in this private quarrel, seem to have formed the only punishment inflicted on this clan for the cold-blooded atrocity displayed in the memorable raid of Kilchrist.[1]

We now approach the time when King James quitted his native country of Scotland to commence his reign as Sovereign of Great Britain. His attention was latterly so much occupied in preparing for his peaceable accession to the throne of England, that the disorders in every part of the Highlands and Isles were allowed to increase to a serious height. This is evident from the number of complaints made to the Privy Council by the Lowlanders adjacent to the Highland line, who suffered severely from predatory bands of Highlanders. The necessity of quieting the districts nearest to the Lowlands must have contributed to withdraw the attention of the Government from the more remote clans. So feeble, however, were the measures pursued for this object, that it was not until the Clangregor, already under the ban of the law, had made an irruption into the Lennox, and, after defeating the Colquhouns and their

---

[1] Sir R. Gordon, ubi supra. The author of the Letterfearn MS. informs us that, in the discussions before the Privy Council, the Mackenzies proved Glengarry "to have been a worshipper of the *Coan*, which image was afterwards brought to Edinburgh and burnt at the Cross."

adherents at Glenfrune with great slaughter, had plundered and ravaged the whole district, and threatened to burn the town of Dunbarton, that the Government was roused to adequate exertions. This happened in February, 1603, two months before the King set out for London; and, as all the power of the Earl of Argyle and his clan, and of many other Highland chiefs, was required to carry into effect the proscription of the Clangregor, it is not surprising that the Islesmen should for some time have enjoyed a respite from Commissions of Lieutenandry, and similar acts of the Royal authority, indicating his Majesty's paternal anxiety for their reformation.[1] In particular, the expedition announced to proceed against the rebels of the Lewis, in order to put the adventurers again in possession of that island, was, owing to these causes, delayed for upwards of two years. James, however, was no sooner firmly seated on the English throne, than his projects for the improvement of the Isles, and at the same time, of his Scottish Crown rents, again occupied his attention, with a better prospect of success than formerly, from the increased resources now at his command. The progress which he made, after becoming King of Great Britain, in reducing the Isles and adjacent Highlands to peace and obedience, will be detailed in the succeeding chapters.

[1] In the Vindication of the Clanranald of Glengarry, App., p. x. there is printed, from the Glengarry Ch. Chest, a warrant, dated 11th May, 1602, to Donald MacAngus of Glengarry, giving him power to press any Scottish vessels in the Isles, to assist him in passing "upon the malefactors and broken men of the Isles, perturbers of the quietness thairof for thair apprehension, &c.," he having previously received a commission for that purpose. The records, so far as the author's information extends, do not allude to this commission to Glengarry; nor does it appear to have been carried into effect in any shape.

CHAP. VII.

FROM THE DEPARTURE OF JAMES VI. FOR ENGLAND TO
THE ACQUISITION OF THE ISLE OF LEWIS BY THE LORD
OF KINTAILL.—1603—1610.

A. D. 1603. THE first event of consequence that occurred in the Isles after the departure of the King for England, was the apprehension and imprisonment of Sir James Macdonald. The proceedings of this restless young chief, from the year 1599 (when he made certain offers to the King's Comptroller, which were approved of by the Privy Council) to 1603, are involved in obscurity. He had before that time liberated his father from the unnatural bondage in which the latter was held; but he seems to have been loath to surrender the power which for some time he had enjoyed in Kintyre and Isla, more particularly as he was popular with his clan on account of his victory over the Macleans at Lochgruinart. Some time in the year 1603, his father having received information that Sir James meditated another plot against him, caused the latter to be apprehended; and after detaining him some time as a prisoner, delivered him to Campbell of Auchinbreck, who placed him in the hands of the Earl of Argyle. Hitherto, the Government had, from the causes alluded to in the last chapter,

23

neglected to interfere in this matter; but after Sir
James had been in the private custody of Argyle for
several months, the Earl was ordered to exhibit him
before the Privy Council. This he did early
A. D. 1604. in 1604, at Perth, when Macdonald was committed prisoner to the Royal Castle of Blackness. From
this prison, with the assistance of some of his clansmen,
Sir James planned his escape, and would have succeeded
but for the disclosure of his intention by some one in the
secret, whereupon he was removed to Edinburgh Castle.[1]
Here we shall leave him for a while. About this time,
Hector Maclean of Dowart, who, among other offences,
had failed to pay the Crown rents for his possessions,
was obliged to give security to the Privy Council that
his Castle of Dowart should be delivered up to any
person whom the King and Council should authorise to
receive it, on twenty days' warning.[2]

In the following summer Lord Scone
A. D. 1605. (formerly Sir David Murray), Comptroller of
Scotland, was directed to repair to Kintyre to receive
the obedience of the principal men of the clans in the
South Isles, with surety for the payment of his Majesty's
rents and duties. Angus Macdonald of Dunyveg,
Hector Maclean of Dowart, and all the principal chiefs
and gentlemen in the Isles, south of the point of Ardnamurchan—together with Cameron of Lochiel, Macranald of Keppoch, Macian of Ardnamurchan, Macian

---

[1] Deposition of Sir James Macdonald, 15th Jan., 1608, and in-
dictment against him, 13th May, 1609, in Pitcairn's Criminal Trials,
III., pp. 10, 7.   Rental Books of Earldom of Argyle, and High
Treasurer's Accounts, ad tempus.

[2] Record of Privy Council (old abstract in library of Skene, the
original Record for the period being lost), 26th August, 1604.

of Glenco, Stewart of Appin, Macdonald of Largie, and Macallaster of Loupe on the mainland—were summoned to appear personally before Lord Scone at Lochkilkerran (now Campbellton), in 'Kintyre, on the 20th day of July, to give their obedience, to find sureties for the payment of his Majesty's rents, and to bring with them and exhibit the title-deeds to all lands claimed by them in the Highlands and Isles. If any of them should fail to obey the proclamation, their title-deeds were at once to be declared null and void, and power was given to the Comptroller to pursue them with fire and sword as rebels to the King. That this might not be considered merely as an empty threat, the fighting men of the western shires and burghs were summoned to attend at Lochkilkerran, well armed, and with forty days' provisions, to support the authority of the Comptroller. Robert Hepburn, Lieutenant of the King's Guard, was sent to the Isles to receive from their respective owners the Castles of Dunyveg in Isla, and Dowart in Mull; and in order to prevent the escape of the Islanders, the inhabitants of Kintyre and the West Isles were ordered, by proclamation, to deliver all their boats to this officer, being at the same time prohibited from using boats without his special licence.[1]

The Council sat at Glasgow while these acts were passed; but the increasing unwillingness of the Lowlanders to be burdened with such expeditions operated on this, as on former occasions, to retard, if not to frustrate the plans of the Government. Angus Macdonald met the Comptroller in Glasgow, and presented to him certain offers (now lost) to be forwarded to the King;

[1] Record of Privy Council (Skene Abstract), June, 1605. Haddington's Collections.

but nothing more was accomplished at this time.[1] A new commission, with most ample powers, was given to Lord Scone early in August, to enable him to carry his former commission into effect.[2] It was not, however, till the month of September that this nobleman reached Kintyre, when he held a court similar to that held in the same place by the Commendator of Pittenweem in 1596. This court, after all these preparations, was only attended by Angus Macdonald and his relations and vassals in Kintyre, particularly the Macallasters, Macneills, Mackays, and Maceacherns; nor does it appear that Lord Scone was able either to compel the attendance of the more distant chiefs or to punish them for their contumacy. He made a roll of the King's lands in Kintyre, and of the occupiers of such of the lands as were not waste; and it is worthy of remark, that, in the nine years which had elapsed since a like roll was made by the Commendator of Pittenweem, the waste lands had considerably increased.[3] He succeeded also in procuring from Angus Macdonald payment of all the arrears of rent due by that chief, both for his lands in Kintyre and in Isla; and, on his departure, he took with him as a hostage for the future obedience of Angus, Archibald Macdonald of Gigha, a natural son of the latter, who was confined in the Castle of Dunbarton.[4]

[1] Offers and Letter of Angus Macdonald in 1606, which mention the former offers alluded to in the text.—See Pitcairn's Criminal Trials, III. 365-6.

[2] Record of Privy Council (Skene Abstract), 8th August, 1605.

[3] Out of one hundred and fifty-one and a half merk lands in North Kintyre, sixty-two were now waste; and out of two hundred and three merk lands in South Kintyre, fifty-one were waste.—See supra, p. 269.

[4] Original Record of Lord Scone's proceedings preserved in

In the summer of this year, the Lewis adventurers, armed with commissions of fire and sword and other high powers, and assisted by some of his Majesty's ships, made another attempt to possess themselves of that island, from which they had been excluded by Tormod Macleod and his followers since the year 1601. The chiefs of the North Isles were ordered to deliver up their castles to such heralds or officers as should be sent to receive them, that they might be garrisoned in his Majesty's name; and in the event of their refusal, warrant was given to the colonists to besiege and take the castles by force. All proprietors of galleys and other vessels in the North Isles and adjacent mainland, were ordered to deliver them up at Lochbroom to the adventurers, who were empowered to seize the boats of such as should disobey. Lastly, the other Highlanders and Islanders were strictly forbidden to hold communication of any kind with the rebels of the Lewis.[1] Having in virtue of their commission summoned together a considerable force from the neighbouring districts, the adventurers landed in the Lewis, and immediately sent a message to Tormod Macleod, offering, if he would submit to them, to convey him to London, where they would not only obtain his pardon from the King, but suffer him, through his friends, to sue for his Majesty's favour, and for some means of subsistence. Much against the advice of his brother Neill, Tormod declined to risk a battle against the colonists and their forces, and yielded to the terms proposed. His brother, however, with those who adhered to him, still held out.

Gen. Reg. House. Letter, Privy Council to the King, 16th March, 1607 ; Denmylne MS., Advocates' Library.
[1] Record of Privy Council (Skene Abstract), July, 1605.

According to their promise the adventurers sent Macleod to London, where, after a time, he made such progress in convincing his Majesty of the injustice of the grant to the Lowlanders of what was properly the inheritance of his nephews, that the colonists began to take alarm lest he should procure its recall. They therefore used all their influence against him; and some of them being members of the Royal household, they prevailed so far that he was sent down to Edinburgh and imprisoned in the castle, where he lay for ten years. Meantime the colonists settled in the Lewis for a time, but were continually annoyed by the attacks of Neill Macleod and those who supported him.[1]

A. D. 1606.   In July, 1606, the Privy Council appointed a committee of its members to meet Lord Scone and hear the offers made through him by the Southern Islanders for their obedience, and for the more sure payment of his Majesty's rents.[2] The result of this conference seems to have been unfavourable to the Islanders; for we find that Angus Macdonald could neither obtain from the Council any answers to his repeated petitions, nor was he permitted to go to Court to lay his case before the King.[3] It was undoubtedly the influence of the Earl of Argyle that guided the Council in slighting these offers, and in the measures afterwards pursued with regard to the South Isles, as it had now been, for some time, his principal aim to procure for himself the King's lands of Kintyre. Accordingly, having proposed himself as a tenant for these lands, he

---

[1] Sir R. Gordon's History of Sutherland, p. 274. Letterfearn MS. History of Mackenzies.

[2] Record of Privy Council (Skene Abstract), 31st July, 1606.

[3] Offers and Letter of Angus Macdonald, dated 8th Sept., 1606. Criminal Trials, III. 365-6.

had various conferences with Lord Scone on the subject.
In the month of November matters were so far arranged between these noblemen, that Argyle agreed
to take in feu, besides the lands of Kintyre, as many of
the King's lands in the Isles as Lord Scone should
require him to accept, paying the same yearly rent as
was fixed in the reign of King James V.; and bound
himself to let none of these lands to persons of the
name of Macdonald or Maclean, without his Majesty's
licence.[1] About this time, Sir James Macdonald,
being informed of Argyle's proceedings, made an
attempt to escape from Edinburgh Castle; but being unsuccessful, he was put in irons to prevent any future
attempt of that kind.[2] Soon afterwards Archibald Macdonald of Gigha, the hostage for the obedience of Angus
Macdonald of Dunyveg, made his escape from Dunbarton,[3] an occurrence which was eagerly laid hold of
by the enemies of the Clandonald of Kintyre and Isla
to increase the general odium against that unfortunate
tribe. The King having signified his appro-
A. D. 1607. val of the agreement between the Comptroller
and the Earl of Argyle, a charter was now granted to the
latter of the lands in North and South Kintyre, and in
the Isle of Jura, which had formerly belonged to, and
were forfeited by, Angus Macdonald;[4] and thus did

---

[1] Original Conditions required of Argyle, with his Answers, dated
in Nov., 1606, and preserved in the Gen. Reg. House.

[2] Pitcairn's Criminal Trials, III. 7.

[3] Letter, Privy Council to the King, 16th March, 1607; Denmylne
MS., Advocates' Library.

[4] Reg. of Privy Seal, LXXVI., fo. 88. The feu-duty, payable
chiefly in kind, for this grant was very considerable; but a large portion of it was permanently remitted to Argyle by Parliament in this
year, for his services against the Clangregor.—Acts of Par., IV. 379.

the legal right to the lands of Kintyre pass from a tribe which had held them for many hundred years. The danger which was threatened to the Clandonald by the terms on which the Earl of Argyle had acquired their ancient inheritance, caused the tribe to draw together in arms under their chief, Angus Macdonald, who now began to despair of obtaining any favourable terms from the Government. Information was brought to the Council, in July, 1607, that the Clandonald and their rebellious associates had lately assembled a number of men in galleys, intending to "invade and pursue his Majesty's good subjects by sea and land, wherever they might find an advantage." If such an intention was really announced, the object was evidently to prevent the men of the western Lowland shires from leaving those districts to follow a Royal commissioner to the Isles; and this object was so far attained, that the inhabitants of Galloway and Carrick were ordered to keep themselves in readiness to defend their own shores from the Islanders; and the Earl of Argyle, who was soon after appointed Justiciar and Lieutenant over the South Isles, was only empowered to call out the militia of Argyle and Tarbert to assist him.[1] As the sheriff-dom of Tarbert, now merged in that of Argyle, was composed of Kintyre and the South Isles, the effect of this limitation was, that the Earl undertook this service with the assistance of his own vassals and friends on the mainland of Argyle alone, since he could not look for much assistance among the very people whom he was sent to reduce to obedience. As the governor, for the time, of the Castle of Dunyveg disobeyed a mandate

---

[1] Record of Privy Council, 31st July and 12th Aug., 1607.

of the Privy Council, ordering him to deliver that fortress to Argyle,[1] it would appear that that nobleman was
not prepared, with such slender means, to attempt a
task so formidable as a siege of that place, more particularly as his commission was only to endure for six
months.   This, therefore, forms another to be added to
the list of abortive attempts at the improvement of the
Isles, which characterise so great a portion of the reign
of James VI.

At the same time that the Earl of Argyle received
this commission over the South Isles, it was directed by
the King that the Marquis of Huntly should be
employed to reduce all the North Isles, except Sky and
the Lewis; and, in consequence, there ensued various
conferences on the subject between that powerful nobleman and the Scottish Privy Council.   The King's
intention was that the Marquis on succeeding in the
duty imposed upon him, should receive a grant of the
Isles in question, to be held of the Crown in fee farm,
for the payment of a certain rent.   It was supposed,
and justly, that the service would be followed out with
more alacrity on this principle, than if Huntly were
employed as a mere officer of the Crown, with no prospect of individual advantage.   At first, however, the
Privy Council could not come to terms with the Marquis, but submitted his offers with their remarks to the
consideration of his Majesty.   In a short time the
King's pleasure was signified to the Council, that certain
conditions, sent direct from the Court, should be proposed
for the Marquis' acceptance.   It is scarcely credible that
such conditions should have emanated from a King of

Reg. of Privy Seal, LXXVIII., fo. 31.

Great Britain in the seventeenth century; and yet there seems no reason to doubt that, if not originally suggested by James himself, they certainly received his approval. They were as follow:—That the Marquis should undertake the service upon his own private means alone— that he should conclude it within a year, and have no exemption from paying rent but for that space—*that he should end the service, not by agreement with the country people, but by extirpating them* — that he should take all the North Isles, except Sky and the Lewis, in feu from the King, as being in his Majesty's hands by forfeiture of the present possession, or otherwise—and that he should pay for these Isles such a rent as should be fixed by the Comptroller of Scotland, according to the principles observed in the rental of the South Isles. The Marquis of Huntly, to his shame be it recorded, accepted nearly all these conditions, undertaking *to end the service, by extirpation of the barbarous people of the Isles, within a year.* He declined, however, to leave the fixing of the rent or feu-duty to the Comptroller, but offered to pay four hundred pounds a-year, of which three hundred were to be for Uist, and the remaining hundred for the other isles specified. This rent the Council refused to accept, as being " a very mean dewtie " for the isles which were to be granted to Huntly, but left this point to the decision of the King as the party chiefly concerned.[1] Before, however, this difference was finally settled, and the vassals of Huntly let loose to massacre the barbarous

---

[1] Record of Privy Council from 26th March to 30th April, 1607. Letter, Huntly to the King, dated 26th March ; and Letters, the Privy Council to the King, dated 26th March, 1st May, and 19th June, 1607; in Denmylne MS., Advocates' Library.

Islesmen, the jealousy entertained by the Presbyterians of any increase to the power of the Marquis, who was an adherent of the Church of Rome, caused this enter- prise to be abandoned altogether. When Huntly appeared before the Privy Council on the 23rd of June, to hear the final determination of the King regarding the amount of rent to be paid for his grants in the Isles, he was, on a complaint by the more violent of the Presbyterians, ordered by the Council to confine himself within the burgh of Elgin, and a circuit of eighteen miles round it; and while in this durance he was enjoined to hear the sermons of certain Presbyterian divines, that so he might be reclaimed from his errors.[1] This acci- dent—for it does not bear the appearance of a scheme concerted to save the Islanders—seems alone to have prevented the reign of James VI. from being stained by a massacre which, for atrocity and the deliberation with which it was planned, would have left that of Glenco far in the shade. But whether the interference of the Presbyterians was accidental or intentional, the Islanders of that day owed nothing to their prince, whose character must for ever bear the stain of having, for the most sordid motives, consigned to destruction thousands of his subjects.

About this time the Lewis adventurers, having sus- tained many annoyances from the persevering hostility of Neill Macleod, who seems to have been assisted by Macneill of Barra, the captain of Clanranald, and Macleod of Harris,[2] began to weary of their undertaking.

---

[1] Record of Privy Council, 23rd June, 1607.

[2] Record of Privy Council (Skene Abstract), 13th March, 31st July (original), 30th Sept., 1606, and 13th August, 1607. Acts of Parlia- ment, IV. 278-281.

Of the original partners, many had for some time withdrawn, some had died, others had spent all their property, and of the remainder, some had more important affairs to call them elsewhere. Thus reduced, and dispirited by the constant attacks made upon them, they forsook the island and returned to their homes. The Lord of Kintaill, who had all along wrought to this end, now began to stir in the matter. By means of his friend the Lord Chancellor, he passed under the great seal a gift of the Lewis to himself, in virtue of the resignation made formerly in his favour by Torquil Connanach Macleod. The surviving adventurers, however, were not so unmindful of their own interests as to suffer this transaction to pass unchallenged. They complained to the King, who was highly incensed at the conduct of Mackenzie, and forced him to resign his right thus surreptitiously obtained. The island being once more, by this step and the consent of the adventurers, at the disposal of his Majesty, he granted it anew to three persons only—viz., James, Lord Balmerino, Sir George Hay of Netherliff, and Sir James Spens of Wormestoun.[1] We shall afterwards have occasion to see the result of an attempt made by these gentlemen to effect the settlement of the Lewis.

After Sir James Macdonald had been put in irons, on his unsuccessful attempt to escape from the Castle of Edinburgh, he made many fruitless applications to the Privy Council for his enlargement. To these applications no answer was returned; nor would the Council even take them into consideration, unless by a special warrant from the King, which they well knew

[1] Sir R. Gordon's History of Sutherland, p. 273-4; Letterfearn MS.; History of Mackenzies.

Sir James, in his present situation, had no prospect of obtaining. Failing in making any impression on those at the head of affairs in Scotland, he attempted to open a correspondence with the Duke of Lennox and the King; but his letters were, in all probability, intercepted —at least, no notice was taken of them.[1] In this state of uncertainty, and anxious to counteract as soon as possible the projects of the Earl of Argyle, Macdonald, in December, 1607, readily joined in a scheme set on foot by the Lord Maxwell, then his fellow prisoner, for escaping from their present durance. The plan was ably conceived and boldly executed. Maxwell made his escape; but Sir James, having injured his ancle by leaping from the wall while encumbered with his fetters, was retaken near the West Port of Edinburgh, and consigned to his former dungeon.[2] The "*treasonable* breaking of ward," as this very natural attempt to escape was styled by the Crown lawyers, was represented in such a light to the King, that instructions were immediately issued for the trial of the unfortunate chief. As a preliminary step, rendered necessary by the forms of the Scottish criminal law, Sir James Macdonald was examined by the Lord Advocate regarding the crimes for which he was to be brought to trial. At this examination he justified his imprisonment of his father by producing a letter from the King approving of that act as good service; but he denied that he had set fire to the house of Askomull. As to the breaking out of Edinburgh Castle, he avowed that he had done so;

A. D. 1608.

---

[1] The Letters are preserved among the Denmylne MS., Advocates' Library.

[2] Pitcairn's Criminal Trials, III., pp. 7, 11.

[3] Record of Privy Council, 11th Jan., 1608.

but denied having hurt with his own hand any of the keepers, some of whom were severely wounded.[1] For some reason which does not appear in any of the State papers of the time, the trial of Sir James Macdonald was now postponed until the month of May, 1609.

The King, having experienced the inutility of trusting to the Scottish militia alone for the furtherance of his projects in the Isles, now determined to employ, in addition, some regular troops and ships of war from Ireland. In the month of March, 1608, this intention was announced to the lieges in Scotland by a proclamation, which (as a sufficient number of troops could not be spared from the Irish garrisons) summoned, to the aid of those intended to be sent, the militia of the shires of Dunbarton, Argyle, Tarbert, Ayr, Renfrew, and Galloway, directing them to meet at Isla, on the first of June, with the forces from Ireland. No lieutenant was yet named to have the chief authority over the expedition; but it was contemplated, at this time, that there should be two of these officers—one for the South, another for the North Isles. Another proclamation was made at the same time, forbidding the chiefs on the mainland opposite the Isles to harbour or give supplies to any of the Islesmen, under the highest penalties. The Scottish Privy Council seem to have neglected nothing which might tend to facilitate the execution of an enterprise implying so much cost and such lengthened preparations. They granted a commission to Andrew, Lord Stewart of Ochiltree, and Andrew Knox, Bishop of the Isles, to meet and confer with Angus Macdonald of Dunyveg and Hector Maclean of Dowart, and to receive offers from these

---

[1] Criminal Trials, III. 11.

chiefs. A month later, this commission was renewed, with the addition of Sir James Hay of Beauly, Comptroller to the Commissioners, who were required to report the result of their conference on or before the 20th of May. Very minute instructions were given by the Council as to the terms to be demanded from the Islanders by the Commissioners. These terms comprehended—*First*, Security for his Majesty's rents; *Secondly*, Obedience to the laws by the chiefs and all their followers; *Thirdly*, Delivery by the chiefs of all "houses of defence, strongholds, and *crannaks*," to be placed at the King's disposal; *Fourthly*, Renunciation by the chiefs of all jurisdictions which they claimed, heritably or otherwise, and submission to the jurisdiction of sheriffs, bailies, justices, or other officers appointed by the Crown; *Fifthly*, That they should be satisfied with such lands and possessions, and under such conditions as the King might appoint; *Sixthly*, That their whole birlings, lymphads, and galleys should be destroyed, save those required for carrying to the mainland his Majesty's rents paid in kind, and other necessary purposes; *Seventhly*, That they, and such of their kinsmen as could afford it, should put their children to school, under the directions of the Privy Council; *Lastly*, That they should abstain from using guns, bows, and two-handed swords, and should confine themselves to single-handed swords and targes. A mandate was issued to Angus Macdonald, his son, Angus Oig, and all others, keepers of the Castle of Dunyveg, charging them to surrender that fortress to the officer bearer of the mandate, within twenty-four hours after his arrival. At the same time, a new proclamation was made, adding to the militia formerly summoned to meet at Isla on the 1st of June the array of Edinburgh and the other southern counties, and of Stirling, Fife, Kinross, Perth, Clackmannan, and Forfarshires. This proclamation proceeded on the ground that the service in the Isles would be a great burden on those formerly charged to undertake it; and that, as the whole country would benefit equally by the success of the enterprise, every county should bear its portion of the burden. This change having rendered delay necessary, the day of meeting at Isla was now postponed from the 1st of June to the 1st of July.[1]

The above proclamations of the Privy Council were, in the month of May, approved of by Parliament; after an attempt, on the part of the Government, to procure a sum of money from the estates in lieu of their personal service had failed. The Parliament declared they were ready to serve his Majesty according to the proclamation; but refused to tax themselves.[2] The preparations for the service in the Isles seemed now to proceed with great vigour. Vessels were ordered to be in readiness to transport the Lowland militia to the Isles; the enlisting of soldiers for foreign service was forbidden during the continuance of the present service; and the burghers of the west were ordered to prepare a number of boats, well furnished with biscuit, ale, wine, beer, and other victuals, for the support of the army, to whom these provisions were to be sold at a reasonable rate for ready money. The Bishop of the Isles was sent by the Council to the King to ascertain finally his Majesty's resolutions on certain important points, and particularly in regard to a recommendation of the Council,

---

[1] Record of Privy Council, from 8th March to 14th April, 1608.
[2] Acts of Parliament, IV. 404.

that only one lieutenant should be employed against all the Isles. A body of five hundred soldiers was ordered to be levied as a guard to the Lieutenant, and the sum of ten thousand merks was allotted for their monthly pay and transport.[1]

Upon the return of the Bishop from Court, it appeared that Lord Ochiltree was the person chosen by the King to act as Lieutenant over the Isles, as being a nobleman of whose "fidelity, courage, and magnanimity," his Majesty had had sufficient proof. The King wrote very fully in answer to the queries proposed to him, enjoining particularly the appointment of a council to assist Lord Ochiltree, and that the Bishop should be at the head of this body; the other members of which, with one exception, were to be chosen from among the gentlemen summoned to attend the Lieutenant on the service. The remaining counsellor was to be named by the Comptroller, "the better to attend to all matters concerning the augmentation or more sure payment of the King's rents in the Isles." Full power was conferred upon Ochiltree to treat with all or any of the Islanders, and encourage them to obedience, according to certain directions laid down, by which the King's opinion was to be taken in each case. Such castles and strengths in the Isles as the Lieutenant and his council should think fit, were to be garrisoned by him—all the others were to be demolished. Provision was made for a body-guard of thirty men to the Bishop at the public cost, on account of the poverty of his see; and while the King remitted to the consideration of the Privy Council the most proper course to be taken with regard to Sir

[1] Record of Privy Council, 21st May to 9th June, 1608; various Letters among Denmylne MS., Advocates' Library, ad tempus.

24

James Macdonald, he gave at the same time strict injunctions for the safe custody of this restless and daring
chief.[1] The further preparations for this insular expedition were not completed till early in the month·of
August, when Lord Ochiltree, with the Scottish division
of the forces, was joined off the island of Isla by some
vessels and troops from Ireland under Sir William St.
John, and the armament was, at a later period, still
further increased by the arrival of an English galley
and another vessel, the latter of which carried a battering train with its necessary ammunition. The Castle
of Dunyveg, in Isla, was delivered to the Lieutenant by
Angus Macdonald without hesitation, along with the
Fort of Lochgorme in the same island. The latter was
instantly demolished; but a garrison of twenty-four men
was placed in the former. On the 14th of August the
armament sailed from Isla, and on the 15th, after a
very tempestuous voyage, reached the Castle of Dowart
in the Sound of Mull. This fortress having been summoned in the regular manner, was surrendered by its
proprietor, Hector Maclean of Dowart, to Lord Ochiltree, by whom it was garrisoned and furnished on the
17th. Ochiltree had previously proclaimed, that as
Royal Lieutenant he would hold a court at the Castle
of Aros in Mull, to which all the chiefs in the Isles were
summoned, and at which he proposed, among other
things, to carry into effect in Mull that part of his commission relating to the destruction of the lymphads,
birlings, and Highland galleys. But in the meantime,
having ascertained that this would be attended with great
injustice to the Islanders, unless the galleys and other

[1] Record of Privy Council, 14th June to 9th July, 1608.

vessels on the adjacent coasts of the mainland were likewise destroyed, so as to secure the Isles from molestation on the part of their neighbours, he wrote to the Council for further instructions on this point, requesting also permission to deal with the mainland castles as he should think proper.[1] The powers he requested were immediately granted to him, under a reservation which saved from destruction the boats and vessels belonging to "obedient subjects."[2] At Aros the following Isles-men assembled to attend the Lieutenant's court—viz., Angus Macdonald of Dunyveg; Hector Maclean of Dowart; Lauchlan, his brother; Donald Gorme Macdonald of Sleat; Donald MacAllan, captain of the Clanranald; Ruari Macleod of Harris; Allaster, his brother; and Neill MacIlduy, and Neill MacRuari, two gentlemen in Mull, followers of Maclean of Dowart; who all, if we may believe the report of Lord Ochiltree, placed themselves at his disposal without condition or promise.[3] It appears, however, from a contemporary author, that this report cannot altogether be depended on. According to this writer, Ochiltree conferred at length with the Islanders, "giving them fair words, promising to be their friend, and to deal with the King in their favour." Having taken very strict order with Angus Macdonald for his future obedience, he suffered that chief to depart home. But not finding the others so ready to accede to all his proposals, the Lieutenant, by the advice of his chief counsellor, the Bishop of the

---

[1] Letter from Lord Ochiltree to the Privy Council, dated at Dowart, in Mull, 18th August, 1608; Denmylne MS., Advocates' Library.

[2] Record of Privy Council, 1st September, 1608.

[3] Ibid, 5th October, 1608.

Isles, invited them to hear a sermon preached by that prelate on board the King's ship, called the Moon, and afterwards prevailed upon them to dine with him on board.   Ruari Macleod of Harris alone refused to enter the vessel, suspecting some sinister design.   When dinner was ended, Ochiltree told the astonished chiefs that they were his prisoners by the King's order, and weighing anchor, he sailed direct to Ayr, whence he shortly proceeded with his prisoners to Edinburgh, and presented them before the Privy Council,[1] by whose orders they were placed in the several Castles of Dunbarton, Blackness, and Stirling.   In the report of his proceedings which Ochiltree on this occasion gave in to the Privy Council, he assigned the lateness of the season as an excuse for his not having proceeded against Macneill of Barra and Macleod of Lewis, intimating at the same time that the former of these chiefs was a depender upon Maclean of Dowart, who would answer for his obedience.   He stated, likewise, that he had, in compliance with a letter from the Comptroller, restored to Maclean the Castles of Dowart and Aros, upon the promise of that chief to surrender them when required; that he had taken surety for the delivery of the Castle of Mingarry in Ardnamurchan; and that he had broken and destroyed all the galleys and other vessels he could find in those parts of the Isles which he visited.[2]

The imprisonment of so many powerful chiefs at one time afforded to the King a fairer opportunity than he had yet enjoyed of improving the condition of the Isles, in conformity with his long cherished projects; nor was

[1] Chronicle of the Kings of Scotland, printed by the Maitland Club, p. 176; Collectanea de Rebus Albanicis, I. 113, 114.

[2] Record of Privy Council, 5th October, 1608.

he backward in availing himself of it. The Islanders, also, finding themselves in his power, presented most humble petitions, submitting themselves entirely to his pleasure, making many offers in order to procure their liberation, and taking credit for having come willingly with the Lieutenant to give their obedience before the Privy Council.[1] A number of Commissioners, selected from the nobility, the prelates, and the officers of state, were appointed to receive the offers of the Islesmen, and to consult and deliberate upon all matters connected with the civilisation of the Isles and the increase of his Majesty's rents. The chief of these Commissioners were, the Archbishop of Glasgow, the Bishop of the Isles, Lord Ochiltree, and Sir James Hay of Kingask, Comptroller; and they entered upon the discharge of their duties under very minute instructions from the King, which expressly provided that, in every case, the result of their deliberations should be submitted for the approval of his Majesty. From these instructions we find that, although James was actively engaged in expelling most of the Irish inhabitants from Ulster, and in granting their lands to settlers from England and Scotland, yet he now hesitated to treat, with like severity, the same Scottish Islanders whom in the preceding year he had actually proposed to extirpate. His chief object now seems to have been to curtail the power of the great proprietors, by procuring from them the voluntary surrender of considerable portions of the estates which they claimed as their inheritance.[2] In

---

[1] Original Petition of Donald Gorme, Maclean of Dowart, and the captain of Clanranald (MS., Adv. Lib., A. 2, 4, No. 17), dated 10th November, 1608. Record of Privy Council, February, 1609.

[2] Royal Commission and Instructions for settling the affairs of

this, as in many of his projects, which sounded well in theory, James was disappointed; but other suggestions made by him at this time, favoured as they were by circumstances, and followed up with zeal by the Commissioners, were productive of so much benefit, that from this time we may trace a gradual and permanent improvement of the Isles and adjacent Highlands.

A. D. 1609. In the early part of the year 1609, many communications took place between the Commissioners for the Isles and the chiefs of the Islanders, as well those who remained in prison as those who were still at large. The offers made by the chiefs were carefully considered by the Commissioners; and the result of the deliberations of the latter was submitted to the King by the Bishop of the Isles, who went to Court as their representative. In case of resistance on the part of any of the Islanders to such measures as might be finally determined on by the Government, the most effectual means were taken to deprive them of shelter or support from the proprietors on the mainland, by binding the latter, under heavy penalties, to oppose the rebels.[1] At the same time, in order probably to strike terror into those chiefs who were supposed to meditate resistance, Sir James Macdonald, who had lain so long in prison, was brought to trial, and condemned to death. The crimes charged against him were, *first*, his setting fire to the house of Askomull, and making prisoner of

the Isles, dated 6th December, 1608, and recorded in the Books of Privy Council, 6th February, 1609.

[1] Record of Privy Council, 6th February to 12th May, 1609. On the latter day, Angus Macdonald of Dunyveg, having presented himself before the Privy Council, was committed to ward in the Castle of Blackness.

his father, which was alleged to be "maist high and manifest treasoun;" and, *secondly*, the treasonable attempts made by him, at different times, to "break ward," or escape from prison. In regard to the first charge, he denied the fire-raising, and produced a warrant from the King approving of his conduct in apprehending his father. This warrant, however, Sir James afterwards withdrew, and declined to use. He then protested that no evidence taken against him by the Earl of Argyle should be admitted at this trial, on the ground that the Earl had seized his estate, and was his enemy, and the enemy of his clan. Nevertheless, Sir James was convicted, on the evidence of his father and mother, not delivered in court, but transmitted in writing to the Lord Advocate by the Earl of Argyle, himself the supreme criminal judge in Scotland, from whom the Justice Depute who tried the case held his commission. The second charge—that of breaking ward—Macdonald admitted, with the exception of the allegation, that, in his last attempt to escape, he had wounded severely some of his keepers; but the evidence of the latter clearly established his guilt in this particular. A verdict of guilty was returned, by a jury composed of Lowland gentlemen of landed property, through their chancellor or foreman, Lord Ochiltree; and after an imprisonment of nearly six years, Sir James was sentenced to be beheaded as a traitor, and all his lands and possessions were declared forfeited to the Crown.[1] He was then conveyed back to his former dungeon in the Castle of Edinburgh, where, instead of suffering the penalty of his treason, he was allowed to

---

[1] Criminal Trials, III., p. 5-10.

linger under sentence of death for six years longer, until, at length, his escape put it out of the power of the Government to bring him to execution. It is not difficult to account for the lenity thus shown towards an individual described in the indictment against him as a monster of barbarity from his youth upwards, and actually convicted of many treasonable crimes. Allusion has been made to a warrant or letter from the King, approving of Sir James Macdonald's conduct in regard to the apprehension and imprisonment of his father, Angus Macdonald of Dunyveg (supra, p. 282). That such a warrant existed, there can be no doubt; and that it would not have represented his Majesty in the most favourable point of view, is very probable; but the precise terms of it are now unknown. It seems clear, however, that the King and his advisers dreaded the publication of it. Hence, in return for the complaisance of the prisoner in withholding from the jury a document of this delicate nature, Macdonald, in all probability, received an assurance that it was not intended to carry into effect the capital part of his sentence. Hopes of an ultimate pardon, too, may have been held out; and, on the other hand, Sir James must have been well aware, that, to persist in exposing the King, would necessarily take away the only chance of life yet left to him, by preventing the exercise of the Royal prerogative of mercy. But in whatever manner we may account for the fact, certain it is that Macdonald was not executed according to his sentence, and that he lay in prison until he effected his escape in 1615, when he once more exerted, although for a short time, a powerful influence over the Islanders, as will appear more fully in the course of the present work.

The Bishop of the Isles, who had, early in the present
year, been sent by the Commissioners of the Isles to
Court, in order to communicate the result of their
deliberations to the King, returned in the end of June,
bearing instructions as to the course which, after a
review of the whole subject, his Majesty considered the
most proper to be followed. This was, that the Bishop
of the Isles and the Comptroller should, in the present
summer, visit and survey the Isles, being accompanied,
both in their voyage thither and in their return, by
Angus Macdonald of Dunyveg and Hector Maclean
of Dowart, who were to be liberated for this purpose.
The other chiefs and gentlemen already in prison were
to remain in prison till the return of the Commissioners
from their survey; and to procure the attendance of as
many of the remaining chiefs as possible before the
Privy Council, the Bishop and Comptroller were to be
empowered to give letters of safe conduct to such as
would promise to come to Edinburgh. The Commissioners for the Isles, however, availed themselves of a
discretionary power given to them by the King, in
regard to the proposed survey, so as to alter materially
the plan suggested by his Majesty. The Bishop of the
Isles was deputed to proceed as sole Commissioner on
this service; and all the chiefs and gentlemen now in
prison were liberated, on finding security to a large
amount, not only for their return to Edinburgh by a
certain fixed day, but for their active concurrence, in
the meantime, with the Bishop in making the projected
survey. Three thousand pounds were allowed to the
latter for his expenses; and in case any of the Islanders
should, after the offer of a safe conduct, still refuse to
come before the Privy Council, the Bishop was armed

with full power to compel their obedience by the assistance of the well-disposed chiefs and their followers.[1] The Bishop set sail on his mission about the middle of July, and so complete were the arrangements made, that, before the end of that month, almost all the principal Islesmen met him in the celebrated Island of Icolmkill or Iona, and submitted themselves to him, as the Royal representative, in the most unreserved manner.[2] Determined to take advantage of this unanimity, the Bishop held a court, in which, with the consent of the assembled chiefs, nine statutes of the utmost importance for the improvement of the Isles were enacted; and the obedience of the natives to these statutes insured, as far as this could be done, by the bonds and solemn oaths of their superiors. The "Statutes of Icolmkill" deserve the particular attention of the lover of Highland history.

The *first* statute proceeded upon the narrative of the gross ignorance and barbarity of the Islanders, alleged to have arisen partly from the small number of their clergy, and partly from the contempt in which this small number of pastors was held. To remedy this state of things, it was agreed that proper obedience should be given to the clergy—(whose number, much diminished by the Reformation, it was proposed to increase)—that

---

[1] Record of Privy Council, June, 1609.

[2] The chiefs and gentlemen who met the Bishop at this time were—Angus Macdonald of Dunyveg; Hector Maclean of Dowart; Donald Gorme of Sleat; Ruari Macleod of Harris; Donald MacAllan Vic Ian of Ilanteram (captain of the Clanranald); Lauchlan Maclean of Coll; Lauchlan Mackinnon of that Ilk; Hector Maclean of Lochbuy; Lauchlan and Allan Macleans, brothers-german to Dowart; Gillespick Macquarrie of Ulva; and Donald Macfie in Colonsay. —Collectanea de Rebus Albanicis, I. 119. Record of Privy Council, 27th July, 1610.

their stipends should be regularly paid—that ruinous churches should be rebuilt—that the Sabbaths should be solemnly kept; and that in all respects they should observe the discipline of the Reformed Kirk, as established by Act of Parliament. By one of the clauses of this statute *marriages contracted for certain years were declared illegal;* a proof that the ancient practice of handfasting still prevailed to a certain extent. The *second* statute ordained the establishment of inns at the most convenient places in the several Isles; and this not only for the convenience of travellers, but to relieve the tenants and labourers of the ground from the great burden and expense caused to them through the want of houses of public entertainment. The *third* statute was intended to diminish the number of idle persons, whether masterless vagabonds or belonging to the households of the chiefs and landlords; for experience had shown that the expense of supporting these idlers fell chiefly upon the tenantry in addition to their usual rents. It was therefore enacted that no man should be suffered to reside within the Isles who had not a sufficient revenue of his own; or who, at least, did not follow some trade by which he might live. With regard to the great households hitherto kept by the chiefs, a limit was put to the number of individuals of which each household was to consist in future, according to the rank and estate of the master; and it was further provided that each chief should support his household from his own means, not by a tax upon his tenantry. The *fourth* statute provided that all persons, not natives of the Isles, who should be found sorning, or living at free quarters upon the poor inhabitants (an evil which seems to have reached a great height), should be tried and punished by the Judge Ordinary as thieves and oppressors. The *fifth* statute proceeded upon the narrative that one of the chief causes of the great poverty of the Isles, and of the cruelty and inhuman barbarity practised in their feuds, was their inordinate love of strong wines and aquavite, which they purchased partly from dealers among themselves, partly from merchants belonging to the mainland. Power was, therefore, given to any person whatever to seize, without payment, any wine or aquavite imported for sale by a native merchant; and if an Islander should buy any of the prohibited articles from a mainland trader, he was to incur the penalty of forty pounds for the first offence; one hundred pounds for the second; and for the third, the loss of his whole possessions and movable goods. It was, however, declared to be lawful for an individual to brew as much aquavite as his own family might require; and the barons and wealthy gentlemen were permitted to purchase in the Lowlands the wine and other liquors required for their private consumption. The *sixth* statute attributed the "ignorance and incivilitie" of the Islanders to the neglect of good education among the youth; and to remedy this fault, enacted that every gentleman or yeoman possessed of sixty cattle should send his eldest son, or, if he had no male children, his eldest daughter, to school in the Lowlands, and maintain his child there till it had learned to speak, read, and write English. The *seventh* statute forbade the use of any description of fire arms, even for the destruction of game, under the penalties contained in an Act of Parliament passed in the present reign, which had never yet received obedience from the Islanders, "owing to their monstrous deadly feuds." The *eighth*

statute was directed against bards and other idlers of
that class.   The gentry were forbidden to encourage
them; and the bards themselves were threatened, first
with the stocks and then with banishment.   The *ninth*
statute contained some necessary enactments for enforcing obedience to the preceding acts.   Such were the
statutes of Icolmkill; for the better observance of which,
and of the laws of the realm and Acts of Parliament
in general, the Bishop took from the assembled chiefs
a very strict bond.[1]   This bond, moreover, contained
a sort of confession of faith on the part of the sub-
scribers, and an unconditional acknowledgment of his
Majesty's supreme authority in all matters both spiritual
and temporal, according to his "most lovable act of
supremacy."   It is a fact which may appear startling
to many, but it is not the less evident on that account,
that the first traces of that overflowing loyalty to the
house of Stewart for which the Highlanders have been
so highly lauded, are to be found in that generation of
their chiefs whose education was conducted on the high
church and state principles of the British Solomon.
There is no room to doubt that the chiefs who followed
Montrose in the great civil war were actuated by a very
different spirit from their fathers; and it is well worthy
of notice that this difference was produced in the course
of a single generation, by the operation of measures
which first began to take effect after the year 1609.

In the month of September the Bishop appeared
before the Lords Commissioners for the Isles in Edinburgh, and presented a report of his proceedings; but,

---

[1] Record of Privy Council, 27th July, 1610.   The statutes and bond
were dated the 23rd and 24th August, 1609.   See also Collectanea de
Rebus Albanicis, I., p. 115-120.

as he proposed immediately going to Court to wait upon his Majesty, the Report was returned to him in order to be shown to the King. In the meantime, until his Majesty's pleasure should be signified, the necessary measures were taken by the Lords Commissioners for securing a general attendance of the Islanders before them in the month of February following. This term was afterwards prolonged till the end of June, on the ground that the King had not as yet resolved what course to take for settling the affairs of the Isles. At the time the Bishop of the Isles returned from his survey a complaint was made to the Lords Commissioners by Maclean of Dowart, Macdonald of Isla, and other chiefs, against an oppressive proclamation, by which the inhabitants of the mainland of Argyle were prohibited from purchasing cattle, horses, or other goods, within any of the Western Isles. It does not appear by whom this proclamation was issued; but as it was calculated to hurt his Majesty's revenue from the Isles, which the tenants could only pay by disposing of their produce to dealers from the mainland, it was immediately annulled by the Lords Commissioners as unlawful, and all the lieges were strictly prohibited from interfering with the trade of the Isles.[1]

We have seen that about the year 1608 the Isle of Lewis had been granted anew to three persons—Lord Balmerino, Sir George Hay, and Sir James Spens. The trial and conviction of Balmerino for high treason in March, 1609, effectually precluded that nobleman from taking any active share in the enterprise of colonising

---

[1] Record of Privy Council, 28th September, 1609, to 15th March, 1610. Collectanea de Rebus Albanicis, I. 153.

the island; but Hay and Spens made very extensive
preparations for availing themselves of the Royal grant.
With their own forces, and assisted by many of the
neighbouring Highlanders, they invaded the Lewis, not
only to set on foot their colony, but to apprehend, if
possible, Neill Macleod, who still held out and opposed
their designs. Neill was secretly encouraged by Mackenzie of Kintaill, who, however, escaped suspicion by
sending his brother (afterwards the Tutor of Kintaill)
to aid the colonists. Having shipped some victuals
in Ross for the supply of the colonists, Mackenzie
secretly procured the vessel to be seized, on her
passage to the Lewis, by Neill Macleod; expecting
that the adventurers, trusting to these provisions
and disappointed, would be forced to abandon the
island. This expectation was fulfilled; for Sir George
Hay and Sir James Spens being unsuccessful in apprehending Neill, and lacking victuals for their followers,
were forced to quit the island and disband their forces,
leaving, however, a small garrison in the fort of Stornoway, until they should send a supply of men and
provisions. The fort was very soon after their departure
surprised and burned by Neill Macleod, and the garrison
taken prisoners. These he sent home safely to Fife:
and thus ended the last attempt made by the Lowlanders to colonise the Lewis. Disgusted
with their want of success, Sir George Hay
and Sir James Spens were easily prevailed on to sell
their title to the Lord of Kintaill, who likewise succeeded in obtaining from the King a grant of the share
in the island forfeited by Lord Balmerino.[1] Having

A. D. 1610.

---

[1] Sir R. Gordon's History of Sutherland, p. 274; Reg. of Privy Seal,
LXXIX., fo. 91; Letterfearn MS.

now at length acquired a legal right to the Lewis,
Mackenzie lost no time in asserting his claims. He
procured from the Government a commission of fire
and sword against the Lewismen;[1] and, landing in the
island with a large force of his clan and followers,
speedily reduced the Islanders to obedience, with the
exception of Neill Macleod and a few of his followers.
As the Siol Torquil never after this succeeded in
making head in the Lewis, it may be proper here to
notice briefly the fate of such of the leaders of that
unfortunate tribe as still survived.

Neill Macleod, the bastard, with his nephews, Malcolm, William, and Ruari (sons of Ruari Oig), and
about thirty others, retired to an insulated rock, called
Berrisay, on the west coast of Lewis, where they maintained themselves for nearly three years.[2] Being then
forced to evacuate this strength by the Mackenzies,
Neill retired to Harris, where he remained for a while
in secret, but at length surrendered himself to Ruari
Macleod of Harris, whom he entreated to take him to
the King in England. This the chief of Harris undertook to do; but when at Glasgow with his prisoner,
preparing to embark for England, he was charged,
under pain of treason, to deliver Neill Macleod to the
Privy Council at Edinburgh, which he accordingly did;
and, at the same time, gave up Neill's son, Donald.
Neill was brought to trial, convicted, and executed, and

---

[1] Record of Privy Council, 19th July, 1610.

[2] While dwelling on this rock, Neill Macleod, hoping to make his
peace with the Government, captured a pirate vessel, commanded by
a Captain Love, who with his crew was afterwards hanged.—Criminal
Trials, III. 100. Collectanea de Rebus Albanicis, I. 48, 49. Letterfearn MS.

died "very christianlie" in April, 1613. Donald, his son, being banished out of Scotland, went to England and remained there three years, under the protection of Sir Robert Gordon, Tutor of Sutherland. From England he afterwards went to Holland, where he died. After the death of Neill Macleod, the Tutor of Kintaill apprehended and executed Ruari and William, two of the sons of Ruari Oig Macleod. Malcolm, the third son, was apprehended at the same time, but made his escape, and continued to harass the Mackenzies with frequent incursions, having allied himself to the Clandonald of Isla and Kintyre, in whose rebellion under Sir James Macdonald, in 1615, Malcolm MacRuari Macleod took a prominent part. On the suppression of this rebellion, he retired to Flanders, whence, in 1616, he made a visit to the Lewis, and there killed two gentlemen of the Clankenzie. He then joined Sir James Macdonald in Spain, and remained there till the return of that chief to Britain in 1620. On this occasion, Malcolm Macleod accompanied Sir James; and of his further history we only know that, in 1622 and in 1626, commissions of fire and sword were granted to Lord Kintaill and his clan, against "Malcolm MacRuari Macleod."[1] Tormod Macleod, the last surviving *legitimate* son of old Ruari Macleod of the Lewis, was imprisoned, as we have seen, in Edinburgh Castle, in 1605 (supra, p. 310). Here he remained for ten years, when the King gave him liberty to go to Holland, to the service of Maurice, Prince of Orange; and he died in that country. His elder brother-german, Torquil Dubh, executed by the Mackenzies in 1597 (supra, p. 271), left

---

[1] Record of Privy Council, 14th November, 1622; 28th November, 1626.

issue by his wife, a sister of Ruari Macleod of Harris, three sons, Ruari, William, and Torquil. The second of these seems to have died soon; and although the others are mentioned by Sir Robert Gordon as youths of great promise at the time he wrote his account of the Siol Torquil, they appear to have both died without lawful issue to inherit their claims to the Lewis, which has now remained for upwards of two centuries, without challenge, in the possession of the Mackenzies.[1] The representation of the ancient and powerful family of Macleod of Lewis devolved, on the extinction of the main stem, on Gillechallum Oig Macleod, or MacGille-challum of Rasay, whose father, Gillechallum Garve, is mentioned, in a charter dated 1572, as heir-male of the family of Lewis, failing issue male of the body of Ruari Macleod, then chief of the Siol Torquil.[2]

---

[1] Sir R. Gordon's History of Sutherland, pp. 270-6. Criminal Trials, III. 244-7. Record of Privy Council, 19th July, 1610, 2nd March, 1613, and 9th February, 1615. Letterfearn MS.

[2] Reg. of Great Seal, Lib. XXXIII., No. 31. This Gillechallum Garve it was, who, when a child, escaped by accident, when many of his family were massacred.—Supra, p. 212.

CHAP. VIII.

A. D. 1610. THE King having signified to the Scottish Privy Council his approval of the Bishop's proceedings, and given certain general instructions for the furtherance of the work so well begun, six of the principal Islanders assembled in Edinburgh, on the 28th of June, to hear his Majesty's pleasure declared to them. Maclean of Dowart, Macdonald of Sleat, Macdonald of Dunyveg, Macleod of Harris, the captain of Clanranald, and Mackinnon of Strathordell, were those who now presented themselves before the Council; and to them was joined Cameron of Lochiel, or (as he is styled in the record) Allan Cameron Mac-Ianduy of Lochaber. The first step taken by the Government was to compel these chiefs to give suréties to a large amount for their reappearance before the Council in May, 1611. The next, was to cause them to give their solemn promise that they should concur with and assist the King's Lieutenants, Justices, and Commissioners, in all matters connected with the Isles; that they should all live together in future in peace, love, and amity; and that they should follow out any questions that might arise among them according to the ordinary course of law and justice. At the same time a particular feud between the captain of Clanranald and Lochiel,[1] was composed by these chiefs "heartily embracing one another, and chopping hands together," in the presence of the Council, and promising to submit their disputes to the decision of the law. A month later, in conformity with his Majesty's instructions, the Bishop of the Isles received a commission for life, as Steward and Justice of all the North and West Isles of Scotland (except Orkney and Shetland), with the homage and service of the King's tenants in these bounds, and all fees and casualties pertaining to the offices conferred upon him. All former commissions of Lieutenandry over the Isles were recalled, and all heritable jurisdictions, real or pretended, which might interfere with the exercise of the Bishop's commission, were suspended. This prelate was likewise made constable of the Castle of Dunyveg in Isla, which it was arranged should be delivered over to him, or those having his warrant, on the 10th of August, by the garrison which Lord Ochiltree had placed in it two years before.[2]

A. D. 1611.   The immediate result of all these proceedings was, that, during the year 1611, the West Highlands and Isles were almost entirely free from disorders or rebellions. The struggle between the Mackenzies and Macleods for the Island of Lewis was not yet at an end; but it was evident that the force of the latter clan was now broken, and that Ruari Mackenzie of Cogeach, the Tutor of Kintaill (on whom, by

---

[1] This feud seems to have regarded the lands of Knoydert.
[2] Record of Privy Council, 8th May to 27th July, 1610; Reg. of Privy Seal, LXXIX., fo. 78.

the death of his elder brother and the minority of his nephew, the command of the Mackenzies had lately devolved), had little difficulty in keeping the island under subjection. The ancient feud between the Macleods of Rasay and the Mackenzies of Gerloch, regarding the lands of Gerloch, which, in the last year, had displayed itself by mutual incursions, was brought to a sudden close by a skirmish, in which Gillechallum Oig, Laird of Rasay, and Murdoch Mackenzie, a younger son of the Laird of Gerloch, were slain, in the month of August, 1611. From this time the Mackenzies seem to have possessed Gerloch without interruption from the Macleods.[1] The Clanchameron and the Clanranald of Lochaber, under their respective chiefs, Allan Cameron of Lochiel and Alexander MacRanald of Keppoch, instead of waging war with each other, or with the captain of the Clanchattan, were employed to assist the Earl of Argyle in suppressing a serious insurrection of the Clangregor.[2] Several gentlemen of the families of Lochiel and Keppoch refused, however, to engage on this service;[3] which, indeed, if carried into effect with good will by the Highland clans employed, would have speedily ended in the utter ruin of the name of Macgregor. The year 1612 was likewise a year of comparative tranquil-

A. D. 1612.

[1] Sir R. Gordon's History of Sutherland, pp. 276-278. Letterfearn MS.

[2] Record of Privy Council, and Treasurer's Accounts, ad tempus. MS. History of Camerons, which narrates fully the means employed by Argyle to procure the assistance of Lochiel in this service.

[3] Record of Privy Council, 25th February, 1612. Many of the Clanchattan also, particularly the Macphersons, assisted to protect the Clangregor at this time. Ibid., 27th September, 1611.

lity in the West Highlands; but the following year was marked by several commotions.

The most important of these was caused by dissensions among the Camerons, which originated in the following manner. The Earl of Argyle, in examining, about the year 1608, his charter chest, discovered the title-deeds which, in the reign of James V., Colin, third Earl of Argyle, had acquired to the lands of Lochiel, through Sir John Campbell of Calder, who had purchased the claim which Maclean of Lochbuy possessed to these lands (supra, p. 126). The successors of the third Earl had hitherto allowed this claim to lie dormant, and it had in fact been forgotten until the evidence of it was accidentally discovered as above-mentioned. The seventh Earl of Argyle, eager to extend the influence of his family, more particularly where this could be done at the expense of his rival, the Marquis of Huntly, to whose party the Clanchameron were attached, proceeded at once to avail himself of his recently discovered claim to the superiority of the lands of Lochiel. Having, in order to obviate any difficulties that might arise, procured from Hector Maclean of Lochbuy, for a small sum of money, a surrender of any title that chief might be found to have to the lands in question, Argyle easily succeeded in obtaining a new charter from the King in his own favour.[1] He then instituted the usual legal process for removing Allan Cameron of Lochiel and his clan from that part of their possessions, much to the astonishment of Allan, who had never been led to suspect any defect in the title-deeds under which

A.D. 1613.

[1] Reg. of Privy Seal, LXXVII., fo. 65.

he and his immediate predecessors had occupied the lands. Hastening to Edinburgh to take advice touching this unexpected suit, Lochiel there met with the Earl of Argyle, who prevailed on him to submit the question to the decision of the lawyers of both parties. That decision was in favour of the Earl, from whom by agreement Lochiel then took a charter of the lands in dispute, to be held by him as a vassal of Argyle. The Marquis of Huntly, who was then superior of a great part of Lochaber, and from whom Lochiel held Mamore and other lands, was highly offended that Argyle should so easily have obtained a footing in that district; and he endeavoured, by all means, to prevail on Lochiel to violate the agreement he had lately entered into. To this demand, Lochiel would on no account consent; qualifying his refusal, however, by many protestations that, although he now held that portion of his estates under the Earl of Argyle, yet that his so doing should not affect his obedience and service to the Marquis of Huntly, but that he should continue as loyal to that nobleman's family as he and his predecessors had formerly been. This answer was far from satisfactory to the Marquis, who secretly resolved upon Lochiel's ruin; and as the easiest way to accomplish his object, he sought to renew the dissensions which had, in the minority of the present chief, caused so much bloodshed in the Clanchameron (supra, p. 228). The Camerons of Erracht, Kinlochiel, and Glennevis, and their supporters, were easily induced to embrace an offer of the Marquis to become his immediate vassals in those lands which Lochiel had hitherto held from the family of Huntly. Accordingly, the Marquis' eldest son, the Earl of Enzie, proceeding to Lochaber with a body of his vassals, put his adherents among the Clanchameron in possession of the lands of which, by the mere will of the Marquis, Lochiel was now deprived. On the departure of the Earl of Enzie, Lochiel appointed a meeting with his hostile kinsmen, at which he pretended that he was perfectly aware that they had been compelled by force to enter into the Marquis' plans; and he therefore requested them to restore the lands to him, when he doubted not he would be able to satisfy the Marquis. At first they made a verbal promise to agree to Lochiel's demands; but when he desired them to subscribe a writing to that effect, they declined, and pressed him to go with them to the Marquis, with whom they engaged to reconcile him; after which they were to restore his lands. " Lochiel," says our authority, " like ane auld subtile fox, perceiving their drift, and being as careful to preserve his head as they were to twine (separate) him from it," promised to take the matter into consideration, and parted from his refractory clansmen on apparently good terms. He then made another journey to Edinburgh, to consult with his legal advisers as to the most proper course he should pursue to recover his lands again. While in that town he received intelligence that his enemies in the clan had appointed a meeting, to resolve by what means they might have his life, and so secure themselves in their new possessions. Upon this he hastened to Lochaber, sending private notice to such as still adhered to him, to meet him at a certain place, on the day appointed for the assembling of the opposite faction, and within a short distance of the spot selected for the meeting of the latter. The chief supporters of Lochiel on this occasion seem to have been the Camerons of Callart,

Strone, and Letterfinlay. Placing the most of his followers in ambush, Lochiel approached the rendezvous of his opponents with six attendants only, and sent to demand a conference with a like number of the other party. His enemies seeing Lochiel with so small a force, and thinking he had only just arrived in the country, and had had no time to collect his adherents, thought this a favourable opportunity for getting rid of him, and accordingly made towards their chief and his attendants, resolving to take the lives of the whole party. The wary Lochiel retreated, so as to lead his pursuers past the wood where the ambush lay, and then, on a given signal, they were attacked both in front and rear, and routed, with the loss of twenty of their principal men killed (of whom Allaster Cameron of Glennevis was one), and eight taken prisoners. The rest were suffered to escape; and Lochiel then replaced himself in possession of the disputed lands, teaching, as our authority quaintly observes, "ane lessone to the rest of his kin that are alyve, in what forme they shall carrye themselves to their chief hereafter."[1] On the news of this proceeding—which even the historian of the family allows was more necessary than justifiable—reaching the Privy Council, Lochiel and his followers were proclaimed rebels, a price was set upon the heads of the leaders, and a commission of fire and sword was given to the Marquis of Huntly and the Gordons

---

[1] Original State Paper in Gen. Reg. House, titled "James Primrois' Information anent the Ilis and Hielandis, Sept., 1613." (Primrose was then Clerk to the Privy Council.) Record of Privy Council, December, 1613; July, 1617. Reg. of Privy Seal, LXXXII., fo. 285.

for their pursuit and apprehension.[1] The Clancham-
eron, or at least that division of it which had followed
Lochiel in the late quarrel, continued for several years
in a state of outlawry; but through the influence of the
Earl of Argyle, it seems to have suffered less than the
Clangregor in circumstances nearly similar.[2]

The next commotion, in point of importance, which
occurred in the west in this year, proceeded from a
dispute among the Macneills of Barra. Ruari Macneill, the chief of that clan, had several sons by a lady
of the family of Maclean, with whom, according to an
ancient practice not then altogether disused in the Isles,
he had *handfasted*, instead of marrying her. Having
afterwards married a sister of the captain of the Clanranald, his nearest neighbour, his sons by that lady
were generally considered as his only legitimate sons, to
the exclusion of the senior family. The latter, however maintained their prior claims, until forced, by the
influence of the captain of the Clanranald, to yield to
their younger brothers. The eldest son of the senior
family having been concerned in an act of piracy committed on a ship of Bourdeaux, was apprehended by
Clanranald in the Isle of Barra and conveyed to Edinburgh, where he died before being brought to trial. In
revenge of this, his brothers-german, assisted by Maclean
of Dowart, seized Neill Macneill, the eldest son of the
junior family, and nephew of Clanranald, and sent him
to Edinburgh to be tried as an actor in the piracy of
the Bourdeaux ship above mentioned. Of this, however,

---

[1] Record of Privy Council, December, 1613; and Denmylne MS.,
Advocates' Library, ad tempus.

[2] MS. History of the Camerons.

he was found innocent, and liberated through the influence of his uncle. Meantime, the surviving sons of the
first family, thinking that their father was too partial to
their brothers, seized the old chief and placed him in irons.
Being charged, by the usual legal process, to exhibit
their father before the Privy Council, they refused, whereupon, being proclaimed rebels, commission was given
to the captain of Clanranald against them. They are
described as great "lymmars," who never professed his
Majesty's obedience, which induced the Council the more
readily to arm Clanranald (who, indeed, was the only chief
who could conveniently undertake the service) with this
commission.[1] Clanranald seems to have used the powers
committed to him in such a way as to secure the peaceable succession of his nephew to the estate of Barra on
the death of the old chief, which happened soon after.[2]

The South Isles still continued tranquil. Angus
Macdonald of Dunyveg, the old chief of Isla, was now
dead, and a lease of that island, or the greater part of
it, had been granted to Sir Ranald Macdonald (afterwards first Earl of Antrim), son of the well-known
Sorley Buy, and brother of Sir James Macdonald of
Dunluce. It is worthy of remark, that Sir Ranald, having endeavoured to introduce various Irish laws and
customs among his tenants in Isla, met with such opposition from the natives, on the ground of these laws
being "foreign and strange," that he was at length

---

[1] "James Primrois' Information anent the Ilis and Hielandis,
September, 1613," above quoted. Record of Privy Council, 27th
July, 1610, 5th December, 1611, 14th January, 1613. Gen. Reg. of
Hornings, Vol. LIII., 15th July, 1629.

[2] Gen. Reg. of Deeds, Vol. CCCCXXVII., 1st June, 1630. Reg.
of Privy Seal, LXXXI., fo. 233. Charter in Ch. Chest of Barra,
dated 16th May, 1622.

compelled, by an order of the Privy Council, to forego all such projects.[1] The difference existing at this period between the Irish customs and those of the Hebrides, while the language of the people was almost identical, must have arisen from the greater progress made by the feudal system in the Highlands and Isles than in Ireland. Some months later, Sir Ranald MacSorley (as he was generally styled) was in treaty with the Scottish Privy Council,[2] probably for an heritable grant of Isla; but the renewal of the disorders in that island, which we shall speedily have to narrate, cut short this negotiation.

Donald Gorme of Sleat, Ruari (now Sir Ruari) Macleod of Harris, Hector Maclean of Dowart, and Donald MacAllan, captain of the Clanranald, are mentioned as having settled with the Exchequer in this year, and as continuing in their obedience to the laws.[3] It was feared, however, that a contemplated grant, by the King, to Sir James Campbell of Lawers, of the lands of Morvern, claimed by the Macleans, would force that clan into rebellion. But, in that event, provision was made that Lawers and his chief, the Earl of Argyle, should reduce the Macleans to obedience at their own charge, or else that the lands should be given up, to be again at the disposal of his Majesty.[4] This transaction appears never to have been completed.

---

[1] "James Primrois' Information," above quoted. Collectanea de Rebus Albanicis, I., p. 160.

[2] Denmylne MS., Advocates' Library, 8th June, 1613.

[3] "James Primrois' Information." Record of Privy Council, January to July, 1613.

[4] Orig. Memorial concerning the Highlands, in the handwriting of Sir Thomas Hamilton, preserved in the General Register House, and dated 13th April, 1613.

In the spring of the year 1614, the Castle of Dunyveg—which, for upwards of three years, had been held by a small garrison placed in it by the Bishop of the Isles, and which, from over security, was carelessly guarded—was surprised and taken by a bastard son of the late Angus Macdonald, named Ranald Oig, and three or four of his associates. The report of this event being carried to Angus. Oig, the younger brother of Sir James Macdonald of Isla, who was then living within six miles of the castle, he immediately sent round the fiery cross to collect the country people to assist him to recover the castle for the King. He then gave it in charge to his kinsman, Coll MacGillespick, commonly called Coll *Keitache*, or Left-handed, to besiege Ranald Oig, who, with his party, evacuated the castle and escaped by sea, after a siege of six days, when the place was immediately occupied by Coll Macgille-spick.[1] Ranald was afterwards apprehended in Isla by Angus Oig; and when pressed to say who had advised him to the enterprise of taking the castle from the Bishop's garrison, told a very improbable story, by which he endeavoured to lay the blame upon one Donald Gorme, a bastard son of Sir James Macdonald. But it was observed that he destroyed a letter which he had previously kept concealed in his sleeve, and which, although he declared it to be of no importance, he yet at the same time admitted was a letter *not to be seen.* For some time the castle remained in the hands of Angus Oig, who professed his readiness to restore it to the Bishop on receiving a remission for any offences

A. D. 1614.

---

[1] Information given to the Privy Council by Sir James Macdonald, 29th April, 1614, compared with the declarations of Angus Oig and others ; Denmylne MS., Advocates' Library.

committed by him and his supporters.   It was said that
at this time he actually offered the castle to the former
garrison, who refused to receive it.[1]

Sir James Macdonald of Isla now presented a
petition to the Privy Council, showing the distress and
misery he had endured for many years past, and desiring to be liberated, and to be allowed to reside in any
place the King might appoint, until an opportunity
should occur of employing him in his Majesty's service.
He offered surety for his appearance before the Council
whenever summoned, and for his not going to Kintyre
or Isla without licence.   As Sir James was still under
sentence of death, never having received a pardon, the
Privy Council declined interfering, until they had
ascertained his Majesty's pleasure.[2]   Before an answer
could have been received from Court, circumstances
occurred which must have influenced many of the Privy
Counsellors in Sir James' favour.   Information was
received from the Bishop of the Isles, who had gone
to Isla to procure the surrender of Dunyveg from the
Clandonald, that Angus Oig not only refused to deliver
up the castle, but had provided it for a siege.   Suspicion was thus excited that both Angus and his brother,
Sir James, were privy to the original design of surprising the castle.   All the papers of the latter were seized
suddenly by a warrant from the Council, and Sir James
himself placed in strict confinement; but on examining
these papers, it appeared that ever since the surprise of
the castle, Sir James had been advising his brother to
give it up.   A letter from Angus Oig to the Council,

---

[1] " Information " above cited, Denmylne MS., Adv. Lib.
[2] Letter, Council to the King, 2nd June, 1614; Denmylne MS.

which Sir James had not yet had time to forward, was also
found, offering to restore Dunyveg to the Bishop, provided
his own conduct in apprehending his bastard brother were
approved of. On a consideration of all these circumstances, the Privy Council, in order to test the loyalty of
Angus Oig, issued a mandate for his immediate delivery
of the castle to the Bishop. The latter was armed at
the same time with a commission of fire and sword,
and a proclamation for the concurrence of the lieges, if
he should find it necessary to attempt the recovery of
the place by force.[1] The Clandonald, however, still
remained in possession of Dunyveg in the month of
August, when the Bishop, who had come to Edinburgh
to consult with the Council, set out on another journey
to Isla, carrying with him a conditional pardon to Angus
Oig and his adherents, provided they gave up the fortress at once. Such was the backwardness of those
appointed to assist the Bishop, owing to the fast
approach of harvest, that he was not able to land in
Isla till the 19th September. He had previously, while
in Arran making his preparations, sent messengers to
Isla with the pardon; but the Clandonald refused to
surrender the castle, unless to himself personally, and
upon receiving in writing a promise of his friendship
to them in future. As the Bishop had formerly incurred
much blame for keeping so insufficient a garrison in this
important place, he was now anxious to redeem his fault,
and, against his better judgment, he proceeded to Isla
with a very insufficient force. He had with him only
seventy men, of whom fifty were soldiers hired at his own
expense, and the remaining twenty were vassals of Sir

---

[1] Minutes of Council Proceedings, Denmylne MS., Advocates
Library, 9th June, 1614.

Aulay MacAulay of Ardincaple. Of the great chiefs
in the Isles, Donald Gorme of Sleat was the only one
who gave the Bishop any support; but as he was on his
way home from Edinburgh, after transacting business
with the Privy Council, he had with him only a small
personal escort. It was thought, however, that his
influence with the Clandonald of Isla would facilitate
the surrender of Dunyveg, and prevent further inconvenience. Before leaving Arran, the Bishop despatched
the chief of Sleat and Sir Aulay MacAulay to warn
Angus Oig of his approach; and, on his way to Isla,
he was joined by many of the Clandonald, who professed
their readiness to support him. On the morning of the
21st of September, however, the Bishop was suddenly
deserted by his new allies; and at the same time the
chiefs of Sleat and Ardincaple returned from Dunyveg,
bearing an absolute refusal on the part of the garrison
to surrender the place. The Bishop was now placed
in a situation of peculiar difficulty. His force was too
small to attempt anything against the Clandonald, who
were hourly increasing in numbers; and he dreaded
the bad effects that might arise from his quitting the
island without effecting his purpose, and as if driven
from it. But his deliberations were cut short by the
promptitude of his opponents, who contrived to seize
and destroy his boats, four in number, and thus made
it impossible for him to quit the island without their
assistance. In these circumstances, the Bishop was
compelled to enter into a treaty with Angus Oig, by
which he promised to use his utmost endeavours to procure for that individual a seven years' lease of the Crown
lands of Isla (then possessed by Sir Ranald Mac-
Sorley), for the rent of eight thousand merks. He

also engaged to procure his Majesty's licence for transferring the Castle of Dunyveg, in property, to Angus
Oig; and to do his best to obtain a pardon to the
Clandonald for all crimes committed prior to the date
of this treaty. To secure the performance of these
conditions, the Bishop was forced to leave in the hands
of Angus Oig his son, Mr. Thomas Knox, and his
nephew, John Knox of Ranfurlie, as hostages. The
Clandonald, on their part, promised to preserve the
hostages from danger; and although the Bishop might
happen to fail in procuring performance of the above
conditions, yet if they should be satisfied that he had
exerted himself to the utmost, they agreed to liberate
the hostages on payment of a ransom. They likewise
engaged to repay such sums of money as the Bishop
should be found to have expended in procuring the
above-mentioned lease and pardon, in the event of his
ultimate success.[1]   Matters being thus arranged for the
time, the Bishop was left at liberty to depart; but, before
doing so, he wrote to the Council, representing the
danger his relatives were in, and how treacherously he
had been deceived by the "pestiferous" Clandonald.
He added, that he proposed remaining in Isla till something could be done for the relief of his son and nephew.
The conclusion of his letter deserves particular notice,
as it serves to throw light on the secret history of the
late events in Isla. "The Clandonald," says the

---

[1] Record of Privy Council, 11th August and 26th October, 1614;
Letters, Bishop of the Isles to Lord Binning, 4th August and 23rd
September; and Letters, Lord Binning to the Bishop and the Court,
8th, 5th, and 28th September; also, Contract between the Bishop and
the Clandonald, dated at Dunyveg, 22nd September, 1614; all preserved
among the Denmylne MS., Advocates' Library.

Bishop, "have built a new fort in a loch, which they have manned and victualled.   Angus Oig, their captain, affirms, in the hearing of many witnesses, *that he got directions from the Earl of Argyle not to surrender the castle*, and that he (the Earl) should procure for Angus the whole lands of Isla, and the house of Dunyveg." [1]   When Angus Oig was afterwards examined in Edinburgh, by the Lord Advocate and other officers of state, preparatory to his trial for high treason, he was asked, "upon his great oath, if he knew that any great man in the kingdom had anything to do with the business of Isla, in any shape?"   To this question, Angus replied, that, soon after the taking of the castle, he had received a message from a gentleman named Malcolm Macneill, uncle to the Laird of Taynish, bearing that Macneill, being lately in company with the Earl of Argyle when the taking of Dunyveg was the subject of conversation, heard the Earl say, "that he was afraid Angus Oig and his friends would give up the castle; and that, if they did so, it would turn to their utter wreck." Macneill then asked the Earl if he might acquaint Angus Oig with what had passed; to which Argyle replied, that he might do so without danger, and that he (the Earl) had spoken as he did on purpose that his words might be repeated to Angus. [2]   A person of the name of Graham, who was afterwards employed by the Lord Chancellor to procure the liberation of the Bishop's hostages, stated that, in conversation with Angus Oig, the latter declared that he never meddled with the Castle

---

[1] Letter, the Bishop to Lord Binning, dated 23rd September, 1614.—Denmylne MS.

[2] Third Declaration of Angus Oig, dated 23rd May, 1615.—Denmylne MS.

of Dunyveg of his own accord, "but that he was induced thereto by the Earl of Argyle, and that he would justify. this with his sword against the Earl." [1]   It would hence appear that Argyle, afraid of the Clandonald at last coming to terms with the Government and procuring a new grant of Isla, had, by various artful representations, induced that unfortunate tribe to rush into a new rebellion. This view of Argyle's policy is further corroborated by a passage in a letter written by an acute Scottish states- man to Court, in which he says, "By many it is thought that if good will did second the duty which they (Argyle and others employed in the Isles) are bound to do, these frequent Island employments would not occur so often.   For when these employments are so profitable in present pay, and a preparative for making suit at Court for service done, how easy a matter it is to have some of these unhallowed people, with that unchristian tongue, ready to furnish fresh work for the tinker; and the matter so carryed as that it is impossible to depre- hend (detect) the plot." [2]

Far from assisting the Bishop of the Isles in obtain- ing performance of the conditions he had promised to the Clandonald, the Privy Council lost no time in pre- paring to reduce the rebels by force.   Having received from John Campbell of Calder an offer of a feu-duty or perpetual rent for Isla, far beyond what any substan- tial person of his rank had ever offered before, they prevailed on him to accept of a commission against Angus Oig and his followers.   This commission Calder undertook to prosecute at his own expense, provided

---

[1] Declaration of George Graham, 16th June, 1615.—Denmylne MS.

[2] Letter, Sir Alexander Hay, Clerk Register, to Mr. John Murray, dated 21st December, 1615.—Denmylne MS.

the artillery and ammunition necessary for battering the Castle of Dunyveg were furnished at the public cost.[1] The project of bestowing Isla on the Campbells was very ill received by the Clandonald, who began, in consequence, to treat the hostages with great severity. It was the opinion of the Bishop that the proposed grant, if carried into effect, would be the source of much trouble and great expense; more than all the Crown rents of the Isles, for many years, would suffice to pay. In the course of the Prelate's remonstrance against the grant to Calder, he observes—"Neither can I, nor any man who knows the estate of that country (the South Isles), think it either good or profitable to his Majesty, or this realm, to make the name of Campbell greater in the Isles than they are already; nor yet to root out one pestiferous clan, and plant in another little better." Instead of this, the Bishop advised a new plantation of *honest men* to be made in Isla, similar to what was then in progress in the forfeited lands of Ulster; and recommended that this colony should be protected by a strong force, to be drawn from the North of Ireland and West of Scotland. In his anxiety to procure the liberation of his relatives, he openly counselled the employment of deceit in the dealings of the Government with the rebels of Isla, whom he characterised as a "false generation and bloody people;" and whom he appears to have thought it perfectly allowable to fight with their own weapons.[2]

[1] Letter, the Privy Council to the King, dated 1st October, 1614.— Denmylne MS. Archibald Campbell, brother to Lawers, and a confidential agent of the Earl of Argyle, was very active in pressing Calder's suit for a grant of Isla.

[2] Letters from the Bishop to Court, 11th and 23rd October, 1614.— Denmylne MS.

Roused by the intrigues of the Campbells, Sir James
Macdonald once more sent from his prison in Edinburgh
Castle to the Privy Council offers, for the performance of
which he named as sureties (each under the penalty of five
thousand merks) the Earl of Tullibardine, Lord Burley,
Sir Ranald MacSorley, the Lairds of Macintosh and
Grant, and John Campbell of Calder.   The appearance of
the latter as one of the proposed sureties is not a little
singular; but it is to be considered that he was brother-
in-law to Sir James Macdonald, and had probably
succeeded up to this period in deceiving the latter as
to his real views.   Macdonald's offers were as follow:—
First, He offered a yearly rent of eight thousand merks
for the Crown lands of Isla, and desired only a seven
years' lease to try his obedience and that of his clan.
But if the King should prefer keeping Isla in his own
hands Sir James engaged, *Secondly*, To make the
island worth ten thousand merks a-year, and to transport
himself, his brother, and his clan, to Ireland, or wherever
the King should appoint, on receiving a year's rent of
Isla to buy land with.   He made other offers relative
to the recovery of Dunyveg without expense, and the
apprehension of those concerned in the taking of that
place from the Bishop, which need not here be more
particularly detailed.   *Lastly*, He engaged, in the event
of all his other offers being rejected, that if his Majesty
would liberate him upon finding such sureties or giving
such hostages as he might be able to do, he would
remove himself, his brother, and all his clan out of
the King's dominions, seeking no conditions of lands
or money; all that he required being a free pardon for past offences, a letter of recommendation to
the States of Holland, and liberty to raise men in

Scotland for the service of the States if employed by them.[1]

No attention was paid to these offers; but, on the contrary, the preparations for despatching Campbell of Calder to the Isles were hastened. Towards the end of October he received, after many communications between the King and Council, a commission of Lieutenandry against Angus Oig Macdonald, Coll MacGillespick, and the other rebels of Isla. At the same time arrangements were made for bringing from the north of Ireland two hundred veteran soldiers and six cannon to meet Calder and his forces at Isla, so as to insure the taking of the Castle of Dunyveg. Very minute instructions were given to the Royal Lieutenant, particularly for the proper victualling of his own men and the forces from Ireland; but he was urged, if possible, to complete the service before the arrival of the latter, so as to save expense. He was also instructed to use all possible care and dexterity to get the Bishop's hostages out of the hands of the rebels. The usual proclamations enjoining the lieges to assist the Lieutenant, and forbidding them to harbour or supply the rebels, were issued at the same time. A free pardon was offered to all of the Clandonald who were not concerned in the taking of the castle, on their quitting Angus Oig within twenty-four hours after the proclamation being made. Pardon was also offered to any of the rebels who should either set one or both of the hostages at liberty, or give up to the Lieutenant an associate of equal rank with himself. A remission was even offered to Angus Oig, provided he gave up the

---

[1] Original offers, cir. October, 1614.—Denmylne MS.

castle, the hostages, and two of his associates of his own rank.[1]

Whilst Calder was collecting his forces, and the troops of Ireland were preparing to embark, the Earl of Dunfermline, Chancellor of Scotland, set on foot an intrigue for procuring the release of the son and nephew of the Bishop of the Isles, who still remained in the hands of the Clandonald. This he did, by his own admission, without consulting with his colleagues of the Privy Council. The individual employed by the Chancellor was a Ross-shire man named George Graham of Eryne, familiar with the Gaelic language, and who had, besides, some acquaintance with the leader of the rebels. Having received his instructions, Graham set off for Isla; and on his arrival there in the month of November, had an interview with Angus Oig Macdonald, whom he prevailed on, by producing his instructions, and by making free use of the Chancellor's name, and giving many promises on his behalf to the rebels, to deliver up to him both the castle and the hostages. Angus Oig was by similar trickery induced to believe that if he obeyed the wishes of the Chancellor, Graham had power to stop all proceedings on the part of the King's Lieutenant, whose arrival in Isla was daily looked for. Having gained his object, the liberation of the hostages, Graham, by way of assurance

[1] Record of Privy Council and Denmylne MS., 21st to 26th October, 1614. At this time Archibald Campbell, brother to Lawers, was appointed Preferrer of Suits to his Majesty from such rebels in the Isles and Highlands as were desirous to obtain remissions, but conceived themselves precluded by legal causes from doing so, in order that such persons might not be forced to continue in rebellion.—Ibid. This Archibald Campbell was Prior of Strathfillan and Bailie, under Argyle, of the district of Kintyre.

that the Chancellor would perform the promises made in his name, and in virtue of his alleged instructions redelivered the castle to Angus Oig, to be held by him as the regular constable until he should receive further orders from the Chancellor. Angus was very unwilling to have more to do with the castle, but was at last persuaded by the Chancellor's subtle emissary to undertake the charge. On his asking what course he should pursue if, contrary to Graham's assurances, he should be summoned by the Royal Lieutenant to surrender the place, he received from Graham strict injunctions to hold it out at all hazards, till he should hear from the Lord Chancellor. At this time a herald was expected to summon the castle in form, previous to the commencement of the Lieutenant's operations. So anxious was Graham (and we may therefore presume his employer also) that the rebels should commit themselves by violent measures, that he advised them to put the herald to death rather than suffer him to approach the castle. This crime he well knew would have authorised the Lieutenant to put all the garrison to the sword. On the approach of the herald, Graham, desirous of preventing any conference between him and the Clandonald, tried to persuade that official to turn back; but failing in this, he returned to the castle before the herald could reach it, and prevailed upon Angus Oig to disobey the summons. Not content with this, he caused Coll MacGillespick to treat the herald very roughly, and conducted himself throughout in a very violent and abusive manner, particularly towards the herald and the Prior of Ardchattan, by whom the latter was accompanied. Graham then took his departure along with the hostages, leaving the deluded

Islanders to their fate. Hearing, on his journey, of
the near approach of Calder's forces, he sent a written
order to Angus Oig, renewing, as if in the Chancellor's
name, the injunctions formerly given to retain the castle
at all hazards. These injunctions his dupes, prejudiced
as they were at this time against the Campbells, too
readily followed.[1] There can be no doubt whatever
that the Chancellor was the author of this notable plan
to procure the liberation of the hostages, and at the
same time to deprive the Clandonald of the benefit of
the pardon promised to them on this account. There
are grounds for a suspicion that the Chancellor himself
desired to obtain Isla,[2] although it is probable that he
wished to avoid the odium attendant on the more violent measures required to render such an acquisition
available. He therefore contrived so as to leave the
punishment of the Clandonald to the Campbells, who
were already sufficiently obnoxious to the western
clans, whilst he himself had the credit of procuring the
liberation of the hostages.

About the end of November,[3] Campbell of Calder

---

[1] This account of Graham's proceedings is drawn from the original minutes of the evidence taken on the subject in the months of
May and June, 1615; from letters of the Chancellor to Court, dated
9th December, 1614; 16th March and 30th April, 1615; all preserved
among the Denmylne MS.

[1] Graham certainly talked in this way. See particularly the evidence taken regarding Graham's conduct, 14th and 15th June, 1615.
—Denmylne MS.

[3] On the 21st of this month, a charter passed the Great Seal,
granting to John Campbell of Calder, and his heirs male, heritably,
in feu farm, "the yle and landis of Ylay and Rynnis, and middle
waird of Ylay, Ilyntassan, as weill rentallit of befoir as unrentallit."
This charter was ratified by Parliament in 1621. Acts of Parliament, IV., p. 675.

arrived with his forces in the neighbourhood of Dunyveg, and remained for fourteen days encamped on two small islands, waiting for the arrival of the troops and cannon from Ireland. Finding his provisions considerably diminished, while nothing had as yet been done towards the reduction of the island, he returned to Duntroon on the mainland, to procure a further supply, and to be in readiness to join the armament from Ireland as soon as he should hear of its arrival. In the middle of December, two days after Calder had sailed for Duntroon, Sir Oliver Lambert, commander of the Irish forces, accompanied by Archibald Campbell, bailie of Kintyre (who had gone to Ireland to expedite the sailing of the Irish division of the expedition), cast anchor in the Sound of Isla. He had with him his Majesty's ship called the Phœnix, a pinnace called the Moon, a hoy to carry the ordnance, and a Scottish bark with provisions; and these vessels carried a considerable number of soldiers. It was not till the 16th of December that Sir Oliver Lambert heard where Calder was, and he then despatched a messenger to inform the latter of his arrival. Meantime, having heard something of Graham's proceedings, and being uncertain what Calder had done in consequence, Sir Oliver, by the advice of Archibald Campbell, summoned the Castle of Dunyveg. This being done, Sir Oliver received a letter from Angus Oig Macdonald, bearing that had he not received a warrant from the Lord Chancellor and Council of Scotland to keep the castle for them, he would have obeyed Sir Oliver's summons. He offered to show his warrant to any person authorised by the General, and protested that if he were attacked by the forces under Lambert's command, he would complain to the Privy Council. To this Sir Oliver replied, that he could not believe that the King would have sent such an expedition at that season of the year to reduce a place already in his subjection; but in order to ascertain the truth of Macdonald's assertions, he sent for a copy of the warrant referred to by the latter. In return he received a copy of Graham's alleged instructions, which seemed fully to authorise the detention of the castle; but being satisfied that Graham had no proper authority for what he had done,[1] Sir Oliver resolved to proceed with the siege as soon as he should be joined by Calder. This junction, however, was not effected, owing to violent tempests and contrary winds, until the 5th of January.

A. D. 1615.   On the 6th of that month, Calder landed in Isla with two hundred men, and the next day his force was augmented by one hundred and forty more. On the 9th and succeeding days, he proceeded to invest the castle and land the ordnance. The rebels now began to be alarmed, and several deserted from the castle, and were pardoned on condition of their doing service against those who still held out. Ranald Mac-James (uncle of Angus Oig), who commanded the fort and island of Lochgorme, surrendered his post to the Lieutenant on the 21st, and, along with his son, received a conditional assurance of his Majesty's favour. On the 27th of January the cannon were all landed, and the battery was prepared to open on the morning of the 1st of February. During the landing of the cannon and erecting of the battery, the Royal forces were fired

---

[1] Graham's proceedings gave great offence both to Calder and Sir Oliver Lambert; particularly the former. Denmylne MS., ad tempus.

upon several times by the rebels, but owing to the fire
being ill directed; the loss inflicted was trifling. Captain
Crawford, one of Sir Oliver Lambert's officers, was
wounded in the leg, and died in consequence soon afterwards; and one of Calder's men was killed on the
spot. Soon after the battery opened its fire on the
castle, a perceptible effect was produced on the garrison.
They sent, in the course of the day, various messages to
the Lieutenant; but their propositions not being satisfactory, the firing was kept up all that day. On the
next day, the battery still playing, Angus Oig had an
interview with the Lieutenant, when it was explained to
him that he had been deceived by Graham; and he
then promised to surrender with as many as chose to
follow him. But he had no sooner returned to the
castle than, persuaded, as there is reason to believe, by
Coll MacGillespick, he again absolutely refused to
surrender. The battery was again opened, and at
length, after many fruitless attempts to procure better
terms, Angus and a certain number of his principal
followers surrendered without conditions. Coll Mac-
Gillespick and others contrived to escape, by night,
in a boat with some difficulty; but their vessel turning
leaky, they were obliged to run ashore in Isla, where
six of them were afterwards apprehended and executed,
Coll himself making his escape. On the third of
February, Calder, having taken possession of the castle,
held a justice court, in which fourteen of the rebels
were tried and condemned to death, execution following instantly upon the sentence. Six of those who had
held the fort of Lochgorme were also condemned.
Angus Oig himself, and a few who were supposed to
be privy to all his proceedings since the first seizure of

the castle, were reserved for examination by the Privy Council. The forces of the rebels were entirely dispersed; and many images connected with the Catholic form of worship were destroyed by the zeal of Archibald Campbell, who describes the island, at this time, as having no religious instructors but one poor man that had been left by the Bishop. It appears that Calder received but little assistance from the country people, who should, in terms of the proclamation, have joined him; and that neither boat nor bark came from the western burghs with provisions, notwithstanding the directions of the Council on that head.[1]

The service being thus concluded, Angus Oig and the other prisoners were brought before the Privy Council to be examined, not only regarding the original promoter of the first seizure of the castle, but as to the treaty between them and Graham. On the first point, the declarations of the prisoners went, as has been formerly noticed, to fix the blame upon Argyle;[2] whilst their evidence on the second created a strong feeling against the Chancellor. Both charges, however, seem to have been smothered. The Chancellor denied most solemnly having given Graham any other instructions than merely to procure the release of the hostages. He

---

[1] Report made to the Earl of Somerset, by Archibald Campbell, of the progress of this expedition.—Denmylne MS., 8th February, 1615. Said MS., 14th and 16th December, 1614.

[2] Supra, p. 354. About this time, the King, writing to Secretary Binning regarding George Graham, who had been sent to England for examination, on a complaint against him by Campbell of Calder, says—"Whereas the said Angus Oig hath promised to reveale an important secrete upon some great man, if he may have assurance of his life;" and urges the Secretary to ascertain the secret, if possible, *without* giving any promise or condition to Angus-Oig.

denied also having authorised him to offer any conditions to the rebels; but a careful perusal of all the documents connected with this affair leaves no doubt that
the Chancellor was much more deeply implicated in
Graham's dishonourable practices than he chose to con-
fess. As for Graham himself, he prevaricated so grossly,
and his statements were so much at variance, not only
with the evidence of the rebels, but with that of Campbell of Calder and many other gentlemen of honour
and credit, that no belief was given to his account of
what had taken place.[1]

During the months of February, March, April, and
May, Coll MacGillespick and others of the Clandonald
who had escaped from Isla, together with Malcolm Mac-
Ruari Macleod, one of the last survivors of the Siol
Torquil, infested the western coasts, and committed
various acts of piracy. In April, a commission of fire
and sword against Coll MacGillespick and his associates was given to eight of the principal chiefs in the
Isles; and one of his Majesty's ships, with a pinnace,
seem to have been employed to assist in this service.[2]
But while the Lords of the Privy Council were occupied in giving directions for the suppression of these
pirates, and in tracing the origin of the late rebellion in
Isla, they were astounded by the intelligence that Sir
James Macdonald had made his escape from prison, and
was on his way to the Isles, where his appearance could

---

[1] Denmylne MS., May and June, 1615. Graham actually received
from the Chancellor 1000 merks for his services; which sum was
repaid to his Lordship by a Royal warrant, before the nature of the
transaction had become public.

[2] Record of Privy Council, February to April, 1516. Denmylne
MS., ad tempus.

not fail to prove the signal for fresh disturbances. It was alleged, on this occasion, by the Council, that Sir James dreaded the result of the inquiry in which they were then engaged; and that his flight proved that he was really the instigator of the late rebellion.[1] But Sir James, in various letters written about this time, denied the imputation, and gave, as a reason for his flight, that he had heard, from the best authority, that Calder, when at Court making a report of his proceedings in Isla, had obtained a secret warrant, charging the Council, on sight of it, to order Sir James to instant execution on his old sentence. Sir James also stated, that he learned this from relations and friends of the Laird of Calder, and he mentioned the names of his informants. Knowing, as he then did, the inveteracy of Calder, who had so lately executed many of the Clandonald, he resolved once more to attempt an escape, as the only chance for his life.[2]

In his escape, Sir James Macdonald was assisted by Allaster MacRanald of Keppoch, by the eldest son of the latter, and the eldest son of the captain of Clanranald. The enterprise appears to have been very skilfully conducted. The fugitives crossed the Frith of Forth in a small boat, from Newhaven to Burntisland, and directed their course thence to the Highlands of Perthshire. On the 24th of May, a commission was given to the Marquis of Huntly and the Earl of Tullibardine for the apprehension of Sir James and his companions; and letters were sent with great despatch to these noblemen, urging them to intercept the fugitives in their passage through Athole or Lochaber. A reward of two thousand

[1] Record of Privy Council, 23rd and 24th May, 1615.
[2] Numerous Letters preserved in Denmylne MS., ad tempus.

pounds was, at the same time, offered for Sir James,
dead or alive.[1]   Archibald Campbell, whom we have
seen exerting himself so much against the Clandonald
in Isla, was ordered to track and pursue Sir James and
his party; and he followed them so closely, by the wood
of Methven and by Murthlie, to Athole, that, had he
been certain of their route, he might have intercepted
them at the east end of Loch Rannoch.   At this time,
the Earls of Athole and Tullibardine, coming from
another direction, were actually in sight of Sir James;
but that chief having been warned of their approach,
escaped with the gentlemen of his party on foot to the
woods, leaving their horses and clothes behind.   Some
of their servants were apprehended, but were afterwards liberated by Tullibardine.   A company of Keppoch's clan now met their chief and Sir James Macdonald, and conducted them from Rannoch through
Lochaber free of all risk of immediate apprehension.
From Lochaber, Sir James and Keppoch proceeded to
Morar and Knoydert, and thence to Sleat in Sky, where
they had a lengthened conference with Donald Gorme.
This chief did not join them openly himself, but a number
of his men of Sleat followed Sir James, who sailed to
the south in a large boat which he procured in that
district.   At the Isle of Eigg he met with Coll Mac-
Gillespick, and such of the Clandonald as followed that
pirate leader.   The reception given to Sir James by
his clansmen was very enthusiastic.   He and those
who had come with him stood in a place by themselves,

---

[1] Record of Privy Council, 24th May, 1615.   Calderwood in his
MS. Church History (Advocates' Library), says, "It was thought
Sir James Macdonald escaped not without the privity of those who
had credit."

whilst Coll MacGillespick's men marched round them, firing volleys of small arms for half an hour ; and afterwards every individual came forward and shook hands with the chief. From Eigg, being now about three hundred strong, Sir James and his followers sailed in the direction of Isla, having previously slaughtered a great number of cattle in the former island, to insure themselves a good supply of provisions. About this time many of the Clanian of Ardnamurchan are said to have joined Sir James ; and the rebellion assumed every day a more formidable appearance.[1]

Meantime the Privy Council were not idle in taking steps to repress this insurrection, before the rebels could have time to do much mischief; but various causes contributed to thwart their intentions. Of these the most important was the absence of the Earl of Argyle, who, being much pressed by his numerous creditors, had lately gone to England without any prospect of an immediate return. His brother, Colin Campbell of Lundy, declined, without a special warrant from the Earl, to undertake the responsibility of keeping the Earldom of Argyle clear of the rebels, or of preventing such of the vassals as were friendly to the Macdonalds from joining Sir James. The Lairds of Calder and Auchinbreck,[2] two of the principal gentlemen of the name of Campbell, were so involved in the embarrassments of their chief, that at this time they dared not

---

[1] These particulars regarding the escape of Sir James Macdonald, and his progress towards Isla, have been drawn from letters of the Earl of Tullibardine, Sir Ruari Macleod, Archibald Campbell, and Sir James himself, all preserved in that valuable collection, the Dunmylne MS., Advocates' Library. See also Criminal Trials, III., pp. 12-22.

[2] Sir Dougal Campbell of Auchinbreck.

repair to Argyleshire. Indeed, Auchinbreck was actually imprisoned in Edinburgh on account of his engagements for Argyle. In these circumstances, the Privy Council wrote to the King, requesting that his Majesty would either order the Earl of Argyle to return instantly to Scotland, to take the command of his clan and vassals, "as being the special person of power and friendship in the Highlands;" or to authorise one of his principal kinsmen to act for him. Calder undertook to keep the island of Isla and the Castle of Dunyveg out of the hands of Sir James Macdonald and his followers; and in the event of their coming to Isla, engaged to use his own force against them, before applying to the King for assistance. A reward of five thousand pounds was now offered for the apprehension of Sir James; whilst five thousand merks each were offered for Keppoch and his son, and Coll MacGillespick; and three thousand merks each for Malcolm Macleod and, Ranald Oig, the bastard brother of Sir James. All harbouring of, or dealing with the rebels, or giving them information, was strictly prohibited. Having received an answer from Court to their application regarding the Earl of Argyle, the Privy Council conferred for several days with the principal gentlemen of the Campbells, who had been summoned to Edinburgh. [1] As they were still ignorant of Sir James Macdonald's motions since he quitted the Isle of Eigg, and never suspected that he would venture into Isla—where there were a number of Calder's men, besides the garrison of Dunyveg—the Council and their advisers were chiefly

---

[1] These were the Lairds of Lundy, Calder, Auchinbreck, and Lawers; the captain of Craignish, and Colin Campbell (of Aberruchill), brother to Lawers.

occupied by their efforts to place the whole of the Isles and adjacent mainland, from Sky southwards to Kintyre, in a posture of defence, so as to deter the rebels from landing. Instructions were accordingly given to the Lairds of Auchinbreck and Ardkinlass for the defence of Argyle Proper, Knapdale, and Kintyre, with three hundred men; to the Laird of Lochnell and Mr. Donald Campbell of Barbreck-Lochow, for the defence of Lorn, with all Calder's vassals not employed in Isla, and one hundred and fifty men out of Lorn and Glenurchy; to the Lairds of Dowart, Lochbuy, Coll, and Mackinnon, for the defence of the coasts from Lorn to the point of Ardnamurchan, with two hundred men; to the Earl of Enzie, for the defence of the coast of Lochaber, with one hundred men; and, finally, to the captain of the Clanranald, Macleod of Harris, and Macdonald of Sleat, for the defence of their own estates, each with two hundred men. The ship and pinnace formerly prepared to act against Coll MacGillespick, were now ordered to pursue the rebels by sea; and the chiefs above mentioned were ordered to communicate with the commander of these vessels as frequently as possible. All the forces called out were enjoined to be at their appointed stations by the 6th of July, furnished with forty days' provisions, and with a sufficient number of boats, to enable them to act by sea if necessary. The Marquis of Hamilton, and the Sheriff of Bute, were, at the same time, ordered to keep the Isles of Arran and Bute clear of the rebels, and to concur with the Argyleshire forces when required.[1]

Scarcely had these orders and instructions been

[1] Record of Privy Council, 8th to 22nd June, 1615. Denmylne MS., 20th to 22nd June. At this time, Colin Campbell of Lundy,

issued, when intelligence arrived from Isla which dis-
concerted all the arrangements that had been made.
Sir James Macdonald and his followers, after leaving
the Isle of Eïgg, proceeded to the south, their destination and intentions being equally unknown to the Privy
Council. About the 18th òf June, Sir James arrived
at the Isle of Colonsay with several hundred men, and
there killed a number of cattle fòr provisions. While
here, he built a fort on a small island in a fresh-water
loch. Four or five days later he landed in Isla, and
having placed a body of men in ambush about the
Castle of Dunyveg, he contrived, by the assistance of a
crafty native of the island, to draw the constable of the
castle,[1] with twelve of the garrison, out of the fortress,
and into the ambuscade. Macdonald's men made their
appearance sooner than was intended; and, upon seeing
his danger, the constable attempted to gain the castle.
About one-half of his escort succeeded in reaching the
inner gate, and closing it against the Clandonald; but
the constable and the rest were overtaken and slain, and
Sir James established himself in the outer court. Having soon afterwards made himself master of the garrison's supply of water, and taken one of the interior
fortifications, the place was surrendered to him next
morning.[2] It does not appear that Sir James com-

---

and Sir John Campbell of Calder, received a licence to go to Court,
to consult with Argyle regarding his debts, and their liabilities for
him; but they were bound, under a penalty of £1,000 each, to return
to Scotland on or before the 25th of July.

[1] The Constable was Alexander Macdougall, brother to the Laird
of Raray.

[2] In a letter to the Earl of Crawford, dated 3rd July, Denmylne MS.,
Sir James states his loss in this affair to have been one man and a boy
killed, and two men slightly wounded.

mitted any excesses on this occasion. On the contrary
he liberated the Prior of Ardchattan and his two sons,
although near kinsmen of the Laird of Calder, who
were in the castle when it was taken; and he seems to
have been satisfied with causing all Calder's followers
to quit the island and return to Lorn. After placing a
garrison in Dunyveg, Sir James Macdonald divided his
force into two bodies; one of which, under himself, was
intended to proceed to the Isle of Jura, and the other,
under Coll MacGillespick, to Kintyre, for the purpose
of encouraging the ancient followers of his family to
rise in arms and assist him. At this time the rebels
were about four hundred strong, chiefly North Islesmen.[1]

Immediately on receiving this intelligence, the Privy
Council wrote to the King, strongly urging him to send
the Earl of Argyle home with all haste, to act as
Lieutenant against the rebels. It was argued that this
was more particularly incumbent on Argyle and his
clan, seeing that the principal cause of the present
disturbances, as alleged by the Clandonald, was the
giving of Kintyre and Isla to the Earl and his relation,
Calder. Besides when they received these grants, it
had been settled that they were to keep their new
acquisitions in subjection without more expense to
Government. As artillery could not be conveniently
carried from Edinburgh to the Isles, the King was
requested to give directions for cannon and ammunition
to be shipped on board the vessels already destined to
act against the rebels, and which were at present under

---

[1] Letter, Hector Macneill of Taynish to Lord Binning, 26th June,
and Letter, Sir James Macdonald to the Earl of Crawford, 3rd July,
1615; Denmylne MS.

the orders of the Deputy of Ireland.[1] All the lieges
within the sheriffdoms of Argyle and Tarbert, were
charged by proclamation to join the forces formerly
appointed to be in readiness under Campbell of Auchinbreck. That baron being liberated from prison, received
a commission as Lieutenant against the Clandonald,
with the chief command over the other gentlemen
employed; but the duration of his commission was
limited to the arrival of Argyle, which was expected by
the 6th of August.[2] Angus Oig Macdonald, and
several of his followers, were tried and condemned for
high treason on the 3rd of July, and executed on the
8th of that month. Their fate excited great com-
miseration, which was mingled with a feeling of indignation that no steps were taken to punish the villanous
conduct of the Chancellor's emissary, Graham.[3]

Soon after his escape, Sir James Macdonald addressed
a number of letters, exculpatory of himself, to various
persons of rank, with whom, when at Court as a hostage
for his father, and afterwards during his long imprisonment at Edinburgh, he had formed an acquaintance.
Among his correspondents, with several of whom he
appears to have been on intimate and even affectionate
terms, we find the Marquis of Hamilton, the Earls of
Crawford, Caithness, and Tullibardine, and the Bishop
of the Isles. His letters are not those of a barbarian,
such as his indictment describes him; but, on the con-

---

[1] Letter, the Council to the King, and Minutes of Council proceedings, 30th June, 1615; Denmylne MS.

[2] Record of Privy Council, 30th June, 1615, and Minutes of Council
proceedings, same date, in Denmylne MS.

[3] Pitcairn's Criminal Trials, III. 364. Calderwood's MS. Church
History, Advocates' Library.

trary, indicated a mind well cultivated for the period.
He seems to have had very good natural abilities, and,
during his long confinement, to have become somewhat
of a student.   Even in his flight to the Highlands,
when his mind must have been occupied with matters of
more pressing interest, Sir James Macdonald contrived
to carry with him a small library; the loss of which,
when he was so nearly surprised in Athole, caused him
great vexation.   Most of his letters breathe a spirit of
implacable hostility against the Campbells, whom he
characterises as a race that "craves ever to fish in drumlie
(muddy) waters;" and he repeatedly declares that he
will die sooner than see them possess Isla.   At the same
time, he wrote an humble petition to the Council, soli-
citing their favourable intercession on his behalf with
the King—offering all the duty of the most loyal subject—and beseeching them not to drive him to despe-
ration by any hasty or violent measures.   It appears
that all Sir James' letters were sent by him to the Earl
of Tullibardine, to be forwarded to their respective
destinations.   That nobleman, however, conceived himself bound to forward the whole to the Privy Council,
who declined, so long as Sir James continued in the
Isles along with avowed rebels, to communicate his
petitions to the King, or to hold any communication
whatever with him.[1]   This resolution was come to
before the Council had heard of the taking of Dunyveg
from Calder's garrison, and was, of course, persevered
in after that event; so that various letters, written by
Sir James to explain his conduct in seizing the castle,

---

[1] Letter, Lord Binning to the Earl of Tullibardine, 13th June, 1615;
Denmylne MS.

failed to produce any relaxation of the severe measures in progress against him.[1]

After the Castle of Dunyveg had fallen into the hands of the Clandonald, Sir James added to the fortifications of the island of Lochgorme a *bawn* of turf of great breadth, at which one hundred and twenty men laboured every day till it was completed. At this time the rebels made many unsuccessful attempts to seize Hector Macneill of Taynish, chief of the southern Clanneill; who, although he and his ancestors followed the Macdonalds while the latter were Lords of Kintyre, had, since the year 1607, become a vassal of the Earl of Argyle, to whom, on the present occasion, he faithfully adhered. Malcolm Macduphie or Macfie of Colonsay, who had likewise, of late years, been compelled to hold his lands of· Argyle, followed a different course, and joined Sir James Macdonald, as the individual to whom, from the old connection between their families, his service was properly due. Donald Gigach MacIan, the principal man in Jura, likewise joined the Clandonald; and the accession of these two chieftains augmented the force of the rebels by sixty-four men. From communications made by the Prior of Ardchattan and Archibald Campbell, his son, to the Secretary of State, it appears that the people of Argyle and Lorn refused to proceed against the rebels till the arrival of a Royal lieutenant; and that, in the middle of July, there were only forty men in arms for the protection of that part of the country against the Clandonald and their abettors. Sir James, deeming the Castle of Dunyveg untenable, was directing all his attention to the fortifi-

---

[1] The letters referred to in the text, written by Sir James Macdonald in June and July, 1615, are preserved in the Denmylne MS. See also Criminal Trials, III., pp. 12-21.

cation of the isle of Lochgorme, and another strength called Dunand, whilst his forces were increasing every day, and the men of Kintyre were now rising in arms to join him. Various reports were in circulation, which, in the absence of their chief, tended much to diminish the zeal of Argyle's vassals. For instance, it was confidently said that Sir James Macdonald had entered into a special bond of friendship with Donald Gorme of Sleat, the captain of the Clanranald, and Ruari Macleod of Harris; and that Hector Maclean of Dowart, if not actually engaged in the rebellion, had announced that, if he was desired to proceed against the Clandonald, he would not be very earnest in the service. These disheartening reports were confirmed to a certain extent by Ardchattan's spies, who declared to him that vassals of the three first mentioned chiefs formed a considerable part of Sir James' force; whilst Maclean's brother had already taken part with the rebels in expelling Calder's men from Isla.[1]

A proclamation was hereupon issued by the Council, calling out the militia of the shires of Ayr, Renfrew, Dunbarton, Bute, and Inverness, in addition to those of Argyle and Tarbert formerly summoned; and commission was given to the Marquis of Hamilton and Paul Hamilton, captain of Arran, for keeping the Clandonald out of that island. The King had now determined to send the Earl of Argyle down as Lieutenant, not only to suppress the insurrection of Sir James Macdonald, but also to take order for the final pacification of all the Western Isles. His Majesty, after giving various

---

[1] Letters, Hector Macneill of Taynish to Lord Binning, 4th and 29th July; and Letters, the Prior of Ardchattan and his son to the same, 15th, 16th, and 29th July, 1615; Denmylne MS.

necessary directions, declared it to be his will that the forfeitures of all those in Argyle and Kintyre, who should be proved to have intercommuned with or assisted the rebels, should belong to the Earl. The number of men, and the amount of stores and money to be allowed to the Lieutenant, and the prices to be paid by the army for provisions, were left to the discretion of the Council. Four days later, the King wrote again to the Council, to say that the Earl of Argyle was on his way to undertake the service in the Isles, and directing them to require of him that, as far as possible, the spoiling of the country might be avoided; and that, in the pursuit of the rebels, no cattle, or other goods, should be taken forcibly by the Earl or his forces, unless from those who had actually taken part with the Clandonald. Such of the rebels as might be taken alive were to be tried by a jury; and such of the tenants of Isla as had fled for fear of the Clandonald were to be restored to their possessions. Generally, the Earl was to be instructed so to proceed, "that civil manners and customs might be established in these Isles, and all their old barbarous customs utterly abolished."[1]

Having finished his fortifications in Isla, and placed his bastard son, Donald Gorme, as keeper of Dunyveg in the meantime, and until a siege should be threatened, Sir James Macdonald and his followers proceeded to Kintyre, where the King's castle at Kinloch (Campbelton) had previously been taken possession of by a detachment of twenty-four men, sent from Isla for that purpose. The rebels landed in Kintyre, four hundred strong, including all the "special men" of Isla, Macfie

[1] Letters, the King to the Privy Council, dated 24th and 28th July, and recorded in the Books of Council, 4th August, 1615.

burgh to consult with the Privy Council. After many conferences, the following arrangements were made, on the 22nd of August, for the suppression of the rebellion in the west. Four hundred hired soldiers were allowed to Argyle, at the rate of four thousand eight hundred pounds monthly pay for that force, including officers. The Earl engaged that these troops were to muster at Castle Sweyn, in Knapdale, on the 2nd of September, from which day their pay was to commence. The following were the prices fixed upon to be paid by the Royal forces for provisions:—Twelve pounds Scots for an ox, two pounds for a stone of butter, one pound for a sheep, and a like sum for a stone of cheese. It was also arranged that there should be a daily communication between the Lieutenant and the Privy Council. Two hundred pounds weight of gunpowder, with the usual proportion of lead and lint, were to be furnished immediately to the soldiers by the Lord Treasurer, that the service might not suffer by any unforeseen delay in the arrival of the ships from Ireland. A letter was written to the Lord Deputy of Ireland, requesting him to give orders that none of the rebels should be allowed to land in that country. The great chiefs in the Isles were enjoined to give their hearty concurrence in the service, according as they should be required by the Lieutenant; and the commission of lieutenandry given to the Earl of Argyle extended over Argyle, Tarbert, and the whole West and North Isles, and elsewhere in Scotland, in pursuit of the rebels, if they should fly from these districts. Among other clauses, it contained one giving him power "to take some good and solid order how the whole West Isles of this kingdom may be retained and holden under obedience." Finally, the usual proclamations were issued, prohibiting any sort of intercourse with the rebels—offering pardon, on certain conditions, to such as should immediately make their submission—and charging all his Majesty's true lieges to concur with and assist the Lieutenant. Matters being thus arranged, Argyle set out from Edinburgh for his own country, satisfied by the Council in all he desired regarding the service he had undertaken.[1]

Having made his preparations, the Earl collected his forces early in September at Duntroon, on Loch Crinan, with his vessels in two divisions, one upon the west, the other upon the east side of the continent, and within a few miles of each other. He first caused the proclamation of pardon, to such as should desert the rebels, to be made; and whilst the time prescribed was passing, he, by his spies, examined Sir James Macdonald's camp, which was on the west coast of Kintyre, near to the Isle of Cara.[2] The force of the rebels was found to be nearly one thousand men, with a number of vessels, most of which were at anchor in Cara. Having ascertained these points, and the time for commencing his operations being arrived, Argyle detached two companies of the hired soldiers, under John MacDougal of Raray, and Mr. Donald Campbell of Barbreck-Lochow, with Sir John Campbell of Calder, the Lairds of Lochnell and Macdougall, and their followers, making, in all, a force of seven or eight hundred men,

---

[1] Letters, Lord Binning and Earl of Argyle to the King, 16th August; and the Chancellor to Mr. John Murray of Lochmaben, 31st August; Denmylne MS. Record of Privy Council, 22nd August, 1615.

[2] This camp was within ten miles of Tarbert by land.

whom he sent by sea on the west coast, with directions to sail straight for the place where Sir James' vessels lay, and, if possible, surprise them by night. Should they fail in this, they were directed to encamp at the point of Ardrissak, to wait the Lieutenant's coming to the east side of Kintyre with the two other companies of hired soldiers, under Captain Boswell, and Robert Campbell, captain of Dunoon, with Colin Campbell of Kilmichael, the Lairds of Ardkinlass, Lamont, and Mac-Lauchlan, and their followers, forming in all a similar force of nearly eight hundred men. Argyle arrived at Tarbert in the evening of the same day he left Duntroon; and was then joined by Auchinbreck, with those under his command.

Sir James' Macdonald, at this time, uncertain of Argyle's movements, had sent his uncle, Ranald, with three or four hundred men, to stop the passage from Tarbert on the east; whilst Coll MacGillespick, with sixty men and three boats, was sent from Cara to West Tarbert, to reconnoitre. Upon learning the near approach of the division commanded by Argyle himself, the rebels retreated as they had advanced; Coll MacGillespick carrying with him Colin Campbell of Kilberry, and three or four of his followers, whom he made prisoners, having found them at some distance from their camp.[1] On his way to rejoin Keppoch and his son, and Sorley MacJames (bastard son of the late Sir James Macdonald of Dunluce), who had been left in charge of the vessels at Cara, Coll MacGillespick was informed that the Laird of Calder and those with him had

---

[1] Kilberry and his followers seem to have been sent out to reconnoitre the rebels.

arrived in the Isle of Gigha. Being incredulous on
this point, he pursued his course so near to that island
that it was with difficulty he made his escape, by landing
on the coast of Kintyre, and abandoning his boats, still,
however, carrying his prisoners with him. He was so
hotly pursued, that fifteen or sixteen of his men were
killed. In the meantime, another party of Calder's
division set out to attack the rebels in Cara; but some
of the Laird of Largie's men having given the rebels
warning, by beacons, of the approach of their enemies,
they took to flight with precipitation. Keppoch fled
towards Kintyre, whither he was pursued by Mr. Donald
Campbell and Lochnell, to the very south end of that
peninsula, and escaped very narrowly with the loss of
his vessels and some of his men; and Sorley MacJames
towards Isla, who in his retreat was pursued by Calder
to within shot of the Castle of Dunyveg. The operations on the east side of Kintyre were not less successful; and Sir James Macdonald perceiving his followers
to be much disordered, forsook his camp and took to
flight. The Laird of Ardkinlass, with four hundred
men, was now directed by Argyle to proceed by land
to the south end of Kintyre, to assist Calder's
division in the pursuit of the rebels, with strict
injunctions to follow them to Isla if they had fled
in that direction. Ardkinlass and his party encamped
for a night on the spot previously occupied by Sir
James; and while there received certain information
that Sir James had gone to the Isle of Rachlin.
This caused a change in Argyle's plans, who now,
with his entire division, crossed over to Jura, and
encamped on the coast of that island, where he was
soon afterwards joined by the ships of war from Eng-

land.[1] About the same time he received intelligence from his spies that Sir James had come over from Rachlin to Isla, and collected his scattered followers to the number of five hundred men, with whom he encamped in the Rinns of Isla, near to a small Island, called Ouersay. Upon this Argyle, with all possible diligence, transported his forces to Isla, where he was joined by the division under Calder, and landed them at the harbour called the Lodoms, being allowed to encamp himself strongly without molestation from the rebels.

Sir James finding it impossible either to resist the Lieutenant's forces, or to escape with his galleys to the North Isles, which was then his principal object, sent a messenger to the Earl, desiring a truce for four days, promising, before the expiry of that time, to surrender himself without conditions. To this request, Argyle yielded conditionally, providing Sir James gave up the two forts he held within twenty-four hours; otherwise, the proposal of a truce would be looked upon in no other light than a scheme for obtaining time, in the hope of a south wind arising in the meantime, which would give the rebels an opportunity of escaping as they intended. Sir James, finding himself now much straitened, urged Coll MacGillespick, who at this time had the command of both the forts, to give them up to Argyle; but this Coll flatly refused to do.

The Earl having received Sir James' answer, that he could not give up the forts, and being, at the same time, secretly assured by Coll MacGillespick

---

[1] These consisted of two vessels under Captains Wood and Monk, and a hoy which carried a battering train.

28

that the latter was willing to surrender them, sent Campbell of Calder, Captain Boswell, and other officers, at night, with a force of one thousand men, by sea, with orders either to surprise Sir James in his camp, or to seize his vessels. Sir James, however, through beacons set by the natives on the O of Isla, received intimation of the intended attack in time to make his escape, along with Keppoch, Sorley MacJames, and forty followers, to an island called Inchdaholl, on the coast of Ireland. It is said that, as the party were going into their boats, some of the principal tenants of Isla earnestly besought Sir James to remain, declaring that, as they had hazarded all for him, and knew there would be no mercy shown to them, they would all die at his feet. Sir James was dissuaded from following this course, as was reported by Keppoch; and he now left the Hebrides and his devoted clansmen, never to return. Those of his men who did not escape with him fled to the hills during the night. The next day, Coll MacGillespick surrendered the two forts and his prisoners, upon assurance of his own life and the lives of some few of his followers; conditions which Argyle did not hesitate to grant, considering the lateness of the season, the sickness of many of the soldiers, and the scarcity of provisions. Coll, likewise, in order to testify his abhorrence of his former behaviour, became an active partisan against his former associates, and crowned his treachery by apprehending and delivering to Argyle Macfie of Colonsay, one of the principal leaders of the rebels, and eighteen others. This conduct soon had many imitators. Macfie himself, and another leader, named John MacIan Vor, who had also been taken prisoner, received a temporary assurance of their lives during

Argyle's stay in the country, on condition of their doing his Majesty service against the remaining rebels. But on his Lordship's departure, not daring to leave such "remarkable ringleaders" behind him without good assurance of their loyalty, he caused them to be presented before the Privy Council. After receiving the Castle of Dunyveg and fort of Lochgorme, Argyle succeeded in apprehending ten of the principal inhabitants of Isla who had taken part with Sir James. These were instantly brought to trial and executed, in virtue of his Lordship's commission.

Having delivered the forts in Isla to Sir John Campbell of Calder and executed nine more of the principal rebels, Argyle proceeded to Kintyre, where there were still a number of men in arms of those who had joined Sir James from this district. Some of the chief of these he apprehended soon after his arrival; and by the severity of his measures, and the number of persons he executed, seemed determined effectually to prevent any chance of a future insurrection in Kintyre. He left Isla for Kintyre near the end of October, and was still in Kintyre on the 10th of November, at which time he dismissed two out of the three King's ships that had assisted him in his operations, retaining the vessel called the Bran, under the command of Captain Wood. In the meantime, he was employed in ascertaining the movements of such of the rebels as had escaped, and in sending parties after them. Sir James was ascertained to be with his son, Donald Gorme, and two followers, concealed by some Jesuits in Galway in Ireland, by whose means he effected his escape to Spain, in spite of parties sent after him both by Argyle and the Lord Deputy of Ireland. Sorley MacJames, with a small body

of men—among whom were Malcolm Macleod and
Ranald Oig, Sir James Macdonald's bastard brother—
was sheltered by his relations in the Glens and Route in
the county of Antrim. Keppoch and his sons were
now in Lochaber, having been sent back to Scotland
by Sir James, with some of the Macallasters and
Mackays of Kintyre, who had accompanied him in his
flight from Isla. The service was not concluded until
the middle of December (at least, the hired soldiers
were not dismissed till that time), having occupied
upwards of three months.[1]

The escape of so many of the principal rebels seems
to have given the Council great dissatisfaction. Lord
Binning, writing to Archibald Campbell in the month
of October says—" Since Sir James and his son, with
MacRanald (Keppoch) and his son, and Glengarry's son,[2]
and MacSorley are all escaped, and Coll pardoned, I
know not what ringleaders these are whom ye write ye
are to bring in. . . . . So long as the heads are all to
the fore, the rebellion will never be thought quenched.
Wherefore, I know my Lord will have such care as

---

[1] The detail of the proceedings has been drawn from two reports
to the Privy Council—one by Argyle himself, the other by his confidential agent, Archibald Campbell—recorded in the books of
Council, 24th November, and 21st December, 1615. Also from
letters, Argyle to Binning, 13th and 29th October, and 7th November; Archibald Campbell to Binning, 20th October; and Captain
Wood to Binning, 2nd November, 1615; Denmylne MS. See also
Pitcairn's Criminal Trials, III. 26.

[2] This young man had been made prisoner by Sir James and
Keppoch in their flight from Edinburgh; had been carried along
with them as a hostage for his father, that the latter should do
nothing against Sir James; and latterly, being released, had taken open
part with the rebels.

agreeth with his own honour and his Majesty's expectation."[1] In the commencement of November, Argyle was directed by the Council to dismiss his hired soldiers, as they conceived he had now no further use for them.[2] But being of a different opinion, he, at his own risk, retained them on service a month and a half longer—his reasons for which he gave in a letter to Lord Binning, in which he expressed his assurance, that when he came to make a report of his proceedings, the Council would approve of what he had. done. In this letter the following remarkable passage occurs:—" My Lord, I thank God that the suppression of this rebellion was in time; for, on my credit, if it had been twenty days longer protracted, few of my countrymen, betwixt Tarbert and Inverary, had proven good subjects : much less could there have been any good expected of further remote places, where there was no true obedience to his Majesty at all."[3]

On the 24th of November, an interim report of Argyle's proceedings was given in by Archibald Campbell, in name of the Earl of Argyle, at which time Macfie of Colonsay was presented before the Council. About a month afterwards, Argyle in person made a full report to the Council. His conduct generally was approved of, except in the retaining of the hired soldiers after the commencement of November; and the Earl was thus obliged to pay from his own resources upwards of seven thousand pounds, being the pay of these troops

---

[1] Dated cir. 16th October; Denmylne MS. ; Criminal Trials, III. 23.

[2] Record of Privy Council, 4th November; Letter, Binning to Argyle, 25th October, 1615.

[3] Dated 7th November, Denmylne MS.

for a month and a half.   In making his report, Argyle
warmly recommended Captain Wood to the notice of
the King and Council, for his services in the late
expedition.[1]

Thus terminated the last great struggle made by the
once powerful Clandonald of Isla and Kintyre, to retain
from the grasp of the Campbells these ancient possessions of their tribe.

[1] Record of Privy Council, 24th November, and 21st December,
1615.

CHAP. IX.

A. D. 1616. THE insurrection in the South Isles being now crushed in the manner above described, the attention of the Privy Council was directed to the apprehension of such of the leaders as had escaped, and were still lurking in the Highlands or Isles. The Marquis of Huntly, and Lauchlan Macintosh of Dunnauchtane, were summoned to give their advice to the Council regarding the steps necessary to be pursued. A commission was given in the month of January to Lord Gordon (Huntly's eldest son), for the seizure of Mac-Ranald of Keppoch and his son, now supposed to be in Lochaber; and proclamation was made, charging the inhabitants of Perthshire above Dunkeld, of Banffshire above Carroun, of Inverness-shire (except the vassals of Lord Kintaill, who were employed in the Lewis), and of Mull, Morvern, and Tiree, to assist Lord Gordon in the service committed to his charge. At the same time, a reward of five thousand merks was offered for Keppoch or his son, alive or dead.[1] In March following, the Privy Council, in the absence of the Earl of Argyle,

[1] Record of Privy Council, 14th and 16th January, 1616.

who had again gone to Court, ordered his brother, Campbell of Lundy, to appear before them in a few weeks, to receive instructions for the suppression of some of the rebels (led by Malcolm MacRuari Macleod, and the bastard son of the late Sir James Macdonald of Dunluce), who still infested the Isles. A commission to Lundy, Auchinbreck, and Ardkinlass, for this purpose was prepared; but the former refused to undertake it, and in the month of June he received a licence to go to Court to confer with Argyle on the subject. It seems to have been considered by the Council that Lord Gordon was not very active in the service against Keppoch; for a second commission against the latter was directed to the Marquis of Huntly, as well as to his son, accompanied by a charge, in the King's name, to these noblemen to undertake the execution of it. In the month of July Lundy returned from England, and still refused the duty attempted to be imposed upon him, stating that he had given, both to the King and to the Earl, satisfactory reasons for his conduct; and adding that his brother might be expected in Scotland in a short time to discharge the service himself. With this answer the Council were obliged to remain contented.[1]

At this time Macleod of Harris, the captain of Clanranald, the Macleans of Dowart, Coll, and Lochbuy, and the Laird of Mackinnon, made their appearance before the Privy Council. This formality had been interrupted by the rebellion in the last year; and very strict measures were now taken to insure the obedience of these chiefs in future. They were obliged to bind

---

[1] Record of Privy Council, 29th March, 28th May, 13th June, and 6th July, 1616.

themselves mutually, as sureties for each other, to the observance of the following conditions:—*First,* That their clans should keep good order, and that they themselves should appear before the Council, annually, on the 10th of July, and oftener if required and on being legally summoned. *Secondly,* That they should exhibit annually a certain number of their principal kinsmen, out of a larger number contained in a list given by them to the Council. Dowart was to exhibit four; Macleod, three; Clanranald, two; and Coll, Lochbuy, and Mackinnon, one of these chieftains, or heads of houses, in their clans respectively.[1] *Thirdly,* That they were not to maintain in household more than the following proportions of gentlemen, according to their rank: viz., Dowart, eight; Macleod and Clanranald, six; and the others three each. *Fourthly,* That they were to free their countries of *sorners* and idle men having no lawful occupation. *Fifthly,* That none of them were to carry hackbuts or pistols, unless when employed in the King's service; and that none but the chiefs and their household gentlemen were to wear swords, or armour, or any weapons whatever. *Sixthly,* That the chiefs were to reside at the following places respectively: viz., Macleod at Dunvegan, Maclean of Dowart at that place, Clanranald at Elanterim, Maclean of Coll at Bistache, Lochbuy at Moy, and Mackinnon at Kilmorie. Such of them as had not convenient dwelling-houses corresponding to their rank at these places were to build without delay, "civil and comelie" houses, or repair

---

[1] At this time Clanranald gave up the names of his brothers, Ranald, John, and Ruari; and Mackinnon gave up those of five of his clan, as disobedient persons, for whom they disclaimed being answerable.

those that were decayed.   They were likewise to make
" policie and planting" about their houses; and to take
mains, or home-farms, into their own hands, which they
were to cultivate, " to the effect they might be thereby
exercised and eschew idleness."   Clanranald, who had
no *mains* about his Castle of Elanterim, chose for his
home-farm the lands of Hobeg in Uist.   *Seventhly,*
That at the term of Martinmas next, they were to let
the remainder of their lands to tenants, for a certain
fixed rent, in lieu of all exactions.   *Eighthly,* That no
single chief should keep more than one birling, or galley,
of sixteen or eighteen oars; and that in their voyages
through the Isles they should not oppress the country
people.   *Ninthly,* That they should send all their
children above nine years of age to school in the
Lowlands, to be instructed in reading, writing, and
speaking the English language; and that none of their
children should be served heir to their fathers, or received
as a tenant by the King, who had not received that
education.   This provision regarding education was
confirmed by an act of Privy Council, which bore that
" the chief and principall caus quhilk hes procurit and
procuris the continuance of barbaritie, impietie, and
incivilitie within the Yllis of this kingdome, hes proceidit
from the small cair that the chiftanes and principall
clannitmen of the Yllis hes haid of the educatioun and
upbringing of thair childrene in vertew and lerning;
who, being cairles of thair dewties in that poynte, and
keiping thair childrene still at home with thame, whair
they see nothing in thair tendir yeiris bot the barbarous
and incivile formes of the countrie, thay ar thairby maid
to apprehend that thair is no uther formes of dewtie and
civilitie keept in any uther pairt of the cuntrie; sua

that, when thay come to the yeiris of maturitie, hardlie
can thay be reclamed from these barbarous, rude, and
incivile formes, quhilk, for lack of instructioun, war bred
and satled in thame in their youthe: whairas, if thay
had bene sent to the inland (the low country) in thair
youthe, and trainit up in vertew, lerning, and the
Inglische tongue, thay wald haif bene the bettir pre-
pairit to reforme thair countreyis, and to reduce the
same to godliness, obedience, and civilitie." *Lastly*,
The chiefs were not to use in their houses more than
the following quantities of wine respectively: viz., Dowart
and Macleod, four tun each; Clanranald, three tun;
and Coll, Lochbuy, and Mackinnon, one tun each; and
they were to take strict order throughout their whole
estates that none of their tenants or vassals should buy
or drink any wine. A very strict act of the Privy
Council against excess of drinking accompanied this
obligation of the chiefs. It proceeded on the narrative
that "the great and extraordinary excesse in drinking
of wyne, commonlie usit among the commonis and
tenantis of the Yllis, is not only ane occasioun of the
beastlie and barbarous cruelties and inhumanities that
fallis oute amangis thame, to the offens and displeasour
of God, and contempt of law and justice; but with that
it drawis nomberis of thame to miserable necessitie and
povartie, sua that they are constraynit, quhen thay want
from their awne, to tak from thair nichtbours." Maclean
of Dowart, and his brother Lauchlan, having delayed to
find the required sureties, were committed to ward in
Edinburgh Castle, whence the former was liberated in
a short time, and allowed to live with Acheson of Gos-
furd, his father-in-law, under his own recognisance of
£40,000, and his father-in-law's for 5000 merks, that

he should remain there until permitted by the Council to return to the Isles. Dowart's brother was not liberated till the following year, when his own bond was taken for the conformity of himself and his son Hector to the obligations imposed upon the other Islanders in July, 1616. His dwelling-place was to be at Ardnacross in Mull; and he was allowed to keep two gentlemen in his household. Donald Gorme of Sleat, having been prevented, by sickness, from attending the Council with the other chiefs, ratified all their proceedings, and found the required sureties, by a bond dated. in the month of August. He named Duntullim, a castle of his family in Trouterness, as his residence; and six household gentlemen, and an annual consumption of four tun of wine, were allowed to him; and he was annually to exhibit to the Council three of his principal kinsmen.[1] These proceedings being communicated by the Council to the King, were approved of by his Majesty; who, at the suit of the Islanders, ordered that the chiefs, and some of their immediate relations, might have licence to use fire-arms for their own sport within a mile of their dwellings.[2]

A. D. 1617. In the following year, Sir Ruari Macleod of Harris, Sir Donald Gorme of Sleat (nephew and heir-male of the late Donald Gorme), Sir Donald MacAllan Vic Ian, captain of the Clanranald, Sir Lauchlan Mackinnon of Strathordell, Hector Maclean of Lochbuy, Lauchlan Maclean of Coll, and Lauchlan Maclean, brother to Dowart, made their appearance before the Council in the month of

---

[1] Record of Privy Council, 11th, 17th, 26th July, 22nd August, 2nd September, 1616; 22nd March, 1617.

[2] Ibid., 18th September, 1616.

July.[1]   About this time, in consequence of great abuses
and oppression, the practice of taking *calps* in the
Highlands and Isles was abolished in the same way as
it had been suppressed by James IV. in Galloway
upwards of a century before.[2]   The *calp* was an acknowledgment of vassalage or dependence on a chief;
and consisted in the best horse, ox, or cow of a vassal,
which, on his decease, was claimed by his superior.
The conflicting claims of different chiefs and landlords
caused, in many instances, great oppression—four or
five calps being sometimes taken from one family on the
occasion of a single death.   This led to the abolition of
the practice.

The chiefs of Keppoch and Lochiel still continued
outlaws; the former for his concern in the rebellion of
Sir James Macdonald; the latter for having, in addition
to his former offences, lately interrupted Macintosh
when the latter was going to hold courts at Inverlochy,
as heritable Steward of Lochaber.[3]   When Lochiel
was forfeited for not producing his title-deeds in 1598,
the disputed lands of Glenluy and Locharkaig were
claimed by Macintosh; and Lochiel had, to save himself from the consequences, entered into a contract with
the latter, by which he agreed to take from that chief
one-half of the disputed lands in mortgage for the sum
of six thousand merks; and to hold the other half
under Macintosh, for the personal service of himself and

---

[1] Record of Privy Council, ad tempus.   Macleod had been
knighted in 1613.   The dates of the knighthood of the other chiefs
are more uncertain, although probably all were knighted after
Macleod.

[2] Acts of Parliament, IV. 548.

[3] Record of Privy Council, June 10, July 31, 1617.

the tenants of the lands. This contract was to endure for nineteen years ; and very severe penalties were imposed upon him who should infringe it. This it was which kept Macintosh from acting against Lochiel when the latter became an outlaw for the slaughter of his clansmen in 1613. Now, however, Macintosh maintained that Lochiel by his late lawless proceedings had forfeited all benefit from the above-mentioned contract ; and he accordingly prepared to carry into effect the acts of outlawry against the latter which were in force.[1]

A.D. 1618. Finding himself unable, in present circumstances, to make head against the Clanchattan, Lochiel was forced to make up his quarrel with the Marquis of Huntly. This he did by surrendering to the Marquis' eldest son the superiority of many lands in Lochaber ; in which lands his own eldest son, John Cameron, and several of his clan were now received as vassals of the house of Huntly. By this sacrifice Lochiel obtained the support of Huntly against Macintosh, whom the Marquis cordially hated.[2] MacRanald of Keppoch and his sons still continued outlaws ; and, in the month of July a commission of fire and sword against them was granted to Macintosh. In the execution of this service Macintosh gave offence to Lord Gordon, who procured the recall of the commission against Keppoch, and received authority himself to act against the latter's eldest son, Ranald—Keppoch himself, and his second son, Donald Glas, having by this time contrived to make their escape and join Sir James

---

[1] MS. History of Camerons.
[2] Ibid. Reg. of Great Seal, L. 144.

Macdonald in Spain.[1]   Here, strange to say, the fugitive Macdonalds were soon after joined by their arch enemy, the Earl of Argyle, whose personal history after the year 1615 is a striking instance of the mutability of human affairs.

In 1616 Argyle had gone to Court to make his personal report of the expedition led by him against Sir James Macdonald in the end of the preceding year. At that time he seems to have been in great favour; for an Act of Parliament was soon after passed dissolving from the Crown the Lordship of Kintyre, granted to him in 1607, and settling it on James Campbell, Argyle's son by Dame Anna Cornwallis, his second wife.[2]   This lady, whom Argyle married when at London in the year 1610, was a Catholic; and she gradually drew her lord over to profess the same faith with herself—although, for some years, his conversion was kept secret.[3]   On pretence of going to the Spa for the benefit of his health, Argyle received from the King permission to go abroad in 1618; his Majesty presuming that the Scottish Privy Council would, before his departure, have taken order for the good conduct of all the vassals and tenants of the Earldom of Argyle. This, however, had been neglected; and, moreover, it was reported, and truly, that the Earl instead of going to the Spa had gone to Spain; that he had there made open defection from the true religion; and that he had entered into very suspicious dealings with the banished rebels, Sir James Macdonald and Allaster MacRanald of Keppoch.   The King upon this wrote to the Scottish

[1] Record of Privy Council, 9th July, 21st October, 1618.
[2] Acts of Parliament, IV. 559.
[3] Douglas' Peerage (Edit. by Wood), I. 94.

Privy Council recalling the licence given to Argyle to
go abroad; and directing that nobleman to be summoned to appear before the Council in the month of
February, 1619, under the pain of treason.[1] In the
meantime various efforts were made to make the
"barons and gentlemen of Argyle" answerable for the
good rule of the Earldom. The result was, that in
December, 1618, twenty of these barons and gentlemen
appeared in presence of the Council, and made the
following arrangement for effecting the desired object:
—Campbell of Lundy undertook the principal charge;
and under him, the Lairds of Lochnell, Auchinbreck,
Ardkinlass, and Kilberry were to answer for the districts
of Lorn, Argyle Proper, Cowal, and Kintyre, respectively. Lochnell, in his district, was to be assisted by
the Macdougalls of Dunolly and Raray, Stewart of
Appin, the captain of Dunstaffnage, Mr. Donald Campbell of Barbreck-Lochow, and Robert Campbell of
Glenfalloch. Auchinbreck was to have the assistance
of the Lairds of Duntroon, Barbreck-Craignish, and
Craignish—all Campbells. The Lairds of Elangreg
and Otter (likewise Campbells) were to support Ardkinlass; and Macdonald of Largie, the Macallasters
of Loupe and Tarbert, Hector Macneill of Taynish,
and Hector Macneill of Carskeay were to assist Kilberry. The latter was to be put in possession of
Argyle's Castle of Kinloch (Kilkerran) in Kintyre,
to enable him the better to keep that district under
obedience.[2]

---

[1] Record of Privy Council, 7th November, 1618. Mem. of Council
proceedings, Denmylne MS., ad tempus.

[2] Record of Privy Council, 17th December, 1618.

A. D. 1619. The Earl of Argyle, having failed to make his appearance on the appointed day, was declared a traitor, by an act which inveighs bitterly against his hypocrisy and dissimulation.[1] He did not venture to return to Britain during the reign of James VI., nor, indeed, until the year 1638; and he died in London, soon after his return in that year. While abroad the Earl of Argyle distinguished himself in the military service of Philip III. of Spain against the States of Holland.[2] From the time of his going abroad, he never exercised any influence over his great estates in Scotland; the fee of which had, indeed, been previously conveyed by him to his eldest son, Archibald, Lord Lorn, afterwards eighth Earl of Argyle.[3]

The fall of Argyle necessarily produced a reaction in favour of the Macdonalds, whose estates had gone to benefit him and his clan. Sir James Macdonald and the chief of Keppoch were recalled from Spain by King James; and, on their arrival in London, the former received a pension of one thousand merks sterling, and the latter a pension of two hundred merks of the same money. The King wrote to the Scottish Privy Council in favour of both these chiefs, sending, at the same time, ample remissions for all their offences, to be passed under the seals of Scotland. To this, however, the Council made many objections, urging the danger of permitting chiefs of such note to be at liberty to go to the High-

A. D. 1620.

A. D. 1621.

---

[1] Record of Privy Council, 4th February, 1619.

[2] Peerage, I. 94.

[3] Letter, Council to the King, 2nd February, 1619; Denmylne MS., Advocates' Library.

lands before proper security had been found for their obedience. Sir James Macdonald's remission passed the seals, however, in the month of October; but some arrangement seems to have been made by which he was debarred from visiting Scotland. He died at London in the year 1626, without issue to revenge his wrongs and those of his clan on the Campbells. At the same time that Sir James Macdonald received his pardon, Keppoch appeared before the Privy Council, trusting to a six months' protection he had obtained from the King. He proposed visiting Lochaber, but was directed by the Council to remain in Edinburgh until he found sufficient security for his obedience to the laws.[1] He seems at length to have satisfied the Council and obtained his pardon; for we find him afterwards settled in Lochaber, in peaceable possession of his estate.

Early in this year, Allan Cameron of Lochiel, and John, his son, were outlawed for not appearing before the Council, to find security, as the Islanders had done, for their future obedience. In the month of July, commission was given to Lord Gordon against Lochiel and his clan, who are described as almost the only persons in the Highlands and Isles who now remained disobedient; and proclamation was made, charging all the men of Badenoch and Lochaber, between sixty and sixteen years of age (except only Sir Lauchlan Macintosh himself), to concur with Lord Gordon in the execution of his commission. The same nobleman was commissioned to apprehend or slay Ranald Macranald, the eldest son

---

[1] Sir R. Gordon's History of Sutherland, p. 238. Reg. of Privy Seal, XCVII. 109. Letters, Council to King, 7th June, 1621; 21st and 28th March, 1622; and Protection to Keppoch, 12th October, 1621—all in Denmylne MS.

of Keppoch, who had contrived to conceal himself in Lochaber ever since the year 1615.[1] It appears that these commissions were not vigorously acted upon; and, indeed, Lochiel and Keppoch being both vassals of Lord Gordon, it is probable he undertook the service in order to prevent the interference of Macintosh, or some other chief who, like him, was disposed to push matters to extremities against both the Clanchameron and the Clanranald of Lochaber. In the following year, Macintosh went to Court, and, by his representations, procured, in the month of June, a commission against Lochiel, directed to himself and twenty-two other chiefs and gentlemen of note throughout the whole Highlands and Isles. The imminent danger which now appeared to threaten Lochiel was averted by the sudden death of Macintosh, which gave an opportunity to Lochiel's friends, particularly the Laird of Grant, to interest themselves on his behalf.[2] By their means Lochiel was induced to submit his disputes with the family of Macintosh, the chief cause of all his troubles, to the decision of mutual friends. The lands of Glenluy and Locharkaig were, by these arbiters, adjudged to belong to Macintosh, who was, however, to pay to Lochiel certain sums of money in compensation of the claims of the latter. Lochiel, although he pretended to acquiesce in this decision, yet delayed the completion of the transaction in such a way that the dispute was not finally settled till the time of his grandson, the celebrated Sir Ewin Cameron of Lochiel.[3] Meantime, he

A. D. 1622.

---

[1] Record of Privy Council, Jan., Feb., March, and July, 1621.

[2] Record of Privy Council, 18th June, 30th July, 17th December, 1622. Douglas' Baronage, p. 352.

[3] MS. History of Camerons.

obtained a pardon for his offences, and his sentence of outlawry was recalled.[1]

Since the year 1617, the Islanders had continued. (with the exception of Hector Maclean of Dowart) to make their annual appearance before the Privy Council with tolerable regularity. In July, 1619, the time for their yearly appearance was, at their own request, altered from July to February; but, in 1621, it was again altered to July, owing to the uncertainty of the weather in spring.[2] In the following year, Sir Ruari Macleod of Harris, Sir Donald Gorme of Sleat, John MacDonald, captain of the Clanranald (son of the late Sir Donald MacAllan), and the lairds of Coll, Lochbuy, and Mackinnon, made their obedience to the Privy Council, as usual, when several acts of importance relating to the Isles were passed. By the first of these they were bound to build and repair their parish churches to the satisfaction of the Bishop of the Isles; and they promised to meet the Bishop at Icolmkill, whenever he should appoint, to make the necessary arrangements in this matter. The Bishop, at this time, promised to appoint a qualified Commissary for the Isles—complaints having been made on this head. By another act, masters of vessels were prohibited, under the penalty of confiscation of the article, to carry more wine to the Isles than the quantity allowed to the chiefs and gentlemen by the act of 1617. The preamble of this act assumes, that one of the chief causes which retarded the civilisation of the Isles, was the

---

[1] MS. History of Camerons; and Original Bond of Caution for Lochiel, dated 21st September, 1623, and preserved in General Register House.

[2] Record of Privy Council, ad tempus.

great quantity of wine imported yearly:—"With the insatiable desyre quhairof the saidis Ilanderis ar so far possest, that, when thair arryvis ony schip or uther veschell there with wines, thay spend both dayes and nights in their excesse of drinking sa lang as thair is anie of the wyne left; sua that, being overcome with drink, thair fallis oute many inconvenientis amangis thame, to the breck of his Majestei's peace," &c.   By a third act, Macleod, Sir Donald Gorme, Clanranald, and Mackinnon, were bound not to molest those engaged in the trade of fishing in the Isles, under heavy penalties.[1]

A. D. 1625.   The last serious insurrection in the West Highlands and Isles which occurred in the reign of James VI., was that of the Clan Ian of Ardnamurchan, in the year 1625, arising out of the following circumstances.   Archibald, fourth Earl of Argyle, had acquired the superiority of Ardnamurchan and Sunart, by resignation of Mariot, daughter and heiress of John Macian of Ardnamurchan.[2]   The heirs-male of the family of Macian continued, however, to possess the estates, without acknowledging the Earl of Argyle as their superior for a considerable period.   Allaster MacDonald Vic Ian of Ardnamurchan is mentioned in the minority of Queen Mary, and John Macian of Ardnamurchan occurs in the early part of the reign of her son (supra, pp. 170, 238).   John Oig Macian, son of the last mentioned John, when on the point of marrying a daughter of the house of Lochiel, about the year

---

[1] Record of Privy Council, July, 1622.

[2] Inventory of Argyle Writs. Reg. of Privy Seal, XVII., fo. 38; XXIV., fo. 29. This lady had married Robert Robertson of Strowan, who consented to her resignation of Ardnamurchan.

1596, was assassinated by his uncle, who was his next
heir, and wished to obtain possession of the estate.
The murderer did not long escape the punishment due
to his crime; for, notwithstanding that he was supported
by Sir Lauchlan Maclean of Dowart, he was soon after
killed in a skirmish with the Camerons. This happened
in the district of Morvern; and the grave of Mac Vic
Ian, as tradition calls the murderer, who is said to have
been a warrior of gigantic size and great prowess, is
still shown in the churchyard of Keill in Morvern.[1] In
1602, John MacAllaster Vic Ian of Ardnamurchan,
now the heir of the family, entered into a contract with
the Earl of Argyle. By this agreement, Macian became bound to exhibit to the Earl the title-deeds of
Ardnamurchan, and to resign the lands to the Earl.
On this being performed, Argyle engaged to receive
Macian as his vassal in the lands, to be holden for
payment of one merk of feu-duty. This shows that,
hitherto, the Macians had possessed upon their old titles
from the Crown, without regard to the conveyance of the
superiority to the fourth Earl of Argyle by Mariot Macian,
the heiress. Argyle likewise engaged to protect and
defend Macian and his clan in the same way as his other
vassals.[2] It does not appear that this contract, so favourable to the Macians (for Argyle's claim to the superiority
was legally good, independent of the proposed resignation), was ever fulfilled, at least on the part of the Earl.
It is clear that the title-deeds were delivered up; but

---

[1] MS. History of Camerons. The author of this MS. calls the
murdered chief erroneously *Donald;* but I find *John Oig* Macian of
Ardnamurchan mentioned in an authentic document, A.D. 1595.—
Collectanea de Rebus Albanicis, I. 200.

[2] Inventory of Argyle Writs.

the history of the Macians after this period, leads to the conclusion, either that Argyle had not acted in good faith, or that the Macians, by some insurrection or similar lawless proceeding, had forfeited the benefit of the laws.   Dying before 1611, this John Macian of Ardnamurchan left a son, Allaster, in whose minority the clan was led by a certain Donald Macian, probably uncle of the minor, styled Tutor of Ardnamurchan.[1]   In 1612, a commission was granted by Archibald Earl of Argyle, to Mr. Donald Campbell of Barbreck-Lochow, "to take and receive the castle and place of Mingarry (in Ardnamurchan), and, upon the Earl's expenses, to put keepers therein;" with power to the Commissioner to summon before him all the tenants and inhabitants of Ardnamurchan, and generally to manage that territory in fixing and collecting with regularity the rents to be paid to the Earl, and punishing, by expulsion or otherwise, the refractory tenants.[2]   This Mr. Donald Campbell was a natural son of that Sir John Campbell of Calder, killed in 1592, by an assassin employed by Ardkinlass and others of the name of Campbell (supra, p. 251).   He was originally bred to the Church, and became Dean of Lismore; but he was of too restless a disposition to confine himself to his ecclesiastical duties.   He first distinguished himself by the zeal with which he endeavoured to bring to justice all those concerned in his father's murder.[3]   The talents and activity of Mr. Donald Campbell recommended him to the notice of his chief, the Earl of Argyle, by whom he was

---

[1] Reg. of Privy Seal, LXXX. 162.

[2] Original in Charter Chest of Airds.

[3] This is proved by many documents in the Charter Chest of Airds.

commissioned, as above, to reduce the district of Ardnamurchan to obedience. He afterwards received from the Earl a lease of Ardnamurchan, and made himself very obnoxious to the natives by his severities. In the end of 1615, or very nearly in the following year, John Macdonald Vic Ian, a son probably of the Tutor of Ardnamurchan, and a principal tenant in the district, went to Edinburgh to seek, on behalf of the Clan Ian, an audience of the Earl of Argyle, or his brother, Campbell of Lundy. Having failed in his object, through the absence of the Earl and his brother, he returned to the Highlands bearing with him a strong letter of recommendation from William Stirling of Auchyle, a confidential agent of Argyle, to Mr. Donald Campbell. In this letter, the following passage occurs:—"It is not without reason and some foirknowledge in preventing further inconvenience, I have written to you; which, I am assured, ye will consider out of your own wisdom. I hope ye will press to win the people (of Ardnamurchan) with [kyndness] rather nor extremitie, speciallie at the first."[1] In July, 1616, the Tutor of Ardnamurchan incurred the forfeiture of two thousand merks, for not appearing before the Privy Council at that time;[2] and it may be conjectured that Mr. Donald Campbell lost no time in enforcing the sentence against Macian. By some error or deceit on the part of Argyle or his agents, a lease of Ardnamurchan had been granted to Sir Donald MacAllan of Moydert, captain of the Clanranald, several years before the expiry of the lease granted to Campbell. In the month of May, 1618, John MacDonald, captain of the Clan-

---

[1] Original Letter in Ch. Chest of Airds, dated 16th January, 1616.
[2] Record of Privy Council, ad tempus.

ranald, son of the late Sir Donald, united with the Clan
Ian, who acknowledged him as their chief, and expelled
Campbell and his adherents from Ardnamurchan.   This
dispute was in the following year submitted to the
decision of Sir George Hay (afterwards Earl of Kin-
noull) and Sir George Erskine of Innerteil, who found
that Campbell's lease was the best in law, and therefore ordered him to be repossessed in the disputed
lands; compensation being made to the captain of
Clanranald for the grassum, or fine at granting of the
lease, paid by his father.[1]   In 1620, some of the principal men of the Clan Ian—with Macleod of Harris, the
captain of the Clanranald, and Maclean of Coll as
their sureties—bound themselves to Mr. Donald Campbell for the dutiful obedience of the Clan Ian to the
house of Argyle, and for their being peaceable tenants
to Campbell, and paying him all rents and damages
that might be found due to the latter.[2]   Two years
later we find Campbell stating to the Privy Council
that Allaster Macian of Ardnamurchan had lately
assembled his clan, and declared to them his intention
of recovering the old possessions of his family, by law
if possible; and should that fail him, had expressed his
determination to resort to force, in which he made his
clan swear to assist him.   Macian, however, making
his appearance before the Privy Council, this accusa-
tion was referred to his oath, when he distinctly denied
the truth of it.[3]

[1] Record of Privy Council, 10th November, 1618; 29th and 31st
July, 1619.

[2] General Register of Deeds, Vol. CCCCXXVI., sub. 15th January,
1630.

[3] Record of Privy Council, 23rd July, 1622.

It is probable, however, that this young chief, whether instigated by his clan, or provoked by the severities of the Campbells, did afterwards resort to force against the latter. In 1624 the Clan Ian were again in rebellion; and in September of that year Macleod of Harris, Clanranald, and Maclean of Coll, as having formerly become answerable for the Clan Ian, were charged to exhibit the leaders of that tribe before the Privy Council in January following. Having failed to do this, these chiefs were denounced rebels, according to the usual forms of Scottish law. At this time the Clan Ian had seized, manned, and armed an English vessel, and had betaken themselves, to the number of five or six score, to a piratical life. In April, 1625, the Archbishop of Glasgow and Sir William Livingston of Kilsyth were commissioned to go to the burgh of Ayr, to provide a ship and a pinnace, properly manned and victualled, for the pursuit of the Clan Ian. At the same time a commission of fire and sword and of justiciary against them was given to Lord Lorn and the Lairds of Calder, Auchinbreck, Lochnell, and Ardkinlass, or any three of them, Lord Lorn always being one. In the month of May a Scottish and a Flemish ship, which had been seized by the Clan Ian, were retaken by Captain John Osburne for the King. From various letters concerning this insurrection which are still preserved, it appears that the pirates of the Clan Ian were for a time the terror of the whole west coast of Scotland, from Isla north- wards. Being hotly pursued from Sky (whither they had probably gone in pursuit of some merchant vessels), by Sir Ruari Macleod of Harris and a body of his clan, they landed in Moydert, the captain of Clanranald's country, and hid themselves in the woods there. Soon afterwards Lord Lorn and his forces arrived at Ardnamurchan, and meeting with Macleod and other chiefs engaged in the service, speedily suppressed the insurrection, and killed or banished the rebels. From this time we never meet with the Clan Ian of Ardnamurchan as a separate and independent tribe; as any survivors of them seem, for security, to have identified themselves with the Clanranald. The services of Lord Lorn were approved of by the Privy Council, and he received the thanks of that body accordingly.[1] Mr. Donald Campbell, originally tenant of Ardnamurchan, became now heritable proprietor under Lorn of that district and Sunart, for which he paid an annual feuduty of two thousand merks. Before the month of January, 1629, he had been created a Baronet, and during the reign of Charles I. was well known as Sir Donald Campbell of Ardnamurchan. He left no surviving male issue; but his title is now enjoyed by the present Sir John Campbell of Airds and Ardnamurchan, the descendant and representative of George Campbell of Airds, nephew to Sir Donald.[2] Of the old Macians, the last trace I have found is a bond, dated at Edinburgh, 22nd April, 1629, by Alexander Macian, son and heir of the late John Macian of Ardnamurchan, to Robert Innes, burgess of the Chanonry of Ross, for the

---

[1] This account of the proceedings against the Clan Ian is taken from the Record of Privy Council, 22nd September, 1624; 27th January, 21st April, 31st May, and 28th July, 1625; and from Letters, Campbell of Calder, the Archbishop of Glasgow to Lord Melros (afterwards Earl of Haddington); from Macleod of Harris to Mr. Donald Campbell—all preserved in the General Register House, Edinburgh; and from the Council to the King, preserved in the Denmylne MS., dated in the months of April, May, and July, 1625.

[2] Documents in Charter Chest of Airds.

sum of forty thousand pounds Scots.[1] From this it may be inferred that Macian had received, or was about to receive, compensation for his claims on Ardnamurchan.

Having now brought the general history of the West Highlands and Isles down to the period proposed in the outset of the present work, I shall conclude by adding such particulars regarding the various tribes of whom I have treated, as may serve to illustrate their position with regard to each other during the reign of Charles I. and his successors.

The *House of Lochalsh* had in 1625 been for about a century extinct in the male line; and while the representation of this family, through a female, had devolved upon Donald MacAngus of Glengarry, its possessions, for the most part, were in the hands of the Mackenzies, whose chief, Colin, Lord Kintaill, was in 1623 dignified with the title of Earl of Seaforth.

The *House of Sleat* which, for several generations after the last forfeiture of the Lord of the Isles, had to struggle with numerous difficulties, and barely succeeded in retaining its possessions from the grasp of the Siol Tormod, was in 1625 in a very prosperous condition. In that year Donald Gorme Oig of Sleat (nephew and heir of the last Donald Gorme, who died in 1616, being the son of the latter's brother, Archibald), after having concluded in an amicable manner all his disputes with the Siol Tormod, and another controversy in which he was engaged with the captain of Clanranald, was created a baronet of Nova Scotia by Charles I. The present Lord Macdonald, his heir-male and

[1] General Register of Deeds, Vol. CCCCXVII.

representative, is the twelfth baronet of the family. In addition to Sleat, Trouterness, and North Uist, Lord Macdonald now possesses the estate formerly held by the Mackinnons in Sky (with the exception of one small property held by Mr. Macallaster of Strathaird), which was purchased in the reign of George III. by his Lordship's grandfather.

We have seen in a preceding chapter the total ruin of the principal house of the *Clan Ian Vor*. It now only remains to glance at the position of the surviving cadets of that powerful tribe. The first of these we shall notice is the family of *Colonsay*. The grandfather of Coll Keitache MacGillespick Macdonald of Colonsay was Coll, a brother of James Macdonald of Dunyveg and the Glens, and of Sorley Buy Macdonald, father of the first Earl of Antrim. Some years previous to the breaking out of the great civil war, Coll MacGillespick was expelled from Colonsay by the Campbells, with whom he had a quarrel. His family was dispersed, and one of his sons, the well-known Allaster MacColl Keitache, having gone to Ireland, returned to the Highlands in 1644 at the head of the Irish troops sent to assist the Scottish Royalists by the Marquis of Antrim. Allaster acted as Lieutenant-General to the celebrated Marquis of Montrose, and received from that leader the honour of knighthood. Although brave to a fault, and, therefore, well qualified to lead irregular troops like the Highlanders, Sir Allaster Macdonald allowed his desire of revenging the wrongs of his family upon the Campbells, to divert him from the proper objects of the war. He was thus a principal cause of the disaster which befel the Royal arms at Philiphaugh —having previously withdrawn many of the Highlanders

from Montrose's camp, to assist him in his private feuds
in Argyleshire; a service in which the western clans
were all very ready to engage. Being driven from the
Isles by General Leslie, and having lost all his followers,
Sir Allaster went to join the Royalists in Ireland, and
was soon afterwards killed in battle there. His father,
old Coll MacGillespick, being left once more in charge
of the Castle of Dunyveg, was entrapped into a surrender by Leslie, and was handed over to the Campbells,
by whom this restless Islander was at length executed.
He was hung from the mast of his own galley, placed
over the cleft of a rock near the Castle of Dunstaffnage.
Dr. Macdonnell, who resides at Belfast, is believed to
be the representative of this branch of the Clan Ian
Vor. Of the *Earls of Antrim* descended from Sorley
Buy we have already spoken (supra, p. 227). This
noble family is now extinct in the direct male line; and
the title of Antrim is enjoyed by the heir of line of the
family. The next branch of the Clan Ian Vor we have
to notice is that of *Sanda* in Kintyre, whose ancestor
was Angus *Ilach,* paternal uncle of James Macdonald
of Dunyveg and the Glens, and of Sorley Buy. The
representative of this family contrived to save his estate
at the time of the forfeiture of Kintyre by James VI.
From him descended in a direct line the late Sir John
Macdonald Kinnear, whose eldest son is the present
representative of the Macdonalds of Sanda. The origin
of the *Macdonalds* or *Clanranaldbane of Largie* has
already been noticed (supra, p. 63). The chieftain
of this branch likewise succeeded in preserving his
estate from forfeiture under James VI. In the direct
male line this family has been for some time extinct—
the estate having gone by marriage to the family of

Lockhart of Lee and Carnwath. The Macdonalds of Sanda and Largie were actively engaged in supporting both Montrose and Dundee.

The *Clanranald of Lochaber*, or Macdonalds of Garragach and Keppoch, were one of the most active clans on the Royal side in the great civil war. Soon after the Restoration, the prosperity of this family received a severe check from the barbarous murder of the young chief of Keppoch, Alexander Macdonald Glas, and his brother, two young men who had received a liberal education, and were exerting themselves for the improvement of their estates. They fell under the daggers of some of their own discontented followers; and although their murder was amply avenged by their kinsman, Sir James Macdonald of Sleat, yet the family did not soon recover from the blow. Coll Macdonald of Keppoch vanquished the Macintoshes, with whom he was at feud regarding the lands he occupied, in the last clan battle that was ever fought in the Highlands. The scene of this conflict was on a height called Mulroy, near the house of Keppoch (for the Macintoshes had invaded Lochaber in the prosecution of the quarrel), and it took place immediately before the Revolution in 1688. Keppoch afterwards joined Dundee, and fought at Killiecrankie; and he likewise joined the banner of the Earl of Mar, and was present at the battle of Sheriffmuir in 1715. His son, Alexander Macdonald of Keppoch, entered eagerly into the rebellion of 1745, and fell gallantly leading on his clan, when the hopes of the Jacobites were finally extinguished at Culloden. There are still numerous cadets of this family in Lochaber; but the principal house, if not yet extinct, has lost all influence in that district.

During the seventeenth century, the *Clanranald of Garmoran* continued to prosper and increase. Donald MacAllan, captain of the Clanranald in the latter part of the reign of James VI., had several brothers. From Ranald, one of these, descended the family of *Benbecula*, which, on the failure of Donald's descendants, succeeded to the barony of Castletirrim and the captainship of the Clanranald, and is now represented by the present Ranald George Macdonald of Clanranald. The *Macdonalds of Boisdale* are cadets of Benbecula, and *Staffa* is a cadet of Boisdale. From John, another of these brothers, descended the family of *Kinlochmoidart*, which is now extinct in the direct male line, the estate being possessed by Colonel Robertson Macdonald, in right of his wife, the heiress of this family. From John Oig, uncle of the above-mentioned Donald MacAllan, descended the *Macdonalds of Glenaladale*. The head of this family, John Macdonald of Glenaladale, being obliged to quit Scotland about 1772, in consequence of family misfortunes arising out of the rebellion of 1745, sold his Scottish estates to his cousin (who is represented by the present .Angus Macdonald of Glenaladale), and emigrating to Prince Edward's Island, with about two hundred followers, purchased a tract of forty thousand acres there, on which his heir-male now resides, while the two hundred Highlanders have increased to three thousand. In that remote colony, the language, manners, and customs of the Highlanders, as in several districts of Upper Canada, are preserved in greater purity than in the mother country. The family of *Knoydart*, mentioned in the Introduction (supra, p. 66), fell into decay about 1611, the lands of Knoydart having previously come into the hands of Lochiel, by whom they were granted to Donald MacAngus of Glengarry, to hold of Lochiel and his successors. The superiority of Knoydart was afterwards acquired from Lochiel by the Marquis of Argyle. The old family of *Morar*, mentioned in the Introduction (supra, p. 66), soon became extinct; and the position of the more modern chieftains of Morar, as heirs-male of Allan Mac-Ruari, chief of the Clanranald in the reign of James IV., has already been noticed (supra, p. 158), and need not here be repeated. The estate of Morar has passed into other hands, but the family still exists in the male line. The family of *Glengarry*, notwithstanding its losses in Ross-shire, continued to prosper in other quarters. Angus, or Æneas, the head of this family, was, at the Restoration, elevated to the Peerage by the title of Lord Macdonnell and Aros, for his services to the cause of the Stewarts. This nobleman, presuming on his Peerage, endeavoured to get himself recognised as chief of all the Macdonalds, in which, however, he failed. He left no male issue, and his title, being limited to heirs-male of his body, died with him. The late Alexander Ranaldson Macdonnell[1] of Glengarry,

---

[1] As some persons attach great importance to the mode of spelling the name "Macdonald," it may be proper to observe here that, until of late, the spelling of Highland names was so lax as to deprive of all weight any argument resting on so uncertain a foundation. It could easily be shown that, on many occasions, the Glengarry and Keppoch families, who have now adopted *Macdonnell*, frequently used *Macdonald*. The most proper way of spelling the name, according to the pronunciation, was that formerly employed by the Macdonalds of Dunyveg and the Glens, who used *Macconnell*. Sir James Macdonald, however, the last of this family in the direct male line, signed *Makdonall*. I have adopted *Macdonald* throughout this work, as being the spelling most generally recognised.

styling himself also of Clanranald, revived the claims of his predecessor to pre-eminence among the Macdonalds; but with no better success—as that honour, by the general opinion of the Highlanders, belongs to the chief who receives from them the title of *MacDhonuill na'n Eilean*, or Macdonald of the Isles; in other words, to Lord Macdonald. The principal families descended of the house of Glengarry, were the Macdonnells of Barrisdale, Greenfield, and Lundie. Of these, the first still occupies its original seat of Barrisdale in Knoydart. It is needless to expatiate here on the devotion which all the branches of the Clanranald have uniformly displayed towards those whom they considered their rightful sovereigns. They engaged in every attempt for the restoration of the Stewarts, and suffered severely in consequence; but after all their sufferings and losses, they still form a numerous and gallant tribe, as attached to the house of Hanover as they ever were to the House of Stewart.

Of the *Clan Ian of Glenco* little remains to be said. The name recalls the dreadful massacre of Glenco, by which it was endeavoured to annihilate this tribe. In spite, however, of the massacre, and of their later sufferings as Jacobites, several families of Macdonalds still possess lands in the vale where their ancestors so long resided. The final ruin of the *Clan Ian of Ardnamurchan* has been detailed in the present chapter; and the name of this ancient tribe is now only to be found in the fast fading traditions of the West Highlands. The *Macallasters of Loupe* continued to possess their lands in Kintyre, until the estate was sold by Colonel Somerville Macallaster, the present heir-male of the old family of Loupe. Many of the name are still to be found in Kintyre and the neighbouring districts.

The family of *Maclean of Dowart*, which, in the reign of James VI., was the most powerful in the Hebrides, had before the end of the seventeenth century lost nearly all its great possessions, and was almost deprived of influence. The seeds of the decay of this important family were sown in the reign of Queen Mary, when the great feud between the Macleans and Macdonalds first broke out. In the reigns of James VI. and Charles I., many debts had accumulated against the barony of Dowart, which enabled the Marquis of Argyle and his successors to establish a claim to that estate; and this claim the Macleans, owing to their exertions in favour of the Stewarts, never had an opportunity of shaking off. Sir Lauchlan Maclean of Morvern, immediate younger brother of Hector Maclean of Dowart, and grandson of Lauchlan Mor (supra, p. 285), was created a Baronet of Nova Scotia by Charles I. On the death of his elder brother, Sir Lauchlan succeeded to the estate of Dowart; and, on the failure of the male issue of Sir Lauchlan, some generations later, the Baronetcy devolved on Allan Maclean of Brolos, descended from Donald, a younger brother of the first Baronet of Dowart. Sir Allan's heir-male, who now bears the title, is Lieut.-General Sir Fitzroy Maclean of Morvern, eighth Baronet. From Lauchlan Oig Maclean, a younger son of Lauchlan Mor of Dowart, sprung the family of Torlusk in Mull. The estate of Torlusk is now held by the heiress of line, Mrs. Clephane Maclean, and will eventually pass to that lady's grandson, the second son of the present Marquis of Northampton. During the seventeenth and eighteenth centuries, the Macleans of *Lochbuy*, *Coll*, and *Ardgour*, more fortunate than those of Dowart, contrived to preserve their estates nearly entire as regarded the property; although compelled, by the power and policy of the Marquis of Argyle, to renounce their holdings from the Crown, and to become vassals of that powerful nobleman and his successors. There were numerous flourishing cadets of all the principal families of the Macleans, too numerous to be noticed in detail in the present brief sketch. The principal of these were— the Macleans of *Kinlochaline*, *Ardtornish*, and *Drimnin*, descended from Dowart; of *Tapul*, and *Scallasdale*, descended from Lochbuy; of *Isle of Muck*, descended from Coll; and of *Borrera* in North Uist, and *Tressinish*, descended from Ardgour. All the Macleans were zealous partisans of the Stewarts, in whose cause they suffered severely; more particularly at the battle of Inverkeithing, in 1652, when this clan lost several hundred men, and a large proportion of officers.

Of the *Siol Torquil*, or Macleods of Lewis, the principal surviving branches during the seventeenth and eighteenth centuries were the families of *Rasay* and *Assint*. The latter property came into the hands of the Mackenzies, who expelled the Macleods towards the end of the seventeenth century; but the family continued to exist, notwithstanding its misfortunes and losses, and was long represented by the late venerable Donald Macleod of Geanies, Sheriff of Ross-shire, whose grandson is now the head of this branch. The Macleods, formerly of *Cambuscurry*, now of *Cadboll*, are cadets of those of Assint. The present heir-male of the old Macleods of Lewis, and chief of the Siol Torquil, is John Macleod, now of Rasay.

The *Siol Tormod*, or Macleods of Harris, Dunvegan, and Glenelg, continued to possess these extensive

estates until near the end of the eighteenth century;
but the estates of Harris and Glenelg have now passed
into other hands. The principal cadets of this powerful tribe were the families of Bernera, Talisker, Griser-
nish, and Hamer, descended from Sir Norman, Sir
Roderick, Donald, and William Macleods, younger
sons of Sir Ruari Mor. Besides these, however, there
were many other most respectable families of the name
settled in Sky, and also in Harris and Glenelg, where
some of them still remain. From the family of Bernera
sprung that of Luskinder, of which the late Sir
William Macleod Bannatyne, formerly one of the Sena-
tors of the College of Justice, was a cadet. The author
takes this opportunity of paying a tribute of respect to
the memory of that lamented gentleman, who, during a
public life of seventy years (for he died at the advanced
age of ninety-one), was ever distinguished by his zeal
in all matters tending to benefit the Highlands and
Isles. He early turned his attention to the history of
the principal Highland families, and to the peculiar
· manners and customs of the Highlanders; in the eluci-
dation of which his progress was so great, at a time
when, from political causes, these subjects were generally neglected, as to make it matter of regret that he
never thought proper to communicate his knowledge to
the world. To Sir William Macleod Bannatyne, the
author of the present work was indebted for much curious
information and many valuable suggestions.

The *Clanchameron*, from the time of the submission of Allan Cameron of Lochiel to the Government
(supra, p. 403), continued to prosper; and, with some
trifling exceptions, the various branches of this tribe
still enjoy their ancient possessions. The celebrated

Sir Ewin Cameron, commonly Ewin Dubh of Lochiel, succeeded, about the year 1664, in making a satisfactory arrangement of the long standing feud with the Macintoshes, by which, in consideration of a sum of money paid by him, he was left at length in peaceable possession of the disputed lands of Glenluy and Locharkaig. This family, like many others, was constrained to hold its lands from the Marquis of Argyle and his successors. The Clanchameron took an active part in all the rebellions in favour of the house of Stewart; and the chivalrous character of the "gentle Lochiel," who led his clan in 1745-6, has left an impression which will not readily be forgotten.

During the seventeenth and eighteenth centuries, the *Clanchattan* was a flourishing clan; and the present Alexander Macintosh, captain and chief of Clanchattan, besides his estates in Badenoch, still possesses the lands in Lochaber so long disputed between his ancestors and the Macdonalds of Keppoch. The *Macphersons*, or *Clanvurich*, have, during the same period, succeeded in establishing themselves as a separate clan from the Macintoshes, although not without a struggle. At the head of the Clanvurich is the present Ewen Macpherson of Cluny, commonly called *Cluny Macpherson*, who styles himself also chief of Clanchattan. It is, however, well known and easily proved that the title of captain and chief of Clanchattan has been enjoyed by the family of Macintosh for at least four hundred years. The Clanchattan (under which term I comprehend the Macintoshes and their followers) and the Clanvurich have both distinguished themselves as zealous and gallant supporters of the claims of the house of Stewart.

The history of the *Clanneill of Barra,* owing to its remote situation, offers little of interest during the seventeenth and eighteenth centuries; nor have there sprung from this ancient stock any branches of importance. Lieut.-Colonel Roderick Macniel, the present representative, possesses Barra and the adjacent Isles, which can be distinctly traced to have been held by his ancestors for upwards of four hundred years; and tradition carries their possession much farther back.

The *Clanneill of Gigha* multiplied much more rapidly. The direct line of the old family, who were certainly in possession of Gigha more than four hundred years ago, failed in the person of Neill MacNeill of Gigha, in the latter part of the reign of Queen Mary. Neill of Gigha, the father of this individual, and many gentlemen of the tribe, were killed in a feud with Allan, Maclean of Torlusk, commonly called *Alein na'n Sop,* prior to the year 1542. Torlusk afterwards disputed, but without success, possession of Gigha with James Macdonald of Isla, to whom Neill, the son, had sold the property. On the extinction of the direct male line Neill MacNeill Vic Eachan of Taynish became heir-male of the family; and his descendant, Hector Macneill of Taynish, purchased from the Macdonalds the Isle of Gigha, in the end of the reign of James VI., or early in the reign of Charles I. Hector's descendants possessed the estates of Gigha and Taynish until the reign of George III., when they were sold. The family however, still exists in the male line, being represented by Daniel Hamilton Macneill of Raploch in Lanarkshire; and while the present work is passing through the press, the Island of Gigha has been purchased by Captain Alexander Macneill, younger, of Colonsay. Next

to the family of Taynish, the principal cadets of the
old Macneills of Gigha were those of *Gallochelly*,
Carskeay, and *Tirfergus*. From Malcolm Beg Macneill, a younger son of John Oig of Gallochelly, in the
reign of James VI., sprung the Macneills of *Arichonan*,
a younger son of which family acquired from the family
of Argyle the Isle of Colonsay, which is now possessed
by his descendant, the present John Macneill of Colonsay. Torquil, a younger son of Lauchlan MacNeill
Buy of Tirfergus, acquired the estate of *Ugadale* by
marriage with the heiress of the MacKays in the end
of the seventeenth century. Many cadets of the Clanneill of Gigha have settled in the North of Ireland,
where several flourishing families of the name are still
to be found.

The *Mackinnons*, after engaging both in the rebellion of 1715 and in that of 1745, lost all their property,
partly by forfeiture, partly by sale; and there is now no
proprietor of the name holding any part of their ancient
possessions either in Mull or Sky. There are still,
however, many gentlemen of the name resident in the
Highlands, particularly in the last mentioned island.
The honour of being heir-male of this ancient family is
disputed between William Alexander Mackinnon, M.P.
for Lymington, and Lauchlan Mackinnon of Letterfearn; nor is the evidence relied on by either party
conclusive on this head.

The old *Macquarries of Ulva* appear to have been
for some time extinct. The principal cadet of this
house was Macquarrie of *Ormaig*, a family which is
likewise believed to be now extinct. Some branches
of the *Maceacherns* still remain in Kintyre. The
estate of Ugadale, the ancient inheritance of the

Mackays in Kintyre, passed by marriage, as above mentioned, to a younger son of Macneill of Tirfergus, in the end of the seventeenth century.

From the accession ef Charles I. to the death of Queen Anne, the power of the *Mackenzies*, under the Earls of Seaforth and Cromarty, was, next to that of the Campbells, the greatest in the West Highlands. The forfeiture of the Earl of Seaforth in 1715, and of the Earl of Cromarty in 1745, weakened that power greatly; yet the Mackenzies are still one of the most numerous and wealthy tribes in the Highlands. The estates of the noble families above mentioned are both, with some exceptions, now held by heiresses—the Hon. Mrs. Stewart Mackenzie of Seaforth, and the Hon. Mrs. Hay Mackenzie of Cromarty; but neither of the titles have been restored. George Falconer Mackenzie of *Allangrange* appears to be heir-male of the Earls of Seaforth; and Sir Alexander Mackenzie of *Tarbat*, descended from Alexander Mackenzie of *Ardloch*, to be heir-male of the Earls of Cromarty. The principal branches of the house of Seaforth, after Allangrange, were those of Gruinard, Kilcoy, Applecross, Coul, Assint, Redcastle, Suddy, Achilty, Fairburn, Devachmaluak, Gerloch, and Hilton. The principal branches of the house of Cromarty, after Ardloch, were those of Prestonhall, Scatwell, Balone, and Kinnock.

The *Macdougalls of Dunolly* suffered much in the great civil war, being stanch Royalists; and, at a later period, their estate was forfeited for joining in the rebellion of 1715. Being restored on the eve of the rebellion of 1745, the Macdougalls were prevented from engaging in that unfortunate attempt; and the estate of Dunolly is now held by Captain Macdougall of

Macdougall, R.N., who appears to be the heir-male of
Dugall, mentioned in the Introduction as the eldest
son of Somerled. The principal families sprung from
the house of Dunolly were those of *Gallanach* and
Soraba. The history of the Macdougalls of *Raray*,
the earliest cadets of the house of Lorn, is very obscure
during the seventeenth and eighteenth centuries. It is
believed, however, that this family is now represented
by Coll Macdougall of Ardincaple.

The *Stewarts of Appin* engaged in all the attempts
made by the Highlanders in favour of the house of
Stewart. The principal family has been extinct for
some time, and their estate has passed into other hands.
But there are still many branches of this tribe remaining in Appin. The chief cadets of Appin were the
families of Ardshiel, Invernahyle, Auchnacone, Fasnacloich, and Balachulish.

It now only remains to glance at the progress made
by the *Campbells* during the seventeenth and eighteenth
centuries. The Marquis of Argyle, commonly called
Gillespick Gruamach, increased the influence of his
family more than any of his predecessors. He succeeded in establishing claims to a great part of the
estate of Dowart, and he caused all the other Macleans,
and also the Clanchameron, the Clanranald of Garmoran, the Clanneill of Gigha, and many other tribes, to
become his vassals, although they previously held their
lands of the Crown. His son, the ninth Earl of
Argyle, consolidated the power thus acquired ; and, as
the forfeitures of this Earl and his father were both
rescinded, the family of Argyle, after the Revolution of
1688, found itself possessed of more influence than any
family in Scotland. This influence was, as formerly,

supported by the willing services of many powerful families of the name, whose distinguishing titles have been sufficiently indicated in the course of the present work, and do not require to be repeated here.

Having now fulfilled the task which, on undertaking this work, he imposed upon himself, the author takes his leave; trusting that he will be found to have succeeded in clearing away ·some of the clouds which formerly obscured the history of the West Highlands and Isles.

THE END.

INDEX.